Fiore dei Liberi's
ARMIZARE
The Chivalric Martial Arts System of Il Fior di Battaglia

Robert N. Charrette

Freelance Academy Press, Inc.
www.FreelanceAcademyPress.com

Number _______ of _______ limited production color copies.

The author and publisher of this book are not responsible for any injury which may result from following the instructions contained herein.

Before embarking on any of the physical activities described in this book, the reader should consult his or her physician for advice regarding their individual suitability for performing such activity.

Freelance Academy Press, Inc., Wheaton, IL 60189
www.freelanceacademypress.com

Printed in the United States of America
by Publishers' Graphics

20 19 18 17 16 15 14 13 12 11   1 2 3 4 5

ISBN 978-0-9825911-7-8
Limited Color Edition

Library of Congress Control Number: 2011932860

For Steve Hick, scholar and opener of the ways

Contents

Foreword vi

Preface viii

Acknowledgements ix

Introduction 1
- The Weapons of Armizare 10
- The Four Openings 12
- The Protection of Armor 13

Il Fior di Battaglia's Organization 14
- Stance 22
- The Way 23
- Four Steps 24
- Three Turns 26

Masters & Scholars 28
- Interplay of Masters and Scholars 34

Lessons of *Abrazare* 36
- *Abrazare* Guards 40
- *Abrazare* Plays 48

Lessons of the Dagger 50
- Dagger Guards 68
- Dagger Plays 70

Lessons of the Sword: Sword in One Hand 96
- Holding the Sword 102
- Sword in one hand Guards 104
- Sword in one hand Plays 106

Lessons of the Sword: Sword in Two Hands 116
- Sword in two hands Guards 132
- Sword in two hands Plays 156

Lessons of the Sword: Sword in Armor 176
- Sword in armor Guards 180
- Sword in armor Plays 192

Lessons of the Axe 198
- Axe Guards 202
- Axe Plays 214
- The Axe is a Sword 221

Lessons of the Spear 222
- Spear Guards and Plays 224

Lessons of Mounted Combat 230

Appendices 234
- Distribution of Imagery in *il Fior di Battaglia* 234
- Glossary 234
- Learning from the Many Faces of *Donna* 235
- Master and Scholars Organization Charts 236

FOREWORD

... there is so much to this art that even the man with the keenest memory in the world will be unable to learn more than a fourth of it without books. And a fourth of this art is not enough to make someone a Master. I, Fiore, know how to read, write and draw, and have books on our subject, a subject that I have studied for over forty years.

Fiore dei Liberi da Premarriacco

They say that necessity is the mother of invention. The book you are holding in your hands proves them right.

I have had the pleasure of knowing Bob Charrette for many years. In a sense, I knew him long before we met; my college bookshelf had more than a few of his novels and games sitting upon it. Once we'd truly been introduced, I knew him as a top-flight living historian who left me realizing how much about daily life in the Middle Ages I did not know; but always in an infectious, "isn't history fun" kind of way. Shortly thereafter, he began to attend my classes on armizare, the medieval martial art taught by that 14th-century master of sword, axe, dagger, and spear, Fiore dei Liberi. Almost like a ritual, Bob would ask me at the end of my class when I was going to get off of my duff and write a training guide of my own, to which I'd reply "don't worry, I'm working on it." And, truly, I am.

It seems that Bob got tired of waiting. You will be glad that he did.

Bob is a modest man, who will tell you that he is a grey-bearded newcomer to the teaching of Western martial arts, and in a sense that is true: he has a few years on the other, well-known armizare instructors in North America and Europe, and until his recent founding of the Forteza Historical Swordwork Guild, he has kept his teaching and training to working with a few personal students. What Bob's comments don't say is that he is a long-time combatant, a professional author and illustrator, and a well-known living historian and experimental archaeologist who specializes in the late 14th century—precisely the period in which Fiore dei Liberi was learning and plying his craft. Thus "knowing how to read, write and draw," as Maestro Fiore put it, he has precisely the right and unique combination of qualifications to make possible the book you are holding in your hands.

Unlike many traditional Asian martial arts, which have passed to us as living lineages, the fighting arts of the medieval knight must be reconstructed. This process involves the study and translation of technical manuals, literature, illumination and hands-on use of the material culture of medieval warfare: the arms and armor through which the art was applied. This is the craft of the experimental archaeologist, and it is precisely what Bob has spent over two decades doing with his organization, La Belle Compagnie. Just as he has meticulously researched 14th-century clothing, woodwork and armor, he has set out to research not just what Fiore dei Liberi taught his students but how he taught them.

Part of this research involves an aspect of historiography much talked about by historians, and little addressed or understood by lay people: context. Nothing exists in a vacuum. Not only is armizare a product of a specific time and place, but so too are the manuscripts in which it was recorded. Therefore, in order to truly understand an author and his art, you must understand the intellectual and social culture in which he was writing. For example, despite all of their similarities in caste, function and fighting disciplines, a medieval knight and a Japanese samurai were products of different ethical, religious and literary cultures, and this is reflected not only in what they say, but how they say it. Closer to home, the Middle Ages were the foundation for our modern society, but in a pre-printing press world, production costs made books luxury items. As such, the form and intention of a 15th-century book can be very different from a 21st-century one. This is especially true of medieval martial arts texts, which are generally a memorial—an aid to memory—and which often follow very different rules of organization and pedagogy than we expect in modern training manuals.

Fiore dei Liberi was a famed master-at-arms, who taught some of the preeminent warriors of his day and whose renown endured for centuries. Reading through his books, it becomes clear that he was an equally thoughtful writer and teacher, who developed a highly refined written instructional method. Unfortunately, that method was written for professional fighting men 600 years removed from us in time, and of a very different culture. Fortunately, you are in the hands of a trained tour guide; someone with the right combination of experiences to take you inside the mind of Fiore dei Liberi (or at least, his written work!) and to use the skills of the modern writer and illustrator to reveal them in a contemporary manner. The end result is not just an "interpretation"—although any translation or analysis of a text is by definition an interpretation—nor is it a "training guide"—although Bob certainly does provide some exercises and suggestions for training. Rather, it is an interpreter's tool kit; an analysis and explanation of both Fiore dei Liberi's system and his training methodology.

As a publisher, I am very pleased to bring this book to press, both for the quality of its content and for the beautiful design Bob has created. As a student and teacher of armizare, I think this book fills a hole and will equally serve the casual reader, the solitary practitioner, the nascent study-group and the seasoned instructor. But as an author, I can't help but swallow furtively and think that Bob Charrette has set a high bar for all of us to clear. That's good; Maestro Fiore deserves no less.

Gregory D. Mele
May 2011
Wheaton, IL

PREFACE

This book is an exploration of the martial art contained in the Getty Ludwig Manuscript XV 13 of Fiore dei Liberi's *il Fior di Battaglia* (The Flower of Battle). Along the way, I will also reference the other surviving works by Fiore where they shed light on details of Fiore's art as presented in the Getty manuscript. While I will be looking at the mechanics of some particular plays, the principal focus is on Fiore's structured teaching, exploring the deeper ordering of plays that goes beyond a simple roll call of "things you can do," for as Greg Mele—a wise man in this matter—often says, "the order of the manuscript is no coincidence." If we wish to understand Fiore's art, we must to look at his plays not just as a collection of tricks, but as the systematic program for learning that it is. This book is not a training regimen, although I give some exercises and make some training suggestions. If you wish to practice the art of arms, you must have sufficient conditioning and I urge you to seek out the appropriate experts to guide you in that endeavor.

Like Fiore's book, this book provides a tool kit, along with some guidance on how and when to apply those tools. It is also a guide to the structure of Fiore's lessons as presented in his master and scholar system as well as in the organization of the sections and plays. It is not a play-by-play interpretation of all the techniques, as that would require a far more extensive volume than this one. Neither is this book a tactical guide to the fight, which is another too-broad topic, as so much of what makes up the flow of a fight must be tailored to the individuals involved and the specific circumstances of each moment and such details are difficult, if not impossible, to cover in a book. The interpretation sections interspersed between the discussion chapters are intended to provide a grounding in some of the core ideas of Fiore's system and an introduction to studying that system. As good as any book might be, even Fiore's, to truly learn the art you must practice it, preferably under the guidance of someone further advanced along the path. If you do not already have such a mentor, I again urge you to seek one out.

As you continue your study, keep in mind that we cannot look at any play in isolation and expect to understand everything Fiore was trying to convey about it. The details of an illustration, the nuances of the text, and the placement of each within the overall treatise must all factor into our understanding of Fiore's teachings. The ordering of the treatise may not be what a modern master might choose, but it *is* a program, and it *does* teach. We must be students of Fiore's *program*, if we truly wish to learn Fiore's *art*.

Much time and effort, as well as the insights of many researchers and practitioners, have gone into developing the material in this volume. It is, however, only a moment in the ongoing process of resurrecting the martial arts of historical masters. Work in this martial arts revival is ongoing and we can expect that time, additional research, and further practical exploration will refine our understanding. This is not the book I would have written five years ago; five years from now, I would likely write it differently. New insights will come, but we need foundations to build upon. I hope that readers will find this volume to be a brick they can lay in their foundation of understanding.

The art is long, says Master Fiore.

Ah, but what a journey!

ACKNOWLEDGEMENTS

Profound thanks are due to Tom Leoni for his kind permission to quote extensively from his translation of the Getty manuscript. Said translation may be found in :

Fiore de' Liberi's Fior di Battaglia M.S. Getty Ludwig XV 13, Italian Swordsmanship Treatise, 2009

Available on www.lulu.com

This book would not have been possible without:

The principal photography team of Joann Socash and Eric Johnson

My partners in interpretation crime: Patrick Carmichael (unarmored, clothed by Revival Clothing) and Tom Taylor (armored by Jeff Wasson and Jessica Rechtschaeffer)

My own long-serving armor made by Robert MacPherson

The staff of Freelance Academy Press

And the help, encouragement, forbearance, and great patience of my wife, Liz.

Many scholars and practitioners have had influence, in large or small part, on my understanding of Fiore's art. Some are likely unaware of their influence, but I am nonetheless thankful for it. They include, but are not limited to, Keith Alderson, Bob Charron, Ilkka Hartikainen, Sean Hayes, Steve Hick, Jesse Kulla, Mark Lancaster, Rob Lovett, Greg Mele, Brian Price, Steve Reich, Mark Shier, Brian Stokes, Jason Vail, Scott Wilson, Guy Windsor, and many other herein unnamed pilgrims met on the road along the way.

Over the years, many have been burdened by my attempts at learning the art, including but not limited to: Andrew Breeden, Patrick Carmichael, Scott Cozad, Scott Nolan, Joann Socash, Peter Taylor, Tom Taylor, and those occasional partners whose names my imperfect memory cannot recall.

You all have my gratitude. Any mistakes and misunderstandings are, of course, my own.

A Note About the Photographs

Like *il Fior di Battaglia*'s drawings, the interpretation photographs in this book are not always shown from a consistent angle, but rather shifted to make the action clear. Unlike the drawings, I am not using crowns and garters. I present the action of the Remedy Master or his scholars, appearing in the red jacket and shiny body armor. My partners (who wear the green jacket and black body armor) are usually the opponent but occasionally get to be a Counter Master. Action usually proceeds from left to right. I will note where we depart from this program in the captions.

Positions (*poste*) are consistently shown with front and side views, even when the drawing shows an angled view.

Some action sequences that appear on *poste* pages have ghostly figures as well as solid ones. The ghost emerges from the solid figure and is on its way to taking the position of the solid figure in the next picture in the sequence. It's not video, but I hope it helps.

... without books, nobody can truly be a master or student of the art ...

INTRODUCTION

Fiore dei Liberi's *il Fior di Battaglia* is not the earliest surviving work on the art of arms. Although we have references to other books, only two survivors are known to predate Fiore's work.

One, a housebook, or collection of disparate material gathered together in a single volume, includes several sections on fencing. This is the so-called Döbringer manuscript (Hs. 3227a which lies in the Germanisches Nationalmuseum in Nürnberg). It appears to have been written about thirty years before Fiore's work, and is the oldest work in the Liechtenauer school of the art. Its text says that the school's preeminent master Johannes Liechtenauer did not invent the art himself, but that the art's practice goes back hundreds of years earlier. It does not have any illustrations.

About a hundred years before Fiore wrote, an anonymous author created the work now known as Royal Armouries MS I.33 (now housed in the Armouries in Leeds, UK). This illustrated book is devoted to combat with sword and buckler. It holds the pride of position as the earliest surviving work on European fencing.

Neither of these earlier works are comprehensive. Both concentrate on sword, either as the longsword or the sword in conjunction with a buckler (which usage Fiore expressly says he is not teaching). Others have written on both these works far better than I can do.[1]

Fiore's work is important to the study of historical fencing, not just because of its early date. The energetic drawings with their close attention to important details far outshine the drawing in I.33 in clarifying details of actions. Fiore's is the first work to cover all of the so-called knightly weapons: dagger, sword, axe, and lance. What makes Fiore's work most valuable is his organized and comprehensive exposition of the art of arms.

This book is an examination of that exposition.

[1] For I.33, see Jeffrey L. Forgeng, *The Medieval Art of Swordsmanship: A Facsimile & Translation of Europe's Oldest Personal Combat Treatise, Royal Armouries MS. I.33*, Chivalry Bookshelf/Royal Armouries, 2003. Although articles have appeared, a comprehensive work on Hs. 3227a remains to be written.

FIORE FURLAN DEI LIBERI

Is this the face of Fiore?
This bearded master executes most of the plays in the Pisani-Dossi's sword in two hands section.

What we know about Fiore comes mostly from his biographical notes in the introductions of his works. He was the son of the "noble" Ser Benedetto[2] of Cividale in Friuli, a small region in what is now north-eastern Italy. At the time portions of the area were under the sway of the Germanic entities that became Austria.

Fiore tells us that he spent more than forty years and possibly as many as fifty before he committed his knowledge to books. One manuscript[3] contains within it the date on which Fiore says he started it in 1409. Based on the professed length of his career, and the usual age when a man might launch a military career, he must have been born some time around 1350. We have no record of either his birth or death.

Fiore says that he grew up wanting to learn all he could about the secrets of weapons and combat. He was a soldier and traveled extensively, seeking to learn as much as possible about the fighting arts. During this time he studied with both German and Italian masters, as well as with experienced warriors of various courts.

He became a *scarmitor*,[4] a sword master, and he trained men for "combat in the barriers." Some of his students were famous, and some fought famous men, and all were "satisfied by my instruction and ... wanted only me as a teacher." The roster includes mercenaries, knights and minor nobles active in northern and central Italy during the latter part of the fourteenth century.

He fought duels, too, because he would not show his secrets to other sword masters. Clearly, he was practiced in the art as well, for in each of those contests he came away victorious and unscathed.

We know more about Fiore than any other early master, but he remains something of a shadow, especially when we look beyond his own words. He is famously associated with the court of the Marquis d'Este because two of Fiore's manuscripts are dedicated to Nicolo, Marquis d'Este,[5] but—as yet—no records linking him to Nicolo's court have come to light.

[2] Noble in this context does not necessarily mean "of the nobility" (otherwise "the noble dagger" would be a member of the nobility) nor does the honorific "ser" necessarily equate with the English "sir" meaning knight. For that matter, knightly rank was somewhat different in England and Italy. It is too complex an issue to address here beyond urging caution in interpretation on the subject.

[3] The Pisani-Dossi manuscript contains the date and the note that it took six months to complete.

[4] Massimo Malpiero (in his *il Fiore di battaglia di Fiore dei Liberi da Cividale*, ribis, 2006) presents an excerpt from the city records of Undine for 1383 that records *Magister Florius scarmitor* as residing in Borgo Gemona.

[5] The Marquis may even have had a hand in the ordering of the material in the Getty, or he may have merely ordered the book produced. The text of Fiore's prolog is ambiguous according to Tom Leoni (private communication).

FIORE'S BOOKS

There are four books attributed to Fiore that are known to have survived to the present day:

- *Il Fior di Battaglia* (Ludwig Manuscript XV 13) resides in the John Paul Getty collection in California and is commonly known as "the Getty."

- *Flos Duellatorum* resides in a private collection and is commonly known as "the Pisani-Dossi" or "the Novati" (after the 1902 facsimile edition).

- *Il Fior di Battaglia* (M. 0383) resides in the Pierpont Morgan library in New York and is commonly known as "the Morgan."

- The last, *Florius de Arte Luctande* (Latin 11269), is pretty clearly younger than the other manuscripts. Unlike the others, its text is in Latin and it has colored illustrations. It resides in the Bibliotheque Nationale of France and is known colloquially as "Florius" or "the Paris."

Each of the manuscripts contains some material absent from at least one of the others. What these differences mean regarding the origin, relationship, and order of creation among the manuscripts is the subject of much debate. It is not a subject that I will go into in this book, although I will be noting some differences among the manuscripts. This will be in order to help explain a specific point under discussion or illuminate something that, while obscure in the Getty, is clear elsewhere.

The first three are vellum manuscripts illustrated with line drawings and date from the earliest part of the fifteenth century. The prolog of the Pisani-Dossi manuscript actually states that Fiore began the book on February 10, in 1409, and in the last verse he complains that it took him six months to write. We do not, however, know whether the surviving manuscript is the original, i.e., the actual pages written as described, or whether it is a copy of the one written in that year. Indeed, the exact dating of all of the manuscripts is unclear and cannot be settled without study of the material by experts in manuscripts and their production.

The Getty and the Pisani-Dossi manuscripts begin with wrestling and move through dagger, sword, poleax, and spear before dealing with combat from horseback. Since Fiore states that wrestling is the foundation upon which the art is built, we can call this approach *foundational.*

The Morgan and the Paris manuscripts start with mounted combat and work down towards wrestling (the Morgan does not actually get there) in what can be termed a *deed-of-arms format,* as that was the common order of fighting in such martial events.

Other elements of Fiore's work still survive in library collections.[6] Although it is unclear how directly

[6] For example, the 1428 collection that is Cod. 5278 at the Österreichische Nationalbibliothek in Vienna has 30 pages of drawings (no text) of plays, including some of Fiore's; Ludwig von Eyb's early sixteenth-century compendium at the Universitäts-Bibliothek-Erlangen in Erlangen, Germany contains what appears to be redrawn versions of some of Fiore's plays; and Matthew Galas reports a 16th-century (?) copy of the Getty prologs in Cod. 224, Collez. Fontanini XXIV, a compilation volume at the Biblioteca Guarneriana in San Daniele.

they relate to Fiore's material, these partial appearances, along with a spate of streets named after him in various cities, indicate that Fiore's work was more widely known in past centuries than in recent ones. Indeed, until Novati's 1902 facsimile edition[7] of the Pisani-Dossi manuscript, Fiore is notably absent from modern fencing histories.

IL FIOR DI BATTAGLIA

The Getty manuscript of *il Fior di Battaglia* is the largest of the survivals and the one with the highest level of organization and presentation. It is a manuscript on vellum of 47 leaves, illustrated with 291 line drawings, some of which have gold or silver leaf details. A few have gold or blue washes.

Fiore says the art concerns "the lance, the axe, the sword, the dagger, and how to wrestle … combat on foot and on horseback, both with armor and without" and accordingly divides his treatise into corresponding sections for each of the forms on foot with an additional section on mounted combat that includes only lance, sword, and wrestling. Between some of the sections he inserts interstitial plays, usually setting up an obvious transition from the weapon of the preceding section to the weapon of the following section.

Within each section, Fiore uses as a system of masters and their scholars to organize and structure the material. It is a sophisticated approach, as I hope to show, but also seems to be an approach which Fiore was still tweaking as he sought a more perfect presentation. For example, the prolog of the manuscript describes four categories of masters and the symbols used to indicate them, yet the body of the manuscript contains some figures who do not carry the symbols appropriate for their role. This is a sign that Fiore's explicative approach to the art was still evolving even as he was making his book.[8] The fact that no Contra-counter Masters appear as Fiore describes them in his introduction is another such sign. *Il Fior di Battaglia*, for all of its masterful presentation of the art, is essentially a work-in-progress, written by a perfectionist continually striving to make his work the best it could be.

All unattributed quotes in this volume are taken from the Getty manuscript in translation by Tom Leoni.

[7] Fiore dei Liberi da Premariacco, *Flos duellatorum in arnis, sine armis, equester, pedester*, Francesco Novati (ed.), Bergamo, 1902.

[8] For example, the Pisani-Dossi has eight Remedy Masters of the dagger while the Getty has nine.

FIORE'S SUBJECT MATTER

Have no doubt that Fiore's art is one of serious martial intent. Anyone who admits that when one is fighting for one's life, one is "... employing every trick, deception and cruelty imaginable" is not talking about pretend fighting. Fiore's understanding of the art was deep and study of his work shows that he understood that the weapons used are, from a certain viewpoint, largely irrelevant. Any fight is a fight against the opponent. It is a fight, not a sword fight or a dagger fight or a spear fight, and in a fight, you will always have four weapons: your mind to judge, assess, and plan; your right arm; your left arm; and your feet, working together to maintain your balance and give you movement.

Some claim that Fiore only taught fighting for within the barriers, and some of these constrain his teaching further as applicable only to judicial dueling. It is true that the prolog of the Morgan seems to emphasize fighting in the barriers which is, given the book's deed-of-arms structure, perhaps not surprising. Also, Fiore's roll call of famous students refers to their deeds at the barriers. And why should it not? A formal deed of arms was the rough equivalent of a modern, televised championship boxing match. Skill was on open display and reputations made, to be spread internationally by the viewers and, more importantly, by the heralds in attendance. This was the high-profile stuff. Certainly deeds of arms are reported from battles, such as in Froissart's *Chronicles*, but such reporting was chancy; and even when the prowess of an individual fighter was reported, who remembered his trainer? By recalling notable public deeds of arms, where one individual fighter strove against another, Fiore could associate himself with the success of his student, making clear his own part in that success. It was, in a way, a classic medieval author's appeal to authority set within the context of a practical art. With it, he validates his quality as an instructor while, on a purely practical level, conducting good advertising.

Il Fior di Battaglia begins with *abrazare*, usually translated loosely as *wrestling*. Fiore tells us that "Abrazare is of two kinds: one is done for pleasure, the other in anger, or for one's life, employing every trick, deception and cruelty imaginable. I want to talk about the second kind and show, in good order, how to come to grappling successfully in the most common situations of life or death combat." The word *abrazare* literally means "to embrace." To put this sentiment in colloquial terms, Fiore is telling us that he is talking about making war, not love.

In the prolog Fiore lays out the structure of how he will explain *abrazare*. At the explanation's end, he tells us that what applies to *abrazare* applies to all of *armizare*, or the art of arms. It follows that his *armizare* is also about "life or death combat." While judicial combats may have mandated the execution of a loser who survived the encounter, other combats within the barriers, such as chivalric deeds of arms, did not. Fiore's use of the phrase "every trick, deception and cruelty imaginable" seems hardly suitable for proper and refined chivalric deeds of arms which, despite the rhetoric occasionally employed, were rarely fought to the death.[9]

---

[9] See Will McLean, *Outrance and Plaisance*, Journal of Medieval Military History, Vol. VIII, Clifford J. Rogers, Kelly DeVries & John France (eds.), Boydell Press, 2010.

Another sign that Fiore is teaching about real combat is that he always remains concerned with fighting in armor. His instruction almost never offers a play that one ought not to try in armor. Only one play in the mounted combat section[10] carries the advice that it ought not be tried in armor.

Further evidence that Fiore's concern is with real fighting is that several plays include obvious civilian circumstances.[11] Fighters rarely sit down or keep their swords sheathed or carry rude clubs in a battle or in the prepared space within the barriers. This clues us in that Fiore's instruction is as much what we today call self-defense as it is a battlefield combat system.

In the prolog of the Pisani-Dossi, while speaking of *abrazare*, Fiore tells us that "these are *prese* and plays that he cannot practice with courtesy, and also these are dangerous plays to practice."[12] This follows a verse in which he seems to suggest that plays should be done in harmony (*concordia*) and with love, not anger. Taken together, this advice suggests that Fiore understood that one has to practice the art to learn it, and that such practice is done with something less than the intensity one needs in combat. Even so, some plays remain very dangerous and cannot be taken to completion in practice.

Furthering this sense of cooperation in training, he often refers to the figures illustrated in the manuscript as companions (*compagni*) rather than opponents. In the translation used herein, Tom Leoni usually translates the term as "opponent" which is a usage more familiar to a modern audience, and makes it a little more clear which player is which. We, as modern practitioners, must think of our training partners as companions. While thinking of the other person as an opponent may help us understand a play, we must always remember that those with whom we train are not our enemies, even when free sparring. Many of Fiore's plays are dangerous and some deadly. We cannot utilize this lethal combat art fully; not if we want to continue to have partners with whom to practice. Are we not all companions on the journey of studying this art?

[10] See the fifth play of the sword on horseback (44 verso A)

[11] The seated scholars refer to specific dagger Remedy Masters, but apparently have their numbers swapped.

[12] Unless otherwise noted, all translations herein from the Pisani-Dossi manuscript are by Rob Lovett, Mark Davidson, and Mark Lancaster via The Exiles' website (www.the-exiles.org.uk).

The Segno Page

QUALITIES OF A SWORDSMAN

On the page known to fencing scholars as the *segno* (sign) page we learn of four virtues that a practitioner of *armizare* must have. Fiore links them to animals to make them easier to remember. All of these animals are the creatures of medieval bestiaries rather than their natural world counterparts, which means they have attributes and qualities associated with them which may be foreign to modern people more familiar with nature films and biological animals studied by science.

The animal at the top of the segno page is a lynx, who declares: “No creature can see better than I, the lynx. And this virtue puts everything in its right place and its measure.” It holds a pair of dividers, a tool used for measurement.

The word associated with the lynx is *avvisamento*, whose most appropriate translation here seems to be caution. In the Pisani-Dossi the words linked to the animals are in Latin rather than Italian. The lynx’s *prudentea* can mean wisdom, prudence, or foresight. This shades the meaning of the Italian and takes us to an understanding that the lynx symbolizes using one’s assessment of the opponent and of the fight to one’s advantage. Is not prudent application of knowledge the wise thing to do? The lynx’s compass enhances this understanding, symbolizing the ability to know and gauge the proper distance for techniques and, by extension, where and when to do them.

The animal on the left is a tiger. As illustrated, this tiger doesn’t look very familiar at all. In truth, it looks more like a rat. The tiger’s depiction in the Pisani-Dossi is somewhat more conventional, if one is expecting a heraldic-style tiger. What this beast looks like doesn’t really matter; what he says does. He says: “I, the tiger, am so quick at running and turning I can’t even be overtaken by a lightning-bolt.“ He holds a double-headed arrow, presumably intended to represent “the arrow of the sky,” or lightning.

Presteza is the word associated with the tiger. It means speed or rapidity. The Pisani-Dossi's word here is *celeritas,* which translates as quickness, as in speed of action. Fiore makes it clearer in the prolog to the Pisani-Dossi, where he counts "quickness of foot and of arms" as one of the seven elements of *abrazare.* This virtue requires one to move quickly, whether with hand to strike or cover or with feet to close and open distance and to avoid attacks.

To the right side of the page is a lion, who comes with this verse: "I am the lion: nobody carries a more courageous heart. I offer everyone battle." Under its paw stands a heart. The lion and the heart are symbols whose association with courage are still widely recognized today.

Ardimento means courage, daring, or boldness. The associated Latin word from the Pisani-Dossi, *audatia,* is similar and means boldness, daring, or courage. It does take courage to step into a fight and face someone intent on doing one harm. The heart under the lion's paw, I think, ties to the lion's last phrase. The virtuous swordsman not only does not shrink from battle, he has the "heart" to place his life and limb at risk.

The elephant at the bottom of the page is the last of the set and he states: "I am the elephant, who carries a castle as freight. I never kneel or lose my stride."

The elephant's word is *forteza,* which is usually translated as strength but in a different context can mean "fortress," which is exactly what the animal carries on his back. The Latin word in the Pisani-Dossi is *fortitudo* and also means strength. Physical strength, as symbolized by the elephant's ability to carry a castle, is certainly useful in the art, and it is one of the elements Fiore lists as necessary for *abrazare.* Yet there is more to find here, and it lies in the nature of the elephant and the surface on which he stands.

According to bestiaries, the elephant has no knees and, if he falls, he can never get up again. Here is an obvious admonition: do not fall. Keeping one's feet requires a good stance and a good ability to shift that stance according to the needs of the moment in a fight. The elephant stands on a surface to direct us towards this consideration, and he lies at the man's feet to tie his virtue to those feet.

Through these virtues we can see that a Liberian swordsman is quick in action. He works from a strong structural base as he bravely confronts his opponent. Perhaps most important of all, he remains always mindful of his circumstances, watching vigilantly for every opportunity to use his abilities and turn the fight to his advantage.

If you want to excel in this art, you must possess these virtues.

The last play of *zogho largo* in the sword in two hands section (left), which is said to be "better in armor," and the same play from the Morgan (right), where it is shown being done in armor.

THE ART: ARMORED OR UNARMORED

In the manuscript, Fiore expresses opinions on some plays as to whether the players should be armored or not. Phrases like "I am good with armor," "If you are in armor, it won't do you any good ...," "... safer in armor than without," "... good both in and out of armor," "to use this thrust you should be in armor," "possible both in and out of armor" are peppered throughout. He renders these judgements regardless of whether the players are depicted as armored or not. As mentioned before, only once does Fiore suggest using a particular play only against an unarmored foe, saying, "Don't use this play against an armored opponent" regarding a counter in the mounted combat section.

Although the occasional helmet shows up on players here and there in the Getty, only four sections have their players shown in armor: sword in armor, axe, spear, and mounted combat. This is not unexpected. It starts with the sword in armor, a subset of the sword instruction focusing on techniques tailored to achieving results against a man in armor. The axe and the spear follow and they are weapons only of the battlefield and the deed of arms, unlike the sword and dagger which can be carried in a civilian context. This point is reinforced when one notices that, once the sword comes into play, the armor mostly disappears from the mounted combat section. The Pisani-Dossi follows this pattern, except in the mounted combat section, where the players remain in armor all the way through.

Curiously, the Morgan only shows players in armor once, in a play for which the Getty tells us "you should be in armor." Even plays which are specifically intended for armored men, such as the sword in armor section, are illustrated showing the players without armor. Indeed, the one play where the players are shown in armor is one which Fiore advises is safer done in armor, but in both the Getty and the Pisani-Dossi, the players are shown without armor.

The Paris manuscript takes a very different approach to expressing Fiore's theme that the art is for both armored and unarmored combat. Players appear in full or partial armor seemingly randomly throughout. For example, the First Remedy Master of the dagger is shown in full armor while his opponent wears no armor at all.

The final illustration in *il Fior di Battaglia* depicts two horses tied to a tree and is Fiore's final statement on the subject. One horse wears a standard saddle and riding tack, the other is armored with a plate chamfron (head piece) and peytral (chest plate) as well as a textile or mail covering for its neck and hindquarters. It is no coincidence that both horses are tied to the same tree. Here Fiore is using a visual memory device to reinforce the message that all of the art taught in this book is for both armored and unarmored combat. It is important for us, as we reconstruct and interpret Fiore's art, to keep this in mind as we learn from his teaching.

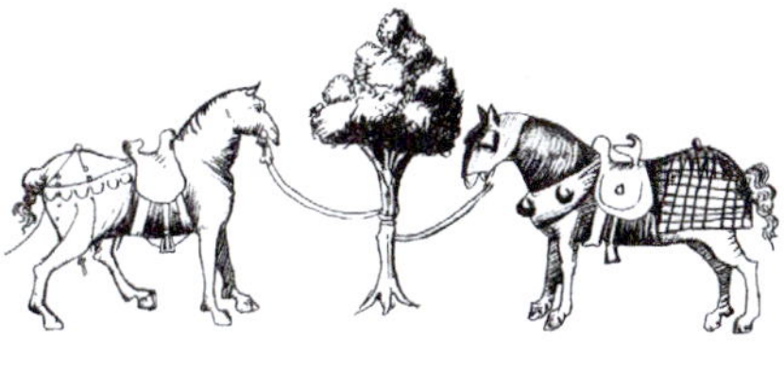

As Fiore ends his book with the horses, so will I end this introduction.

THE DAGGER
(DAGA)

The daggers in the manuscript have longish, tapering *blades*, implying a sharp tip. None are shown being used to slice or cut, although the blade is used to apply pressure during a lock. Although most appear to be what is now called a rondel dagger, the *pommels* and *guards* depicted vary and several of the stylistic variants recognized today show up. Filipo Vadi is the first to recommend a length, suggesting a blade that reaches to the user's elbow is best. This would give a blade length of 10 to 13 inches for an adult male.

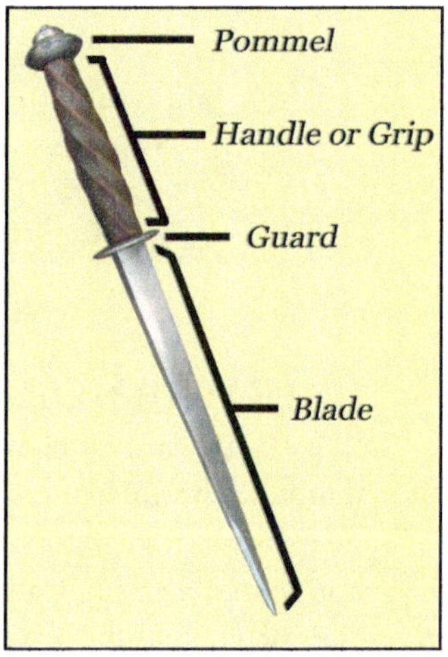

THE SWORD
(SPADA)

Fiore makes no distinction between swords used with one hand and those used with two. The lengths of the swords depicted vary, but this is more likely due to artistic issues than an attempt to render weapons of a specific length. *Blades* are often shown tapering steadily from *hilt* to point, but some show more parallel edges that change abruptly to a point at the tip. Most swords are depicted with grips longer than what is today considered a single-handed sword. Wheel-shaped (or possibly globular) and pear-shaped *pommels* appear. Preserved swords and archaeological finds suggest a blade length of 34 to 38 inches for this sort of sword.

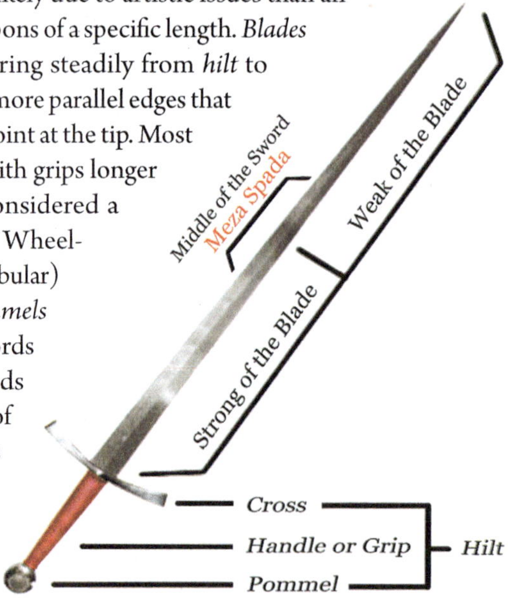

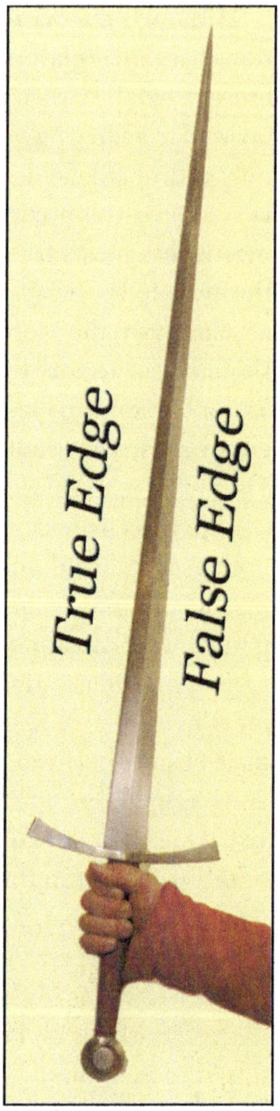

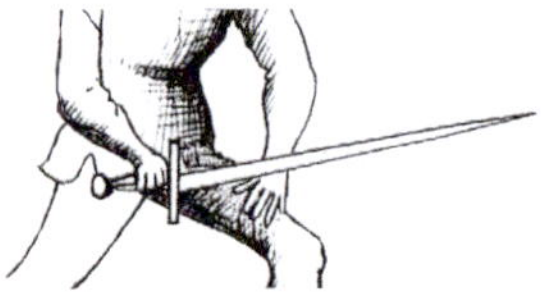

Sword in one hand

Sword in two hands

Sword in armor

THE AXE
(AZZA)

The axe, as depicted in the manuscript, is a shafted weapon of varying length, even in sequential pictures (again most likely due to artistic issues). Fourteenth-century illustrations depict a weapon that varies from about shoulder height to about head height. Later axes can be considerably longer. Surviving axes and pole-hammers suggest a weight of about six pounds. The axe has a heavy head with a *hammer* face on the true side and a *beak* on the false; together the two are sometimes called the *cross* of the axe. A *spike* projects from the head end which functions like a spear head. It also usually has a pointed cap on the butt end called a *butt-spike*. In the late fourteenth century, when Fiore was a soldier, weapons that more closely resemble an axe (reproduction at right) are far more commonly illustrated in the hands of men-at-arms. These weapons replace the hammer head with an axe blade and sometimes omit the beak or replace it with a blunt face similar to the hammer.

THE SPEAR
(LANZA)

Fiore uses the same word for a spear used on foot as he does for one used while mounted, although he does refer to a heavy and light distinction for mounted combat and long and short versions for foot combat. The foot combat version seems to have been 6 to 8 feet long. Some of the spears in the manuscript are shown with small crossbars or knobs or a collar of fringe below the head. The spear's *head*, which is shown in various shapes, is used exclusively for thrusting. At the other end of the shaft Fiore recommends an "iron," also used for thrusting. The shaft can deflect the opponent's weapon to exchange a thrust and the Counter Master tells us to strike with the butt when the head is deflected.

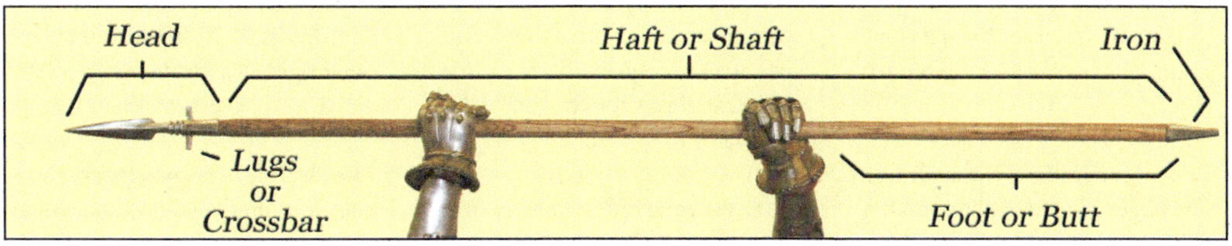

The earliest description of the four openings of medieval combat theory comes from Hs. 3227a, the so-called Döbringer text. In it, the author describes four openings that divide a target body into quadrants. The vertical dividing line runs through the body's midline. The horizontal dividing line is at approximately navel level.

Fiore's work connects with this breakdown in his description of the five thrusts of the sword. One, he says, comes in the middle, apparently anywhere along the vertical line. The other four are divided into upper thrusts, one from the left and one from right, and lower thrusts, also one from left and right. Implicit in this is the idea that cuts will also come into those quadrants, which is something explicitly stated by Liechtenauer tradition masters.

For blows with a sword (or other weapon), Fiore seems to have preferred angles and target areas within these quadrants. The sword attacks are noted below. They also apply to axe, but the dagger works a little differently due to its short length and reliance on the point, as will be detailed later.

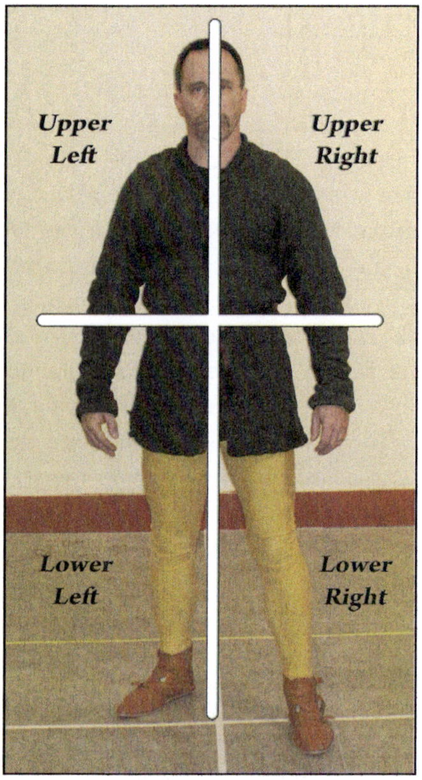

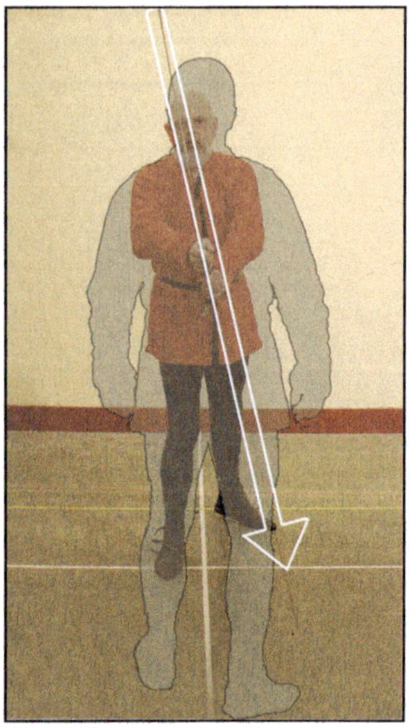

The *fendente* cut comes from above, cutting down into one of the upper quadrants. You can throw it from your right (*mandritto*) or your left (*riverso*).

Its ideal path follows the angle from the target's jaw to the knee on the opposite side.

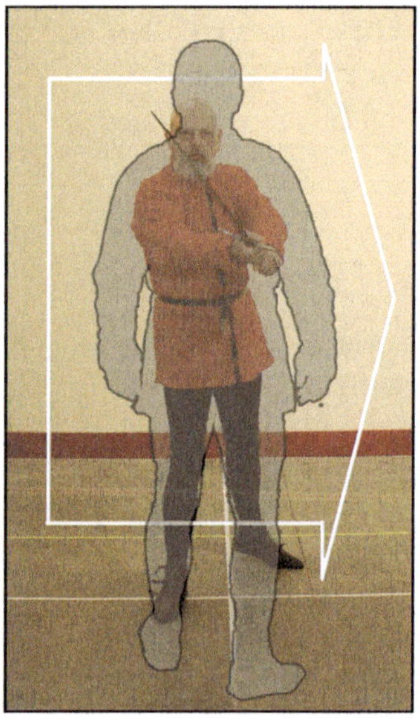

The *mezzano* cut comes between the zones of the *fendente* and *sottano* cuts. It can come into either an upper or a lower quadrant on its side. You can throw it from your right (*mandritto*) or your left (*riverso*).

Its target zone is described as from the temple to the knee.

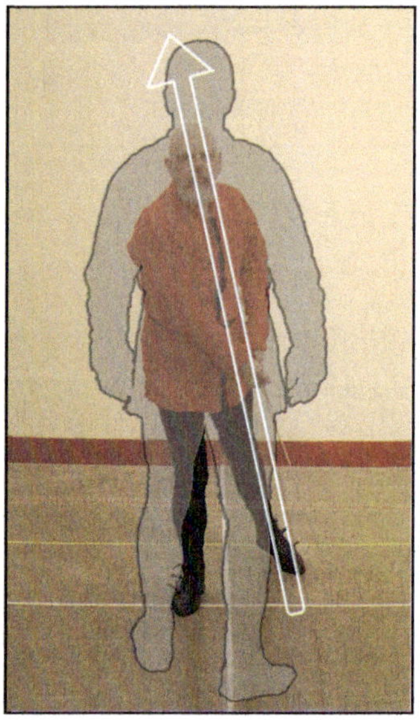

The *sottano* cut comes from below, cutting up into one of the lower quadrants. You can throw it from your right (*mandritto*) or your left (*riverso*).

Its ideal path reverses that of the *fendente*, from the target's knee to the jaw on the opposite side.

Plate armor was in wide and increasing use during Fiore's career. By the time he wrote, nearly complete body coverage would have been expected for a man-at-arms. Of course, the more complete the armor, the heavier it is and the more a man's mobility and agility are compromised. Men-at-arms would seek to protect themselves well, but they might not wear as much as they could. Apparently, for example, it was a popular decision to leave off a visor to avoid the severe restrictions to vision and breathing that a visor imposed.

Throughout this period, weapons had to deal with the increasing protection. Swords, for example, cannot cut or pierce good plate armor and are less effective against it than against the interlocked rings of mail, which for centuries was the staple armor of men-at-arms. Techniques such as those Fiore shows for the sword in armor were developed to use an existing weapon—the sword—in ways designed to maximize its effect against an armored man. Meanwhile, weapons that were more effective against plate—such as the poleax (Fiore's *azza*)—were developing and coming into wider use.

Whatever weapon he used, a fighter looked for the weakest points in his opponent's protection and sought to bring his best combination of weapon and technique to bear against such points.

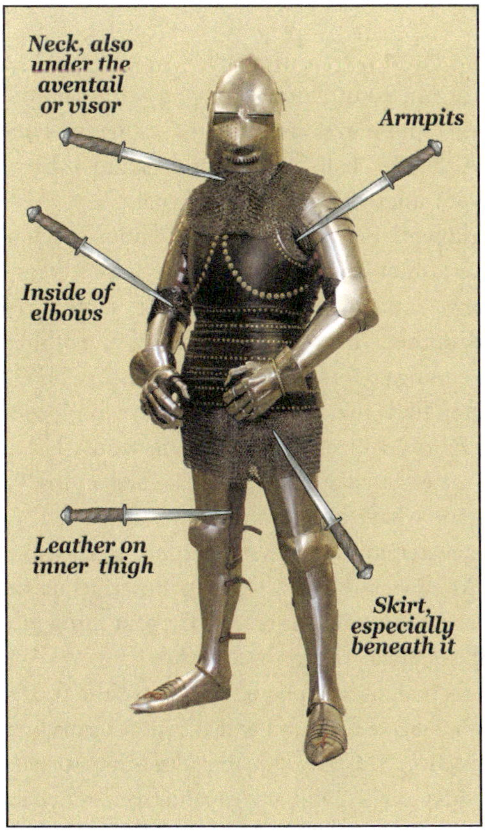

The weaker points in the armor are where the wearer is only protected by mail, leather, or cloth. Any place that presents a significant gap, such as behind the cuff of the gauntlet, is also a weak point.

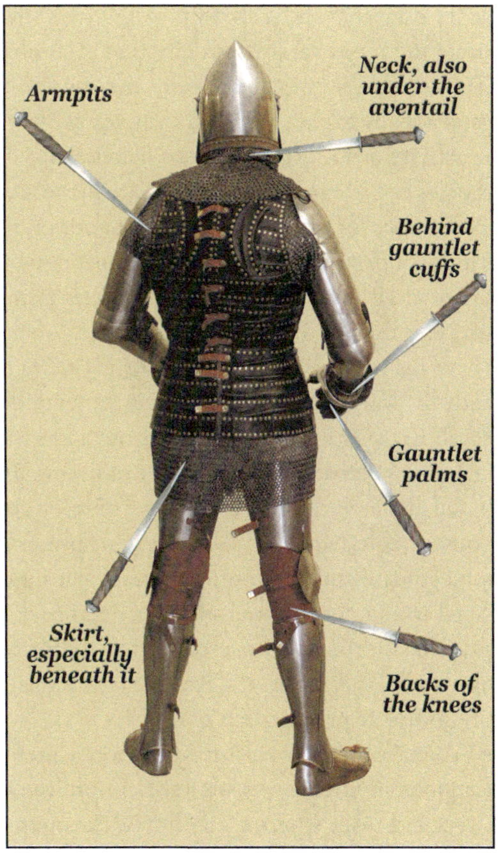

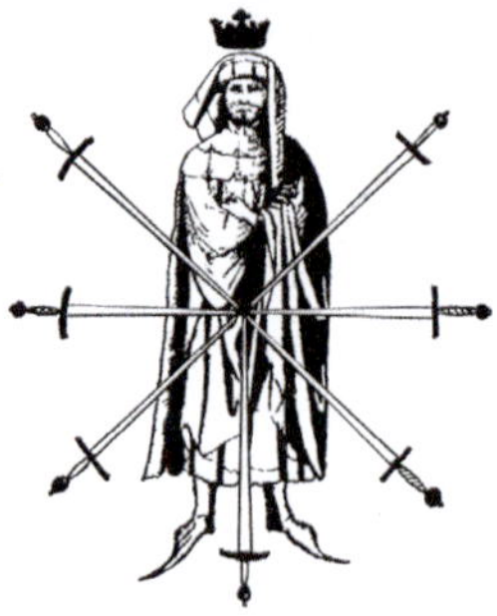

The colored letters, the illustrations and the plays will show you all the art clearly enough for you to understand it.

IL FIOR DI BATTAGLIA'S ORGANIZATION

The Getty manuscript is the longest and most highly organized of Fiore's surviving works, and it is the primary basis for this book. Within it, Fiore's structured presentation of the art uses many devices to explicate the multi-variable activity that is combat. Although challenging to understand, *il Fior di Battaglia* is no "da Vinci codex." Clarity and simplicity were among Fiore's admitted goals.

Organizing any explanation of a complex activity is difficult. For any written explanation of a multivariate activity one must present the material in a linear fashion and, in doing so, the presenter must make choices concerning when and how to present information. Due to the nature of the subject matter, a good choice for one aspect may be a poor one for another. Thus, almost invariably, one or more aspects make perfect sense from one point of view while ending up "out of order" from another. Should one work to clarify that sense of out-of-ordering one often finds the original aspect's previously clear presentation is muddied and makes less sense. We have Fiore's choices preserved in his works, but we do not have his reasoning. The organized nature of his material makes it clear that he had a plan. We must study his works carefully in order to better understand what that plan was.

Il Fior di Battaglia's introduction lays out a key for its material, stating that the information will be presented in a way that is clear and easy to follow. The Morgan and Pisani-Dossi manuscripts do this also, but the details vary. The Pisani-Dossi's prolog goes so far as to take the reader on a tour through all the various sections, while the Getty's prolog presents the *abrazare* section as a model.

Careful study of the manuscript reveals that Fiore was making a strong effort to have the treatise streamlined and compact as well. He often refers back to previous sections rather than repeating material. The repeats he does make are part of his structured presentation. This, as we shall see, leads him to insert bridging material that allows the reader to extrapolate from a single point and expand that connection to a more complete presentation of the art.

Even when we think we have grasped Fiore's intent, we must look closely at our conclusions because preconceptions are always an issue. Furthermore, the strength and skill of a practitioner may allow a solution to work in a place where it may not be the optimal—or even a possible—solution for a less gifted or less learned practitioner. Fiore's work seems to be trying to offer what might be called mainstream solutions which do not rely on exceptional performance by the practitioner.

THE COLORED LETTERS

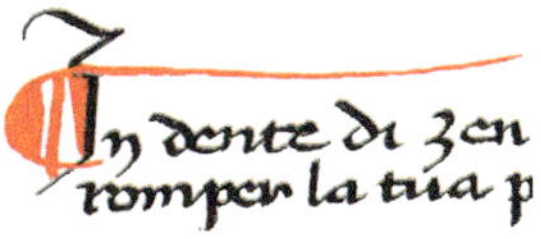

In his injunction that the treatise is designed to be understood easily, Fiore references "the colored letters." This looks to be a reference to what manuscript scholars called *paraphs*. These symbols mark breaks in the text, usually but not exclusively in verse presentations. They also usually alternate colors.

Fiore's paraphs are red and blue, but they do not strictly alternate. What, if any, meaning this non-alternating arrangement has is not currently known. Certainly the breaks in the flow of the words will help understanding, just as our modern system of punctuation does.

MASTERS AND SCHOLARS

Fiore tells us that "these Masters and students support the whole art of arms." He is referring to the system of masters and scholars he describes in the prolog. These named and numbered masters are part of his exposition on *abrazare*. At the end of that exposition he states that "they support the art of the lance" and do the same for "the axe, the single and double-handed sword, and the dagger" so it is clear that we are to take the master-scholar program as applying to weapon combat and mounted combat as well. Masters and their scholars appear in all of *il Fior di Battaglia's* sections. We will look at them in detail in the next chapter.

PLAYS: PRINCIPLE BY EXEMPLAR

A play is a particular action or instance of doing something. In Fiore's manuscript, plays are placed in a context. They are usually shown in response to a specific action on the part of the other fighter, such as an attack or a cover. Thus a play presents an example of something that might happen in a fight.

Fiore uses his masters and scholars as related examples to teach specific lessons. The scholars of the First Remedy Master of the dagger explore actions to the inside of the attacking dagger's line, while the exploration of action to the outside of that line belongs to the Third Remedy Master.

In keeping with common medieval practice for teaching an activity, Fiore shows us an action (the play) and expects us to learn many things from it. The first, most obvious layer is the action itself. How is it done? By practicing the action, the student internalizes it and its nuances. As he does, he grows closer to understanding the principles that govern it. When can it be done? Why is it done? When should it not be done? When the student can, in different but appropriate circumstances, apply the principle behind the example, he demonstrates that he has mastered that principle. Thus, from specific example, the student is expected to learn the underlying principle. Understanding this explicative approach is key to understanding what Fiore is teaching and how much more there is to his art than what is depicted in the illustrations or mentioned directly in the text.

For example, Fiore several times refers back to one specific play of the dagger, that scholar of the First Remedy Master who performs the Middle Bind (*ligadura mezzana*). In plays with other weapons, he tells us that the scholar can perform this action. This links one example to another, extending the play while keeping the instruction compact. The linkage itself is an example, offering us the principle that one can use actions from other portions of the manuscript when the correct positioning and circumstances arise. This means that the student is expected to find other connections between specific actions, applying then when they are appropriate.

ORGANIZATION BY WEAPON

Fiore tells us that the art of arms includes "the lance, the axe, the sword, the dagger, and how to wrestle" and he says combat takes place "on foot and on horseback, both with armor and without." Thus, it should be no surprise that he devotes sections of his work to each of the weapons mentioned. Throughout the treatise he uses phrases like "safer if I wore good armor" which indicate his constant awareness that combat can occur "both with armor and without."

The first section deals with wrestling, or *abrazare,* of which he says he is talking about the sort of unarmed techniques used when fighting for one's life. *Abrazare* can be translated as "the art of the embrace," but Fiore's wrestling is not limited to embraces (holds). It is a lively art of strikes, grips, and throws more akin to unarmed combatives than Olympic wrestling. Due to the complex nature of this portion of the art, I will use the Italian term *abrazare* to refer to it rather than the more limiting English terms like wrestling or grappling.

The largest and most comprehensively organized section of the treatise is that concerning the dagger (*daga*). Here Fiore lays a lot of groundwork for handling attacks by weapons. Many *abrazare* techniques are first illustrated here. This has more to do with making specific actions easier to see in a drawing than with their being exclusive to dagger play.

The sword (*spada*) section is subdivided into three parts according to how the weapon is used. The sword in one hand (*spade a una mano*) section covers use of the sword with one hand on the grip. The sword in two hands (*spade a due mano*) section has techniques for using a sword with two hands on the grip and is further subdivided into *zogho largo* and *zogho stretto* plays. (See page 129 for more on the *largo/stretto* distinction.) The sword in armor (*spada in arme*) section covers techniques specialized for dealing with an armored opponent. Fiore makes no distinction among physical differences of swords. A sword is a sword. What matters is how you use it.

The next section concerns the axe (*azza*). This is a weapon designed for armored combat and the players using it are depicted in armor.

The last of the foot combat weapons is the lance (*lanza*), which we modern practitioners are more likely to call a spear.

Having laid out the art of combat on foot, Fiore proceeds on to fighting on horseback (*a cavallo*), where he looks at using lance, sword, and *abrazare* while mounted.

Above: Fiore's first baton play.
Below: A dagger play from Talhoffer's 1467 *Fechtbuch*.

TRANSITIONS BETWEEN SECTIONS

Between most of the weapon sections there are transitional elements. Most of these elements consist of mixed weapon plays where elements of the preceding section are used, usually against the weapon of the following section (and, in this context, I'll be considering the empty hand as a weapon).

Between the *abrazare* section and the dagger section there are four *bastoncello* (baton) plays. The first two show a scholar (although whose scholar he is remains unclear) using a baton against an unarmed opponent. These plays can just as easily be done with a dagger. Indeed, several later German fighting treatises illustrate the so-called scissors trap on the neck being done with a dagger.

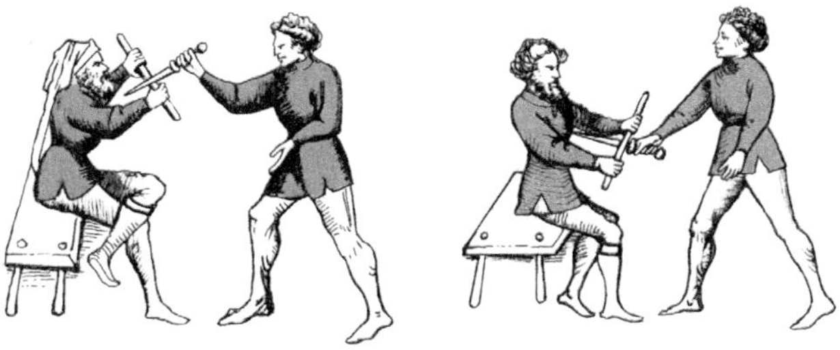

In the second half of the page between *abrazare* and dagger, Fiore identifies these scholars as belonging to dagger masters (eighth and sixth, respectively). This seems to be an error. The Sixth Remedy Master is the one to deal with downward-grip attacks while it is the Eighth Master who deals with upward-grip attacks.

The second two plays show the scholar in a seated position. This is very unusual in fighting treatises and, even in Fiore's work, appears only in the Getty manuscript. Fighting while seated on a bench is hardly a battlefield option. It is, however, a situation that might arise in an assassination attempt, something that was a concern of nobles in the Italian states during Fiore's time.

These seated scholars use a baton to cover against dagger attacks but are specifically identified in the text as scholars of two of the Remedy Masters of the dagger—albeit apparently mistakenly coded as to the numbers.

Between the dagger section and the sword section, and spread across three pages, are plays matching a dagger against a sword. The first page has a dagger-armed master dealing with attacks by a swordsman. The second and third pages have a sword-armed master, whose sword starts in its scabbard, playing against an attacker with a dagger. What weapon the master holds changes during these plays, and on the third page Fiore begins the instruction for the sword in one hand with three opponents facing a master as he stands ready to receive them.

The subdivisions of the sword section are interrupted by several plays using sticks. These appear between the sword in two hands section and the sword in armor section. The master with seven swords, or segno page, also appears here.

As a break between the sword in armor subsection and the axe section, Fiore gives us two drawings of specialized swords, rather than matching the sword against the axe. No obvious transitional material appears between the axe section and the spear section. Possibly this speaks to an attempt to unify the armored foot combat sections by not interrupting these sections whose weapon use is clearly very closely related.

One would expect to find some transitional material between the spear and mounted combat sections, but the plays of a spear-armed man on foot facing horsemen do not appear until the end of the mounted combat section. Why it is there and not elsewhere is unclear.

The general pattern of placement of these transitional elements makes it clear that Fiore is using them as punctuation between the sections. This approach is clearest in the Getty. The Pisani-Dossi places them differently while the Morgan groups what it has of them at the end of the manuscript, right after the truncated plays of sword in one hand. They are absent from the Paris manuscript.

DISPERSED AND LINKED INFORMATION

Fiore does not give us all the information about his art that we—from our viewpoint some 600 years later—would wish he did. Some information that he does present is not where we would expect it. For example, modern martial artists usually feel that footwork and body orientation are basics that should be taught at the beginning of study. Fiore does not do that. Other than specific stepping instructions in some plays, he does not present any explanation of the *volte* (turns of the body) and the "four things" (i.e., steps) until the first text of the sword in two hands section, well into the manuscript.

This is not an unknown technique in some modern teaching methods. Sometimes having students perform an action before giving them a name or definition for that action works well. Was Fiore aware of this? Is the presentation deliberately ordered according to such an idea, or is the placement of this information so deep in the manuscript simply a question of being included when he remembered to include it. After all, haven't we all had one of those "Oh, yeah, I forgot to mention ..." moments when explaining a subject? Fiore could tell us, but as he is unavailable for consultations, we can only guess at his reasons.

Certainly Fiore disperses information within the manuscript. Sometimes he makes explicit reference to the connections, other times he merely infers or implies. As noted before, the seated players with batons are noted as being scholars of dagger masters. These scholars are using batons rather than daggers, but their techniques belong to dagger masters. By making this connection Fiore tells us that similar tools work in similar ways. Similarly, in the mounted section he makes it clear that alternate weapons that share the crucial characteristics have the same effect, saying, "What I do here I could do with my *ghiavarina,*[1] with my staff or sword."

Several plays in the sword section refer back to the third play of dagger and the Middle Bind that is executed by that scholar. There are also immediate textual references to other plays, such as in the connection between the Ninth and Fourth Dagger Remedy Masters, and the Fifth Dagger Remedy Master's statement that he can do what the preceding masters do. Additionally, visual cues in some of the illustrations also offer links between sections, as I will comment on later.

The overall result of all these connections is something not too unlike a hypertext, leaving us with the inescapable conclusion that *il Fior di Battaglia* is an amazing, sophisticated work of expository presentation.

PICTURES IN *IL FIOR DI BATTAGLIA*

The illustrations in the treatise are drawn with great skill and attention to detail, but they should not be thought of as the medieval equivalent of photographs. Fiore's illustrations are more like diagrams, intended to convey important details of an action, rather than rendering a realistic view of a technique as it might be executed in a fight. It is, as part of the instruction, important to show the mechanical details of a fighting action and to show those details "clean" so the reader can appreciate the necessary components.

Experimentation and experience suggest that what may at first appear to be a case of a multi-moment illustration is a depiction where part of the body is poised for an accompanying action, rather than executing that action. If the action were illustrated in its proper timing, it might partly or completely obscure the important action details from the reader's angle of view. Fiore does not give us views of a single action from both sides (at least not within the same manuscript), as we often see in modern martial treatises, nor does he give us supplementary detail pictures of important parts of a technique. Those tools were not in his arsenal.

Another interpretive issue is that artists of the time were still struggling with perspective. Which foot is in front? Is the arm extended directly toward the opponent or at an angle? This problem is especially troublesome in the sword section, but it does occur in the dagger section as well.

Another problem which dogs interpretation of the sword section is that swords are occasionally drawn as though they were transparent, making it difficult to understand which blade should be nearer

[1] A specialized spear with a wide blade and flange-like spikes below the head.

From the Pisani-Dossi (carta 6A)

From the Getty (10rD)

The same dagger Instruction Master from the Pisani-Dossi (left) and from the Getty (right). The Getty masters wear progressively more elaborate clothing and are represented as progressively older (and presumably wiser) men. The Getty's illustrative approach may be encoding an understanding that the groups of techniques are progressively more advanced. Certainly some modern masters of Asian martial arts believe throws are for more advanced students than breaks.[2]

the viewer. This is not a trivial matter since it affects how follow-on action will work. One must use judgement, experience, experimentation, and—with caution—even material from other sources to reach an interpretation.

The line drawings in this volume are traced from the illustrations in the Getty. Adjustments have been made to clarify body positions, make weapons straighter and more visible, adjust hands so they have the normal five fingers, and get the correct hand on the correct arm. Great attention was paid to the details and I think you will find them reliable regarding the details of the actions depicted.

That said, you will find that drawings sometimes differ from reality. For one thing, the drawings are not done from a consistent angle, but rather present whatever angle informs of whatever detail(s) is (are) significant for the circumstance depicted. This will be noticeable in this books interpretation photographs, especially regarding the positions (*poste*), which are presented in front and side views relative to the opponent and do not always look exactly like the drawings.

HOLES IN THE SYSTEM?

Just how complete is Fiore's *armizare* system? This is a difficult question to answer, as *complete* and *system* mean different things to different martial artists. Fiore tells us his book "will show you all the art clearly enough for you to understand it." Yet some of the "all" seems to be missing. For one, where are the basics? Stance and footwork are considered absolute basics by modern martial artists, but Fiore says nothing about the latter and doesn't get around to mentioning the former until the middle of the sword section, although several specific stepping instructions appear scattered throughout the treatise. What about how to hold a sword? Fiore shows us places to grip one for various effects, but says nothing about how tight to hold it or when to loosen or tighten the grip. What about how to swing a sword, or any other weapon for that matter? The closest he comes to this is with his instructions for cutting and thrusting, and they are more along the lines of a corrective to improve one's understanding of the best

[2] In Sang H. Kim, *Teaching Martial Arts, The Way of the Master*, Turtle Press, 2nd. ed. 1997.

path for particular cuts to take. And what about horsemanship? Dom Duarte, king of Portugal, avid practitioner of arms, tells us[3] that the better horseman will win an engagement. Where is Fiore's advice on handling your horse in combat?

I think that the answer to the question of the missing basics lies in the nature of Fiore's audience. *Il Fior di Battaglia* is dedicated to Nicolo d'Este and was, as we are told in the prolog, written at his order. Elsewhere in the book Fiore addresses comments directly to Nicolo. This book was written for him and for his use. By the time Fiore wrote, Nicolo was a prominent figure with a reputation as a formidable swordsman. To suggest he needed to learn the basics could well be considered an insult. On the other hand, offering him a framework for the art of arms as he would have already learned it and presenting the fruit of a master swordsman's long study of the art would be a valuable service. Remember that Fiore, by his own admission, was an old man when he wrote and he was unlikely to be around much longer to teach his hard-won secrets, secrets for which he fought duels in order to keep them that way. Those secrets would be a valuable commodity to Nicolo. But basics? Nicolo was well past needing instruction in those.

So it seems that Fiore's book is an advanced text and not one for beginners. As such, according to some definitions, it is *not* complete since it lacks the basics. As reconstructors of an art to which we have lost our connections, we crave instruction in those basics. To find them, we must look to other texts and other arts and carefully adapt what we find to what we learn from Fiore's books.

Specific missing actions and types of actions are often pointed out as holes in Fiore's art. As noted earlier in this chapter, Fiore's use of the medieval process of teaching principle by exemplar fills those holes, I believe. We must understand Fiore's exemplars more completely and understand them in the context of their presentation. I hope this book will open some of those doors.

A WORK IN PROGRESS?

As noted before, there are differences in detail between Fiore's books. Some, I believe, illuminate an ongoing thought process on Fiore's part. For example, he seems to be struggling with how to best represent the equal nature of the two players in the crossing of the swords in a bind.

Below, we see the first Remedy Master of the sword in two hands as presented in the various manuscripts. Note the figure on the left is rendered as a Remedy Master (shown wearing a crown) in all

From the Getty
(25rC)

From the Morgan
(27rA)

[3] In Antonio Franco Preto & Luis Preto (trans.), *The Royal Book of Horsemanship, Jousting and Knightly Combat, Dom Duarte's 15th century Bem Cavalgar*, Chivalry Bookshelf, 2005.

four, but the figure on the right is treated differently: in one, he is simply a player (with no identifying markers), in the next, a Counter Master (who wears both a crown and a garter), and the other two, a Remedy Master himself.[4]

Is the right-hand player a Remedy Master (as in the Pisani-Dossi and the Paris) because he too can do the plays? Is he a Counter Master (as in the Morgan) because he does the plays if he acts first? Or is he best presented as simply a player (as in the Getty) with text covering the two figures' equality? This last approach is helpful, as it does not disrupt the primary-variant scholar organization as detailed on page 30.

Further evidence of the imperfections in Fiore's body of work comes from the obvious mistakes within the manuscripts. I've already pointed out the incorrect assignments to dagger Remedy Masters for the seated scholars of the baton. Other mistakes, or perceived mistakes, may not be so easy to see and, even when found, not all interpreters will agree on their existence, let alone their nature.

One apparent mistake is, I believe, more a case of Fiore suffering from second thoughts about an element of his organization—an occupational hazard for those trying to explain complicated activities and processes. In the text for the last scholar of the Sixth Remedy Master of the dagger, Fiore says "Although I have been placed after the counter of the sixth play, I logically belong before it, since I am a student and this play belongs to the Sixth Master." You will note that he does not accuse the artist of having drawn the picture in the wrong place. He says a similar thing about belonging to a master in the twelfth play of the First Remedy Master of the dagger. As I will detail further later, I believe that the nature of these plays and their placement after Counter Masters is a feature of the organization of the treatise rather than a mistake.

Second thoughts may also be the explanation behind variations in the organization of some of the plays when compared across the manuscripts. One example is the change from four to three Counter Masters for the First Remedy Master of the dagger. In the Pisani-Dossi, the first Counter Master hits the arm of a scholar who makes his cover badly. This is not really an action on the master's part, which could be why it is missing in the more tightly arranged Getty manuscript.

More could be said in this subject, but space is lacking in this book, so we will move on.

From the Pisani-Dossi
(carta 19B)

From the Paris
(14rA)

[4] For definitions of the types of masters, see Masters and Scholars beginning on page 28.

Fiore's art requires a stance that is strong and stable, both in armor and out of armor. It also requires a stance suitable for moving in any direction with equal facility.

Stand with your weight on the balls of your feet, knees slightly bent. At first, this is tiring for modern feet and legs, especially your calf muscles. Persevere. You will ultimately find yourself better able to move, and to move quickly.

Your feet should be about shoulder width apart. This is wide enough to be stable and narrow enough that you are not limited to a preferential movement direction.

Your lead foot should point straight at your imaginary opponent, and your trailing foot should point away from that line by about 45 degrees.

Keep your hips tucked in beneath your head and let your weight settle down evenly through both legs. You should feel very stable in this position.

If you shift more of your weight to your leading leg, you will find your body and head move slightly closer to your imaginary opponent.

If you shift more of your weight to your trailing leg, you will find your body and head move slightly away from your imaginary opponent.

You can vary your weight distribution according to tactical needs. It will also vary naturally as you seek to move from this stable position.

When you seek to move from the stable, evenly weighted position, you must first shift some of your weight to one foot or the other. The foot from which you shift weight becomes lighter-weighted and you can lift it from the ground without falling over. Once off the ground, you can move that foot wherever you wish, transferring weight to it again to achieve the stable position or even more weight to it to allow the first heavy-weighted foot to become lighter-weighted and then to move.

Going through this weight-shifting sequence while moving one foot forward then the other is usually called *walking*.

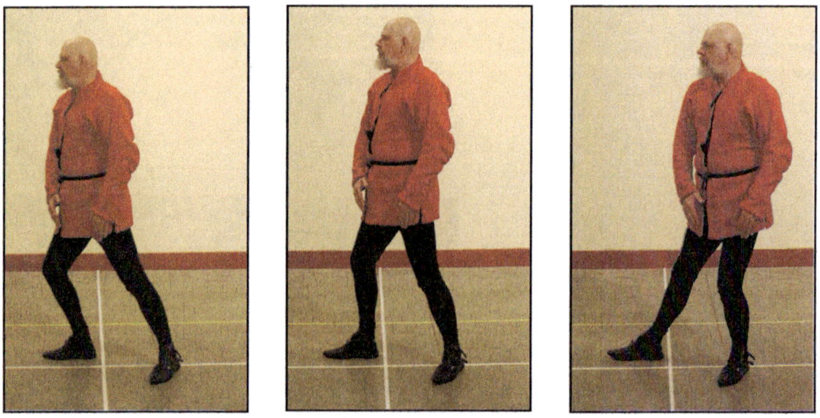

Iron Gate Position held with the weight forward (left), centered (center), and backward (right).

Fiore uses the term *strada* meaning *way* or *path* in reference to the relative positions of the two fighters. His use of the concept seems to have strong similarities to what, in modern fencing, is called the line, but it is not identical.

In fencing, if you are primarily facing your opponent's chest, you are on the inside line. If you are facing his flank or back, you are on the outside line. This is a definition built on a linear stance with the sword presented forward.

Fiore's art, unlike modern fencing, is not linear and the sword, or other weapon, can be held in a variety of ways. Fiore's is an art in which wrestling is integral and squared-up, orientation-changing, full-body forward motion is too. The notion of a path wider than the weapon's line is consistent with his art.

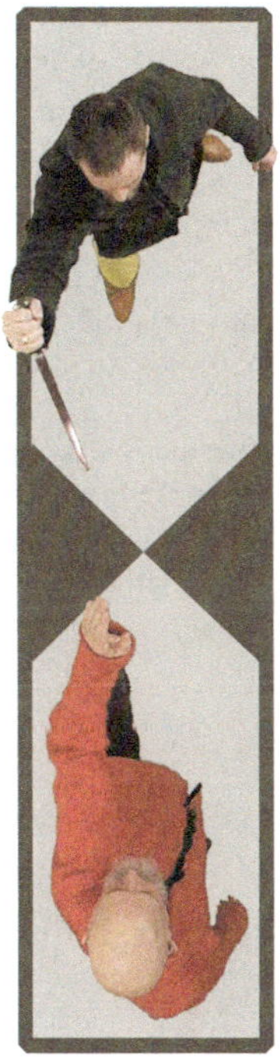

You can think of the Way as an imaginary path connecting the two opponents who are facing each other. This is the space through which one would move to attack the other.

Stepping out of the Way creates a new Way for the moving player, one in which he has a direct line toward the opponent and the opponent is left facing air.

Moving to the outside **Moving to the Inside**

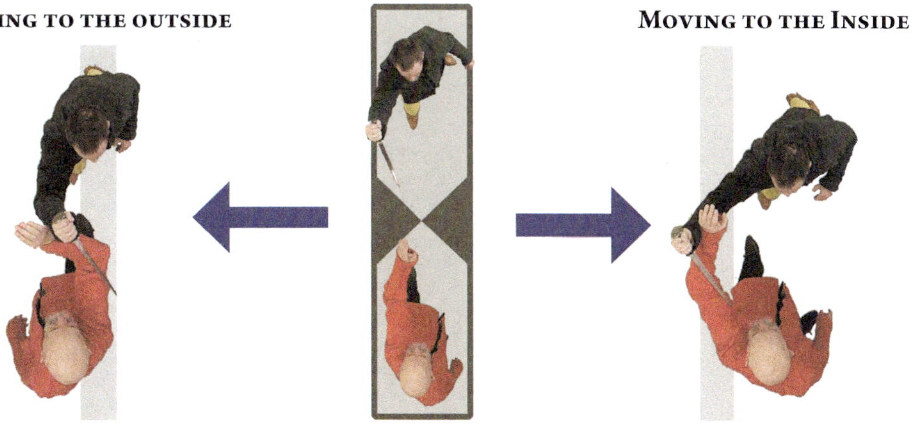

When you respond to an attack, you will end up either remaining in the Way or moving to the inside or outside of weapon's path as it comes forward within the Way.

Regarding steps, Fiore says there are four things in the art: *passare* and (*re*)*tornare* plus *accressere* and *discressere*, rendered here as pass, return (or pass back), increase and decrease. There are two pairs, each distinguishing a foot's movement relation to the other foot.

Fiore seems to have chosen to lump steps together rather than split the possible steps, and he has chosen a single dominant aspect to name his stepping categories. All the various possible steps can be built from these blocks. Fiore gives examples in some plays with explicit instructions as to which foot does which step and sometimes he even gives the general direction, as in "pass across" and "adjust forward out of the way." We learn that the pass (*passare*), and by inference the return (*retornare*), is not confined to motion directly forward. While making either, the moving foot may shift slightly, or significantly, to one side or the other.

PASS
(*PASSARE*)

The rear foot moves forward, past the front and becomes the new front foot.

INCREASE
(*ACCRESSERE*)

One foot shifts. Your other foot does not move. The moving foot *increases* the distance between it and the non-moving foot. The moving foot moves in a direction appropriate to the tactical circumstances.

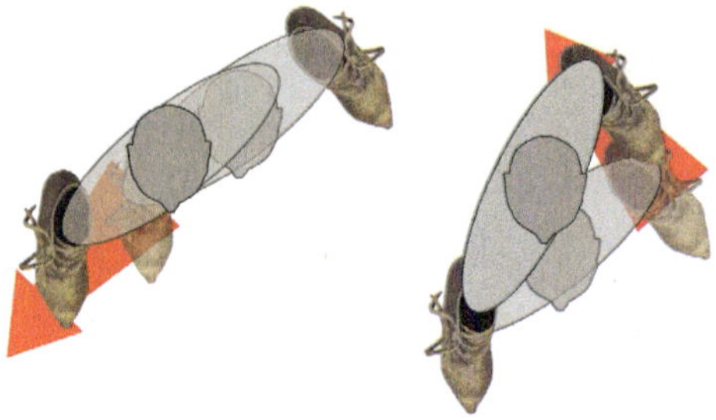

RETURN
(*RETORNARE*)

The front foot moves backward, past the rear and becomes the new rear foot.

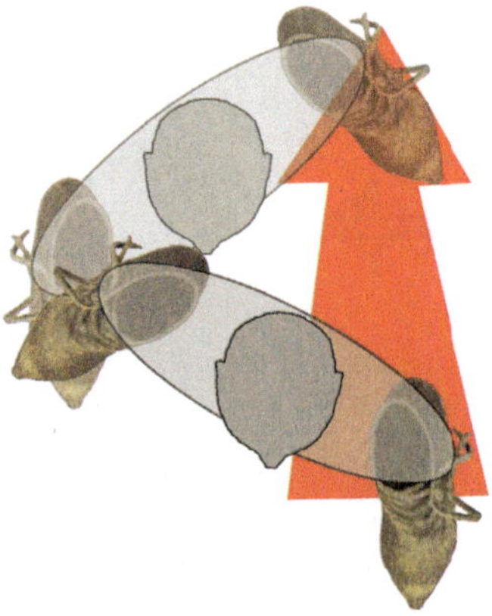

DECREASE
(*DISCRESSERE*)

One foot shifts. Your other foot does not move. The moving foot *decreases* the distance between it and the non-moving foot. The moving foot moves in a direction appropriate to the tactical circumstances.

Here the oblique pass is taken across the line. Note how this takes the body away from anything moving through the center.

Here the oblique return moves away from the line through the center. The head is clear but the body is not. Both move further away.

Normally a pass (or return) changes the distance between you and your opponent, but it need not do so. Stepping obliquely while passing (or returning) can change your orientation to your opponent as well as possibly changing the measure. Stepping this way is often called a slope pass or an oblique pass.

Other steps can be built with the basic foot shifts as well. An increase of the front foot followed by a decrease of the rear (A) gives an advance. A decrease of the back followed by an increase of the front (B) yields a gathering step. A compass step is the footwork to the Full Turn (*tutta volta*). A slope pass comes from a pass followed by a decrease of the new back foot (C).

Tactical necessity and the player's intention will govern the length of steps and their direction, which makes it hard to explain in a book. The proper choice requires judgement honed by practice and experience.

That said, Fiore seems to prefer stepping into an opponent's attack. But he also seems to want to have his students safe in the fight. The good scholar must recognize when to choose one preference over another. For example, one can use retrograde steps to effectively create time to react to the opponent's action and thus stay safe, at the expense of following the precept to move into an attack.

However you step, you want to maintain good body structure and orientation. In an attack, you want your moving foot to point directly at your opponent, as this defines your body's orientation and your structure. You want to be aligned directly toward where you will focus your energy: your opponent. If your intent in the motion is not a direct or immediate attack, but rather a preparatory, re-positioning move, your moving foot should point in the direction of your motion, again to preserve your structure and alignment.

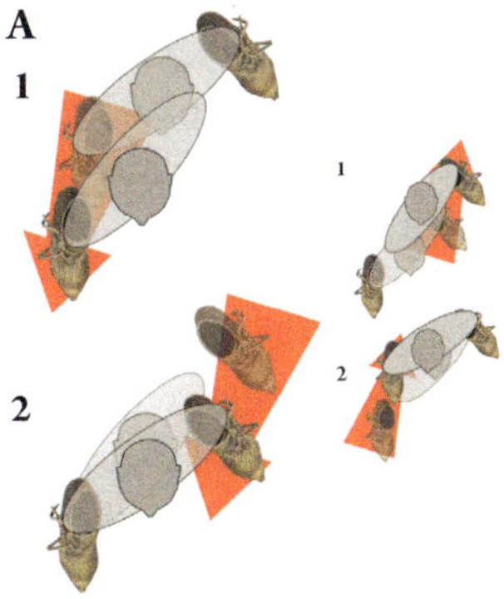

An oblique *accressere* of the front foot advances the body toward the opponent, increasing the width of the player's stance and lessening his stability. A follow-up *discressere* of the rear foot restores his stability. A front foot *discressere* followed by a rear foot *accressere* yields a retreat.

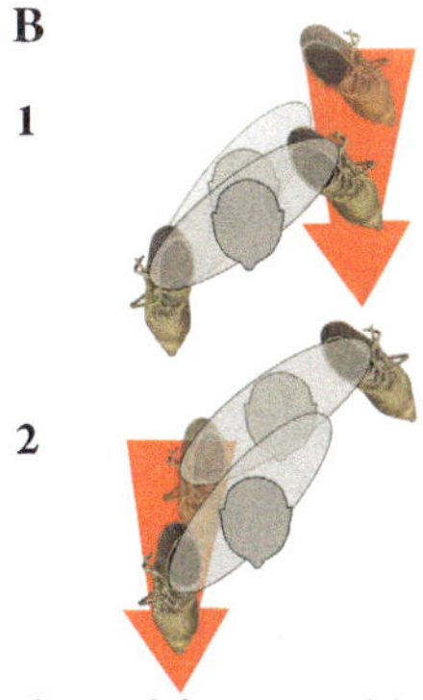

A forward *discressere* of the rear foot does not shift the body in relation to the opponent, but lessens stability. A follow-up *accressere* of the front foot restores his stability and advances closer to the opponent.

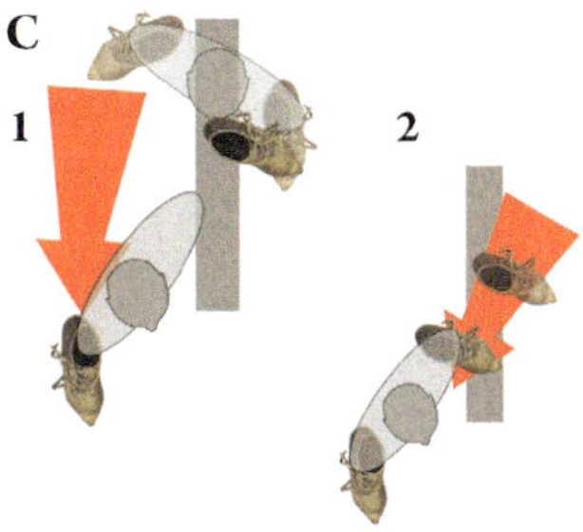

An oblique forward *passare* of the rear foot retreats the body off the line but increases the player's foot separation and lessens his stability. A follow-up *discressere* of the new back foot restores his stability.

Fiore says there are three turns (*volta*): the *volta stabile,* the *mezza volta,* and the *tutta volta,* rendered here as the Stable Turn (or turn in place), the Half Turn, and the Full Turn.

Fiore says that the turns involve "playing" and this means they are more than just footwork. They all involve re-orienting your body position, shifting the hips and shoulders in ways that add power to whatever action you are attempting to do.

The turns change the direction of the energy which you are bringing to bear. It is this change of direction that makes them so effective in powering throws.

You can also change distance with the turns, allowing you to move out of the way of an attack or to bring your own attack to bear. The Stable Turn has a particularly subtle effect of apparent measure change. If you are in the heels-forward stance and the opponent only reads your body position, he will likely believe that you are further away than you are. This can lure him into your measure so that, with a quick Stable Turn, you can strike him before he realizes he has entered your measure.

Two of the turns, by definition, require movement of a foot. All require reorientation of both feet. However, experienced practitioners find that they can generate much of the same effect (and power) by shifting their hips without moving their feet. Whether Fiore would see such an action as one of his *volta* remains a question we cannot answer.

STABLE TURN
(VOLTA STABILE)

A volta stabile ***lets you play forward or backward (from one side only), without moving your feet.***

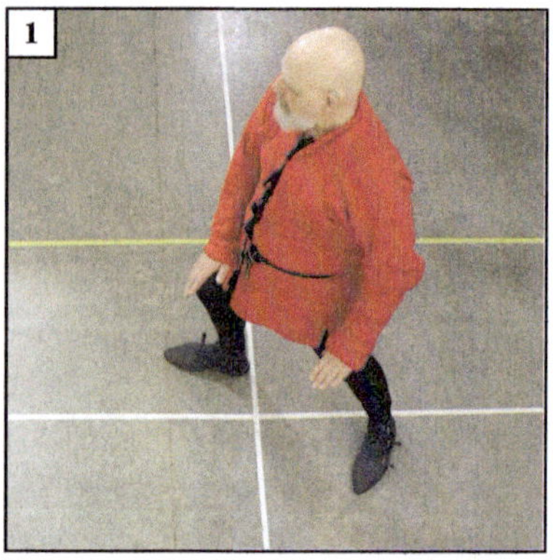

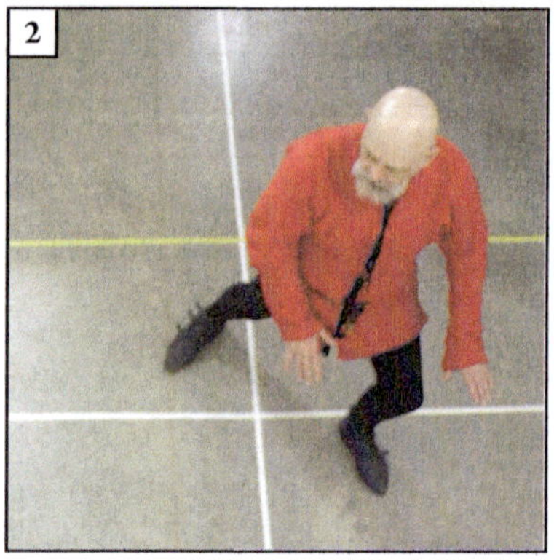

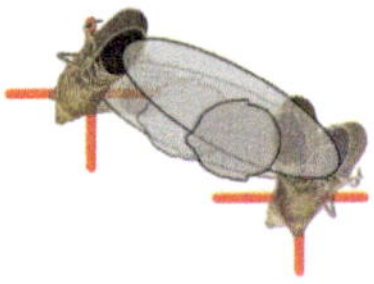

To make a Stable Turn, pivot on the balls of both feet. If, as here, you start with your front foot pointing at your opponent, turn until it points about 45° away from your opponent. This produces a heels-forward stance as seen in many of Fiore's illustrations.

Where you play before

Where you play after

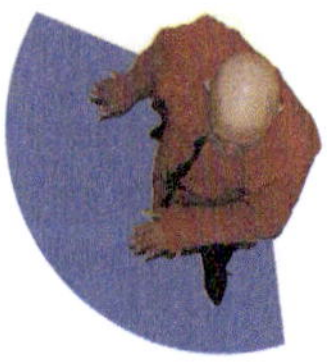

HALF TURN
(MEZZA VOLTA)

A mezza volta *is when you pass forward or backward, letting you play on the opposite side forward or backward respectively.*

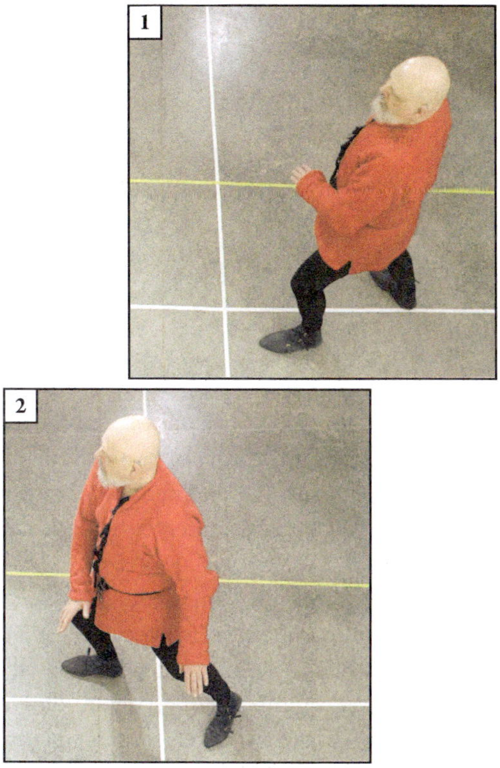

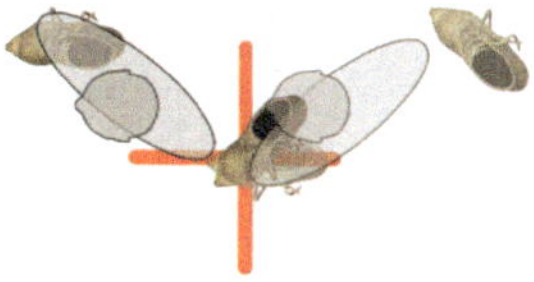

Fiore's description makes it clear that the footwork of a Half Turn is a pass or a return and that it is the change in where you play that makes it a *volta* rather than a simple *passare* or *retornare*.

Where you play before

Where you play after

FULL TURN
(TUTTA VOLTA)

A tutta volta *is when you use one foot to describe a circle around the other foot; in other words, one foot stays in place, the other circles around it.*

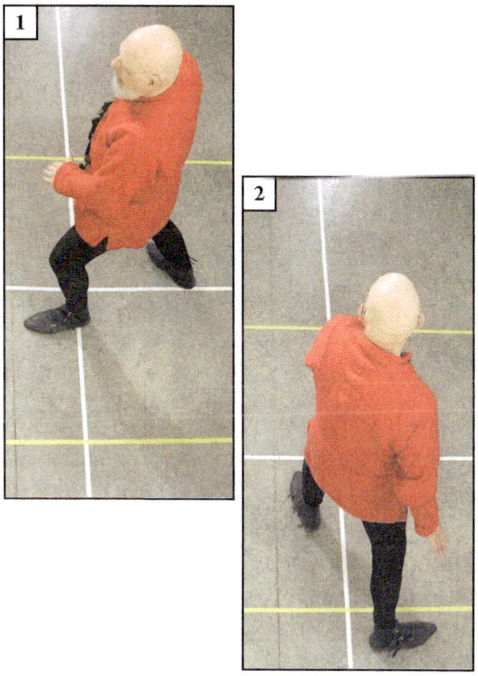

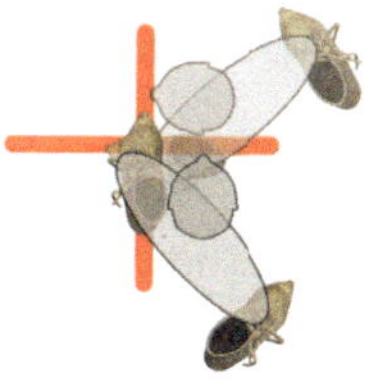

Fiore's description of the Full Turn is quite clear. You pivot on the ball of one foot (here the front one). The other foot and leg moves around it. In making a Full Turn, your circling foot moves a little or a lot, depending on the time available and the intent of the action.

Where you play before

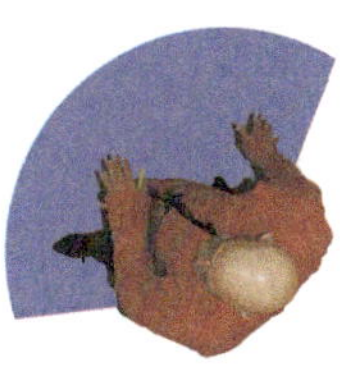

Where you play after

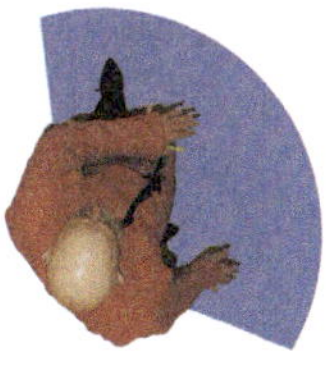

Overall, these Masters and students support the whole art of arms—on horseback and on foot, armored and unarmored ...

MASTERS & SCHOLARS

Fiore lays out his system of masters and scholars in *il Fior di Battaglia's* prolog. He names and numbers four types of masters, though the numbering apparently only applies to their order of presentation in the prolog. The first is the Fight Master, the second is the Remedy, the third is the Counter, and "in some places, the art admits a Fourth Master or king who counters the Third king or Counter to the Remedy. I call this the Fourth Master or Contra-counter."

The Morgan manuscript, like the Getty, names the masters (except for the Contra-counter Master who is not described), but the Pisani-Dossi prolog neither names nor numbers the masters. Instead, it lays out the organization of the manuscript in a manner more like a modern table of contents. Although this listing is sometimes annotated, it uses the appearance of masters essentially as chapter headings. Most of the Pisani-Dossi masters fall into the Getty manuscript's categories of masters despite not being given names.

In the Getty, Fiore sets out this system for *abrazare*, or wrestling, and says the same system applies to other weapons supporting "the whole art of arms." In the *abrazare* section, no Contra-counter Master appears, despite such a master being described as part of the model. In fact, Contra-counter Masters are very rare throughout Fiore's body of work. None[1] appear as described in the Getty, although a couple appear in the dagger section of the Pisani-Dossi. Clearly Fiore's planning does not always align with his practice.

I believe that this discrepancy in design-realization of Fiore's master and scholar organization is another sign of the evolution of concept that occurs across Fiore's work. The Getty, the most evolved, essentially eliminates the Contra-counter Masters, possibly because, as Fiore says in the prolog, "Few plays, however, can go beyond the Third Master, after which lies danger." The missing Contra-counter Masters could be part of a streamlining process resulting in the Getty manuscript's content.

Though all types of masters do not appear in all weapon sections, this system of masters and scholars lays out a teaching program. It allows the reader to recognize the flow of instruction and understand when the pedagogy shifts from one phase to another.

1 One scholar in the mounted combat section is described as the counter to the previous play, a Counter Master's play, and should therefore be a Contra-counter Master.

Fight Masters

The first type of master that Fiore introduces is the Fight Master. These masters wear their identifying crowns and stand in a position (*posta*) or guard (*guardia*), terms Fiore seems to consider equivalent. A *posta*, Fiore says, "is what you use to defend or 'guard' yourself against the opponent's attacks. A *posta* (or *guardia*) is a 'posture' against the opponent, which you use to injure him without danger to yourself."

Fight Masters wear a crown (9rA)

Fight Masters offer instruction in how the fight flows and what can be achieved from a given position. Primarily, they note what sort of attacks can be launched from the position. Unfortunately for us, they often speak in obscure generalities, leaving interpreters to seek out what Fiore meant through experimentation and by correlation with other fencing masters and traditions.

Remedy Masters

The second category of masters is the Remedy Masters. They wear their crowns and present a remedy, which is an "antidote against your opponent's attacks together with the ability to strike him." Strike, in this context, may not be literally a striking attack but rather the opportunity to use some technique such as a grapple, disarm, or throw against the opponent. Sometimes the technique to use *is* an actual strike.

Remedy Masters wear a crown (10vA)

Remedy Masters are usually followed by scholars who execute a specific follow-on action. I'll say more about scholars shortly.

In what may be a space-saving measure, the Remedy Master is often shown already moving into a follow-on action and thus becomes his own first scholar. This peculiarity can make it tricky to understand the technique of the remedy itself, leading an unwary interpreter to conflate remedy and follow-on technique.

Counter Masters

Next come the Counter Masters, who wear crowns and garters and respond to the Remedy Master and his scholars. Sometimes a counter is only described in text.

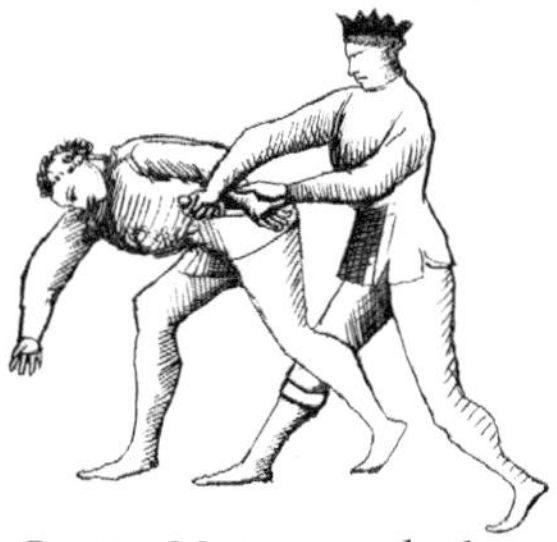

Counter Masters wear both a crown and a garter (11vA)

Some Counter Masters work against the particular play of a scholar and appear directly after that scholar. These I call *specific Counter Masters*. Others make their play directly against the cover of the Remedy Master, acting before the follow-on action takes place. These I call *general Counter Masters*.

Masters, in general, function as punctuation points in Fiore's pedagogy. As we'll see, these general Counter Masters have a special place in separating one section of instruction from another because, in some cases, scholars belonging to the Remedy Master do not appear until after the general Counter Master. *Il Fior di Battaglia* is a carefully structured work, so this placement likely means something significant.

CONTRA-COUNTER MASTERS

Contra-counter Masters wear both a crown and a garter (the same symbols as a Counter Master) but they stand on the side of the drawing that their fellow scholar's stand on.
(carta 8a position E, Pisani-Dossi)

Last among Fiore's listed masters are the Contra-counter Masters, who also wear crowns and garters. These masters respond to the Counter Masters with a technique that foils the counter. Fiore himself tells us these are rare and the art rarely progresses past the Counter Master stage.

Fiore's comment "after which lies danger" seems to me a rare statement of Fiore's assessment of how a fight can progress and what makes for a fight one can survive. On a practical level, it is easy to see how a fight is over, reset to an earlier phase, or devolved into unscientific roughhousing by the time the Contra-counter master's turn comes around.

OTHER MASTERS

(10rA)

Several other crowned figures appear in the manuscript that do not quite fit into Fiore's categories. They wear crowns, the sign of a master. They also appear like chapter headings in the Pisani-Dossi prolog's tour of the manuscript. It follows that they must be masters.

Here's the problem: They don't fit with any one of the descriptions in the prolog. They do not stand in a position (*posta)* like Fight Masters. They do not wear garters like Scholars, Counter Masters, or Contra-counter Masters. They can't be Remedy Masters because they do not make a cover or execute a technique. Instead these masters stand casually and offer advice or instruction. The ones in the dagger section mostly speak in general terms but those associated with the sword section get somewhat more specific in their advice.

I call these undescribed masters *Instruction Masters* for their role in the manuscript. Despite not appearing in Fiore's roll call of masters, these Instruction Masters are important to his presentation of the art. The sword section masters, in particular, distill aspects of *armizare* that are vital to understanding the art. One cannot help but wish Fiore had given us more of them.

One of the Instruction Masters is different from the rest because he does actually stand in a *posta*. It is the same *posta* as the first Fight Master: Full Iron Gate, although we see it here from the front which, in itself, is an unusual thing.

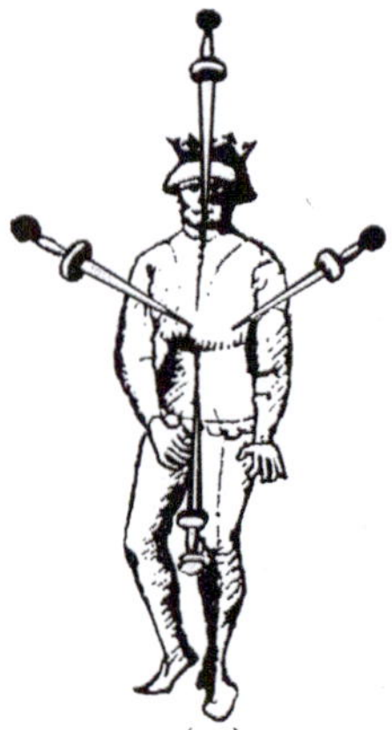

(9v)

This fellow (shown left) is doing a lot of jobs. His inclusion suggests an attempt to parallel the segno, or seven-swords page, but to do it for dagger because he is quite similar to the segno shown later in the manuscript. In both, the weapon under discussion lies over the figure on angles assigned to certain blows. The text accompanying him covers similar ground to the four illustrations in the sword section which detail the attacks that can be made with a sword, showing their paths and targets. In addition, this page contains paragraphs of text in Fiore's style of Fight Master introductions and even some trash talk about the superiority of the dagger—Fiore tends to talk up a weapon when introducing it.

This unique figure is a combination Fight-Instruction Master for the dagger and he appears only in the Getty manuscript.

PLAYERS AND COMPANIONS

Fiore refers his practitioners, scholars and masters alike, as players (*zugadori*). Those with whom they practice he calls companions (*compagni*). This is an important point of mind-set, for in learning the art we must work together.

Fiore's reference to training in harmony is something we modern practitioners should take to heart, striving to do so as we work to interpret his teachings and as we strive to understand and practice his art.

As important to our understanding of his art is his statement that real fighting will show nothing of this concern.

A VARIETY OF SCHOLARS

Scholars wear a garter on one leg. (10vC)

Scholars are the students of the masters. They are the players who make the action of a Remedy or Counter Master and execute his plays. They wear a garter on one leg to show their relationship to the master. Usually, they appear on the same side of the drawing as their master, but several times they switch sides so that the action can be drawn clearly.

Previously, I noted that some Remedy Masters have the flow of their scholars interrupted by general Counter Masters. Looking at the Dagger section, we can see that five of the general Counter Masters of dagger appear at the end of their Remedy Master's section and are immediately followed by the next Remedy Master (or in the case of the last one, by the next section). This is as one would expect from Fiore's description of Counter Masters in the prolog.

However, the other four general Counter Masters (First, Second, Sixth, and Eighth) are followed by additional scholars before the next Remedy Master appears, and two of their scholars specifically state that they are students of their Remedy Master. The scholar of the Sixth Remedy Master, as noted before, may be ambivalent about his placement but the sixth scholar (12th play) of the First Remedy Master just says that he belongs to the First Remedy Master. He is followed by four more scholars. That's a few too many to lay at the feet of an artist who misplaced a picture, especially as they are all accompanied by their own specific Counter Masters. This arrangement suggests that there might be something different about the scholars that follow general Counter Masters, and that these Counter Masters function as a punctuation point to alert the reader to a difference.

Here the Sixth Remedy Master's scholar makes a move very similar to that used in the cover of his master, yet it is not that cover but a direct attack to the incoming dagger hand. Fiore himself is ambivalent about the play's location in the treatise, saying "Although I have been placed after the counter of the sixth play, I logically belong before it, since I am a student and this play belongs to the Sixth Master." Yet in the end, he is where he is.

The Sixth Remedy Master (16rA)

This scholar's attack is another sign that the post-Counter Master scholars do not make the cover of their Remedy Master, and here it is quite clear that they take an action with mechanics strongly related to that cover.

Last scholar of the Sixth Remedy Master (16vD)

The Eighth Remedy Master
(17rC)

His first scholar
(17vA)

His second scholar
(17vB)

Neither of the scholars of the Eighth Remedy Master holds a dagger—a major difference from their master. This tells us that these scholars are definitely different from the usual follow-on scholars. Not only has their dagger disappeared, but they are making a cover rather than a follow-on play. Even though the text describes plays they can do, Fiore is clearly giving us something different here.

One of separated scholars belonging to the First Remedy Master (14th play) is very clear about not being a direct follow-on play. In the text of this scholar (18th play), it says "If I was unable to bend your arm ..." which is to say, if I am unable to do the first play where the scholar bends the arm and disarms the attacker, "this is the disarm I would choose."

This makes it obvious that the 18th play is not simply an alternative choice for a disarm, but only comes into play when the basic disarm fails. Thus it is not a direct play from the Remedy Master's cover.

Similarly, the very name that Fiore gives the seventh scholar's play (14th play of the First Remedy Master), "More Strength," tells us that it is circumstantial in its application. One uses it when one needs more strength, as when facing a more powerful opponent whose blow cannot be stopped by the Remedy Master's single-armed cover.

I could detail each variant scholar, but these examples should make it clear that Fiore's ordering of plays uses the punctuation point of a general Counter Master to separate scholars who do the Remedy Master's cover and a direct follow-on play from scholars whose play either involves a disruption to the normal follow-on play, a notable circumstance to employ the play, or a variant cover whose mechanics, while different, are strongly allied to the Remedy Master's cover.

Another distinction between scholars needs to be made. Some, as noted, make their play as a direct follow-on of the Remedy Master's cover. Others complete the play of a scholar who precedes them rather than making a play entirely of their own. Thus, in some portions of the manuscript, the number of plays is less than the total of *direct* (those who make a play) and *follow-on* (those who complete a play) scholars.

The First Remedy Master
(10vA)

Fourteenth play of the First
Remedy Master (12rB)

Eighteenth play of the First
Remedy Master (12vB)

PRESENTATIONAL STRUCTURE: FIRST REMEDY MASTER OF THE DAGGER

Here is the ordering of the plays of the First Remedy Master of the dagger. You will find a larger version in the Appendix, along with charts for the other Remedy Masters of all sorts.

A solid line connects the master to his primary scholars. A dashed line connects to secondary scholars. A diamond shape or line connects to Counter Masters. Alternatives are represented by a branching of the lines.

The illustrations of masters of all types are boxed in.

One element of the program absent from the First Remedy Master of the dagger is what I call follow-on scholars. These are scholars who continue the play of the scholar before them as indicated by the text. Their connection is shown by a solid line.

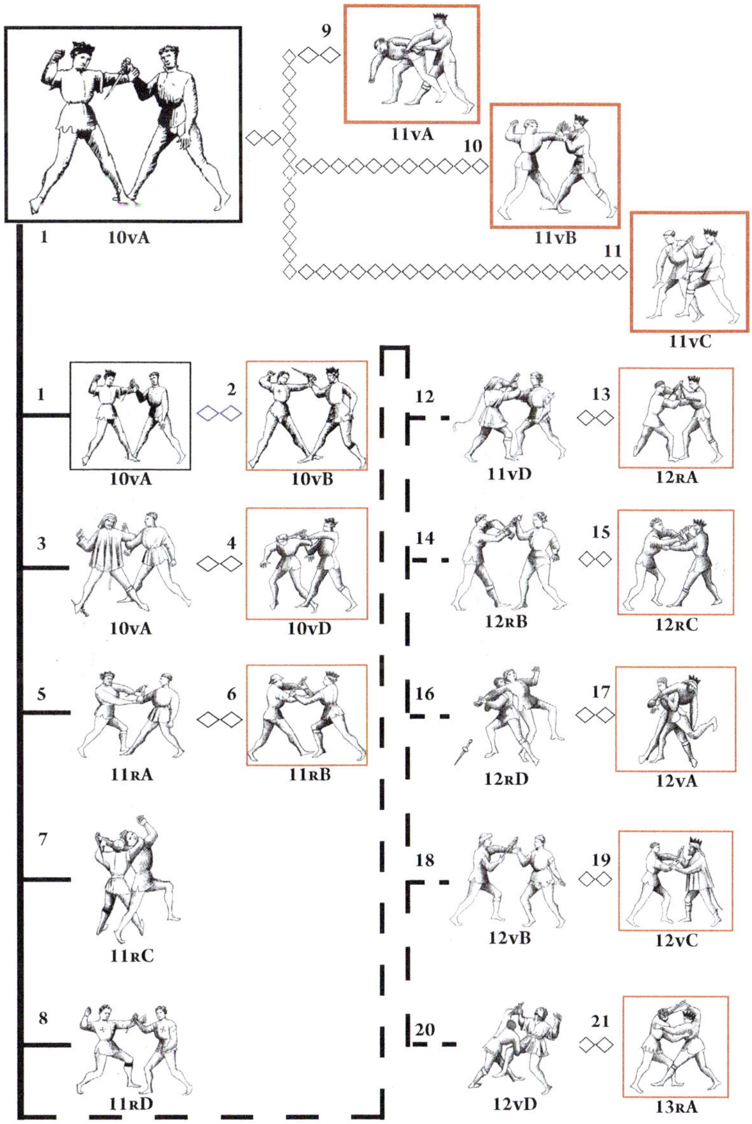

This page spread takes the First Remedy Master of the dagger as an example. Play begins with the Remedy Master making the cover. The action can proceed through the various scholars as dictated by the circumstances (five are shown here). The follow-on actions of the players can also affect the flow of play.

Some of the scholars' plays admit specific Counter Masters as indicated by the double headed arrows.

The last sequence at the bottom of the opposite page moves through Remedy Master to general Counter Master to Contra-counter Master.

REMEDY MASTER

The scholars of the First Remedy Master of the dagger each present one of the five elements of dagger fighting: disarms, breaks, binds, throws, and strikes. This pattern, coming first, reinforces the understanding that all elements of the art are present (at least *in potentia*) at all times.

The first four also offer paired options. The first two offer a closed and open space response while turning away from the attacker and the second two offer the same options while stepping into the attacker.

FIRST SCHOLAR

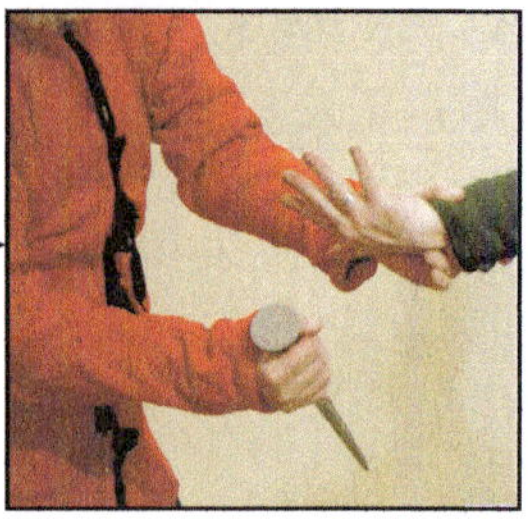

The first scholar grips the wrist of the attacker and turns it. This action levers the dagger from the attacker's hand, disarming him.

SECOND SCHOLAR

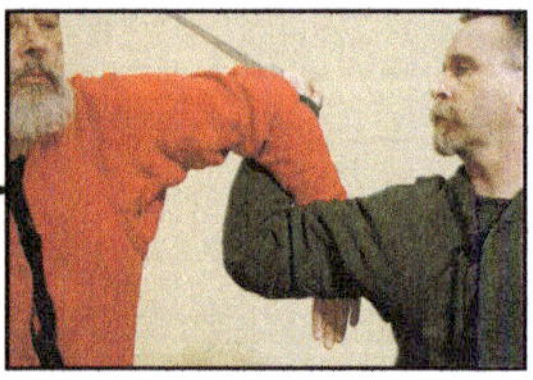

The second scholar slips his hand outside the attacker's elbow then brings it back in and up to break or dislocate the limb. This is easier if the attacker's arm is forced wide.

THIRD SCHOLAR

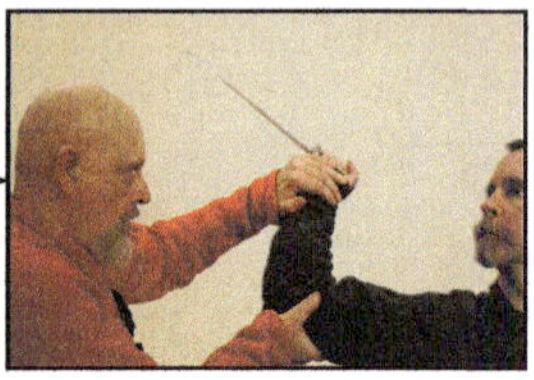

The third scholar grips then steps in, as he brings his other hand up to cup the elbow, forcing the limb into the Upper Bind.

FOURTH SCHOLAR

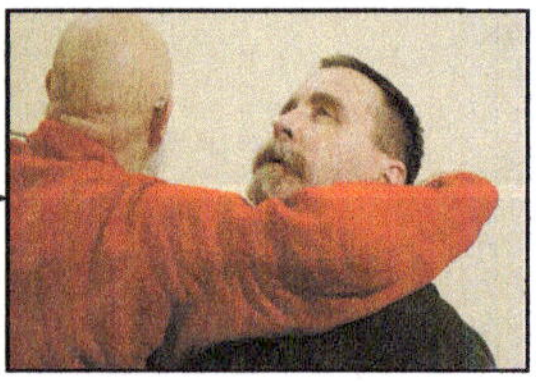

The fourth scholar grips, steps in and puts his upper right arm into the attacker's throat and his leg behind the attacker's, throwing him. This is easier if the attacker's arm is forced wide.

FIFTH SCHOLAR

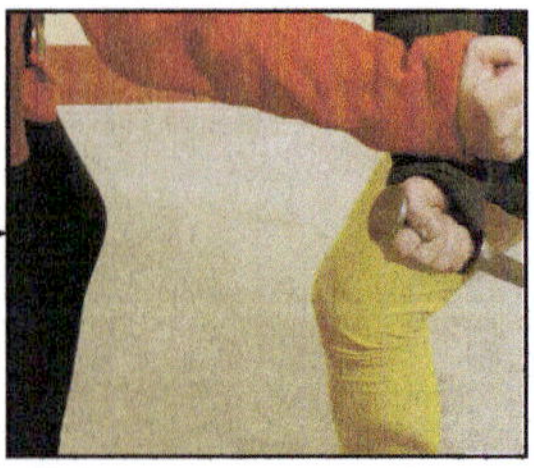

The fifth scholar strikes with his left hand into the outside of the attacker's arm. He follows this immediately with a right-hand strike to drive the dagger down and into the attacker.

Counter to First Scholar

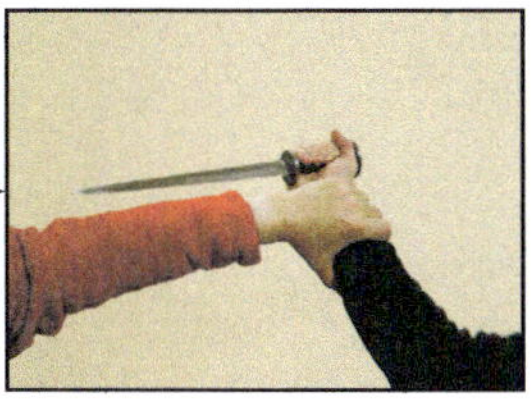

This Counter Master turns his blade up and over the scholar's arm. This action removes the leverage point for the disarm.

Counter to First Scholar

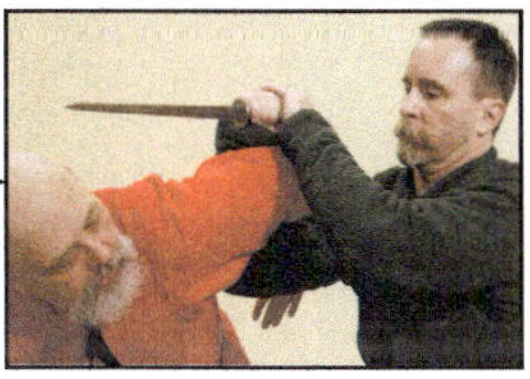

This Counter Master brings his left hand up and grabs his own dagger hand. This action gives him two hands against the scholar's one and a superior leverage position.

Counter to First Scholar

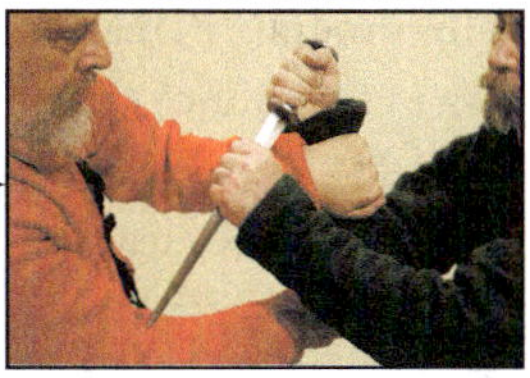

This Counter Master grabs his dagger blade with his left hand. This action gives him two hands against the scholar's one and allows him to redirect the point into the scholar's elbow.

Remedy Master

Counter Master

Embedded details may be hidden in the drawings. Note how the Remedy Master/scholar's foot is nearer to the viewer than the attacker's foot in one and further in the other. There is no time for the scholar to shift about while the Counter Master acts. This indicates, I believe, that the Remedy Master may or may not step off line as he makes the cover. Naturally stepping helps, but it may not be possible. The scholar must be ready to make the play in either case.

Not all Remedy Masters set the same patterns. Each offers something specific to his weapon or his place in the overall program while remaining within the overall master-and-scholar approach.

Remedy Master

The Remedy Master makes the cover and prepares for his follow-on action.

Counter Master

The Counter Master interrupts the Remedy Master, preventing the follow-on action.

Contra-counter Master

The Contra-counter Master interrupts the Counter Master's action, regaining the initiative and allowing a follow-on action after all.

Abrazare is of two kinds: one is done for pleasure, the other in anger, or for one's life, employing every trick, deception and cruelty imaginable. I want to talk about the second kind and show, in good order, how to come to grappling successfully in the most common situations of life or death combat.

LESSONS OF *ABRAZARE*

LESSONS IN THE PROLOG

Fiore begins his lessons of *abrazare* in the prolog. He uses *abrazare* to outline his program of masters and scholars, going on to say that they "act as pillars of the art of *abrazare*—both in and out of armor. Similarly, they support the art of the lance, with their weapon, guards, masters and students; the same they do for the axe, the single and doubled-handed sword and the dagger." He makes it quite clear that the program applies to all of *armizare* "through the principles they follow in *abrazare*." *Abrazare* is, thus, the foundation of the whole art, and the pedagogy of *abrazare* is the foundational teaching structure for *armizare*. What we learn here will apply throughout our entire course of study.

THE QUALITIES OF ABRAZARE

In the prolog, Fiore tells us that *abrazare* calls for eight[1] qualities:

- Strength
- Speed
- Knowledge of grapples
- Knowledge of breaking an opponent's arms or legs
- Knowledge of binding up an opponent's arms so that he cannot act
- Knowledge of where to strike
- Knowledge of throwing an opponent to the ground without danger to oneself
- Knowledge of dislocating an opponent's arms and legs

Most of these qualities are knowledges; only two are physical attributes. Unsurprisingly, they are the two physical attributes (personified by the elephant and tiger, respectively) in the seven swords page. It should also be no surprise that knowledge of the details of each element of the art—whether wrestling, dagger, sword, axe, or spear—is vital.

[1] In the Pisani-Dossi, Fiore only cites seven, skipping grapples.

Even though strength is the first listed quality, it seems unlikely that Fiore prizes raw power. While there can be no doubt that general body strength is necessary for pursuing martial arts, many arts emphasize technique over brute strength and Fiore's art seems to be one of those. A little bit later he notes that "whether you are stronger or weaker, use the grapples that arise from the binds and be sure to know how to defend against those which your opponent uses on you." Fiore seems to be saying that knowledge can overcome deficiencies in strength; exactly as is espoused in many other martial arts such as *jiujutsu.*

As what is surely general advice, Fiore urges his students, when assessing an opponent, to look to see if he is "stronger or bigger than you, and whether he is much younger or older." These characteristics will play into assessing what sort of strength you will encounter, but they have a role to play in what sort of speed you will encounter as well.

Speed is the second necessity Fiore calls out. The Pisani-Dossi clarifies that he speaks of arm and leg speed in this context. Certainly, being able to shift and turn your arms and legs is a virtue in wrestling. Striking with your limbs also requires speed for effectiveness, and striking is a part of the art.

Clearly, knowledge of the art is important in Fiore's mind. He advises his students to "take note of whether he places himself in any of the guards of *abrazare.*" This prudent advice is echoed in the instructions accompanying several plays throughout the manuscript, where he says a scholar executes a play because the opponent does not know the counter. Once again, Fiore's advice extends beyond *abrazare.* The same caution applies to other weapons forms within the art.

Of all the knowledges of *abrazare,* the least well illustrated in the treatise is that of striking. It is clear, however, that striking is an important part of the art, for Fiore tells us to strike. He offers targets, some of which are obvious to modern practitioners and some of which are more obscure. "Under the chin" would seem to be the neck, often called God's gift to martial artists for the many exposed and vulnerable bits of anatomy found there, but Fiore might not be so expansive in his definition. We cannot know. "The flanks" is equally obscure. It likely means all along the side of the torso, but could have had a more limited application, such as striking into or below the short ribs.

> ***If your opponent is not in armor, strike him in the most painful and dangerous spots, such as the eyes, the nose, the temples, under the chin and in the flanks.***

Fiore is not very specific about how to strike at these targets, but he gives us a hint of his thinking in the dagger section where he suggests going at an attacker with "your arms, hands and elbows." Certain other strikes are shown in the plays, such as the knee to the groin—a target notably not listed among the "most painful and dangerous spots"—and a Counter Master's eye gouge.

Binds are an integral part of *abrazare.* In the course of his book Fiore describes three arm bindings: the Upper Bind (*ligadura soprana*), the Middle Bind (*ligadura mezzana*), and the Under Bind (*ligadura sottana*). The names seem to be based on the direction in which you drive the joint you are locking up.

Each type of bind can result in a lock, and sometimes a dislocation or a break if applied forcefully. Fiore says they will apply "whether or not you and your opponent are wearing armor." Indeed, some of them are more effective against a man wearing plate armor, which can limit his flexibility. The curious thing about Fiore's presentation of the binds is that he does not show most of them here nor does he name them until after the *abrazare* section. Binds appear and start getting names in the dagger section. I think this displacement out of *abrazare* may have to do with the need to illustrate their mechanics. Fiore shows no closing in *abrazare*; the players are already in contact and striving for good grips. For all that it is close-range play, dagger fighting at least starts at a greater distance than *abrazare.* This separation allows the artist to show details that would be obscured by the close body positions of grappling wrestlers.

Many have noticed the absence of ground fighting in Fiore's art. The reason for this absence can be speculated upon, but Fiore is silent on the subject. However, his comment in describing the qualities of throwing an opponent to ground includes the caution "without danger to oneself." Fiore's message could well be: send him, but don't go yourself. We can all wish we had a definitive answer on this point, but we don't.

LESSONS BEFORE THE PLAYS: THE GUARDS

The illustrated portion of *il Fior di Battaglia* begins with the guards of *abrazare*, which are shown below. Fiore tells us that these four guards are the best. I agree with him because they encapsulate the basic energy flow of action for Fiore's art and represent its fundamental body mechanics. Each of these positions, along with movement to and through them, will define actions throughout the system. Knowledge of their form and their capabilities is vital to understanding Fiore's art. In the interpretation pages I will be presenting them along with most of Fiore's positions and guards, but these four are vitally important to understand clearly.

One can pair these guards in different ways to look at some of their capabilities. The first and most obvious pairing is as they stand in the book as pairs facing each other. Each of these pairs can generate a counter action to defeat the one facing it. Although he doesn't say it here, Fiore will also tell us that, save for positions which rely on having a point in line with the opponent, all guards can counter themselves. Wrestling guards don't have points, but a principle worth noting is that the fellow with the longer arms, like the one with the longer sword, will win when Long confronts Long or Frontal meets Frontal.

A second observed pairing is that there are two single-arm guards and two double-arm ones. This sounds trivial, but the change in body position is significant when shifting from a single-arm position to a double-arm one.

The third pairing dovetails with the second. Long and Frontal project linear energy while Boar's Tooth and Iron Gate project circular energy. Each of these pairs groups a single-arm guard with a double-arm position. Look to the interpretation pages for more on this.

In this first presentation of guards, Fiore tells us that "these guards don't remain fixed for long." Here it is because of the "immediate grapples that follow them" but the caution to avoid remaining in a fixed position is valid. Staying in one position gives your opponent time to refine his own intention and act. Fiore doesn't explicitly articulate this principle of *freqens motus* (roughly translatable as *constant motion*) as expressed in Hs. 3327a, but I think he understood it very well. We should keep this thought in mind as we study other guards.

These four guards make it possible to do all the things we listed in abrazare ...

Long Position (6rA) | Boar's Tooth Position (6rB) | Iron Gate Position (6rC) | Frontal Position (6rD)

A LESSON WITHIN THE PLAYS

The first *abrazare* plays, taken as a set, encapsulate an unarticulated principle of the art. The oldest fighting treatise still extant, the sword and buckler book known as I.33, speaks of this principle in one of its two oft-repeated verses: "Where he flees, I seek to follow."

The Remedy Master begins the sequence. The text says that he can come to the point illustrated in the first drawing from "every guard of *abrazare,*" which is as close as Fiore gets to commenting on how to effect closing in *abrazare*. Upon achieving the position shown, the instruction is to immediately perform the action of the second play.

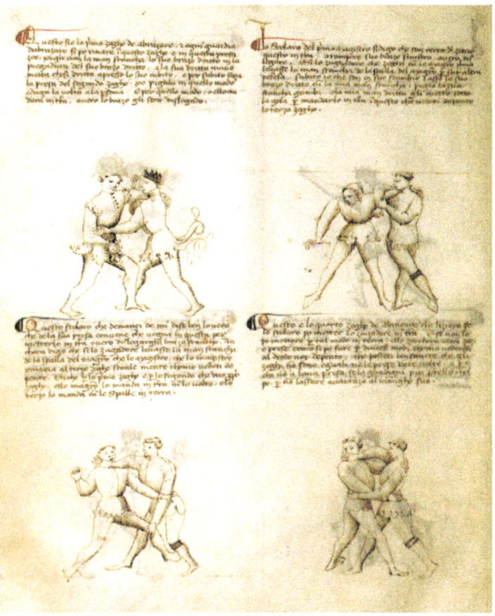

A page (6v) in *il Fior di Battaglia* is read in a "z." That is from upper left to upper right to lower left to lower right. A drawing's position is assigned a letter in that order.

The text of the second play confirms that the action is a break or dislocation of the arm, but goes further to consider what happens if the opponent slips his hand from the scholar's neck and makes the play ineffective. The opponent is "fleeing" the grapple. The text's instruction to move to the position shown in the third drawing sets the scholar to following the opponent's movement.

This action uses the opponent's attempt to free his arm to the scholar's advantage. As the opponent's chest turns from directly facing the scholar to a more outwardly directed position (something that comes with slipping his arm free), the scholar amplifies that motion and turns it against the opponent with a hand under his chin that forces his head back.

If the opponent starts to shift his body back to a straight-on stance before the scholar can achieve the position in the third play, the scholar can shift to the fourth play. His right hand is already seeking the position on the neck. His left hand, unable to reach the leg that has been removed from reach, shifts to the opponent's hip. In a push-pull motion the scholar amplifies the opponent's changed motion. All that the opponent has achieved is to change how he will be thrown.

You will find more detail on this sequence in the following interpretation section.

The lesson here is twofold. First, you must learn to read the opponent's intention through what you can feel of his body starting to move. Second, you must use that knowledge to shift ahead of him—preferably taking advantage of his direction of movement— and change the play to your advantage. This is Fiore's first lesson and one we are meant to carry through the whole work.

You will learn that the plays are not all the same, and grapples are seldom identical; therefore if you don't have a good grip, try to gain one as quickly as you can, or else the advantage may go to your opponent.

ADAPT

The quote to the left makes it clear that the fine details of a move will change in a real fight. While you cannot expect to execute any play in picture-perfect imitation of Fiore's drawings, you can expect the principles to work for you. In addition, you must be mentally and physically agile enough to move "as quickly as you can" from a failed action in search of a successful play.

LONG POSITION
(POSTA LONGA)

Fiore's illustration shows the player from the back. He is turned to oppose Boar's Tooth. The lead foot angle varies slightly in the Pisani-Dossi.

To find Long Position, your hand will lead. As your hand rises your palm should face inwards or downwards. Your foot, on the same side, moves forward as well.

It is important that your hand does not just drift forward, but shoots toward your opponent. Your arm ends straight, but not locked at the elbow.

Your arm should be in good, straight-line alignment with your shoulders. Shoulder and hips should be in the same plane.

ABRAZARE GUARD DRILL 1

Stand in Iron Gate, left leg forward.
Pass Forward into Long Position.
Move arms into Iron Gate.
Pass Forward into Boar's Tooth.
Move arms into Iron Gate.
Pass Forward into Frontal Position.
Move arms into Iron Gate.
Repeat sequence.

You can step into this position on either side.

You can also form this position by stepping back with your lead foot and bringing the hand on the other side forward.

Once you have mastered the correct posture, you will find that you can form the position without stepping by achieving the correct arm-shoulder-hips alignment.

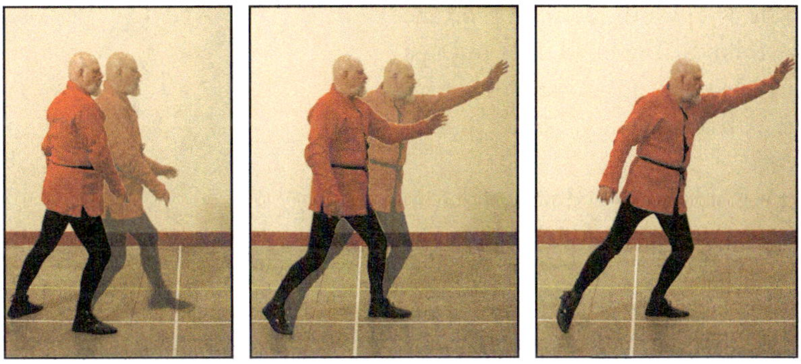

Here the scholar rises from Iron Gate Position, passing forward into a front-weighted Long Position.

Long Position is primarily linear. Your body aligns along the extended arm, through the spine, and (with shoulders and hips in the proper plane) down through your rear leg into the ground. This alignment (A) allows you to stand firm against pressure, passing it downwards.

It also allows you to project forward in the same line (B), as is used for striking.

B

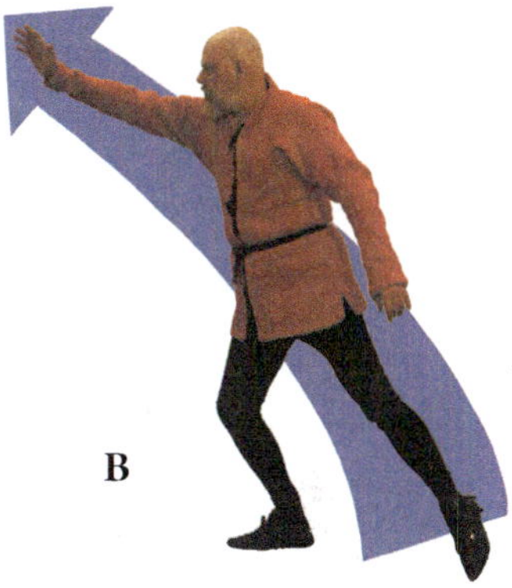

Here Long Position is used as a strike against the opponent's face.

Here Long Position is used to disrupt the opponent's structure and throw him.

BOAR'S TOOTH POSITION
(POSTA DI DENTE DI CINGHIALE)

To find Boar's Tooth, your hand will lead.

As your hand comes up, your palm should face inwards or upwards. Your foot, on the same side, follows. The hand does not just drift forward, but rises up into your opponent or into the path of his action, usually coming across as well.

Your arm should be in good alignment with your shoulder. Shoulder and hips should be in the same plane.

The figure is shown up on the balls of his feet, strongly suggesting the circular motion that is part of this guard.

A contemporary of Fiore, Edward of Norwich,[1] had this to say about how a boar attacks:
"For some men have seen him slit a man from knee up to the breast and slay him all stark dead at one stroke so that he never spake thereafter."
and
"The wild boar slayeth a man with one stroke as with a knife ..."

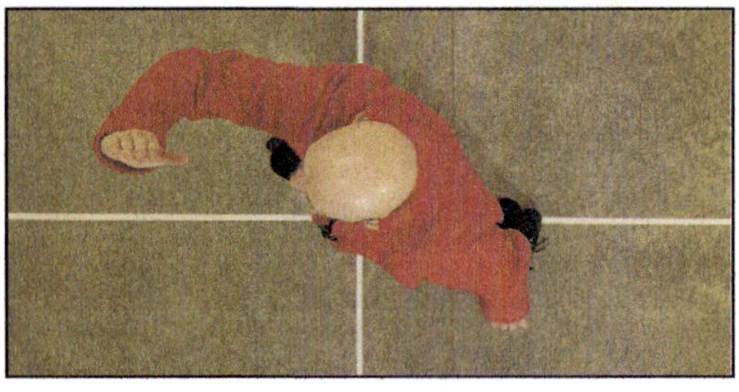

1 Edward of Norwich, William A. & F. N. Baille-Grohman (ed.), *The Master of Game*, University of Pennsylvania Press, 2005.

You can step into this position on either side.

You can also form this position by stepping back with your lead foot and bringing the hand on the other side forward and up.

Once you have mastered the correct posture, you will find that you can form the position without stepping by achieving the correct arm-shoulder-hips alignment.

And just like the boar strikes at an angle, from this guard ... always strikes at an angle...

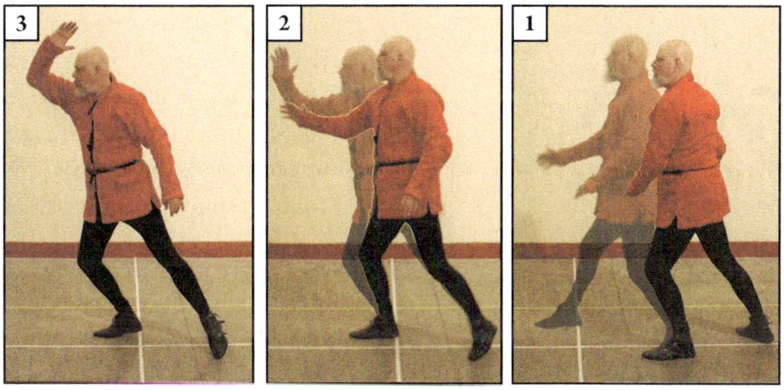

Here the scholar (moving from right to left) passes forward from Iron Gate Position into a front-weighted Boar's Tooth Position.

A

Boar's Tooth Position primarily projects circular energy. It also uses body alignment similar to Long Position's to pass energy down through your skeleton into the ground.

It can project energy upwards (A) to deflect an opponent's action or disrupt his structure.

When formed moving across, it can direct the energy upwards or downwards (as in B moving into Iron Gate for the throw). Boar's Tooth and Iron Gate are linked in their primarily circular nature.

B

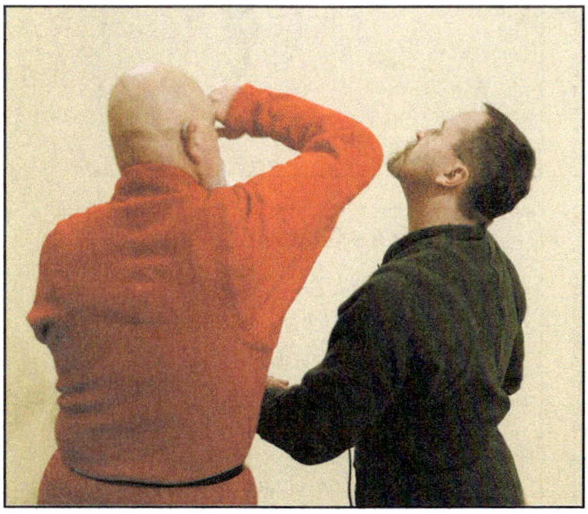

Here Boar's Tooth is used as an elbow strike against the opponent's head.

Here Boar's Tooth is used to move an attacker's arm to the side, opening him up to an immediate attack.

IRON GATE POSITION
(POSTA DI PORTA DI FERRO)

To find Iron Gate, both hands lead, palms downwards.

Your foot, on the side towards which you are moving, follows. The hands drop down, lead hand inside lead knee, arms straightening if they started bent. Your hips turn slightly in the direction of movement as your hands move and sink down slightly.

You can step into this position on either side.

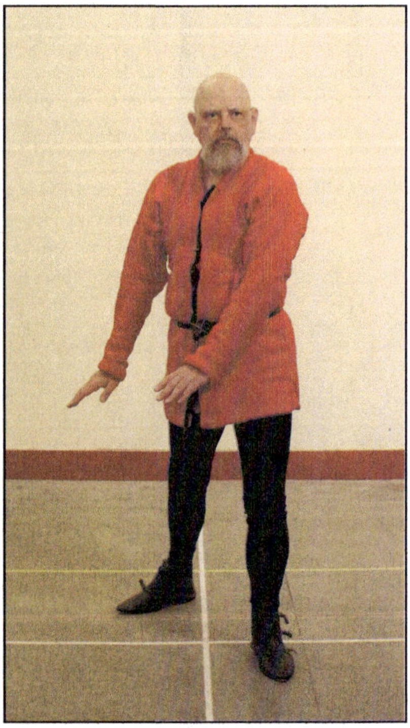

ABRAZARE GUARD DRILL 2

Perform *Abrazare* Guard Drill 1 but do so by stepping backwards rather than forwards.

ABRAZARE GUARD DRILL 3

Perform *Abrazare* Guard Drill 1 but accompany all moves to Iron Gate with a Stable Turn (*volta stabile*).

You can also form this position by stepping back with your lead foot.

Once you have mastered the correct posture, you will find that you can form the position without stepping.

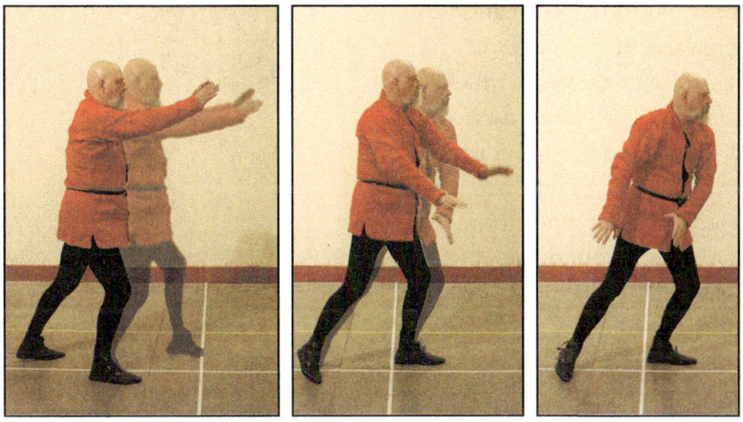

Here the scholar steps forward from a Frontal Position to a front-weighted Iron Gate Position.

Iron Gate Position primarily projects circular energy, using it to deflect an opponent's action or disrupt his structure.

Whether rising up from it or falling down into it, this position provides the structure to create throws, especially when utilized with a turn (*volta*).

The scholar moves his arms across and down towards Iron Gate. His right hand grasps his opponent's wrist and his left comes behind the elbow, setting up an arm bar.

The scholar makes a Stable Turn (*volta stabile*) as he moves into Iron Gate. He uses body structure to unbalance and throw his opponent.

FRONTAL POSITION
(POSTA FRONTALE)

To find Frontal Position, your hands lead, palms facing inwards or forwards.

Your foot, on the side towards which you are moving, follows. The hands do not just drift forward, but shoot outward (or upward) toward your opponent. Your arms finish straight, but not locked at the elbow. Your hips end squared up to your opponent.

You can step into this position on either side.

ABRAZARE GUARD DRILL 4

Perform *Abrazare* Guard Drill 3 but step backwards rather than forwards.

ABRAZARE GUARD DRILL 5

Perform *Abrazare* Guard Drill 3 but accompany all moves to Iron Gate with a Full Turn (*tutta volta*).

You can also form this position by stepping back with your lead foot.

Once you have mastered the correct posture, you will find that you can form the position without stepping.

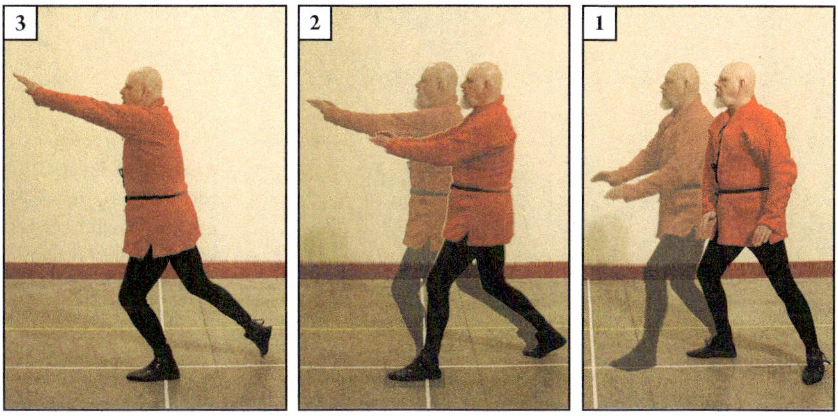

Here the scholar (moving from right to left) rises from Iron Gate Position, stepping forward into a front weighted Frontal Position.

Frontal Position projects primarily linear energy, aligning your body to maximize its passage. It can channel it outwards or pass energy down through your arms and torso into your legs.
Frontal and Long Positions are linked in their primarily linear nature.

The scholar uses Frontal Position as a strike.

The scholar uses Frontal Position to disrupt a similar strike by the opponent and place himself in control of the center line.

A core lesson of *abrazare* is to sense and respond to your opponent's positioning and moves.

1

The players begin already grappling.

2

The scholar (on right) makes the action of the Remedy Master.

To make the action of the Remedy Master, the scholar's left hand strikes down into the inside of his opponent's right elbow, to break his grip, while bringing his right hand up and over the opponent's left elbow, as he steps to seek Boar's Tooth. This would result in the second play. (See B on next page.)

3

The opponent slips his left hand from the scholar's neck before the scholar can step, avoiding the bind or break action of the second play.

4

Following in response to his opponent's action, the scholar immediately shifts towards the third play. (See C on next page.)

5
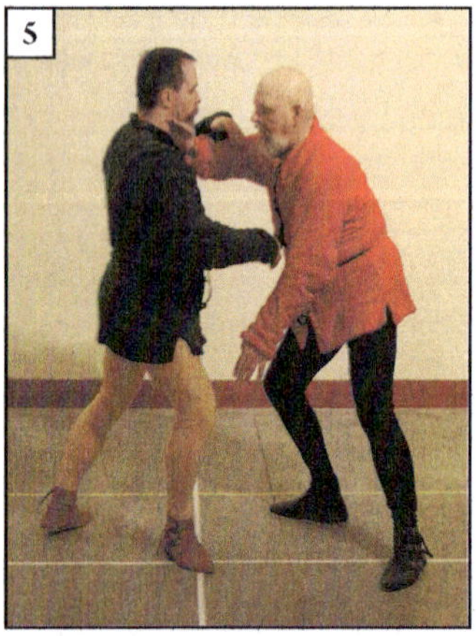
Again the opponent reacts too quickly, shifting his leg away and avoiding the third play's throw.

A: Fourth Play

The scholar in the fourth play discomforts his opponent by pushing his head in the opposite direction that he is pulling the hip.

The scholar moves in response to his opponent's action and shifting into the position of the fourth play. (A)

Grabbing his opponent's jacket, the scholar unbalances his opponent and achieves the fourth play's throw.

B: Second Play

The leverage applied against the opponent's arm can be used to control the arm or break it. The kick out indicated by the scholar's right foot position in the drawing is a violent, full force option that can result in the scholar dropping the foe to the ground and falling on top of him, causing additional damage.

C: Third Play

Slipping his arm under his opponent's chin, the scholar can lever his head backwards and set him falling. Extending towards Long Position, the scholar can grab the rising leg to ensure a dangerous fall. Adding a turn to this action can direct the angle of the opponent's fall.

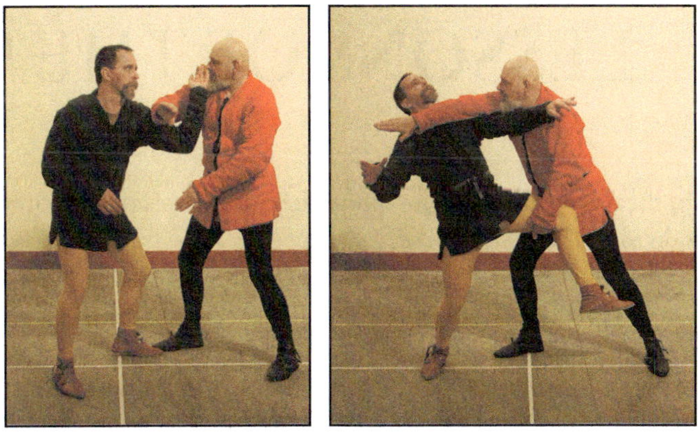

Actions similar to those of the Remedy Master may be set up while closing to grips as well. Here, the scholar (right) rises from Iron Gate and slips into Boar's Tooth while avoiding one of the opponent's hands,

Here, the scholar (right) rises from Iron Gate and strikes into his opponent's neck as he moves toward Long Position, catching his opponent's rising leg. The throw occurs as the scholar achieves Long Position.

I am the noble weapon called the dagger, and I'm in love with close play. If you know my deceptions and my art, you will be skilled at every subtlety of the art of arms.

LESSONS OF THE DAGGER

With the dagger section, Fiore introduces the issues of weapon range and distance as well as relative position to the opponent. *Abrazare* play is so close that there is only one measure and thus the need for cover on an approach is greatly reduced or eliminated. As in *il Fior di Battaglia*, this book's dagger section will be the longest one in the book, because so many basics are laid down and encoded in the plays and their organization.

Fiore begins the dagger section with Fight Masters, presenting five positions (*poste*). Each is a variation of Iron Gate and we must look to their differences to find their place in Fiore's teaching.

The most obvious differences among them are in the hand positions and whether and how they grip a dagger. Only two guards are shown with the player holding a dagger, and each of these is directly

DOWNWARD GRIP

The most common dagger grip shown in medieval treatises is one where the pommel of the dagger sits near the user's thumb and the blade projects from the fist on the side away from the thumb.

Today this is widely known as the *icepick grip* or, in reference to the modern preference for the upward grip, the *reverse grip*.

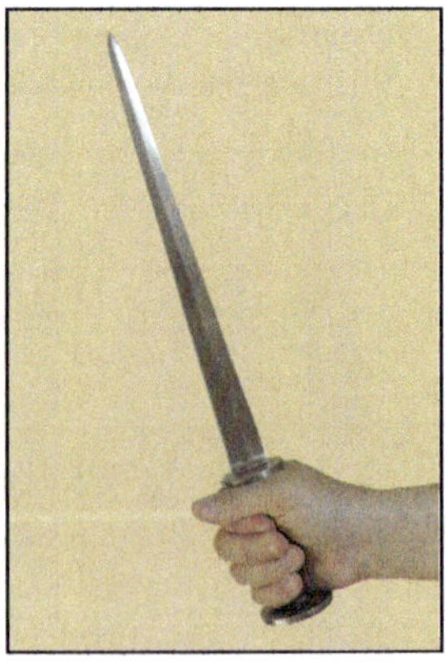

UPWARD GRIP

The pommel of the dagger sits at the base of the user's fist and the blade projects from the fist on the side nearest the thumb.

Today this is widely known as the *standard grip*, but it is not standard in medieval dagger fighting, and use of that term is inappropriate in reconstructing medieval dagger fighting.

Full Iron Gate, Simple
(*Tutta Porta di Ferro Sempia*)

Full Iron Gate, Doubled
(*Tutta Porta di Ferro Doppia*)

Half Iron Gate, Doubled
and Crossed
(*Mezza Porta di Ferro
Doppia et Incrosada*)

Middle Iron Gate, Doubled
(*Mezzana Porta di Ferro Doppia*)

Full Iron Gate, Crossed
(*Tutta Porta di Ferro Incrosada*)

related to one of the Dagger Remedy Masters. The text says that Full Iron Gate, Simple plays with and without a dagger, and experience shows that Full Iron Gate, Crossed can also play with a dagger, easily becoming either Middle or Half Iron Gate. Only Full Iron Gate, Doubled cannot use a dagger.

Foot position also varies among the five guards. All but Half Iron Gate show an open-hip position where the hip on the side of the trailing foot is turned slightly away from the opponent. This maximizes the player's ability to shift position and distance quickly, and sets the player up to generate power through movement from that side. Half Iron Gate is different. This Fight Master has his hips squared up to the opponent. This is tied directly to his grip on the dagger. An open-hip position would reduce the player's ability to parry to the left, as the text says he can do. Movement ability is deliberately reduced in favor of improved ability to cover against attack.

Two of the guards have the wrists crossed and Fiore says that they (and all remedy plays using "crossed" positions) cannot perform extended covers and so are "better" when in armor than without. The same problem exists for Full Iron Gate, Doubled, because of the wrist grip.

THE DAGGER INSTRUCTION MASTERS

Fiore gives us a double page spread with a single figure on the left page and four figures on the right page. Together, they instruct about the five things that Fiore says makes up dagger fighting: strikes, disarms, breaks and dislocations, binds, and throws.

This is a slight variation of the five knowledges which he says (in the Pisani-Dossi) are needed for *abrazare*. There, breaks and dislocations are separate items and there are no disarms, which have no place in *abrazare* as no weapons are in play. Here we see Fiore working the important mnemonic number five to his advantage. We get five things to remember, even though they are a different five things. These same five things will come into play in all the weapons of *armizare*.

This Instruction Master says "... I will disarm anyone attacking me ..." and points to the dagger he has taken from his opponent. Note that his own dagger is sheathed at his belt.

This Instruction Master says "... I have broken and dislocated a good share of them ..." referring to the arms he holds.

This Instruction Master says he has the knowledge "... of opening and closing ... the arms of whoever comes against me ..." and points to the keys he holds. Keys control locks.

This Instruction Master says "... I've put thousands in that situation ..." referring to the man he has thrown to the ground, who now lies, defeated, at his feet.

This Instruction Master says "... against me defensive arms and armor are useless ...." He is the master of strikes.

Most of the dagger Instruction Masters really aren't terribly helpful on a practical level. It is, however, interesting to note that they appear in progressively more elaborate clothing and are rendered as progressively older men. The four that appear in the Pisani-Dossi do not follow this pattern. Is this a hint that the various things of the dagger are progressively more sophisticated or advanced? Fiore has nothing to say about the meaning, if any, of this obvious pattern.

The one Instruction Master of the Dagger who is helpful stands in a position (*posta*), unlike his fellows. He does this because he is pulling double duty as the Fight Master of dagger strikes. His page, which has but the single illustration, is also very hard working. The first paragraph associated with him is characteristic of other Fight Masters, with its generalized instructions for what to do. Surrounding the figure are paragraphs corresponding to those of the four categories of sword attacks which each get their own drawings. The page ends with another paragraph that follows the style and rhythms of other weapon introductions.

While this master does not appear in the Pisani-Dossi, both manuscripts do have a version of what is commonly called the segno page which shows seven swords superimposed on the image of a man. The seven swords represent the seven attacks available to the sword. Two blows from above, left and right; two horizontal blows, left and right; two blows from below, left and right, and the thrust (of which there are five), depicted by the sword pointing vertically. That last sword, if it were to be positioned in a physically appropriate position, should be standing perpendicular to the man; but that is always a challenging perspective to illustrate, and perspective was still developing in the art of Fiore's time.

The Master of Seven Swords (also known as the *segno*)

A sword is long enough to create different measures, depending on how it is employed. A sword's blows cover a wider volume of space, but its point, coming in a thrust, still closes on the centerline even though it can come from five directions: above left, above right, below left, below right, and through the middle.

Fendente
Instruction Master

Sottani
Instruction Master

Mezzani
Instruction Master

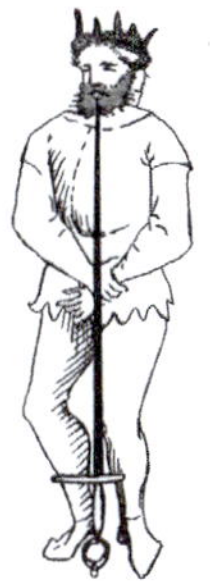

Punte
Instruction Master

A dagger is far shorter and one only employs it at close range. Whereas the sword may strike with edge or point, in Fiore's art the dagger is only shown striking with the point. This gives it a strong relationship to a sword's thrust, yet its attacks follow an arc, albeit often a shallow one, toward the target. Along with the close range, this means that a high attack on the side has more in common with a low attack on that side than it does with one along the centerline, whether high or low. The master's four daggers draw this distinction. One comes from above, one from the right, one from the left, and one seems to come from below. There is no descriptive paragraph for an attack whose primary vector is straight through the middle and is neither directed downwards or upwards.

I can strike fendente to the head or body, from the elbow to the top of the head. Below the elbow, however, I don't have the same freedom without getting into a lot of danger, so I am reluctant to strike there.

From the riverso side, I can strike anywhere between the elbow and up to the temple. These strikes are called mezzani. These riversi strikes cannot be delivered when you are ready to execute a parry against an opponent.

On the mandritto side, you can strike and parry if you need to, and can hit your opponent from the elbow to the temples. This can be done more safely on the mandritto than on the riverso.

A dagger going in the middle towards your head can strike as high as under the chest, but no higher; the left hand can be used to defend.

On the sword segno page, this sort centerline thrust is accounted for with a point-up sword. On the dagger master's page, its place is preempted by the weapon representing the rising *sottano* blow. A dagger on this trajectory, drawn in proper perspective, would appear as a simple and uninformative circle. Fiore's artist answered the challenge of illustrating something that should extend from the plane of the page with a point-up sword in the segno page, but here he is unable to use his previous solution, so he draws nothing.

STRIKES FROM ABOVE

When the text says strikes come from above, it says they come *de sopra,* but Fiore explicitly calls these dagger strikes *fendente* rather than using the directional terminology he uses for the left and right attacks. *Fendente* is the same term he uses for downward attacks with the sword.

The target zone is from the top of the head to the elbow. Specifying the top of the head defines the basically downward motion of this attack.

Fiore cautions "... Below the elbow I don't have the same freedom without getting into a lot of danger ..." As with the attacks from the right and the left, a downward-grip attack has problems below the horizontal centerline of the body. One can strike to a lower target but one's posture is compromised, a serious issue if in armor.

STRIKES FROM THE RIGHT

When the text says strikes come from the right, it says they come *de man dritto,* or from the straight hand or the forehand. In the dagger instruction, Fiore explicitly calls these strikes *mandritto.* He also says they are *mezzani,* which in the sword section is a blow that comes between the *fendente* and *sottani,* which is to say a mostly horizontal blow.

The target zone is from the temple to the elbow. Specifying the temple as a target clearly indicates the primarily horizontal nature of the blow and its path from the outside.

Downward-grip dagger attacks thrown toward targets below the elbow level get progressively weaker, mechanically, as the arm rotates downward. Also, the elbow is increasingly presented and it is a prime target for attack.

STRIKES FROM THE LEFT

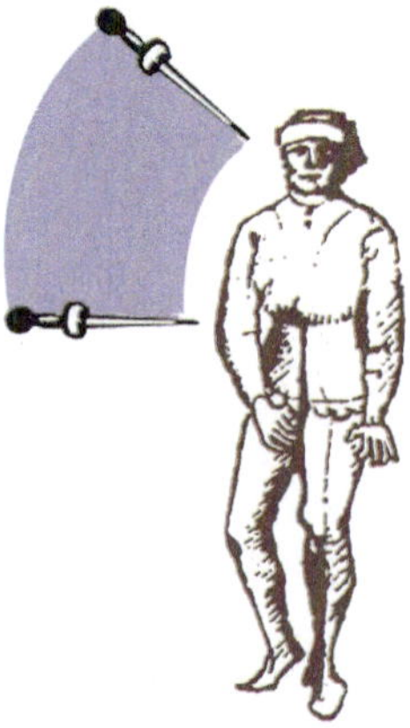

When the text says strikes come from the left, it says they come *de man riversa,* or from the reversed hand. In the dagger instruction, Fiore explicitly calls these strikes *riverso.* He also says they, like the *mandritto* strikes, are *mezzani,* or mostly horizontal blows.

The target zone is from the temple to the elbow. Specifying the temple as a target clearly indicates the primarily horizontal nature of the blow and its path from the outside.

Downward-grip *riverso* dagger attacks thrown toward targets below the elbow level offer the defender an easier countering move because as the arm rotates downward it presents progressively more of the elbow and pre-rotating the arm should the target manage a grip to create a bind.

AN ARC OF STRIKE POSSIBILITIES

Time, by our experience of it, is a continuity, one moment blending into the next. A dagger fight is a place of continuity, and all the possible angles of attack blend into each other. For example, strikes from the right can rise higher and become more vertical until they are no longer coming from the right but coming from above. At some point, the best response to the attack will change to a different cover more suited to the changed angle.

The Upper Arc

From Above

Fiore says nothing about how this attack affects your ability to cover. However, like the attack from below, it is a centerline attack. As it is a centerline attack, your body will be squared up against the opponent and your shoulder position will allow easy use of the off-hand to cover.

The Fourth Remedy Master deals with this attack.

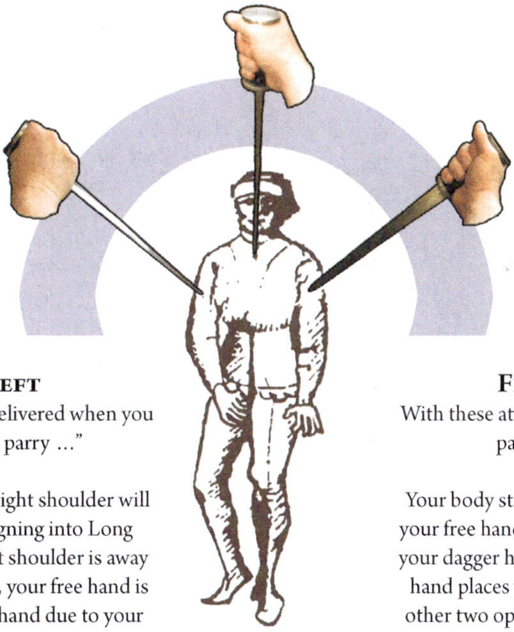

From the Left

These attacks "... cannot be delivered when you are ready to execute a parry ..."

As you make the strike your right shoulder will be leading; your body is aligning into Long position. This means your left shoulder is away from the opponent and, thus, your free hand is moving behind your dagger hand due to your body's position.

The Third Remedy Master deals with this attack.

From the Right

With these attacks, Fiore says that you can "... parry if you need to ..."

Your body structure during this attack allows your free hand to move ahead, behind, or with your dagger hand. Moving ahead of the dagger hand places your off hand in danger, but the other two options offer differing tactical possibilities.

The First Remedy Master deals with this attack.

Nine Remedy Masters of the Dagger

1

2

3

4

Master has empty hand and faces one attack

5

Master has empty hand and faces two attacks.
Master is held by opponent

6

7

8
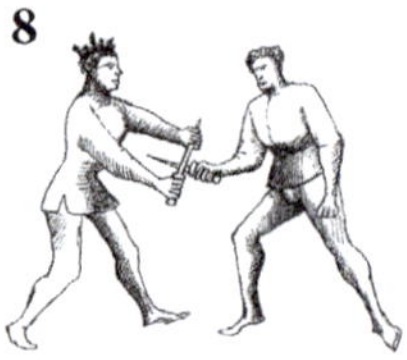

Master has own dagger, gripped with both hands

9

Master has empty hand and faces one attack

ORGANIZED INSTRUCTION OF RESPONSE

Let's look at the pattern of Fiore's Remedy Masters. Fiore gives us nine Remedy Masters. Six play empty-handed and three play with dagger gripped in both hands. All except the Fifth Remedy Master play against an attacker who wields his weapon either in a downward or an upward grip; the Fifth Remedy Master has attackers using both grips. He also plays against an attacker who is gripping him with the off-hand. This grip is the defining element for the Fifth Remedy Master and makes this master distinct. It also makes him a punctuation point. So we get four empty-handed masters, Fifth Dagger Master, then the three who have daggers, and lastly another empty-handed master. This arrangement is not coincidence.

The first four empty-handed masters deal with an attacker using a downward grip. The last, the Ninth Remedy Master, deals with an attacker using an upward grip. It is easy to see why the one might be separated from the others. Yet Fiore's Fight Master tells us that there are four attacks: from above, from the left, from the right, and from below. The Third Remedy Master is quite clearly dealing with the attack from the left, just as the Fourth Remedy Master deals with an attack from above. The First Remedy Master is a good fit for the attack from the right and his placement as the first remedy, against what is likely to be the most common attack, confirms this. The Ninth Remedy Master would seem to be a perfect match for the attack from below. Four attacks and four Remedy Masters would seem to make a perfect set. Yet we get five empty-handed Remedy Masters. Four attacks and five remedies doesn't seem to add up.

Additionally, the Remedy Master dealing with the attack from below is not one of the first four, but the last of nine. Why isn't he grouped with the three masters that deal with the other, apparently basic, attack vectors that Fiore sets out? Is the reason for separation as simple as how the attacker grips his dagger? If so, why are those other three grouped with another empty-handed master who doesn't deal with a described attack? We need to look more closely.

With the First Remedy Master Fiore first gives us a response to attacks from the right, probably the most common form of attack. It is easy to see why this master goes first. The Second Master, at first, appears to be the odd man out or, as some practitioners believe, just a different response to the same attack the First Remedy Master is dealing with. The Third Remedy Master handles the reversed attacks from the attacker's left, while the Fourth Remedy Master responds to attacks from above.

As we saw before, the attacks faced by the First, Fourth, and Third Remedy Masters describe the upper arc, a continuous arc in the plane of the opponent's body, starting on one side, rising over the head, and then down the other side.

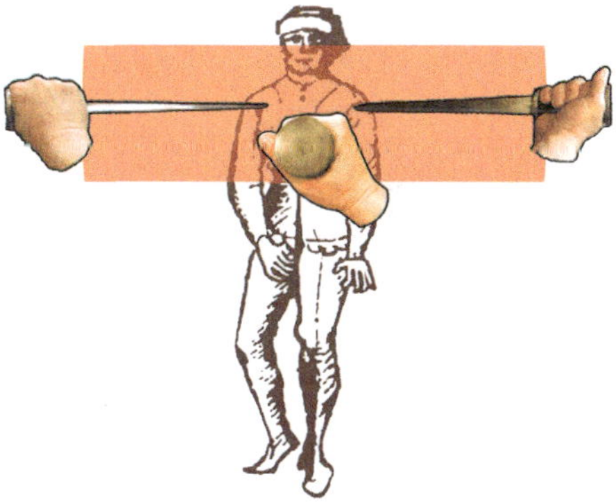

The Horizontal Band

What happens when the attacker shifts his line of attack from the outer circle in toward the center? What if he wants to throw an attack that will travel on a shorter path, closer to the centerline of the body? Certainly a horizontal attack (*mezzano*) from the left or right can be thrown closer to the center line. If the angle continues to shift in that direction, it will eventually become an attack from the other side. Again we find a zone of attack, this time a horizontal band. This creates a horizontal plane through the body of the target which, like all planes seen edge on, appears as a line. And again, when we try to defend we find a point of transition where the standard response to a horizontal blow becomes less effective as the path of the blow comes closer and closer to the centerline.

Fiore does not describe the centerline, transitional attack for the horizontal range, but he gives us a response to this center line attack and it sits right between the attack from the left and the attack from the right: the Second Remedy Master.

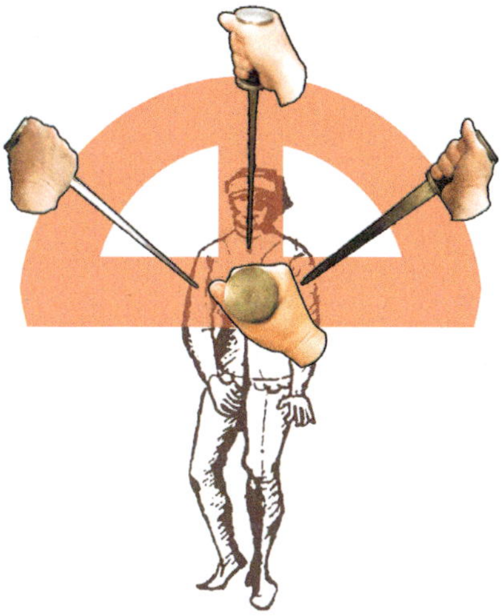

Combined Upper Attack Zones

The upper arc and the horizontal band cover the target zones of downward-grip attacks. They make a logical grouping, as when they are taken together they represent the two upper quadrants of the standard medieval division of the body into four target zones.

STRIKES FROM BELOW

When the text says strikes come from below, it says they come *de soto*. In the dagger instruction, Fiore does not give them a clear name. To parallel Fiore's usage of *fendente* for dagger attacks from above, dagger attacks from below I suggest referring to them as *sottani*.

Mechanically, the best way to strike from below is with an upward-grip attack and Fiore dedicates a Remedy Master to deals with just such an attack. It seems safe to conclude that the *sottani* attacks are, at least primarily, upward-grip attacks. Like the *sottani* blows of the sword, the weapon user's thumb, rather than his fingers, leads the hand toward the target.

Fiore says that strikes from below are "... going through the middle towards your head ..." and that they go "... as high as under the chest ..."

These attacks go on the centerline. As the sword *sottani* are paired with *fendente*, the dagger *sottani* are partnered with the downward attacks. Fiore explicitly makes a connection between his Fourth and Ninth Remedy Masters, telling us that the covers against attacks from above are nearly the same for those from below but that their plays are different.

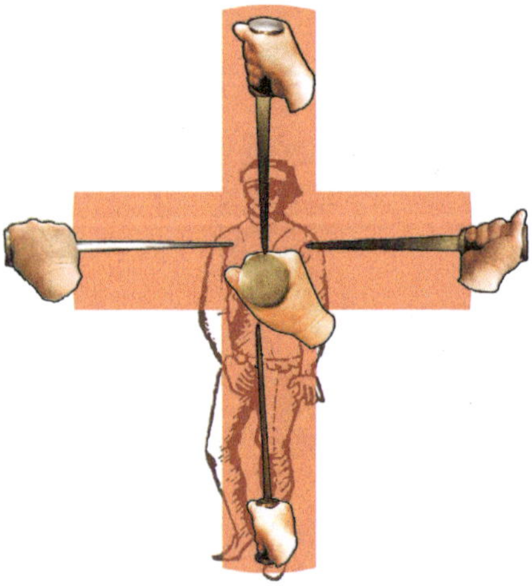

THE CROSS

Looking at what he shows us for these attacks and responses, we see that the mechanical details of what one needs to do (whether attacker or defender) change at about the midline of the body. Nevertheless, this connection creates an intellectual continuity of vertical, centerline attacks describing a new, vertical plane defined by the relationship of the attacker and defenders's bodies and the centerline attacks.

When you join the horizontal band, defended by the first three Remedy Masters, to the vertical band, defended by the connected masters who cover above and below, you get the cross that divides a body in the four targeting zones.

OPENING THE LOWER WINDOW

THE LOWER ARC

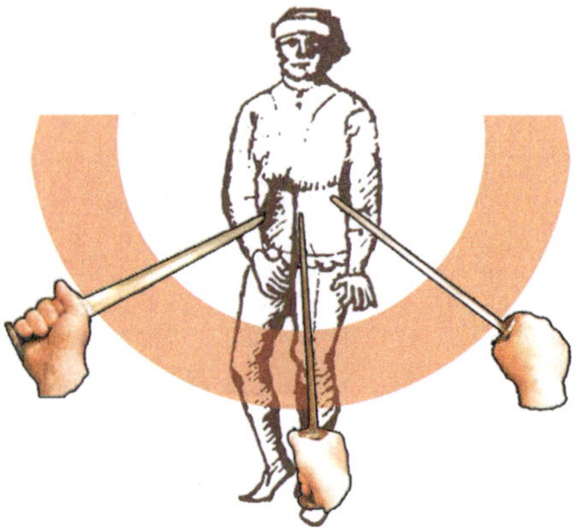

As we have seen, the first four Remedy Masters set up defenses for approximately half of the zone though which dagger attacks can come. We have also seen that the Ninth Remedy Master, playing below and against an upward-grip attack, completes the vertical arm of a cross. It is this master, the very one separated from his companions who make up the responses to the upper arc of attack possibilities, that opens a window into a lower arc of attacks that mirrors the upper-arc Masters.

Attacks from the right and left with an upwards-grip dagger are recorded in other traditions and have proven effective in modern knife play, so they are real. Other than the one directly in the center line, Fiore does not show us these attacks explicitly but their place in the spectrum of possible attacks is built into the organization of his work.

Fiore tells us that the attacks of the downwards grip cannot stray below the horizontal divider of the target zones "without getting into a lot of danger." Likewise, the upwards-grip attacks also should not stray above that line. The attacker's arm position once past the line is similar in both cases: halfway turned into a lock already, an easy target to an experienced grappler.

The body structure used to make attacks into the dangerous zones (whether upwards-grip going high or downwards-grip going low) offers less power for the attack, making them sub-optimal for armored fighting. The upwards-grip attacks suffer especially from this, which may partly explain why Fiore gives them little attention.

THE CIRCLE AND THE CROSS

When taken all together, the target zones of all the attacks give us a circle and a cross. These are powerful mnemonic aids. They are also potent symbols to the medieval mind. The circle represents unity. The cross upon which the Savior died was an instrument of salvation to medieval Christians, just as in fencing the cross made with your weapon brings you salvation in an immediate and more secular fashion.

With our modern eyes, we can easily see that by combining the angles around the arcs along with shifts along the horizontal and vertical axes plots out a hemispherical volume of space representing the total range of attack angles. Even without medieval symbolism, in the circle and the cross, we have a powerful conceptual tool to aid us in our understanding of the art.

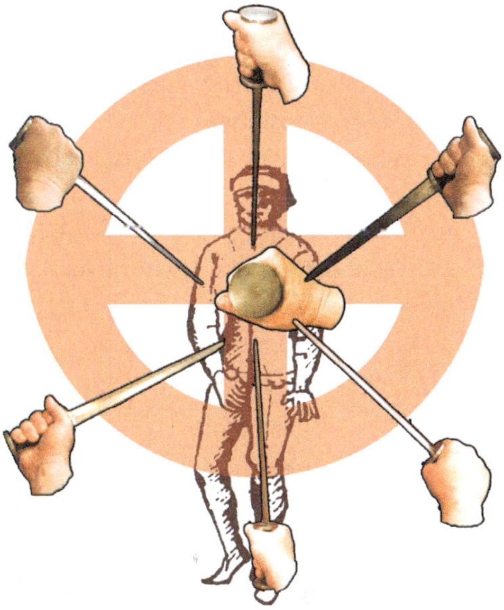

THE CIRCLE AND THE CROSS

A MECHANICAL LINK

It is worth noting that the hand holding a dagger in the upward-grip grasps the weapon the same way one holds a sword. The dagger is a weapon that relies on its point, as does a sword when making a thrust. Placing a sword thrust into the five targets of Fiore's Thrust (*punte*) Master puts one's hand into the same positions as making upward-grip dagger attacks. Try it and see.

Once off the center line, you will find your hand moving into positions very familiar to modern fencers: First (palm right, thumb down), Second (palm down, thumb left), Third (palm left, thumb up), and Fourth (palm up, thumb right). Going above the horizontal line is not a serious problem for a sword because the weapon's length protects the wielder from getting his arm grabbed by a grappler.

FIRST REMEDY MASTER: WORKING INSIDE

I am the First Master called "Remedy." A remedy is an antidote against your opponent's attacks, together with the ability to strike him. ...

Fiore's illustration of the First Remedy Master combines the master's cover with the first play almost as if he considered the cover itself as elementary. The cover is, indeed, elementary—or rather, foundational—as it is Long Position, the very first position he presents in the treatise.

In the illustration, the Remedy Master's foot is clearly inside that of his attacker. Interestingly, in the illustration of the specific Counter Master in the second play, that foot is clearly outside the attacker's foot. The countering action is not one that involves footwork. Did the artist make a mistake? Given the attention to detail throughout the treatise, this seems unlikely, especially because one can find a lesson in the different foot positions.

The text of this play gives no instruction on stepping. Modern knife defense encourages stepping into an attack to intercept it and reduce its force. Also, it is wise to step off line and out of the way of a dagger attack, as this gives you an additional level of protection should your attempt at a cover fail. This is not always possible, especially in a quick, close-quarters dagger fight. The cover may need to be made without a step, as is shown in the Remedy Master. Of course, it can also be made with that step, as the scholar apparently did against the Counter Master.

First Scholar (play 1)
Disarm

Second Scholar (play 3)
Break/Dislocation

With the First Remedy Master, Fiore first gives us five scholars, each one specializing in one of the five elements of dagger fighting. As this is Fiore's first presentation of important concepts in the *armizare* sections, I'll detail each in an interpretation spread (starting on page 69).

Most of these plays allow other actions beyond the one illustrated, but they all have one thing in common: their actions are working on the inside line of the initial attack. Yes, even the fifth of these scholars (the eighth play). His strike is set in motion and moves into the space that would be inside line even as his covering arm moves the dagger and makes the strike seem to go against the outside line.

A fight is not a tidy exercise and small changes in the position of one or the other fighter can have large effects on the success of an action. Likewise, differences in impetus or intention on the part of either or

Third Scholar (play 5)
Bind

Fourth Scholar (Play 7)
Throw

Fifth Scholar (Play 8)
Strike

both combatants can change how actions play out. Fiore's plays represent idealized actions, designed to make clear the mechanics of the technique demonstrated. The student is left to figure out how, in real world conditions, to apply the principle taught in the play.

Working with the first scholar's disarm action, I find that alternate footwork on the part of the scholar can deal with responses from the attacker and allow him to complete his action when things don't "freeze" in the illustrated position. If the attacker is still trying to force his blow through, the scholar can pass back with his left foot and complete the disarm in the space between them. If the attacker presses in, the scholar can circle his right foot back, pivoting on the left to clear space and complete the disarm. If the attacker backs away, the scholar can pass forward, maintaining extension on the attacker's dagger arm, and complete the disarm.

Fiore sometimes states that his scholar can throw the opponent without specifying an action to power that throw, and with good reason. Throws can be powered through structural positioning by creating a solid one for yourself as, or after, you break down your opponent's structure and through the three turns (*volta*). The choice is usually tactical, with the chosen method determining the direction and violence of the throw.

SECOND REMEDY MASTER: DEFENDING THE CENTER

At first glance, second Remedy Master and the scholar in the fourteenth play of the First Remedy Master seem to be the same, but look closer. The positions of the attackers are different, because the attackers are making different attacks. In response, the defenders are making different, although similar, responses.

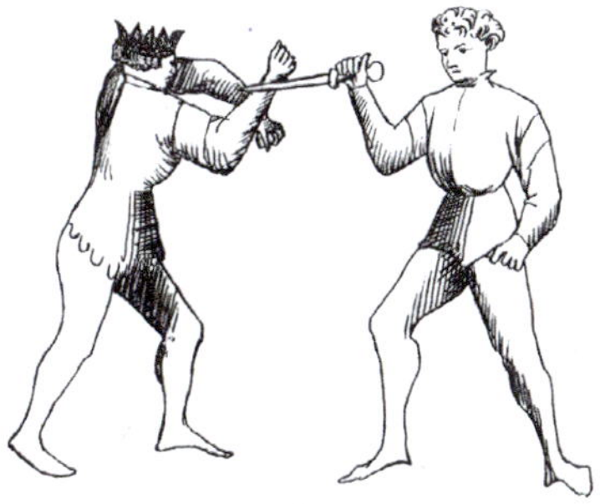

I play with my arms crossed so that I can perform the remedies we just saw. ... I can play mandritto and riverso and cross below and above.

The attack being made is a centerline horizontal blow. It is very quick and, in a fight, often reinforced with a second hand on the dagger's pommel. As we learn in other places, the response to a doubled-up attack is to double-up yourself.

The cover of the Second Remedy Master is a modified form of Frontal Position, played with the wrists crossed right over left. As the scholar moves his crossed wrists into the cover, he raises his left elbow high, bringing his upper arm near his head. At the same time, his right shoulder drops and shifts forward while his right elbow pulls in toward his own center.

Fiore tells us that the crossed covers cannot cover long, and apparently illustrates that by showing the cover made against the dagger blade rather than the attacker's arm. This seems to be a warning that you must form this cover very quickly. The longer the weapon's blade, the more dangerous it is in this circumstance.

Fiore is also consistent in telling us that crossed covers are good in armor. He sometimes goes so far, as here, to say you can't do better. Certainly armor would help if you make the cover against the blade, protecting your arms and hands from the blade. It will also help if you do not quite clear the point away from yourself, or if you fail to halt all of its forward progress and it hits you.

THIRD REMEDY MASTER: WORKING OUTSIDE

The Third Remedy Master of the dagger is shown already well into the follow-on action. To find the basic cover, we must look to the general Counter Master (14 recto D). Since this Counter Master plays against the Remedy Master before he makes a follow-on action, the Remedy Master must be depicted in something close to the position of his cover. And so it is here: Long Position on the right.

Here we start with the strong plays of the riverso side, ... My students will follow with the plays deriving from the defense I am performing with my right hand. ...

The illustration depicted here of the Remedy Master is a composite (and labeled as such to avoid confusion with Fiore's actual illustrations). It uses elements of the Counter Master drawing to produce it."

The play shown as the Third Remedy Master is done to the outside of the dagger's line of attack, as are all of this Remedy Master's scholars. Together they present a variety of techniques available when the attacker's arm is between you and his body. These are difficult techniques to counter, as indicated by the lack of specific Counter Masters. There is only the general Counter Master playing against the Remedy Master himself. This is a lesson in itself: being outside the line of attack is a relatively safe place to be.

The first three of the Third Remedy Master's scholars have a further lesson to teach that arises from the natural reaction of an attacker whose blow has been thwarted, and it is one that will be expanded on with the Fourth Remedy Master's scholars. With these three we see responses to the basic reactions of the thwarted attacker.

Remedy Master 3 Play 1 (13vB)

The first scholar (play 1, at left) responds to an attacker who stays in the center of his way, either because he is momentary surprised his dagger has been stopped or is pressing his attack through. The scholar steps into this, extending into Long Position on the left and throwing his opponent in a fashion similar that used by the First Remedy Master's fourth scholar (play 7), but on the other side of the attacker's arm.

Remedy Master 3 Play 2 (13vC)

The next two scholars use techniques best applicable if the attacker either retreats from the block to the side from which his attack came (play 2, at right) or tries to pull back to his left from his now blocked attack (play 3, below left). The first scholar moves into the opening space and placing his right arm around the attacker's throat (and probably grasping his own arm with his left hand) converts the attacker's retreat into a takedown by adding a rotational element. The second scholar follows the movement and uses it. He steps in, striking with his hand to the attacker's elbow, either breaking the arm or forcing him to the ground.

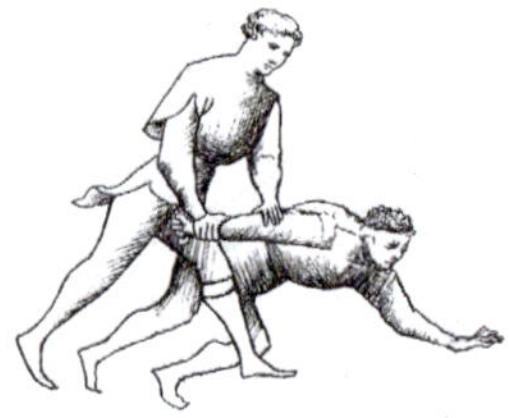

Remedy Master 3 Play 3 (13vD)

Not coincidentally, the Pisani-Dossi has its version of this scholar followed by a very similar play where the scholar uses his forearm instead of his hand to make contact with the attacker's arm. Either will do the job. It may be less a deliberate choice on the part of the scholar than the result of the closeness of the combatants and/or the time available to complete the action. An understanding of this may be the reason behind the omission of the Pisani-Dossi play from the Getty as, essentially, a case of circumstantial rather than universal application.

These scholars bring into dagger fighting specific applications of the principal of following your opponent's reaction that was first demonstrated in the sectrion on *abrazare*.

THE FOURTH REMEDY MASTER: FOLLOWING ON

The Fourth Remedy Master is shown making his cover. A follow-on action, a disarm, is described in the text. Apparently Fiore considered it more important here, as he did with the First Remedy Master, to show the cover than the follow-on play. As we did for the First Remedy Master, we should consider this play the first scholar of this Remedy Master.

I am the Fourth Master, and I perform this grapple. ...

As mentioned above, the Fourth Remedy Master's scholars expand on the issue of responding to the attacker's reactions. With the attack coming from above, the range of reactions possible to the attacker is greater than it was with a more horizontal attack, in part because he is playing in the center of the way. He might pull to either side, he might try to go up or down, or he might try to pull back or to push through. The attacker has six directions of response and Fiore gives us six scholars. All of them use the attacker's energy to their advantage.

The written play that accompanies the Remedy Master himself uses the energy of the attacker trying to push home his attack. A common tactic for the attacker here is to try to direct the dagger point toward the scholar's face and reinforce his attack with his left hand, doubling up to force the point home. The scholar responds to this quickly by turning his whole body to isolate the attacker's arm and force the attacker's reinforcing arm out of play.

Remedy Master 4 Play 2
(14vB)

The first scholar illustrated (play 2, left) deals with the attacker's move to his left. By doing this, he opens up space for the scholar to enter. While keeping control of the attacker's wrist with his left hand, the scholar releases his right hand grip and shifts his right hand under the attacker's arm. He grips his own wrist or hand, doubling his advantage over his opponent's arm as his own right arm becomes a fulcrum over which to lever the attacker's arm.

Remedy Master 4 Play 3
(14vC)

The second (play 3, right) responds to the attacker pulling back along the line of his attack. The scholar follows the attacker's motion. Releasing his left hand grip, he shifts that hand behind the attacker's arm and grabs his own wrist, creating a doubled grip that overwhelms the attacker's arm.

Remedy Master 4 Play 4
(14vD)

Both of these play partake of Fiore's two-beats-one principle. Both also can vary their effect. The vehemence of the attacker's withdrawal or that of the scholar's advance can decide whether this action will be a bind, break, or throw.

If, instead, the attacker reacts by pulling up from the line of his attack, perhaps to prepare for another strike, the third scholar (play 4, left) is the response. Shifting his left hand to the attacker's elbow, he amplifies the upwards motion. As the attacker starts to lose his balance, the scholar's right hand seeks out his knee to complete the throw in an emphatic manner.

Remedy Master 4 Play 5 (38rA)

With an attacker who tries to pull his dagger arm to his right, a different response is necessary (play 5, right). Blocking the movement of the dagger or grabbing it allows the scholar to use the attacker's own action to help strip the dagger from his hand.

Remedy Master 4 Play 6 (38rB)

If the attacker should drop his arm down, typically accompanied by an attempt to move his body back out, the fifth scholar (play 6, left) comes into play. Holding the attacker's wrist in place with the left hand, the scholar can grasp the dagger and shove it in the direction the attacker is moving. This will disarm him and, because the attacker has started backwards, minimize the danger for the scholar whose right hand will be moving closer to the attacker.

Together the scholars of the Fourth Remedy Master present a complete set of responses designed to play against the likely reactions of a thwarted attacker. The student of the art must develop his ability to feel the change that will come as the attacker reacts and follow after it with a decisive action.

THE NINTH REMEDY MASTER: COVERING BELOW

As the Fourth Remedy Master dealt with attacks from above, the Ninth Remedy Master deals with attacks from below. Saying, "My underhanded grapple is like the one the Fourth King does overhanded, although my plays are nothing like his …" Fiore tells us the two masters are related.

I am the Ninth King, the last one of dagger. My underhanded grapple is like the one the Fourth King does overhanded, although my plays are nothing like his. …

An attacker, finding his upwards-grip attack thwarted has the same set of possible reactions as the downwards-grip attacker of the Fourth Remedy Master. However, the different mechanics involved in the upward versus downwards grip make the plays of the Remedy Master's scholars different.

Discounting the scholars whose actions elaborate on another scholar's play, the Ninth Remedy Master has six scholars. When Fiore says "my plays are nothing like his" he seems to be referring to the mechanics of the plays rather than the triggers, for like those of the Fourth Remedy Master, these scholars make their plays following after the responses of a thwarted attacker.

These plays are built around an upwards-grip centerline attack. Earlier, I described how this attack opens up the possibility of upwards-grip attacks coming from the left or right. Even when they do, the cover is the same. The follow-on play changes little, although once off the centerline an attacker is unlikely to try to withdraw his dagger hand to the side from which he attacked. Mechanically, such a withdrawal is uncomfortable and awkward.

REMEDY MASTERS WITH DAGGERS

I am the Sixth Master ...

Fiore presents us with three masters who hold daggers: the Sixth, Seventh, and Eighth Remedy Masters. All hold the dagger's grip in their right hand and the blade in their left. The first and last of these three hold the dagger in the same way, while the middle one holds his dagger with his wrists crossed, right above left. These are the two dagger grips depicted among the Fight Masters.

The Sixth Remedy Master is shown blocking with his body twisted (note the center seam of his garment showing), indicating he is squared up against his attacker. The block is strong and, against an unprotected arm, painful.

This is, however, but one of his responses as he "can defend to all sides." This certainly means he can cover to the left and right, and as he is shown covering above, he can cover below, making his defense a suitable one for an attack coming from any point on the circle. The Middle Iron Gate Fight Master, who holds his dagger the same way, defends "below, above and on all sides."

This master has five scholars, who confine themselves to demonstrating circumstances relating to the illustrated upper attack. The first three deal with the most likely attack reactions, shifting left (play 3) and right (play 1) and one not seen before (because we have not seen a scholar with a dagger before): the second scholar's response to an attempt to pull down and break his two-handed grip.

It is important to remember that your hand is not welded to your dagger blade (or to the grip, for that matter). The cover of the Sixth Remedy Master brings your left hand, your grabbing hand, close to your opponent. The first scholar (Remedy Master 6 Play 2) reminds us of this by grabbing the attacker's arm to free the scholar's dagger for an attack of his own. That same grab opens up the possibility of the plays of the First Remedy Master. Fiore, having covered them there, need not repeat them here.

I am the Seventh Master and I play with arms crossed. ...

In his ability to cover on all sides, the Seventh Remedy Master is like the Sixth. Unlike him, this master has no scholars at all. Yet Fiore tells us that he can do "the previous plays" and specifies the Middle Bind with a specific reference to the third play of the First Remedy Master. This block puts one in good position to release one's grip on the blade, leaving the left hand in good position to make a number of grips and plays. What you do will depend greatly on where you covered, taking your lead from whichever of the first four Remedy Masters deals with the attack you are covering against.

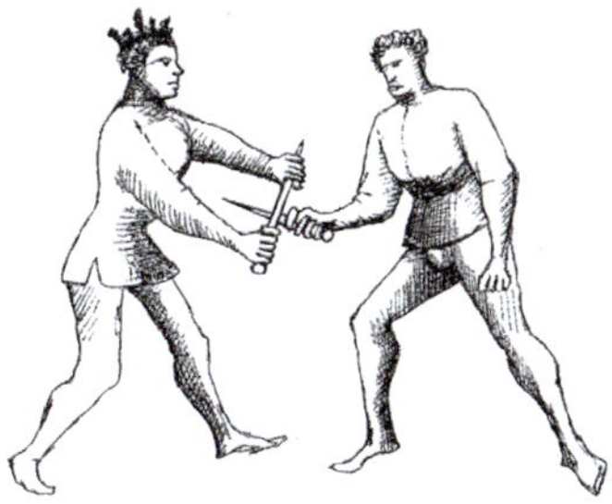

I am the Eighth Master, and I cross with my dagger. ...

The Eighth Remedy Master appears only in the Getty. He makes a cross below, apparently illustrating what the Sixth Remedy Master told us he could do. Why show this? If the reason is to make clear that the dagger grip can be used to cover against an upward-grip attack, why not also provide a master who uses the Seventh Remedy Master's grip to cover below? Doesn't he also cover in all directions? Interestingly, the Paris manuscript offers a Remedy Master using the Seventh Remedy Master's grip while making cover below. Why aren't both in the Getty to complete the set?

To further confuse matters, the Pisani-Dossi offers a scholar who plays from this master's cover, but the master himself is absent. There are other oddities about the material in the Pisani-Dossi's dagger section that contribute to the sense of unfinished pedagogy there, but the presence of a scholar with a dagger must make us wonder why he is not present in the Getty.

So what is the Eighth Remedy Master up to? Obviously, he needs to be present to tie in with the references in the baton plays. But what else does he offer? He has no primary scholars, just two variant scholars appearing after the general Counter Master. The master himself is holding his dagger Doubled and Crossed, and he stands in Half Iron Gate. Neither of his variant scholars carry daggers and both stand in Full Iron Gate; one holds his arms Doubled and the other Crossed. This is the only place in the Getty that we see an empty-handed scholar playing Crossed against a dagger. Notably the empty-handed Doubled grip, which we were told the Second Remedy Master could "cross below and above," appears here covering below. This all implies a strong relationship in mechanics.

With the empty-handed Ninth Remedy Master, who covers below, we were told he was similar to the Fourth Remedy Master, but that his plays were different. We are given scholars to illustrate that. Yet with the Eighth Remedy Master we get no scholars to show us how the plays differ as, given the mechanics of the upward-grip attack, they must. As noted before, the Pisani-Dossi has a scholar for this master's cover that makes a play, but he is missing from the Getty. Instead we have the Eighth Remedy Master saying, "some of my plays come afterwards, some we already saw," and specifically referring to plays belonging to the Sixth and the Ninth Remedy Masters.

If the Eighth Remedy Master had been left out, one could argue that the omission fits within the space-saving paradigm that flows though Fiore's work. After all, his cover is within the purview of the Sixth Remedy Master, isn't it? But he does appear, and it is that very same parsimonious paradigm that explains his presence. He acts as a space-saving bridge, linking several disparate aspects of dagger play together. He is a sign post to point the way for the reader to make connections within the art that Fiore does not take the time to make explicit.

As we will soon see, this is not the only time that Fiore leaves it to the reader to use these linkages to open out a major part of the art while leaving the reader to explore and understand for himself the breadth of the art.

HIDDEN DAGGERS

Unlike many other fencing works, *il Fior di Battaglia* has little in the way of knife dueling, where two combatants face one another with a dagger grasped in one hand. There is one instance: the ninth play of the Ninth Dagger Remedy Master where that dagger is drawn and then discarded as ineffective in the following play. This pair of plays, the last in the dagger section, is saying "if I need a dagger, I can take yours" and may simply be a closing statement certifying the effectiveness of Fiore's empty-handed techniques against a dagger-wielding opponent.

Dagger against dagger from Hans Talhoffer's 1467 *fechtbuch*.

Nevertheless, later masters show men holding a dagger with one hand, fighting against men also holding a dagger in one hand. Fiore doesn't. This seems a curious omission, especially since Fiore lists the dagger among the weapons in his arsenal. Does striking someone with his own dagger, which Fiore shows several times, count as fighting with a dagger? Or did Fiore only advocate fighting with a dagger when you have both hands on it, as is shown among the Remedy Masters? I would argue that both circumstances are part of Fiore's art, as is the more conventional dagger fighting shown by later masters.

In the text accompanying the very first Fight Master of the dagger, Fiore tells us "I can execute the plays with and without the dagger." Here the empty-handed Fight Master is explicitly telling us he can do the plays with a dagger. Fiore leaves us to understand enough of the art from our study of the plays to know how to execute those plays with a dagger in our right hand.

Why the right hand? Because, in the second Fight Master, he tells us that master cannot fight with the dagger because if you are holding your wrist with your right hand, you can't also hold your dagger.

While the fifth Fight Master, who is the third of the three empty-handed masters, says nothing about using a dagger, it is worth noting what the third Fight Master has to say. He, like the fifth, plays with his wrists crossed and he can parry "both with the dagger and without." This strongly implies that the fifth Fight Master can also play with a dagger in his hands.

Inference can be flimsy ground upon which to interpret the art. Fortunately, Fiore has left us more links to support the connection. The very obvious one is that he assigns the two seated scholars in the baton plays to Remedy Masters of the dagger. And since a baton can be used as a dagger, a dagger should be able to be used as a baton—at least in some applications. Fiore's first play of the baton shows the rather vicious triangle trap on the neck. Later masters, such as Hans Talhoffer,[1] show this same play executed with a dagger.

Baton plays from Fiore with corresponding dagger plays from Talhoffer (above right) and Codex Wallerstein[2] (below right).

One obvious application of using a dagger instead of fighting empty-handed is in the simple strike. So, where a empty-hand strike is implied or called for, one can easily substitute a dagger strike.

But Fiore also gives us hints about how he would use a dagger were he holding one. The first illustrated scholar of the Sixth Remedy Master (Remedy Master 6 play 2) demonstrates how a dagger blade can be used to replace a hand grip in the formation of a bind, where the blade is used to apply the pressure where a hand would normally be used to create the Middle Bind.

Further, by using the hook created by the angle between the dagger blade and your fist you can use your dagger hand wherever you use a hook grip. If gripping the dagger tightly, especially if making contact with the part of the blade nearest your hand, you can use it where you would use your empty hand to push. The pommel of the dagger can also be used to do this.

I believe that diligent application of these techniques to the empty-hand dagger plays will reveal Fiore's hidden daggers to the inquisitive student.

1 Hans Talhoffer, *Medieval Combat: A Fifteenth-Century Illustrated Manual of Swordfighting and Close-Quarter Combat*, Mark Rector, ed. and trans., Greenhill Books, 2000.

2 Zabinski with Bartlomiej Walczak, *Codex Wallerstein: A Medieval Fighting Book from the Fifteenth Century on the Longsword, Falchion, Dagger, and Wrestling*, Paladin Press, 2002.

FULL IRON GATE, SIMPLE

(*TUTTA PORTA DI FERRO SEMPIA*)

Standing in Full Iron Gate, Simple seems no different from the Iron Gate of *abrazare.* This is not surprising, as the instructional device of the dagger section is how to play empty handed against the dagger, a close-in weapon.

The text says that this guard plays with and without a dagger. This provides the treatise's opening, which allows us to understand that all of the scholars of the open-handed Remedy Masters can make their plays while wielding a dagger.

Fiore presents these five dagger guards, each a variation of Iron Gate. All hold the hands down, making them harder targets for the opponent while reserving the player's options of response.

The most obvious differences among them are in the hand positions and whether (and how) they grip a dagger. Only two guards show the player holding a dagger, although the text says that Full Iron Gate, Simple plays with and without a dagger.

Foot position also varies, and all but Half Iron Gate show an open-hip position where the hip on the side of the trailing foot is turned slightly away from the opponent. This maximizes the player's ability to shift position and distance quickly. It also sets the player up to generate power through movement from that side.

Half Iron Gate is different. This Fight Master has his hips squared up to the opponent. This is tied directly to his crossed grip on the dagger. An open hip position would reduce the player's ability to parry to the left, as the text says he can do. Movement ability is deliberately reduced in favor of improved ability to cover against attack. This is very important, as when using this grip he cannot cover long.

MIDDLE IRON GATE, DOUBLED

(*MEZZANA PORTA DI FERRO DOPPIA*)

Stand in the Iron Gate of *abrazare* and hold the dagger is in your right hand, upwards grip. Your left hand holds the blade. Direct the point towards the centerline.

This guard is called the "best and strongest of all" and Fiore tells us that it can parry "below, above and on all sides." Middle Iron Gate moves easily into the cover of the Sixth Remedy Master.

FULL IRON GATE, DOUBLED

(*TUTTA PORTA DI FERRO DOPPIA*)

Your right hand grasps your left wrist. Blocks from this position are strong, but it cannot cover long, a common problem with the crossed guards.

You stand in Full Iron Gate, Doubled as you would for the Iron Gate of *abrazare* except for hand position.

The text says that Full Iron Gate, Doubled cannot play with a dagger. This is because the player is presumed to be right handed and his right hand is busy holding his wrist.

HALF IRON GATE, DOUBLED & CROSSED

(*MEZZA PORTA DI FERRO DOPPIA ET INCROSADA*)

The dagger is in your right hand, downwards grip. Your left hand reaches under your right arm and holds the blade. Though covers from this guard are short, they are very strong when they block and they can cover to all sides.

You can easily move into the cover of the Seventh Remedy Master and can parry "above and below, right and left, with dagger and without."

As a "half" position, this guard is more squared up and centered in order to cut down on response time against threats.

FULL IRON GATE, CROSSED

(*TUTTA PORTA DI FERRO INCROSADA*)

Cross your wrists, right over left. Otherwise, you stand in the Iron Gate of *abrazare.* Covers from this guard are short, a common problem with the crossed guards. Fiore says this guard is "strong," another common feature of crossed guards.

Experience shows that Full Iron Gate, Crossed can also play with a dagger. With a dagger, it can shift easily to Half Iron Gate.

The cover of the First Remedy Master is Long position on the left

The scholar's hand strikes into incoming attack. Speed is important here as the attack will be coming in fast. An aggressive cover also helps shift the attack out of line and off its target while opening up the attacker's body position to follow-on techniques.

The target of the scholar's strike is the attacker's wrist, with the intent to catch it against the scholar's own wrist. This can be against the outside of the arm or the edge, which one you elect may be intentional and based on which technique you have in mind as a second intention. Whether the cover is made with the arm's back or edge, the scholar must be prepared to follow on with a technique that suits the cover he has achieved.

The portion of the scholar's arm that makes contact may also be out of his control, as a result of the match-up of the speeds of attack and cover. The scholar must still be ready to execute a follow-on technique that suits the position of his arm relative to the attacker's arm and the pressure he will be feeling.

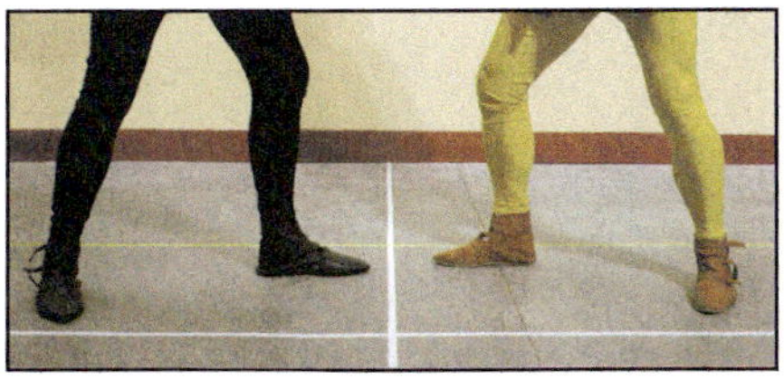

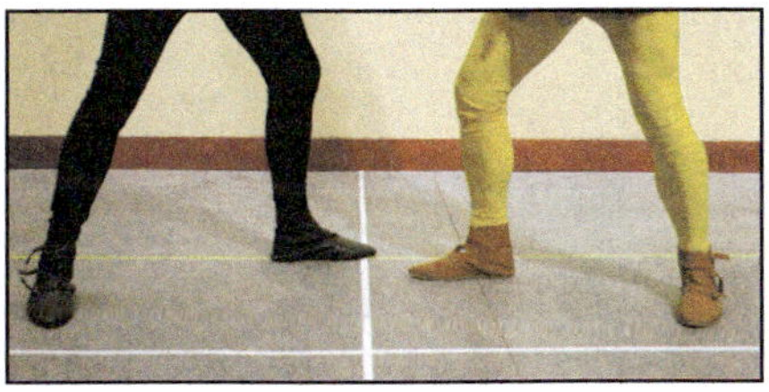

Fiore's illustration shows the Remedy Master's left foot in front of the attacker's lead foot, essentially on the centerline. The master may or may not have made a step.

The main instruction here seems to be: adopt Long Position, setting your structure to defeat the incoming attack. Note that the foot position is shown differently in subsequent scholars, including the scholar playing against the Counter Master who deals with the Remedy Master's cover.

The exact position of your lead foot is less important than the aggressive cover.

If the Remedy Master makes no step, his knee straightens to form a structured, sound Long Position against the attack.

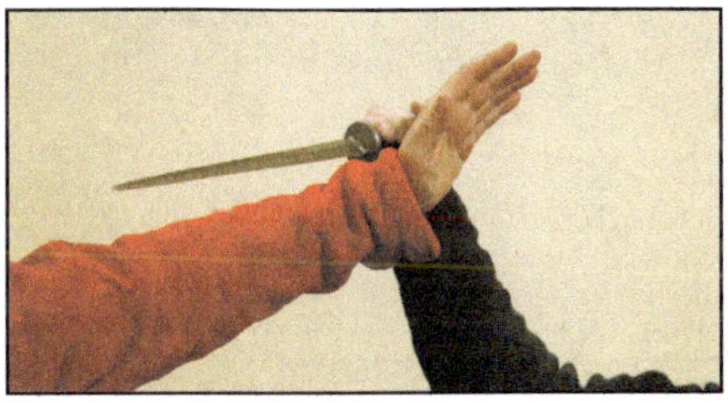

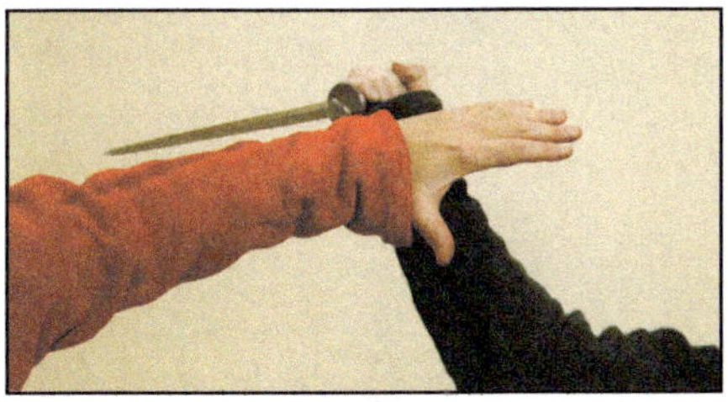

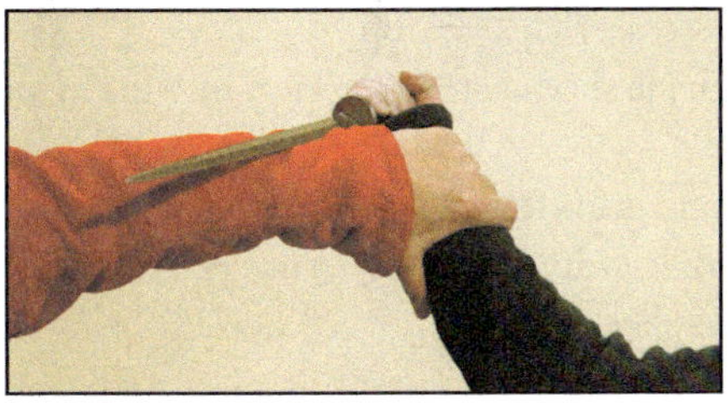

Fiore's drawing shows the Remedy Master's hand gripping the opponent's wrist. This illustrates part of the first play as well as the master's cover.

A grab is a natural follow-on from a rotation of the wrist. The Remedy Master's cover may include the start of the rotation that goes into the grab but the grab itself is probably part of the first play.

Rotation should only begin after the cover is established. You must have the contact with the opponent (which is analogous to a bind with swords) to know what to do next.

If you go right for the grab that Fiore shows, you might miss and the result will be bad for you. Such an attempt also exposes the hinge that is your wrist to the hyperextension that a powerful blow can create against it.

Making the block first increases your safety margin during the move. Also, not committing to the grip until you have a feeling from the contact against him positions you better to execute some of the other plays more quickly.

Fiore's illustration shows the Remedy Master's right hand raised and ready to strike. This is a prime example of the diagrammatic nature of Fiore's illustrations.

Dagger fighting is fast, and the player must be fast, too. The follow-on strike must be on its way as soon as you set the structure of your cover.

You probably never actually get your right hand raised and ready. This is instruction, not a photographic illustration of a moment in the technique.

Also, using strikes as a method of softening up the opponent to ease the execution of techniques is almost certainly a part of Fiore's art. The posing of the Remedy Master could simply indicate readiness to execute one of the techniques displayed by the master's scholars.

The first play of the First Remedy Master is a disarm

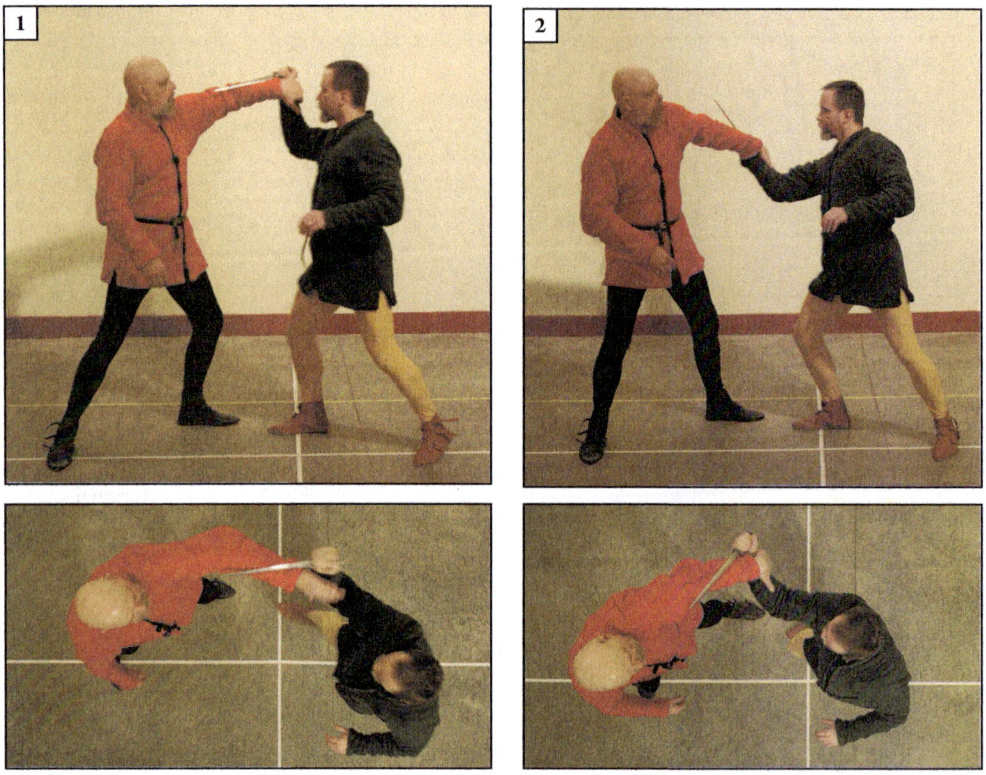

The scholar makes the cover of the Remedy Master. He should strike strongly into the incoming attack.

Achieving good contact, he rolls his hand over and grips the attacker's wrist.

The attacker's dagger lies over the scholar's arm. If it does not, it will not provide a lever point and the scholar will not be able to execute the play.

As the scholar makes his cover, he should strike at the opponent with his free hand as shown to the right. This step is omitted in the interpretation plays, as it is in the manuscript drawings to make clear the action of the particular play.

By continuing to roll his hand to the left, the scholar will pry the attacker's dagger from his hand.

As the scholar rolls his hand, that lever point begins to apply force against the attacker's fingers, opening up his grip.

The scholar uses his free hand to collect the dagger as it leaves the attacker's hand. He may now use it to strike the attacker.

... Here is the absolute best thing I can do: making you drop your dagger by turning my hand to the left.

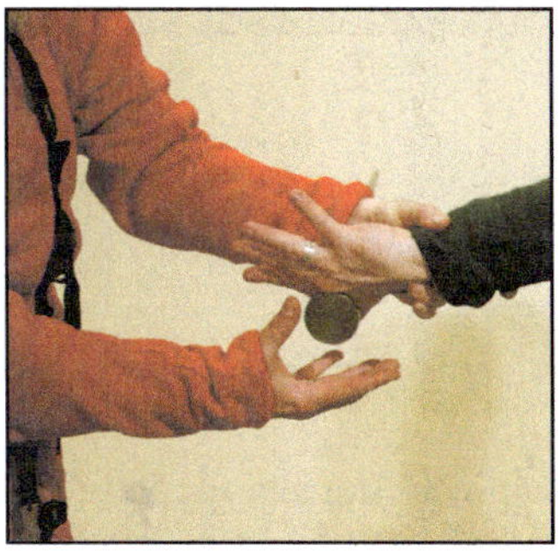

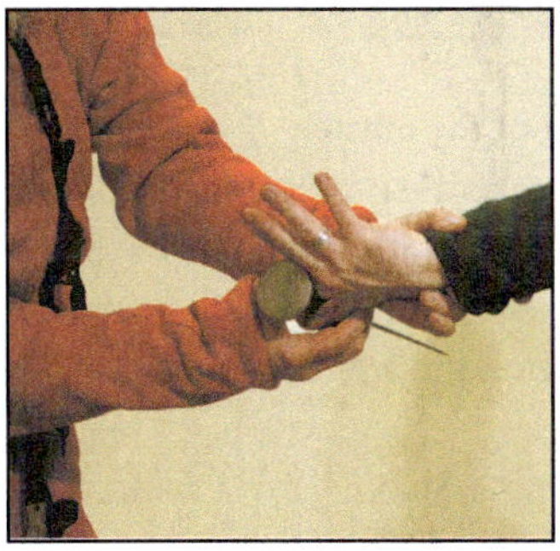

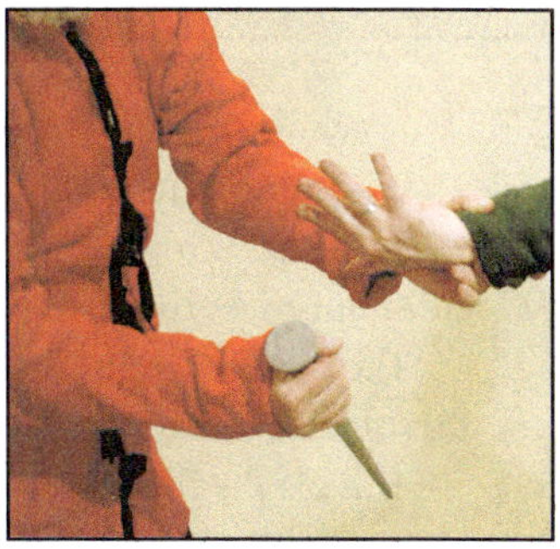

The attacker's fingers open up as the blade levers across the scholar's arm. Done quickly and violently, the dagger is ripped from the attacker's hand and goes flying away.

Done more slowly and with a clean technique that successfully torques the attacker away from him, it enables the scholar to use his free hand to collect the dagger as he strips it from the attacker.

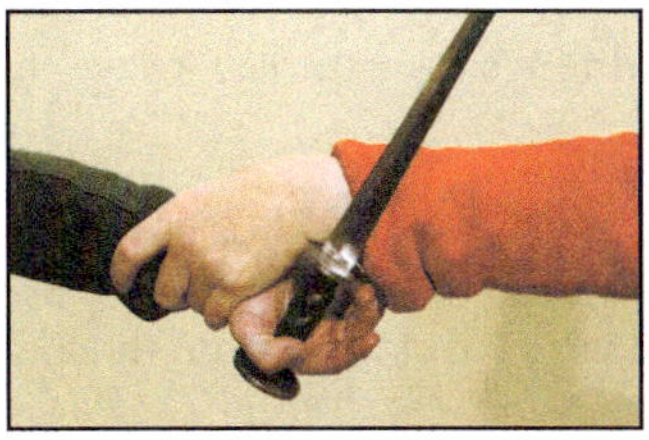

The scholar's effectiveness in the disarm is increased if the base of his palm lies across the base of the attacker's palm, where his grip will lock up the attacker's wrist and limit his ability to rotate it.

The third play of the First Remedy Master is a bind that breaks the arm. It can also be translated into a hold or a takedown

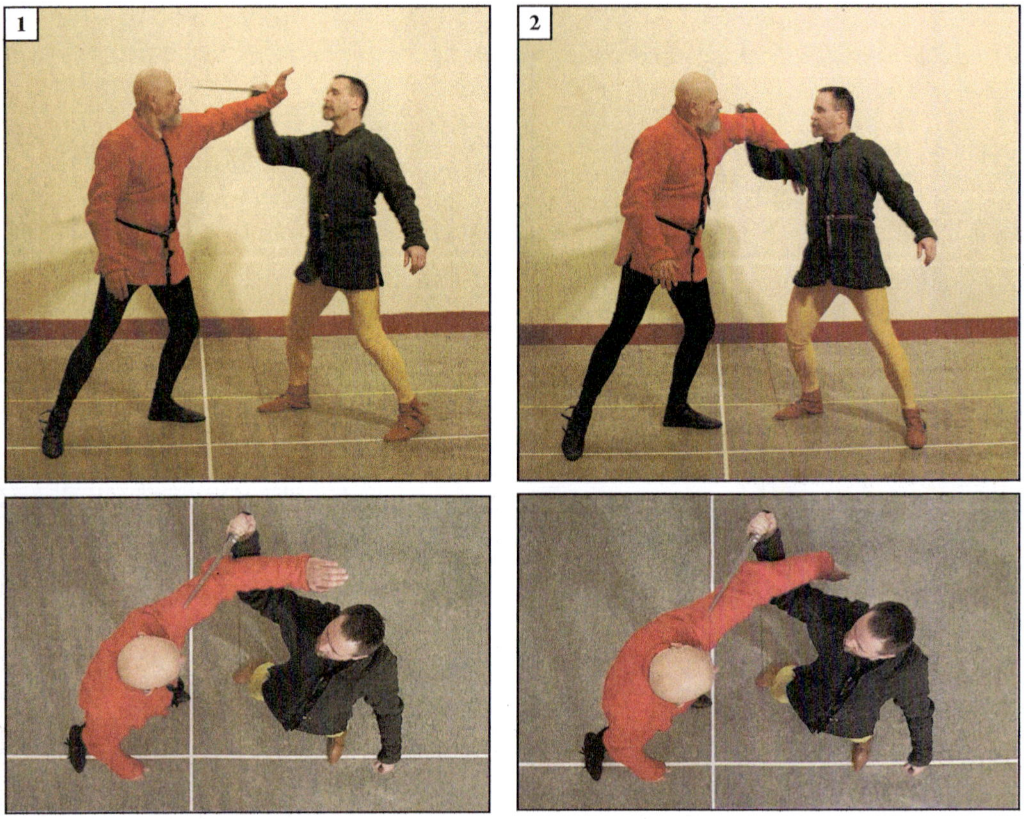

The scholar makes the cover of the master.

It is important that the attacker be presenting a bent elbow.

The scholar may simply await the attacker or adjust forward (*accressere*) into the attack. The latter improves the chances that a bent elbow will be presented.

The scholar begins to envelop the attacker's arm, moving his hand, thumb leading, behind the attacker's arm.

The play is illustrated using a Stable Turn (*volta stabile*) to power the action. Note the change in the orientation of the scholar's feet in the detail pictures. This turn reorients the body, powering the action.

The scholar could also execute a Full Turn (*tutta volt*a), pivoting on his left foot with his right circling back. Done gently, this spirals the attacker down to the ground. A more violent expression snaps the arm and flings the attacker away. The scholar completes the move by moving into Boar's Tooth.

In training, the play halts before going to Boar's Tooth.

Note: Although the Stable Turn is show in use, movement on the attacker's part may require a Half or Full Turn on the scholar's part to maintain the lock and complete the move.

I have locked your arm in a middle bind, so that you won't give me any trouble. If I decide to throw you to the ground, I'll do so with no trouble at all. And don't even dream of freeing yourself from me.

The second, partly transparent arm in the pictures above represents the final position that the scholar is seeking.

The scholar's hand emerges from behind the attacker's elbow. Then his arm starts to rise into the bent arm of Boar's Tooth as he makes his Stable Turn. This can snap the attacker's arm or dislocate his shoulder, the primary goal of this action.

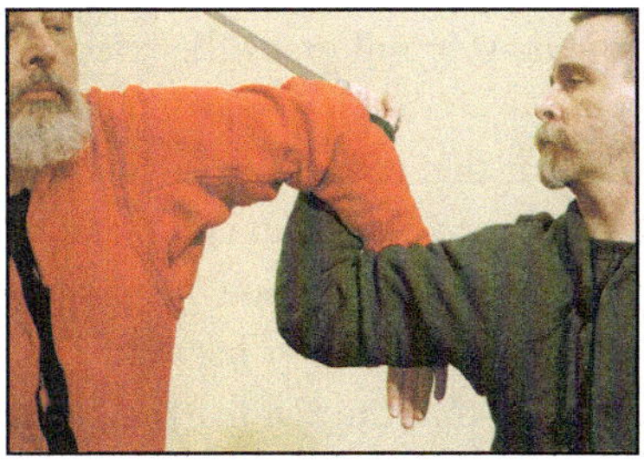

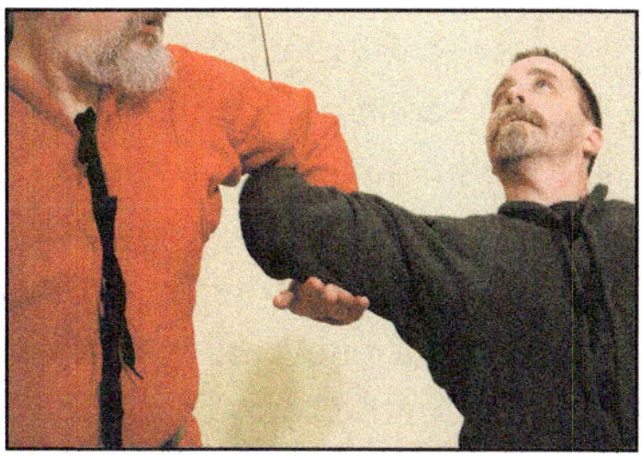

The scholar's back becomes the lever point allowing the dagger to be stripped from the attacker's hand.

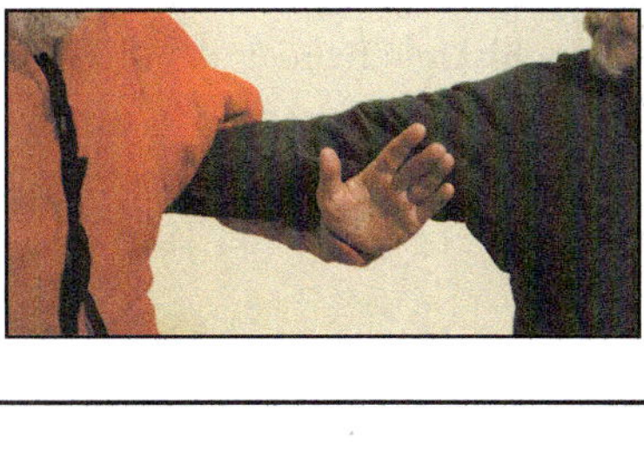

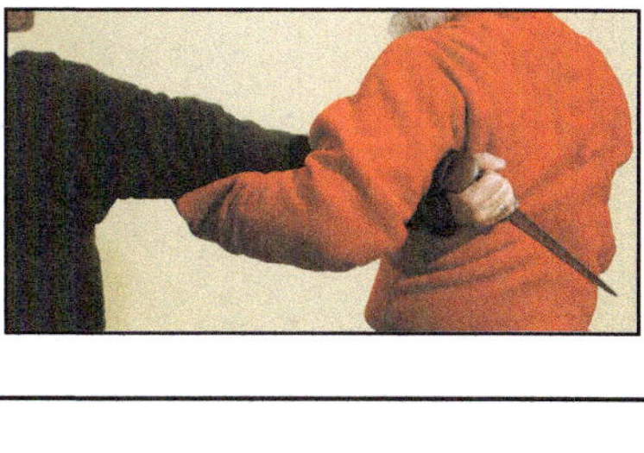

THE FIFTH PLAY OF THE FIRST REMEDY MASTER IS A BIND THAT CAN BE TRANSLATED INTO A THROW. IT ALSO FUNCTIONS AS A DISARM

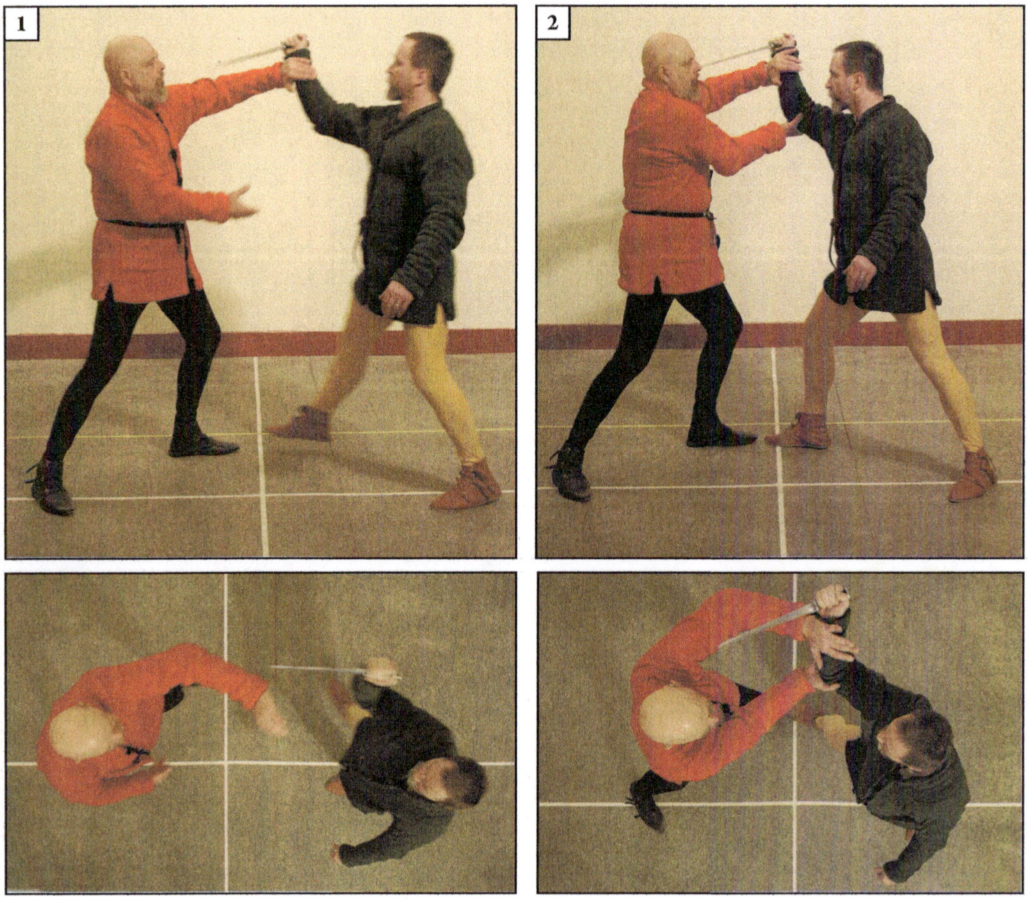

The scholar makes the cover of the master and grabs the attacker's wrist while bringing his right hand forward.

Fiore's illustration shows clearly that this cover is made with the left foot out of the way. Moving offline helps push the attacker's arm out wider and make his elbow an easier target.

The scholar brings his right hand to the attacker's elbow, keeping his arms extended so that the attacker cannot easily reach his own right elbow. Shove his wrist away and keep his elbow close.

From the counter to this play, we see that the scholar passes back with his left foot as he executes the bind to maintain distance from his opponent.

Once the attacker's arm is twisted and he is going off balance, the scholar can, as the text suggests, leave his grip at the elbow and put his right hand under the attacker's right knee and throw him. Lifting the leg encourages the opponent to land head or neck first, a potentially lethal fall.

The throw in the alternative ending is best powered by passing forward with the right foot. Other throws can be powered by a Stable Turn, or a Full Turn with the left foot circling back.

Here's a good parry to get your dagger from you. I can also use this grapple to put you in a good bind. If I put my right hand under your right knee, I can quickly make you fall, since I am an expert in this art.

THE TEXT OFFERS AN ALTERNATIVE CONCLUSION TO THIS PLAY.

Pushing the wrist back and toward the opponent's shoulder locks up the arm, allowing the scholar to release his right hand grip and move that arm toward the opponent's knee. The scholar's step breaks his opponent's structure by taking his shoulders back past his center of gravity. This results in a backwards fall for the opponent. Grabbing the knee helps the scholar ensures his victim will fall on the back of his head.

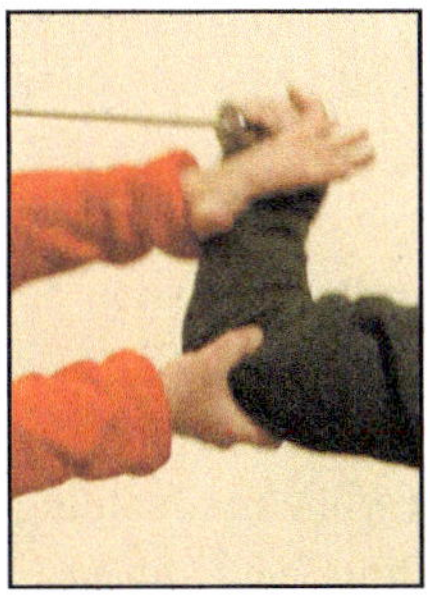

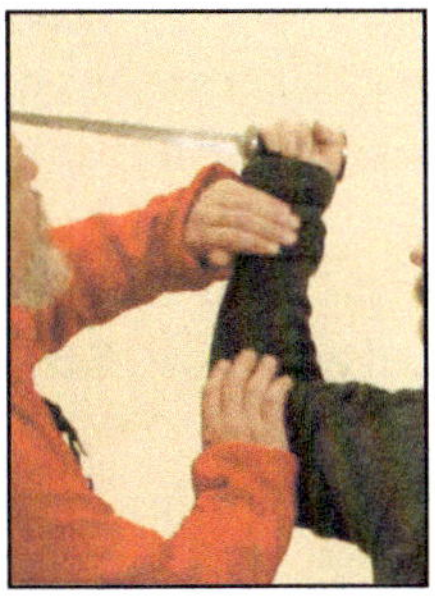

The grip on the left is the one shown in the interpretation play above. The one on the right is an alternative grip. Fiore says "the grapples are seldom identical." In other words, you will use the grip that allows you to get results. Both of these grips do the important task of getting the opponent's elbow moving in an opposite direction from his wrist.

SAFETY NOTE: Falls directly backwards like this are very dangerous and difficult to make safely. Spare your partner and only take this action to the point where his balance *starts* to fail.

The seventh play of the First Remedy Master is a throw

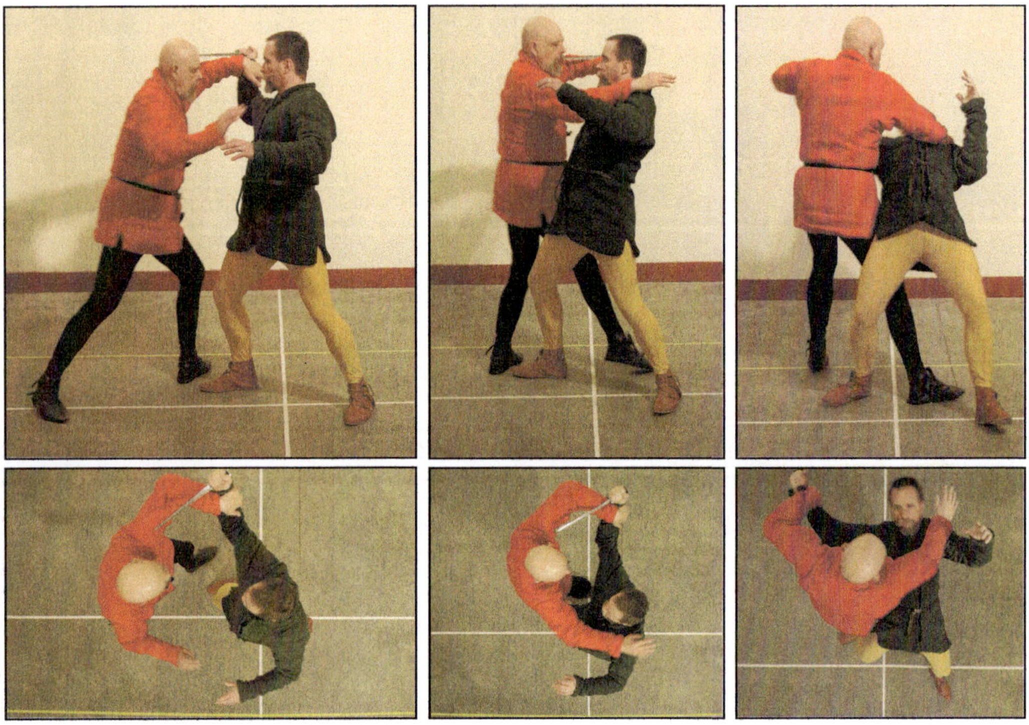

As with the previous play, the scholar will find more success if he steps out of the way as he makes his master's cover.

The strike into the attacker's arm drives his arm wide.

The grab helps control the dagger but is not absolutely necessary if the technique is executed quickly enough.

The scholar passes forward, stepping past the attacker's lead leg. Ideally, this will position the scholar with his knee behind the attacker's knee to create the pivot point over which the scholar will break the attacker's structure.

As the scholar moves, his right arm comes forward, driving over the attacker's shoulder.

The scholar drives his upper arm into the attacker's throat. Executing a Stable Turn (*volta stabile*) he throws the attacker onto his back.

As the scholar makes his turn, he should be extending his left arm while maintaining his grip on the attacker's wrist. The scholar is striving to attain Long Position (*posta longa*), and his left hand should be trying to reach the position shown in the illustration of Long Position.

Extending the Stable Turn into a Full Turn results in a more powerful throw.

This is a play that admits no counter. The opponent will surely go to the ground and be disarmed, since the student can do this to him as you can see. And once he is on the ground, the student can finish the play with other actions.

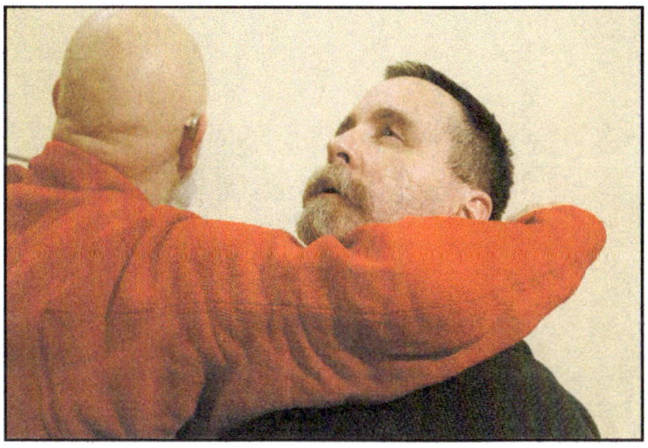

Hooking the neck with an arm is an easier action than trying for something like a throat grip and much easier to execute while in armor.

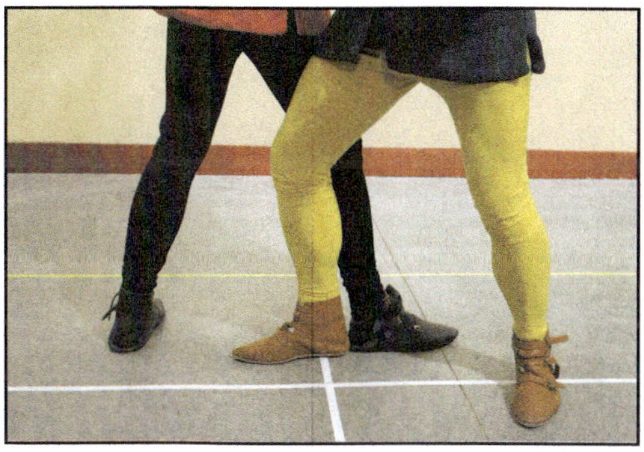

The scholar places his leg so that his knee is behind his opponent's knee, setting up a fulcrum for the throw.

If the attacker's step puts him past the attacker's leg, the throw can be made as a hip throw.

If the attacker's arm is driven wide enough, the scholar can simply walk past him, bowling him over.

The eighth play of the First Remedy Master is a strike against the attacker

The scholar has stepped out of the way and moved into the cover of his master. Whether by intent or accident, his covering arm has come behind the incoming attack.

Because he is behind the attacker's strike, the scholar can amplify the motion of the attack, forcing the attacker's body to continue turning.

The scholar strikes with his right hand, aiming into the attacker's center. It will come against the attacker's arm.

He can pass forward with his right foot to do so or make a Stable Turn (*volta stabile*). The choice will be tactical, driven by the attacker's response.

The scholar's strike re-directs the momentum of the attacker's own strike and sends his dagger into his own leg or body. Fiore notes the stomach or thigh as the target of this attack.

Little done?

Fiore says this play is not commonly done, leading one to wonder why it is uncommon. Is it hard? Unsafe? Or just something that few fencing masters know?

This play is not very common in the art of the dagger, but it is a defense worth knowing. The student can employ this parry and then strike his opponent either in the thigh or in the stomach.

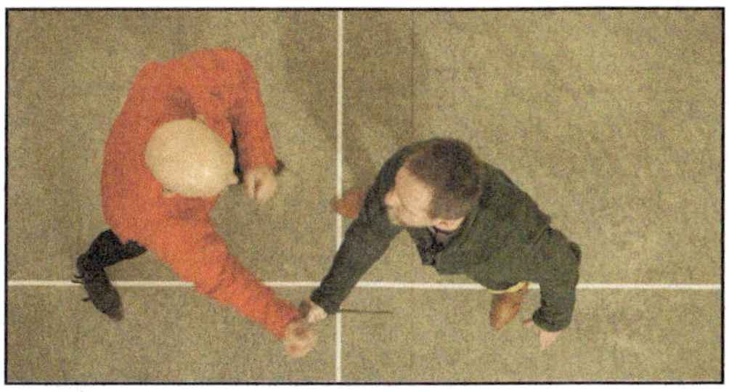

The scholar must use his left hand to control the attacker's dagger arm and ward against a sudden reverse (*riverso*) strike.

The scholar's hand strikes to the attacker's hand, driving it down and inward.

The cover of the Second Remedy Master is a modified Frontal position

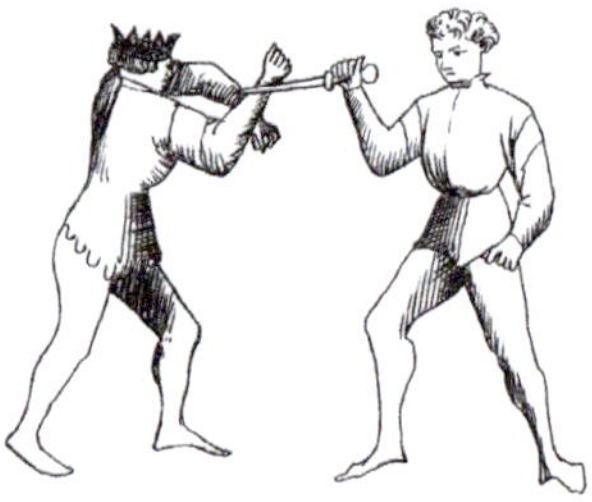

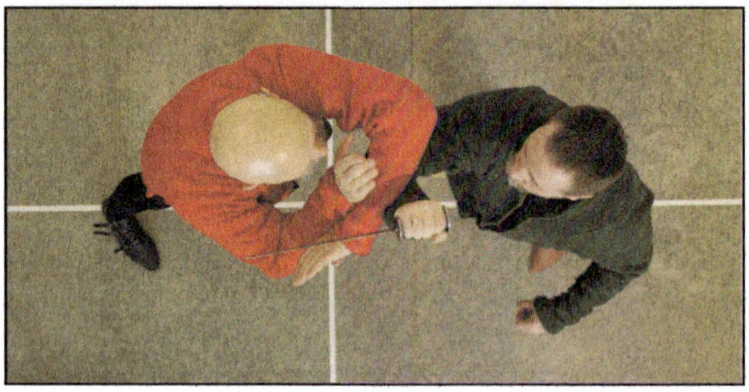

This cover is made against an attack not explicitly detailed among the four that accompany the dagger's Fight-Instruction Master. This attack is, however, a common and dangerous attack.

When an attacker has a downward-gripped dagger and starts making his attacks (from either side) closer toward the centerline, he creates these through-the-middle attacks. Like the primarily horizontal (*mezzani*) blows from the left and right, they have a target zone from the temple (the forehead, when in the center) to the elbow. Going lower results in the same problems one encounters with the other downward-grip attacks.

In the text, a strike through the middle is said to come *per mezo*. Following Fiore's pattern of shoving the words together (as with *de man dritto)* the rendering herein will be *permezo* for this category of strikes.

Since the attacker's body can be squared up along the centerline, his off hand can be ready to cover as in the attack from below.

Permezo attacks must be dealt with differently than attacks from either side and the Second Remedy Master is Fiore's answer to them.

The Second Remedy Master's cover is a modified form of Frontal position, played with the wrists crossed right over left.

As the scholar moves his crossed wrists into the cover, he raises his left elbow high, bringing his upper arm near his head. At the same time, his right shoulder drops and shifts forward while his right elbow pulls in toward his own center. Twisting the torso as the cover is made provides additional help in taking the dagger point off target, while simultaneously reducing the possible targets for the incoming point.

I play with my arms crossed so that I can perform the remedies we just saw. If we were both in armor, I wouldn't look any further for a better defense. There's no remedy stronger than I who wear a crown, since I can play mandritto and riverso and cross below and above.

With the cover made, the scholar has both hands near the attacker's dagger wrist and is ready to play to either side, as the attacker's pressure dictates. The plays of the First and Third Remedy Masters are available from this position, which may have something to do with the placement of this master between those masters in the order of presentation.

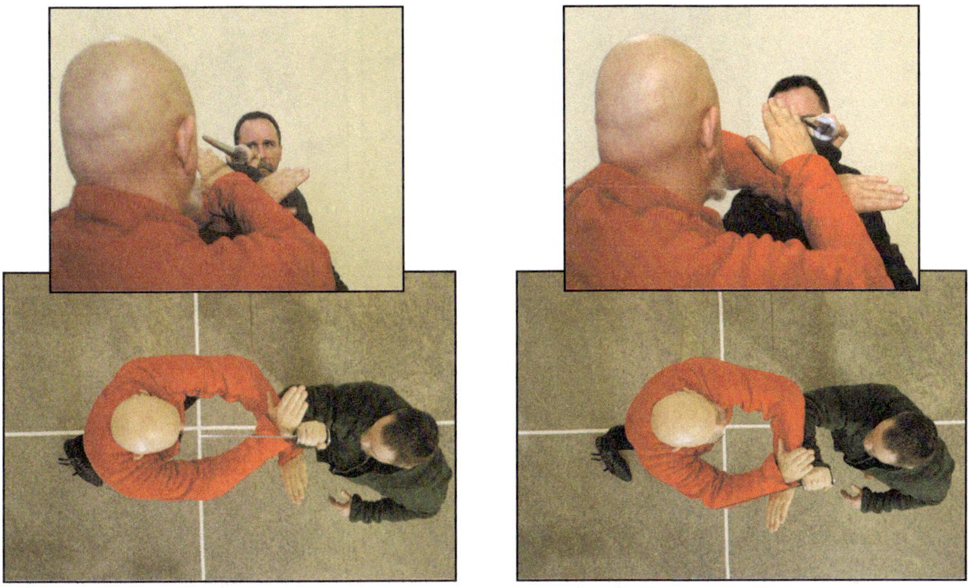

The crossed wrists cannot cover long. A long dagger blade will reach past the cover and score. If the cover is made (left) without the shoulder-elbow shift, the blade remains on line; a long blade will reach its target. The shoulder-elbow shift (right) changes the line of travel for the dagger.

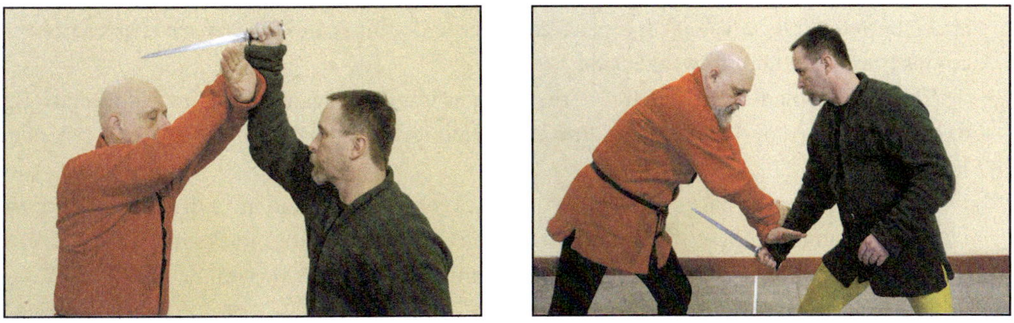

Fiore states this cover can make the cross above (left), which he illustrates, as well as making it below (right) which he does not illustrate.

The cover of the Third Remedy Master is a Long position on the right

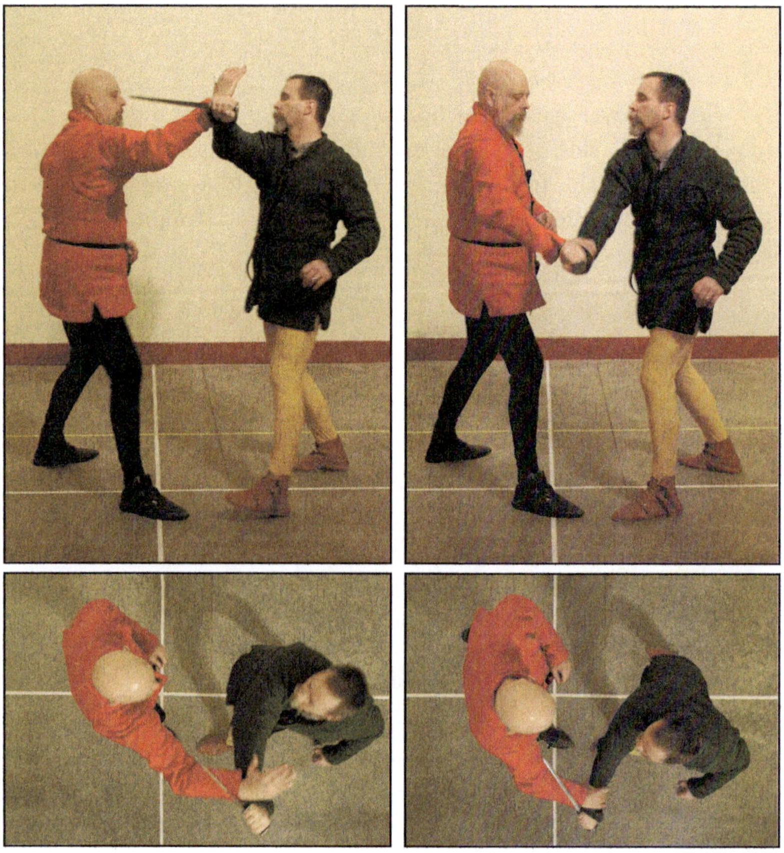

The illustration of the cover of the Third Remedy Master is labeled *composite* because Fiore's illustration shows the master already deep into the play. The illustration is taken from the general Counter Master who, like the other general Counter Masters, is shown in play against the Remedy Master's cover. The heads have been swapped to put the crown on the Remedy Master.

The scholar steps off line, toward the attacker, to make his cover. This helps shut down the attack before it fully develops. It is generally safer to do this against the *riverso* attack since this comes from the attacker's weaker side.

The cover is made with the edge of the hand, as was done against the *mandritto* attack. The palm faces inward or downward, thumb tucked alongside the palm to minimize the risk of its being broken.

The hand rolls and makes the grip on the attacker's wrist in a fluid motion as contact occurs.

With the attack stopped, the scholar stands on the outside of the attack line, a relatively safe position. Moving in to attack with *abrazare* techniques is the obvious follow-on.

Here we start with the strong plays of the riverso side, which caused countless to lose their lives. My students will follow with the plays deriving from the defense I am performing with my right hand. This is an easy action used to throw someone to the ground.

Locking hands makes the throw more secure.

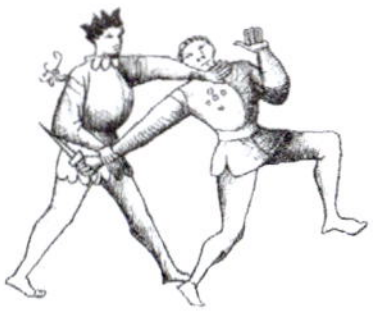

After the grab, the scholar passes forward. His left hand softens up the opponent by driving the edge into his throat. While pulling down with the right hand, the left hand hooks the throat and forces the head back. As the scholar achieves his stance, striving for Long Position, the attacker falls on his back

The scholar abandons his grab, presumably because the attacker is trying to withdraw (or maybe he just failed to achieve it). He steps toward the opponent with his right leg, throwing his right arm around the throat. With a turn, he can throw his attacker much as the fourth scholar of the First Remedy Master does.

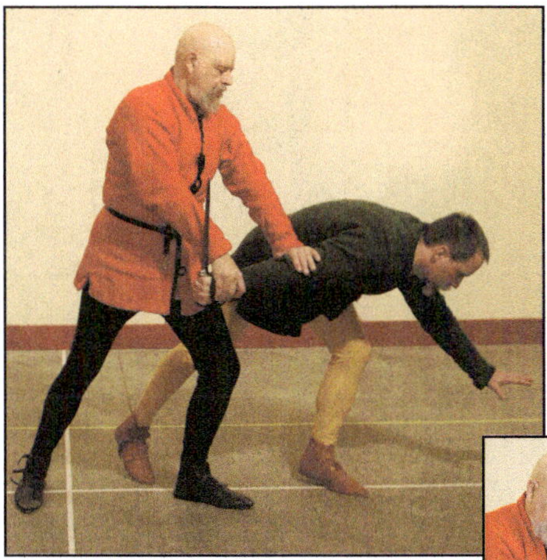

Pull his wrist behind his back for another variation of the lock.

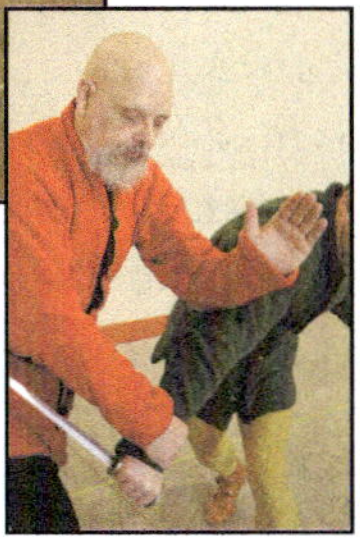

After the grab, the scholar drives his right hand forward with a pass. A soft strike creates a straight arm-bar, locking up the arm, which can be used to force the opponent to the ground. A hard strike can break the arm.

The elbow can do what the hand misses.

Fiore shows several variations on the *ligadura sottana*, the Under or Lower Bind, made from this cover. In this one the scholar forces the attacker's elbow down and out while using his wrist grip to bring the dagger hand in and up to create the lock.

The cover of the Fourth Remedy Master is a Frontal position

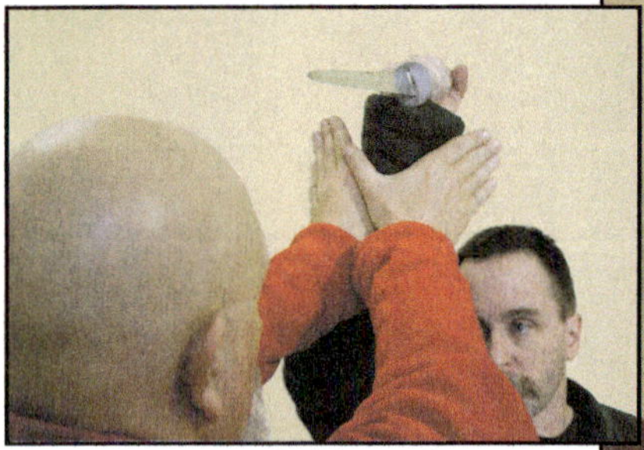

Detail of the catch

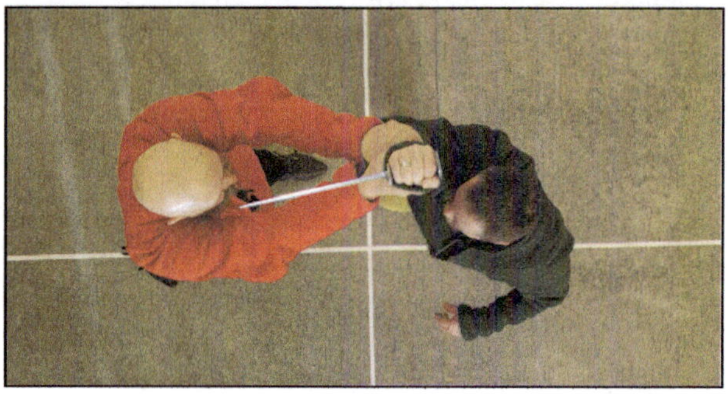

The Fourth Remedy Master responds to the *fendente* attack. Since this attack comes in the center zone, it is best defended with two hands.

The scholar extends both arms to meet the attack. The hands are together. The left thumb lies against the palm of the right hand, snugged up against the right thumb. The right thumb lies along the top of the left hand. Fingers extend outwards. This positioning protects the thumbs, unites the hands in their endeavor, and creates a funnel to help bring the attacker's wrist to where it can be gripped.

Closing the fingers over the attacker's arm, the grip is made immediately. Equally quickly, the scholar must respond to the attacker's pressure.

While each of the six scholar's of this master offer responses to the six axes of movement, the scholar can force a direction if he is faster. He may also influence the attacker's response with his own action, such as stepping off line and discouraging the attacker from responding in that direction or covering slightly softly to encourage the attacker to press the attack and thereby allow the first play.

I am the Fourth Master, and I perform this grapple. With a similar one, my students can hurt many men …

Following the attacker's response to the cover

If I turn right without letting go of your arm, I'll take your dagger away …

If the attacker presses forward, turn and disarm. Based on the master's first play of in the Pisani-Dossi, this turn becomes a disarm once the arm is controlled.

Bring your right forearm hard against his upper arm.

If the attacker shifts to his left, use the space. Your right hand slips under his arm and grips your own/his hand. Set your elbow against his, turn, and bind/break his arm.

Use your left arm as a fulcrum over which you bend his arm backwards.

If the attacker pulls back, amplify his motion. Keeping his arm bent, slip your left hand behind his arm and grab your own arm to bind his. This can become a takedown.

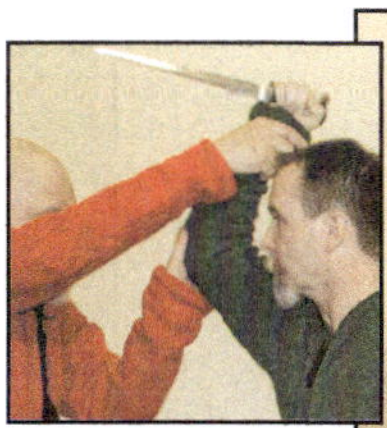

Folding his arm at the elbow helps over balance him.

If the attacker pulls up, amplify his motion. Shift your left hand to his elbow and over-balance him. As his structure breaks, shift your right hand down and grab his rising leg.

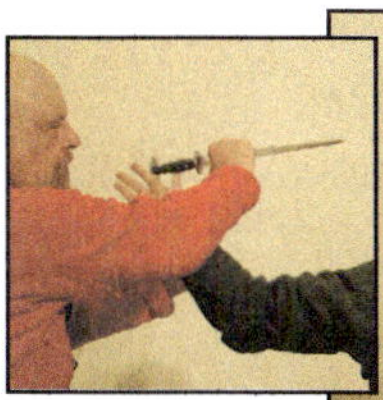

Rotate the dagger parallel to the ground, around his thumb.

If the attacker shifts to his right, use his motion to power a disarm. Release your right-hand grip and use that hand to turn and grip his dagger.

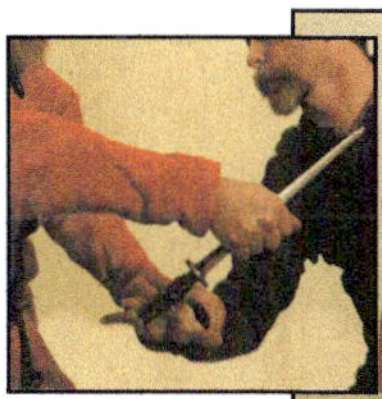

Rotate the dagger in the plane of his arm.

If the attacker pulls down, go along with his motion and disarm. Release your right-hand grip and use that hand to turn and grip his dagger.

The cover of the Sixth Remedy Master is a modified Frontal position

Detail of the cover

The Sixth Remedy Master is shown making his version of the cover of the Fourth Remedy Master, but he can "defend on all sides."

The scholar extends both arms, dagger gripped with both hands. The goal is to place the dagger blade perpendicular to the incoming arm. As always, your arms must be extended enough to keep the attacker's dagger from reaching you.

This is a very strong cover, and potentially a painful one to an attacker's arm.

In follow-on play, remember that even though "I can also perform other plays without letting go of my dagger" your hand is not welded to that dagger.

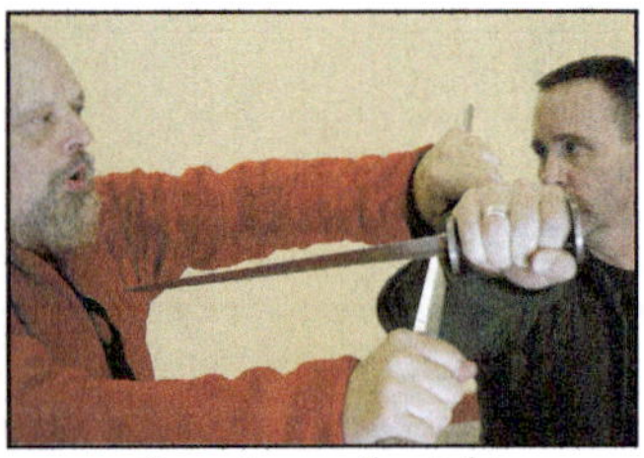

Covering on the right.

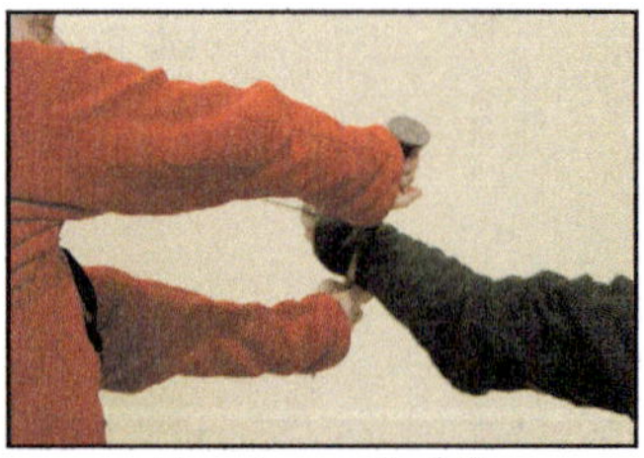

Covering on the left.

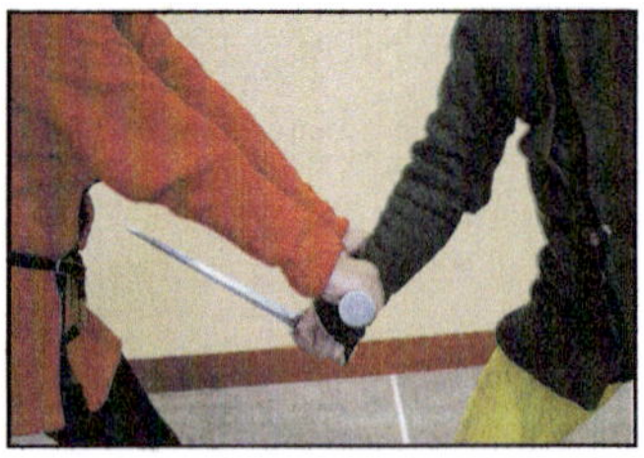

Covering below. Note that this is the Eighth Dagger Master's cover.

I am the Sixth Master and I declare that this parry is good both in and out of armor, since I can use it to defend on all sides and enter all the binds. I can also perform grapples and strike according to the way my students will do. Every one of my students should execute this parry, and then follow with the plays that are possible.

Fiore instructs that the scholar can shift to the grip for disarming and immediately strike. He doesn't make explicit reference to the first play of the First Remedy Master, but he goes on to directly reference that master's next scholar, who does the Middle Bind. Further, he says, "I can also perform other plays without letting go of my dagger." Shown below are ways to make some of the First Remedy Master's binds with dagger in hand.

Middle Bind.

Upper Bind: A.

Upper Bind B.

This master's scholars also make plays while maintaining "the position of the Sixth Master," which is to say while maintaining their double-handed grip on the dagger and the opposition of the blade against the attacker's wrist.

... if you were in armor, ... I could nicely hit you in the face ...

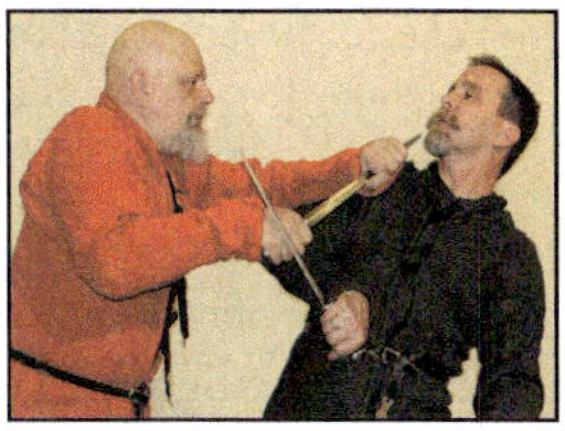

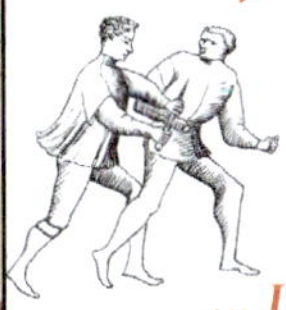

... I have struck you in the chest, since you are not wearing armor and you don't seem to know your close play.

The cover of the Seventh Remedy Master is a modified Frontal position

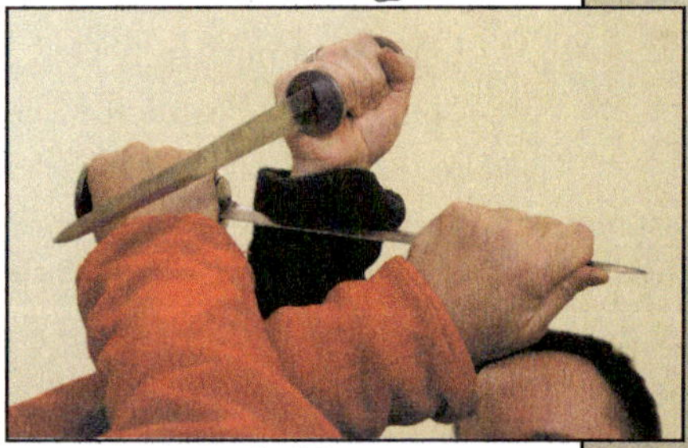

Detail of the cover

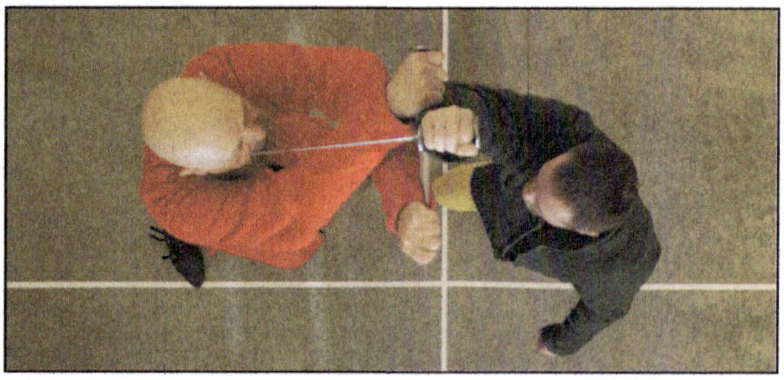

The Seventh Remedy Master is shown making his version of the cover of the Fourth Remedy Master, but like the companion dagger-wielding Sixth Remedy Master, he can make his cover against all sides.

The scholar extends both arms, dagger gripped with both hands. The goal is to place the dagger blade perpendicular to the incoming arm. This cover cannot be extended out as far as the Sixth Master's and the danger of a long blade's point reaching you is real. Fiore says this parry is "better in armor," presumably for the protection armor affords against that threat.

This is a very strong cover, possibly the strongest.

Fiore offers no scholars for this master. He has already covered what can be done from this position with other masters.

As with the Sixth Master, your hand is not welded to that dagger. Fiore makes it clear in the one play he specifically suggests in the text accompanying the master.

I am the Seventh Master and I play with my arms crossed. This parry is better in armor. What I can do from this parry are the previous plays, i.e., the middle bind, which is the third play of the first Remedy Master of dagger. ...

... I can also turn you by pushing your right elbow with my left hand, then immediately strike you in the head or shoulders. ...

The cover.

The slip.

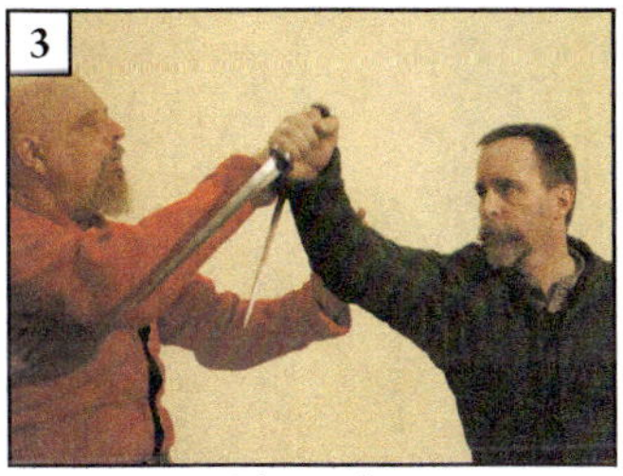

The push.

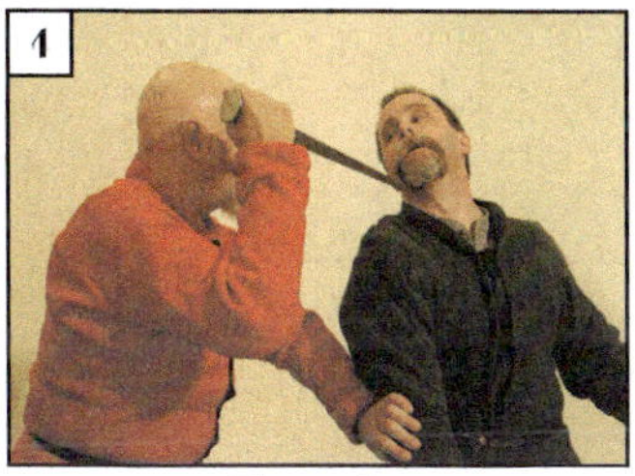

The strike.

... This parry is done mostly to get into binds ...

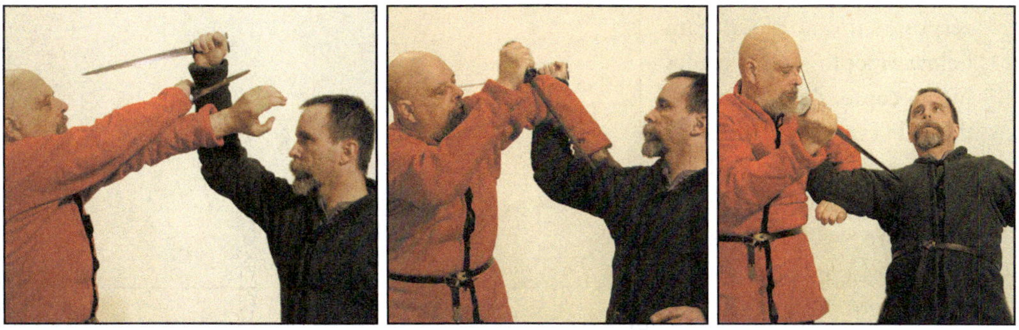

Here, the cover unfolds into the Middle Bind of the third scholar of the First Remedy Master. The dagger maintains pressure to keep the arm bent for the binding.

Here, the cover unfolds into the Under Bind of the Third Remedy Master. Downward pressure from the dagger hand and upward pressure from the empty hand must be maintained as you turn to your right to make this bind. With the Under Bind happening, you transfer the pressure from your dagger hand, using your chest to maintain the bind as you prepare to strike with your dagger.

THE COVER OF THE NINTH REMEDY MASTER IS A MODIFIED FRONTAL POSITION

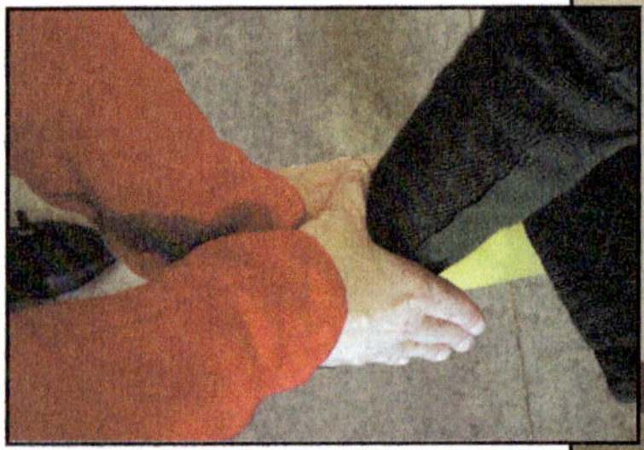

Detail of the cover

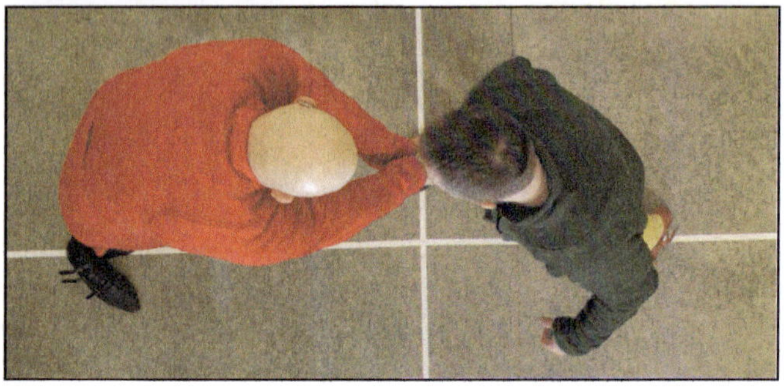

The Ninth Remedy Master responds to the attack from below. Since this attack comes in the center zone, it is best defended with two hands.

The scholar extends both arms to meet the attack. The hands are together. The left thumb lies against the bottom of the right palm. The right thumb lies along the top of the left hand. Fingers extend outwards. This positioning protects the thumbs, unites the hands in their endeavor, and creates a funnel to help bring the attacker's wrist to where it can be gripped.

Closing the fingers over the attacker's arm, the grip is made immediately. Equally quickly, the scholar must respond to the attacker's pressure.

Fiore says, "My underhanded grapple is like the one the Fourth King does overhanded, although my plays are nothing like his." The cover is constrained by the physical mechanics of making it downward rather than upward. Likewise, the plays are affected by these same inherent mechanics. The actual grab, however, is quite similar.

As with the Fourth Master, this master offers responses to the six axes of movement. Fiore's "nothing like his" comment most likely refers to the downward orientation and the consequently different body structures of the players that force different responses, rather than any deep difference in play mechanics.

As before, the scholar can force a direction if he is faster or uses his stepping to influence the attacker's response.

I am the Ninth King, the last one of dagger. My underhanded grapple is like the one the Fourth King does overhanded, although my plays are nothing like his. This grapple, good with and without armor, leads to many strong actions, especially the ones shown right below. I am positive about them—with or without armor.

Following the attacker's response to the cover

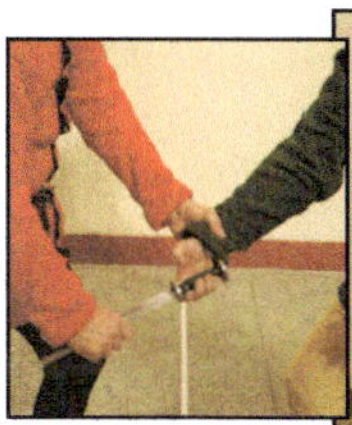

Rotate the blade toward his elbow.

If the attacker pushes through, encourage his energy with your wrist grip while using your right hand to force the blade back against his motion to disarm him.

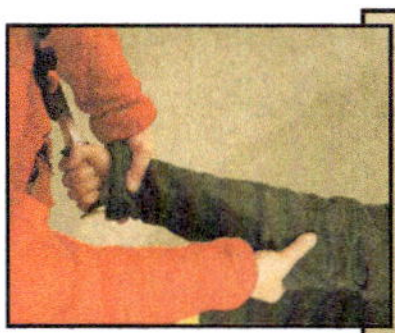

Push down on his wrist and pull up on his elbow.

If the attacker shifts to his right, move into the space. Pull up against his elbow while pushing down against his gripped wrist.

Push down on his elbow and pull up on his wrist.

If the attacker shifts to his left, move into the space. Pull in and down at his elbow while pushing out and up on his gripped wrist.

Your upper arm jams into his above his elbow or into his armpit

If the attacker tries to go up, use his energy to guide his arm up as you turn. Ram your shoulder into his upper arm as you make a Stable Turn. If his arm does not break, apply pressure.

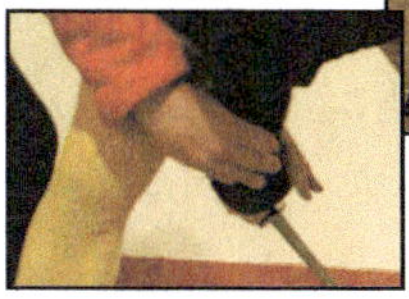

Exchange gripping hands beneath him.

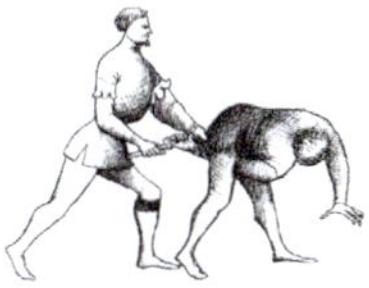

If the attacker pulls back, guide his arm back between his legs, Shift behind him and gather up his wrist. Disarm him at your leisure.

Hold his dagger down while drawing yours.

If the attacker pulls down, he doesn't really have any where to go and will be weak. Maintain your superior structural positioning and keep his hand away from you while you draw your own dagger and strike him.

These exercises will give you a feel for where the transitions occur and when you have to abandon one response in favor of another one. Of course, differences in strength between opponents, as well as differences in the strength of the attack or cover, will also affect the tipping point.

Around the Circle

The two partners stand arms length apart.

One partner (the attacker) closes his fist as if holding a dagger and positions that fist halfway to a completed *mandritto* attack.

The other partner (the defender) positions his wrist against the attacker's wrist on the inside as if he has executed a Long Position block against the attack.

The attacker applies pressure and the defender feels how his posture resists that pressure.

Keeping the pressure steady, the attacker begins to move his arm up and around the circle toward his partner's head.

The defender will find it becomes increasingly harder to prevent the imagined dagger from coming closer. When this happens, the defender brings his other arm into play, placing a second wrist against the attacker's wrist. This doubling allows the defender to resist the pressure with much less effort.

The attacker continues moving around the circle, shifting toward a *riverso* attack line. As he does this, the defender will feel that his first arm is less and less engaged in the cover until he can remove it from play and maintain his cover with only the second arm that he brought in.

As the attacker continues his progress around the circle, he will reach a point where he must apply more pressure to keep his fist at the same distance from the defender. At this point, he rolls his wrist over. Note that his hand's grip position will go from a downward to an upward one at this point.

At about the same point, the defender will find it easier to maintain cover against the pressure by rolling his own hand over, going from wrist-to-wrist contact to palm-to-wrist contact.

As the attacker moves along the circle towards the center, the defender will find that he again needs a second arm to resist the pressure. He brings his other hand in, palm to wrist, to his cover, as Fiore says, "doubled."

The attacker continues circling and, as before, the defender will find a point where he no longer needs both arms to maintain the cover.

As the attacker's arm rises along the circle, he will come to a point where rolling his wrist will allow him to maintain his relative position without increasing pressure. He does this, shifting his hand's grip position again.

The defender will soon find a shift from palm-to-wrist back to wrist-to-wrist is more comfortable and effective.

Try circling with different levels of pressure. Also try circling with the attacker's arm at different extensions, both tighter and looser, as well as having the attacker move around the circle in the opposite direction.

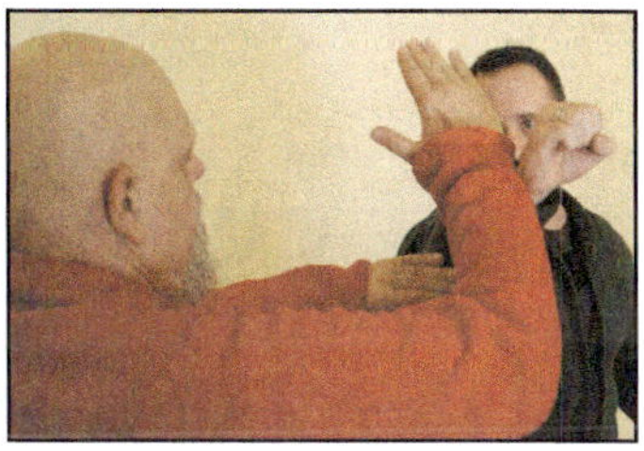

Across the middle

Attacker and defender start as before.

Instead of going around the circle, the attacker shifts his fist toward the centerline between the two partners.

The defender will find a point where his arm begins to collapse under the pressure and he must bring his other arm in to maintain the cover.

As the attacker continues moving across, one of the defender's arms will no longer be necessary and he can transfer to a single-arm cover.

Move back and forth, allowing the defender to seek smooth transitions that keep the attacker's fist at a constant distance from him.

Up and Down

The attacker starts high, at the top of the circle.

The defender, as you might suspect, immediately finds that a single arm cover is not good, so he must make his cover with crossed wrists.

As the attacker moves down along the centerline, he will find he reaches a point where his hand's grip position no longer allows him to apply adequate pressure.

About the same time, the defender will find that he reaches a point where he feels the attacker's fist will slip through his cover.

You have found an inflection point.

The same thing happens if you start from below and the attacker rises along the centerline. You are experiencing a boundary line related to body mechanics.

I am the sword and I am lethal against any weapon; lances, axes and dagger are worthless against me. I can become extended or withdrawn; when I get near the opponent I can enter into close play, perform disarms and abrazare. …

LESSONS OF THE SWORD

SWORD IN ONE HAND

Fiore does not give a set of Fight Masters to begin the sword in one hand section as he does for other weapons. Instead, he shows a single, crowned swordsman facing three figures, a situation very similar to that of the dagger master facing a sword, as well as to that of the master who faces paired opponents at the end of the sword in two hands section. The latter two, Fiore says, stand in named guards, but the position in which this sword-armed master stands is given no name, making it unclear whether Fiore considers this position to be a *posta*. Fight Masters, as you will recall, stand in *posta* and Remedy Masters make a cover. Which is he meant to be? The scholars who follow seem to act from his position, making his cover, which would make him a Remedy Master. This fits well with the fact that he is clearly responding to one of several kinds of attack. If he is just a Remedy Master, that would mean the sword section has no Fight Masters to begin it.

Yet in the mounted combat section, Fiore calls a very similar position *Coda Longa* (Long Tail). The horseman holds it on the left, like this sword master, and not on the right as the *Posta di Coda Longa* is shown for the sword in two hands. The action of the mounted combat master is similar to that of this sword master, which argues that this master is indeed a Fight Master and that the name of his *posta* has simply been omitted.

Whatever was in Fiore's mind, the sword in one hand section does not begin as other weapon sections do. Some of that may have to do with the sword's split personality of multiple ways to grip and use it, and with Fiore's apparent desire not to repeat obvious lessons except where a punctuation point is necessary.

The sword in two hands section ends with a picture quite similar to the one beginning the sword in one hand section, to bracket the unarmored sword plays. Between the two subsections, there are four sets of figures. The first set is a pair of *Posta di Donna* (Woman's Position) variants and is accompanied by instruction not specifically related to those two *poste.* The second set is a series of positions showing how the sword can be held. Fiore calls them guards (*guardia*) but, except for the two occurrences of *Posta di Donna,* he does not name these positions. Third come four Instruction Masters who explicate the blows and thrusts of the sword. The last set is a series of twelve *poste* for the sword held with both hands on the hilt. All are named and all look and instruct like the Fight Masters they are.

Posta di Donna appears in all three sets showing guards, uniting them. The position (still unnamed) of the master from the sword in one hand section appears in the second set. His inclusion in one set links him to the other sets, offering us the chance to incorporate the instruction from the other sets into our understanding of the sword used in one hand.

Today, we like to get our definitions up front, but Fiore doesn't use that approach. His instructions for how the Master of the Sword in One Hand should step use terms he doesn't explain until the text of the paired *Posta di Donna* set. He might have provided definitions at this point during personal instruction, but we will likely never know if he did. We have only his book, and must draw our lessons from it. He seems to have felt that setting much of the instruction regarding swordplay in the middle of the sword section was a better way to do it. Because of this, we find ourselves having to look forward as well as back to understand much of the art. And perhaps that is part of the lesson he is imparting.

Having recognized that there are lessons pertaining to sword in one hand in places other than the sword in one hand section, we suddenly realize that the subsection is not as small as it first appears. Let's look at the doors this realization opens.

The Instruction Masters, who speak of sword attacks, do not distinguish whether the sword is held in one hand or two. They tell us of the paths of their attacks and what they can do. In the course of this instruction three guards are called out: *Posta Longa*, *Porta di Ferro,* and *Posta Breve.*

The last of these is illustrated as a guard for sword in two hands (below left). Note how similar it is to the position of the rightmost attacker facing the Master of the Sword in One Hand (below center). That attacker would appear to be holding *Posta Breve* for sword in one hand. His companion in the middle seems to stand in the position corresponding to *Posta di Donna,* allowing for perspective shift and the variations in sword position inherent in the illustrations of *Posta di Donna* for Sword in two hands (an example below right). The key element here is that the sword is held near the shoulder with the blade

Posta Breve

Posta di Donna

behind the head. Certainly the attacker's position is one from which he could cut, making a *fendente* blow, and end in the position of the Master of Sword in One Hand.

Fiore tells us that "We *fendente* are not slow to strike, and recover in guard with each step." *Fendente* are paths along which the sword travels, beginning in one *posta* and ending in another. A later Italian swordsman, Angelo Viggiani, makes the practice of moving from position to position clear in his *Lo Schermo* (1575), saying, "every strike or motion lies between two guards (or instances of stillness), and every guard lies between two strikes."[1] It is a practice that is at the heart of fencing and Fiore's art clearly partakes of it, even if he does not express it as clearly.

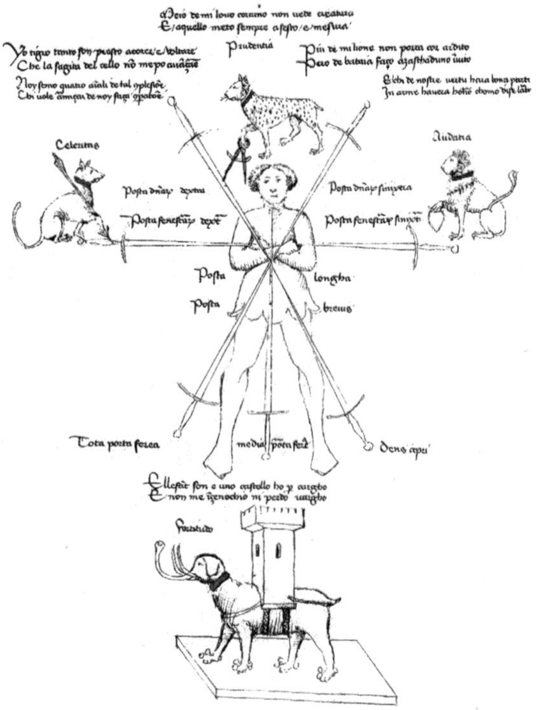

The Pisani-Dossi's version of the segno page has some additional notations absent from the Getty's versions. Each of the swords is assigned a *posta* from which that blow can be thrown. Indeed, such a blow may even be the most expected, if not the best, blow that can be made from these *poste. Posta di Donna* (left and right) is assigned to the swords pointing down along in the direction of *fendente*; *Posta Dente di Cinghiale* and *Tutta Porta di Ferro* to those pointing upwards along the path of *sottani*; the swords between, the *mezzani* blows, get *Posta di Fenestra* (left and right); and the sword belonging to the thrust gathers in *Poste Longa, Breve,* and *Mezzana Porta di Ferro.*

The opposed swords imply that a blow departing from one *posta* is likely to end in the *posta* belonging to the opposite sword. Thus a *fendente* blow beginning in *Posta di Donna* on the right will move downwards into *Posta Dente di Cinghiale* on the left side of the swordsman's body. And we do find a *Dente di Cinghiaro*[2] among the *poste* in mounted combat's sword section.

The connections to the mounted combat section just reinforce our understanding from the connections within the sword section. Using both we can construct a full suite of *poste* for sword in one hand to parallel the guards for sword in two hands. Interpretations of these guards can be found on pages 103 and 104. The usefulness and applications of these hypothetical guards for the sword in one hand need further research as the possibilities exceed those envisioned by later fencing masters.

Through this process of interconnection and extrapolation from the exemplars, we see that Fiore's material for sword held in one hand is not so sparse after all, and that the master for the subsection is both a Fight Master (he does stand in a *Posta di Coda Longa*) and a Remedy Master who provides a cover from which scholars will play.

---

1 Translation of quote from Viggani's *Lo Schermo* 76R by Tom Leoni in *The Complete Renaissance Swordsman,* Freelance Academy Press, 2010.

2 *Cinghiaro* is a dialect spelling of *Cinghiale.*

A SWORD IS YOUR SHIELD

The Master of the Sword in One Hand makes what might be called a universal parry, although our understanding of the interplay of the sword sections shows that this is not the only action to be made successfully with a sword held in one hand. The parry is designed to deal with three different modes of attack: a blow, a thrust, and a thrown weapon. The master is shown facing three opponents,[3] each ready to make one of those attacks, and the master can deal with each of them using the same action.

It is in this play that Fiore first specifies what many take as the signature footwork of his art. The master says, "I'll step with my front foot a little off the line, and with the left foot I'll pass at an angle ..."

The step off the line provides a measure of safety by taking the master out of the direct line of the attack. The "pass at an angle" is used to orient the master for his follow-on action. Like the step off the line, the exact placement and direction will depend on the circumstances when the play is made. If the footwork is performed perfectly, no other action is necessary to avoid the attack.

How rarely is everything perfect? As the master makes his steps, he says, "... I'll cross and beat away your swords, find you open and strike you for sure." The cover is the master's protection in an imperfect world. Having protected himself first, and well, the master is positioned to end the fight with a well-placed attack.

MEASURE AND THE FIGHT

With this subsection Fiore introduces a new concept in his presentation of the art. A simple comparison between the sword in one hand's Fight-Remedy Master and the dagger master who plays against multiple attacks makes it clear. Once the sword comes into the game, there's a greater distance between the combatants. The illustration for the Master of the Sword in One Hand even takes up two illustration spaces, signalling a much wider measure.

It is important to note again that the illustrations are not photorealistic. Once should not try laying a ruler on the drawn figures to try to reach conclusions about whether one combatant is in or out of measure or to quantify some perfect assessment of measure. Simply appreciate that the engagement range with the sword is greater than that of the dagger. Weapons, even of the same type, will vary in their dimensions, as will people. Those differences may be small, but they can make the difference in whether you engage safely or not.

Fiore, having made his point about the different measure of sword and dagger play, uses the plays of this subsection to teach several differences in your actions that arise from having a long, sharp rod of metal sticking out of your fist.

---

[3] Although it may appear so at first glance, the attackers are not attacking simultaneously. "Go ahead and come one by one," the master says, making it clear that each attack type is dealt with separately.

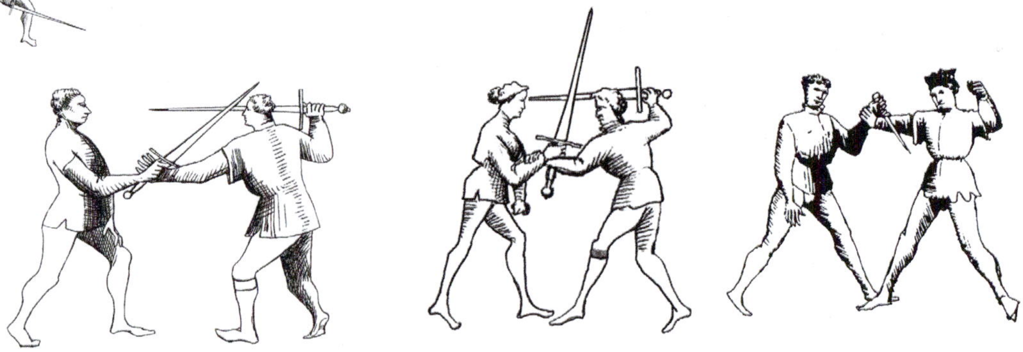

The first scholar (left) of the Master of the Sword in One Hand compared to the same play from the Pisani-Dossi (center) and the Remedy Master/first play of the dagger (right). The dagger master's image is flipped so as to emphasize the similarity of the positions. The scholar's sword provides safe passage for him as he closes to where he can reach his opponent's wrist.

A SWORD BRINGS VARIATIONS

Having a long bar of steel extending from your hand means you cannot move your hand the same ways that you can if your hand is empty. Some of this change is to the good and some requires adaptation on your part, especially if you want to take advantage of techniques you've already learned.

The first play of the sword offers a variation on the first play of the dagger. First the scholar's sword must move into the cover, otherwise he will be hit. With cover achieved, the scholar's left hand comes forward and makes a grip like that of the First Remedy Master of the dagger.

Note that the Getty picture shows the scholar's hand inside the attacker's arm and sword, awkwardly placed to "throw his sword to the ground with my left hand." The Pisani-Dossi version clearly shows the scholar's hand passing between the attacker's arm and the grip and pommel of the sword. This is the necessary positioning for the disarm, which will work with the sword as it did with the dagger.

The sword scholar's right hand is raised, ready to strike. "Now I can place a thrust in his face without trouble." Here, with the sword, the scholar can reach his opponent more easily than with the hand strike indicated by the dagger master.

With the link to familiar territory established, the second scholar presents a new option made possible by the sword. The sword has an edge that is good for wounding, something that Fiore's daggers seem not to have. Having made the cover, and driven the opponent's sword wide, the scholar can turn his blade and strike from a measure outside the distance for true close play.

Note that the scholar passes forward as he strikes and that he strikes to the equivalent of Long Position. The step aligns the skeleton, providing power for the strike.

Having made cover, the basic advice of Fiore's plays is to hit him with a blow or a thrust as the opportunity presents itself. If you cannot hit him with the sword, don't waste time. Grab him and end the fight.

Second scholar (20vB)

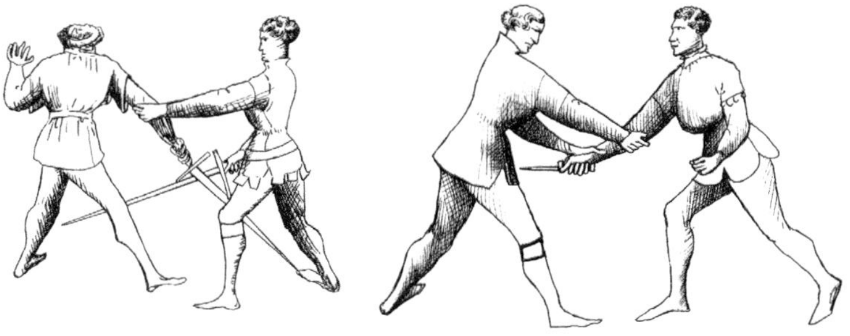

The sixth scholar of the Master of the Sword in One Hand uses his sword to hold down the sword or hand of his opponent like the dagger scholar uses his hand against the hand of his opponent.

A SWORD IS YOUR HAND

In the dagger section we learned that the dagger can be used to make plays without relinquishing it. Here in the sword in one hand section, Fiore makes the point that this same principle applies to the sword. You can use parts of the sword to fill the function of a grip in *abrazare*. The lesson reflects back on understanding what you can do with Fiore's hidden daggers as well.

One scholar (shown above left), having made his master's cover and then transported the attacker's sword to the ground, maintains pressure against that sword with his own. The blade pressure replaces the grip on the wrist as used by a scholar (above right) of the Ninth Remedy Master of the dagger. The scholar's left hand reaches behind the attacker's elbow and applies upward pressure, creating an arm bar.

Fiore only shows one exemplar of this principle. He leaves it to the student to internalize it and, having done so, to recognize when and how to apply other variations of it. It should be easy, for example, to see how the grip and pommel projecting beneath a swordsman's hand can potentially be used as if he were gripping a downwards pointing dagger in his hand.

IT'S ALL RELATED

The last play in the sword in one hand section[4] calls for the scholar to take the blade of his sword into his left hand. This is a grip called *mezza mella,* or half blade. The corpus of German *fectbucher* refer to the same grip as *halbschwert,* or half sword. Fiore's use of the term best translated as half sword (*mezza spada*) applies to the crossing of the swords in a bind at the middle of the blade. I will deal with it in the sword in two hands section.

It is worth noting that Fiore points out that this last play is better in armor than without. In part, this is surely because of the exposure to a counterattack the scholar risks as he shifts to the *mezza mella* grip. An additional point could be that playing with the sword in this grip is better suited for armored combat. Certainly it is the grip Fiore shows most often in the sword in armor section. Whatever the reason for Fiore's cautionary statement, it should be obvious that play could continue from this point using plays and techniques from the sword in armor section. The placement of this play as the last of the sword in one hand makes its the linkage to that section easier to see.

[4] This play comes second after the master in the Pisani-Dossi and the Paris, possibly indicating different thoughts about how it plays and certainly a different approach to its placement in the teaching program.

Six positions demonstrate the different ways a sword can be held. On a deeper level they demonstrate the connections between sword in one hand, sword in two hands, and sword in armor. The last one also connects sword to axe.

This guard is "set to throw my sword." This is a specialized grip of limited application. While some might consider throwing the sword to be something one would never do, Fiore presents a thrown sword as a threat to both the Sword in One Hand and Sword in Two Hands Masters.

This guard is "set to deliver a long thrust: the way I hold the sword makes it possible to extend the thrust considerably." The text goes on to expand on its usefulness in armored combat. Not coincidentally, it is paired with the next guard, one also presented in the sword in armor section.

This guard is *Posta di Donna*. It is a guard of sword in two hands. The text notes that this position is separate from the others in the set (despite its similarity to the one that follows, shown here on the next page) which helps clarify that these illustrations are about showing the ways one can hold a sword.

This is a guard "useful both in and out of armor against a lance or a sword that is thrown at me." As it is the guard of the Master of the Sword in One Hand it is useful for more, but as presented here it is paired with the one for throwing a sword and its application in that context is given priority.

This is "a good guard against sword, axe and dagger in armor." It's not surprising therefore that it is one of the guards of the sword in armor. Note that unlike the previous guard (shown here on the opposite page), the thumbs of the scholar's hands both face inwards. (The inset picture shows a three-quarters view of the same position.)

This guard is also *Posta di Donna*. Noting that the sword is more like an axe in this grip, Fiore dispenses the following fortune cookie advice, "Weighty things can be of great impediment to those that are light." A strike with the relatively more massive hilt end of the sword can bash aside a weakly held defense.

Using illustrations of attackers and some players in the mounted combat section, I have put together some composite illustrations of guards for using the sword in one hand. The illustrations are appended to the interpretation photos. Given that the basic actions of strikes should move from guard to guard, there ought to be positions beyond those illustrated. The rest of those presented

WOMAN'S POSITION ON THE RIGHT
(POSTA DI DONNA LA DESTRA)

WOMAN'S POSITION ON THE LEFT
(POSTA DI DONNA LA SINISTRA)

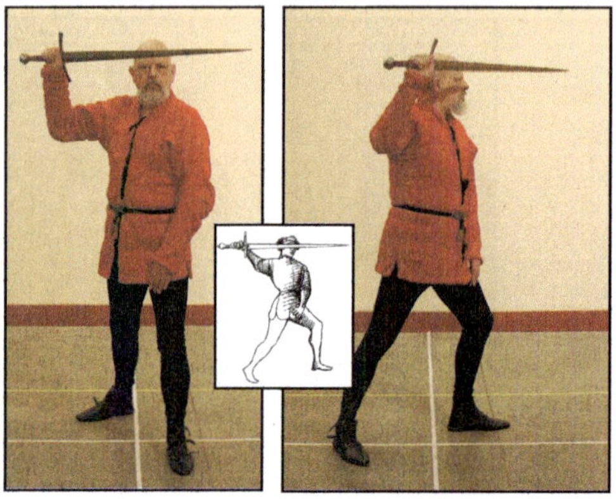

WINDOW POSITION ON THE RIGHT
(POSTA DI FINESTRA LA DESTRA)

SHORT POSITION
(POSTA BREVE)

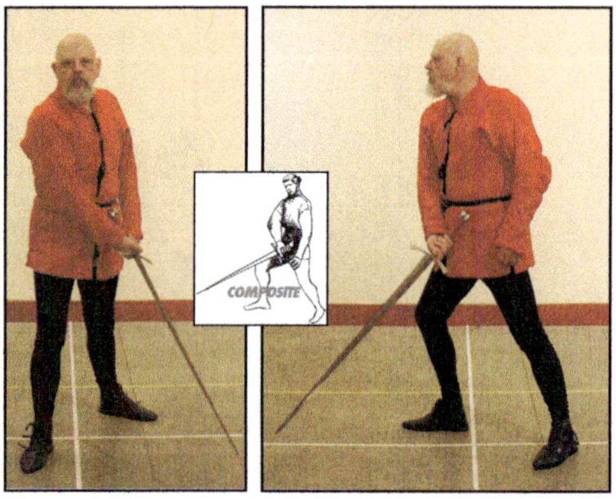

BOAR'S TOOTH
(POSTA DI DENTE CINGHIARO)

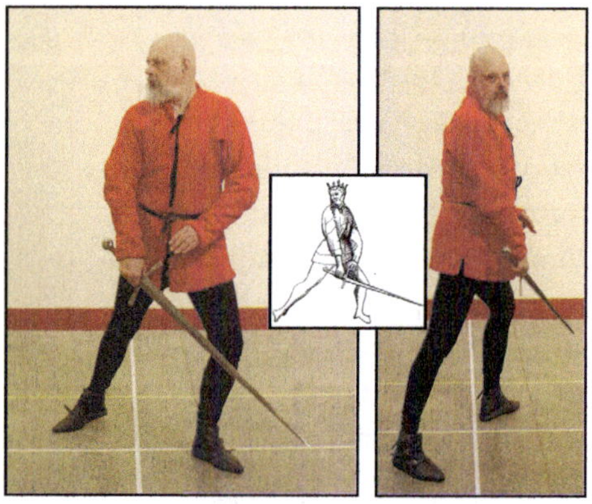

LONG TAIL ON THE LEFT
(POSTA DI CODA LONGA SINISTRA)

here are drawn from the sword in two hands section in order to make a more complete set. The names should look familiar. The actions and options should also follow those of the sword in two hands.

Middle Iron gate
(Porta di Ferro Mezzana)

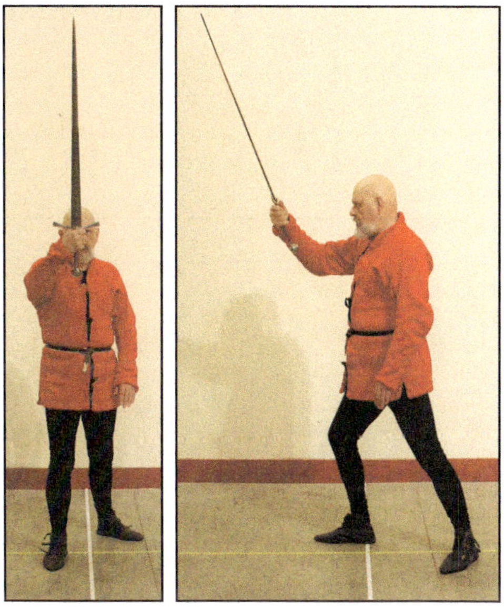

Frontal Position
(Posta Frontale)

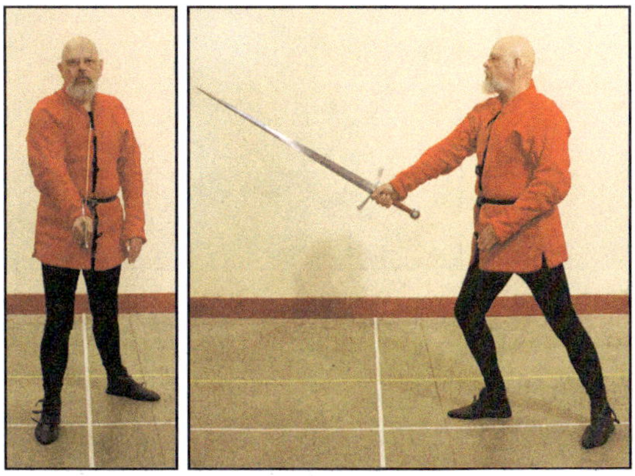

Long Position
(Posta Longa)

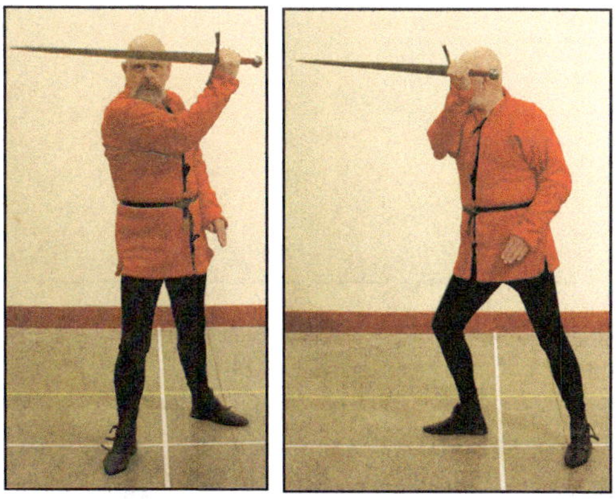

Window Position on the left
(Posta di Finestra la Sinistra)

Long Tail on the right
(Posta di Coda Longa Destra)

Full Iron Gate
(Tutta Porta di Ferro)

The cover of the Master of the Sword in One Hand is Window Position on the right

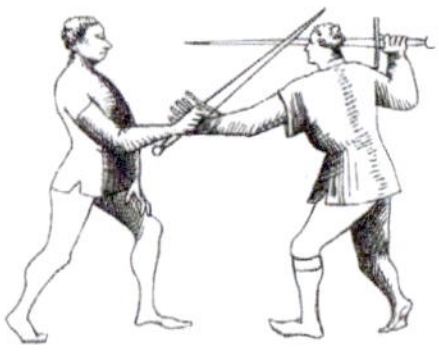

The scholar begins the play by making the cover of the Master of the Sword in One Hand. He steps off line with his front foot. His sword rises into the cover, opening a path for his left hand to move in. The sword may move with either edge leading. If the false edge leads, the scholar's hand must turn when this arm extends to provide strength against a blade that stays in contact.

The scholar's hand moves into the space under the attacker's hand, between the sword's grip and his arm. See the first play of the First Dagger Remedy Master (page 78) for the mechanics of the disarm.

A stab to the face can precede the disarm attempt. This is especially useful if the sword is needed to maintain cover until the disarm action removes the threat of the opponent's sword.

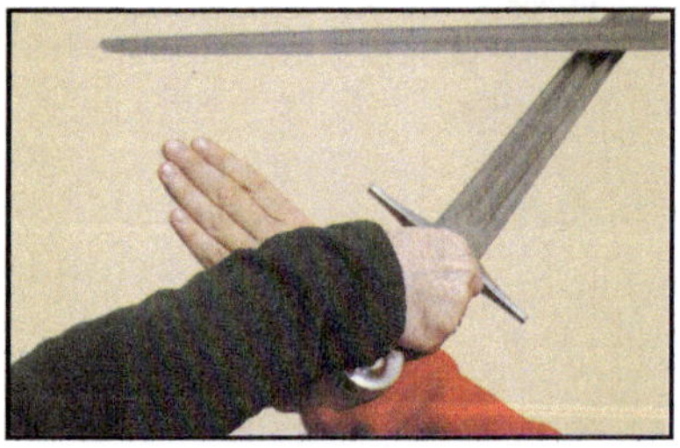

Note how the scholar sets his hand against the attacker's. This is the same stop as is used against a dagger as is shown below (from the other side). The hand then rotates to a grip and rotates further to create the disarm.

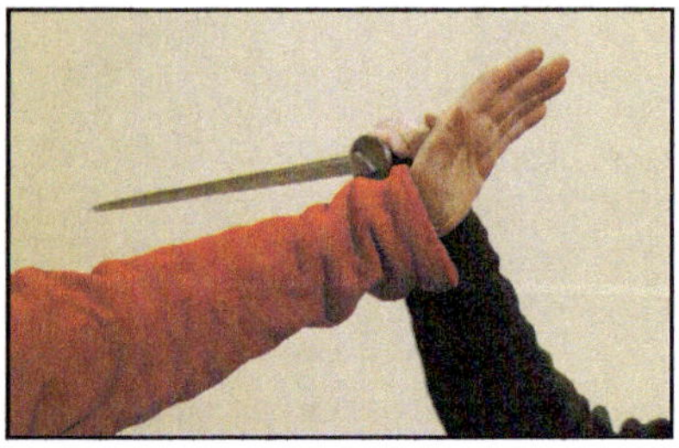

I've followed to the letter what my master said. I've passed off the line making a good parry, finding the opponent open. Now I can place a thrust to his face without trouble, while seeing if I can also throw his sword to the ground with my left hand.

Here the scholar strikes with the point of his blade. He has made his cover with his sword's true edge and won the bind, but his opponent's sword is still present.

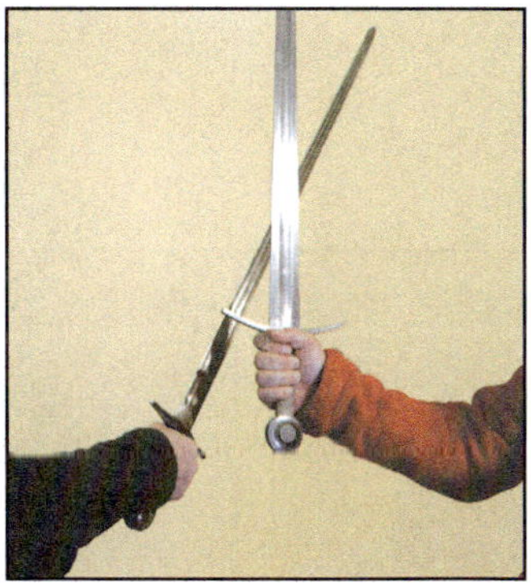

Here the scholar, having strongly deflected the attacker's sword, strikes with the edge of his blade. This effect is more easily achieved when the scholar makes his cover with his sword's false edge, striking the opponent's blade wide in the crossing.

Here the scholar has not driven the opponent's sword away, and must keep his blade in place as cover while attempting the disarm. If the scholar's cover was made with the false edge, he must turn his blade and make true edge contact to be stronger against pressure from his opponent.

The illustration of the Master of the Sword in One Hand shows him in the heels-forward stance. As this is Fiore says that all sword guards (*poste*) can make the Stable Turn (*volta stabile*) and the Half Turn (*mezza volta*), using the former will produce a heels-back stance. The same applies to the other guards.

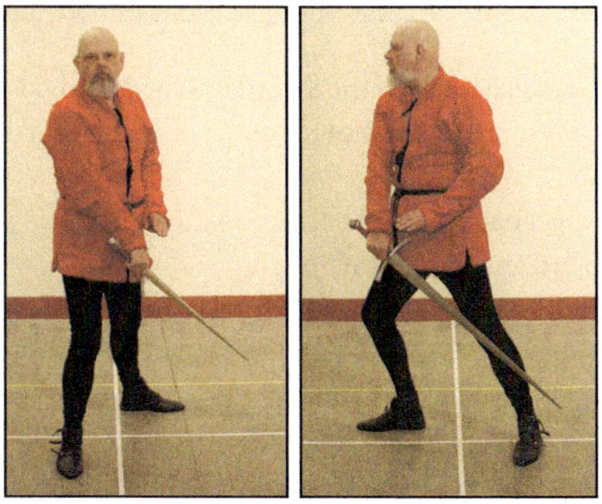

Long Tail on the left
heels back

Long Tail on the left
heels forward

The cover of the Master of the Sword in One Hand is Window Position on the right

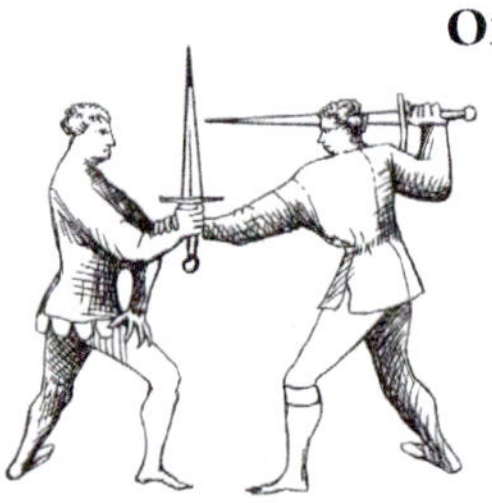

I can easily hit you with a cut or thrust. And if I step forward with the front foot, I'll put you in the middle bind, shown in the third play of the first Remedy Master of dagger. Or I can do the play that's after me, hitting you and putting you in a bind.

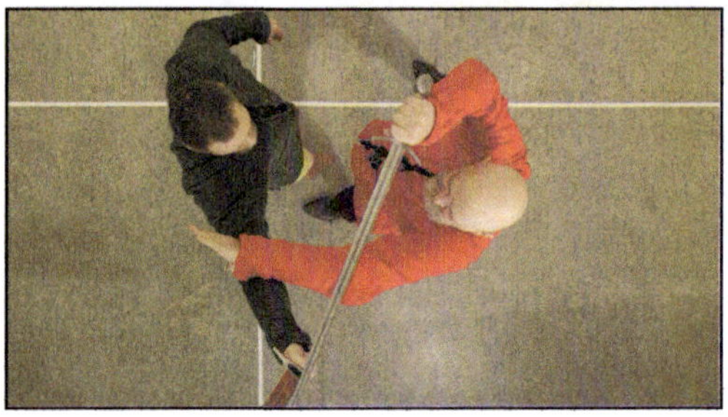

The scholar begins the play by making the cover of the Master of the Sword in One Hand. He steps off line with his front foot. As noted previously, the direction of the step is chosen based on the attacker's direction of attack.

The scholar's sword rises into the cover, opening a path for his left hand to move in.

That hand moves past the opponent's sword hand and over his elbow.

As the scholar steps in with his front foot (*accressere*), two things happen. His left hand continues moving, preparing to come up around the opponent's elbow and into the Middle Bind (see the second scholar of the First Dagger Master on page 73) and his sword point drives into the face of his opponent. Note that the scholar's sword covers him throughout this move.

Once the Middle Bind (*ligadura mezzana*) is set, his sword is no longer necessary as a cover. The bind twists the opponent's sword away and negates it as a threat. With the scholar's sword free, he can use it to continue to strike his opponent.

Your sword and your arm are nicely trapped and you can't get away without me striking you like this, because you've shown so little knowledge of this play.

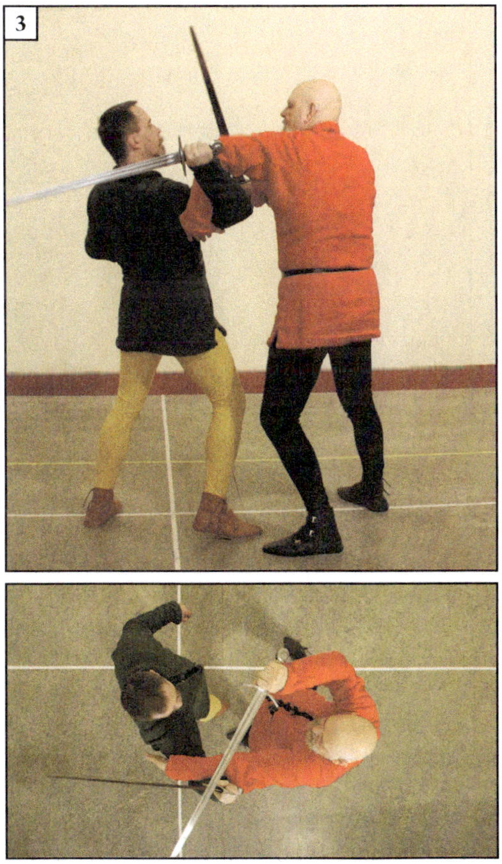

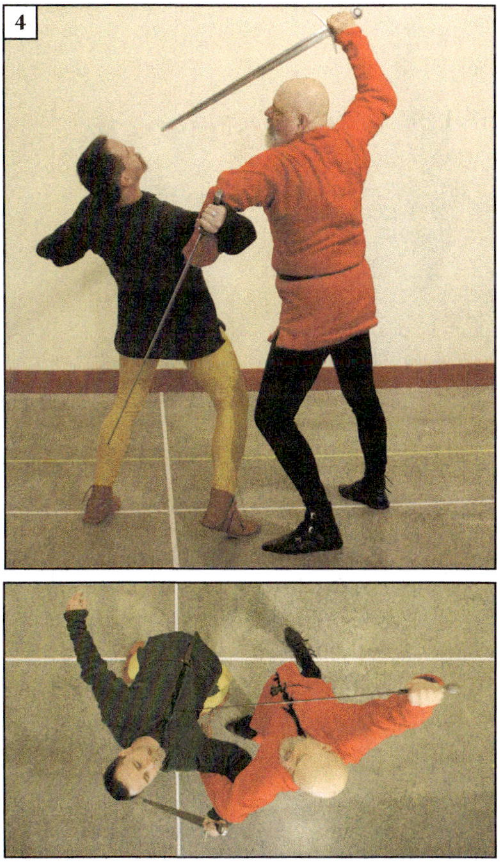

Note that this play and the preceding two parallel the opening plays of the First Remedy Master of the dagger. His scholars do a disarm and strike, then a Middle Bind. There, as here, the follow-on technique may be determined by how deeply the scholar's hand comes relative to the opponent's arm. The further away from the opponent's hand, the more likely the scholar is to go to the Middle Bind.

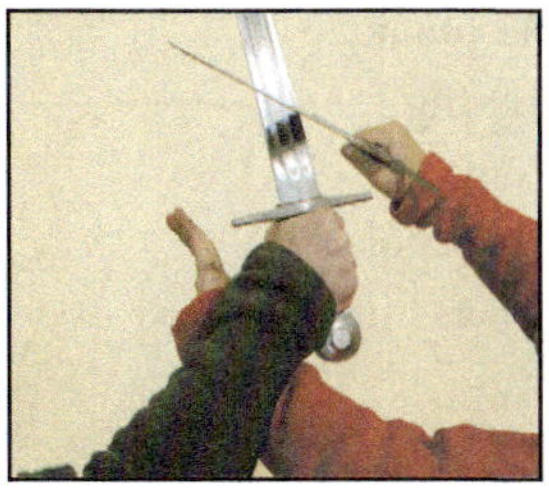

The scholar's hand is close to the opponent's so he begins the disarm.

The scholar's hand has driven deeper and so he begins the Middle Bind.

The cover of the Master of the Sword in One Hand is Window position on the right

The scholar begins the play by making the cover of the Master of the Sword in One Hand. He steps off line with his front foot. As noted previously, the direction of the step is chosen based on the attacker's direction of attack.

The scholar's sword rises into the cover, opening a path for his left hand to move in.

That hand moves to the outside of the attacker's arm, reaching for his elbow.

Pushing on the elbow, the scholar turns his opponent and strikes him.

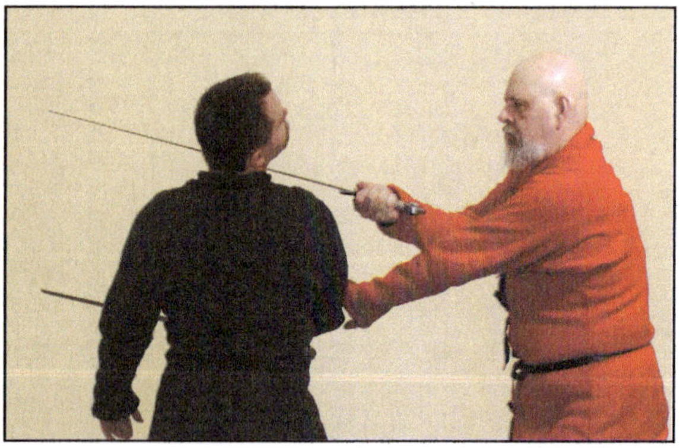

The elbow push opens your opponent to attack

Here I can strike you in front, but this is not enough. I give your elbow a push, turning you to strike you in the back. I can whip my sword to your neck, and you won't be able to help it.

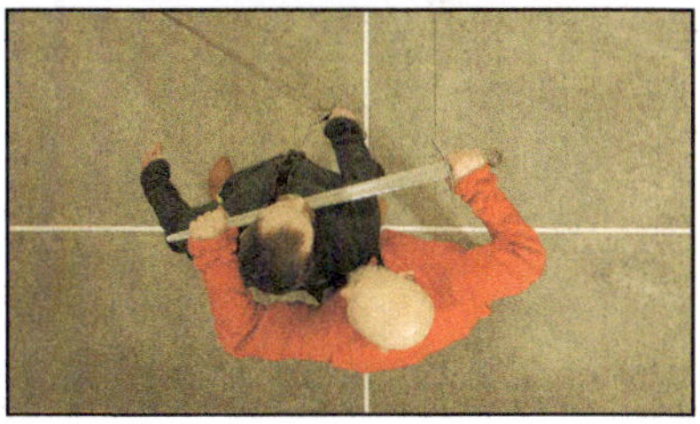

After the elbow push, this scholar chooses to get up close and personal. He advances (*accressere*) behind the turning opponent. As he does so he moves his sword blade up to the throat and reaches behind his opponent's head. The scholar grasps the tip of his sword as it emerges over the shoulder. If instead of a simple advance, the scholar uses his left leg to strike into the back of the opponent's left knee, the unbalancing effect is enhanced. Doing this can threaten the scholar's own balance since it usually results in a very deep advance. He can restore his own balance once his left foot lands by bringing his right foot forward (*discressere*).

Against an unarmored opponent, a throw is not necessary to finish him. Pressure and a slight slide of the edge across his throat will result in the opponent's gory demise.

With the sword against the throat, the scholar can also turn (*volta stabile*) and seek Iron Gate Position to get a dangerous throw that is also good against any opponent, even one with good throat armor.

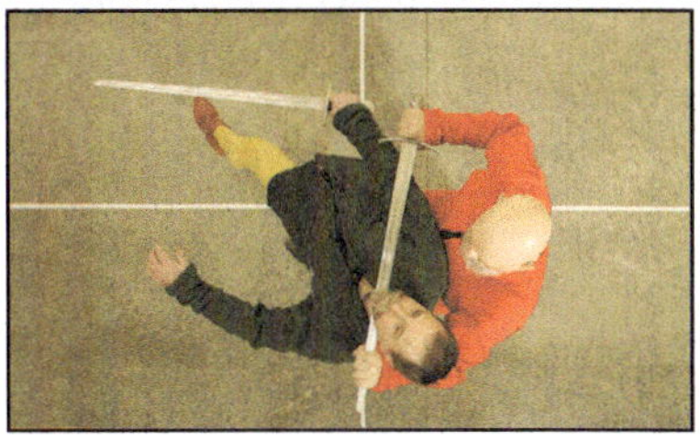

The cover here moves through Window position and ends in Iron gate

You attacked with a thrust and I beat it to the ground. Look: now you're open and I can hit you. I can also turn you and do even worse, while hitting you in the back.

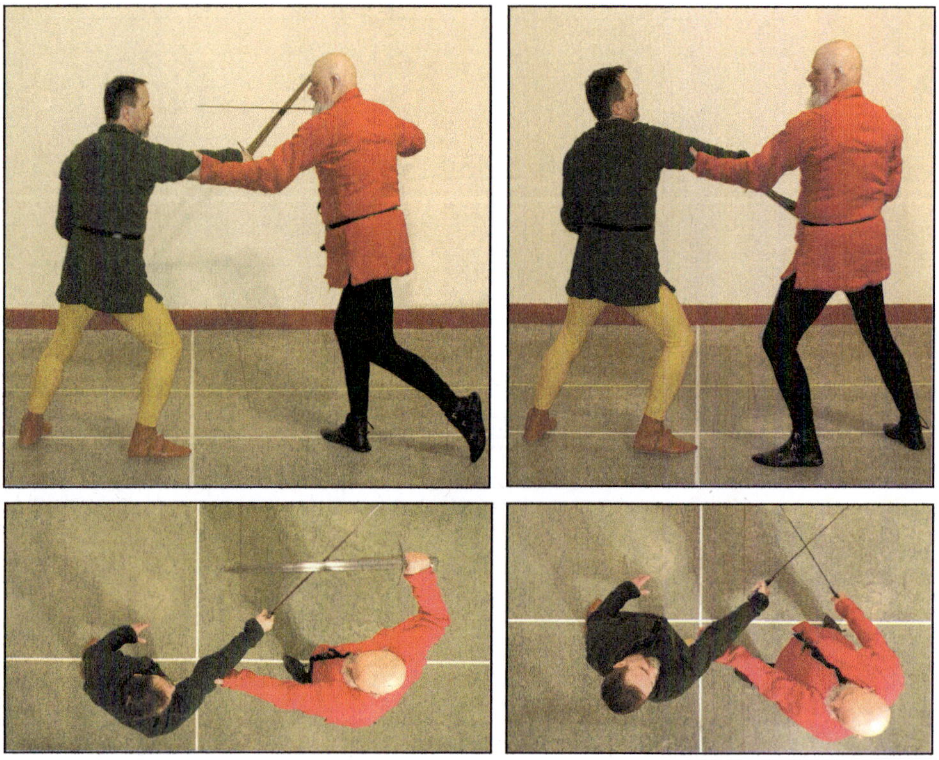

This play is a response to a thrust rather than a cut.

The scholar begins the play by starting the cover of the Master of the Sword in One Hand, seeking to deflect the thrust.

The scholar steps off line with his front foot (*accressere*) and cuts into the incoming blade.

The scholar's sword contacts that of his attacker and bears it down, transporting it to the ground. This is the "breaking" of the thrust.

The cover opens a path for the scholar's left hand to move in to catch the attacker's elbow.

Pushing on the elbow, the scholar turns his opponent.

Once the scholar has control of the opponent's elbow, he may strike him with the sword.

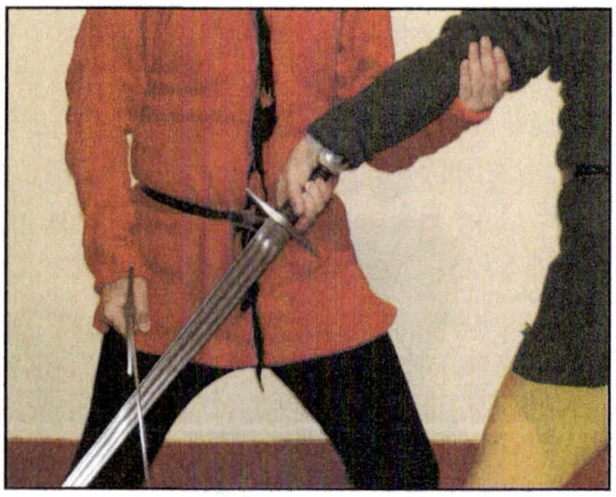

It is important to keep pressure on the opponent's blade until his elbow is controlled.

The elbow push opens your opponent to attack

I have quickly come to this situation after turning you by pushing your elbow. I did this to throw you to the ground so that you can't pick any more fights with me or anyone else.

Here, the scholar pushes the elbow and immediately kicks into the back of his opponent's right knee. As he recovers from his strike, the scholar falls forward and extends into Long Position on the left. His left arm may strike into the throat of the unbalanced opponent, or he may simply extend into Long Position and use his body structure. Either way, the opponent is headed for the ground.

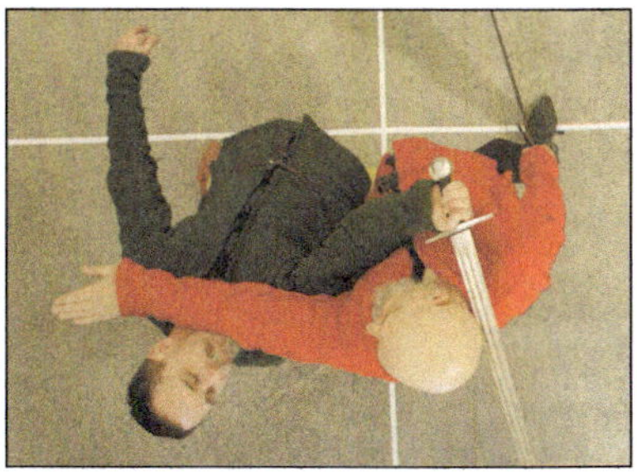

The scholar, perhaps because he was too eager to strike or used too much strength in the deflection, has neglected to leave his sword as cover. The opponent's blade comes up as the throw begins and strikes him.

The scholar must keep his sword in position to cover against a counterstrike (possibly only reflexive, but dangerous nonetheless) on his opponent's part.

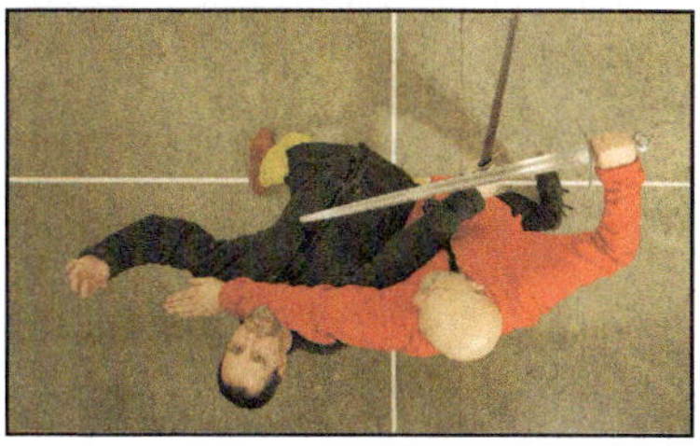

The cover of the Master of the Sword in One Hand is Window Position on the right

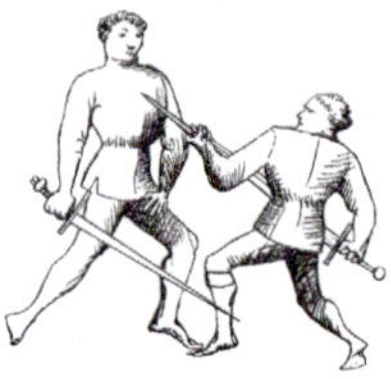

This is a play in which, to use this thrust, you should be in armor. If the opponent attacks you with a thrust or cut, parry and immediately do what's shown in the illustration.

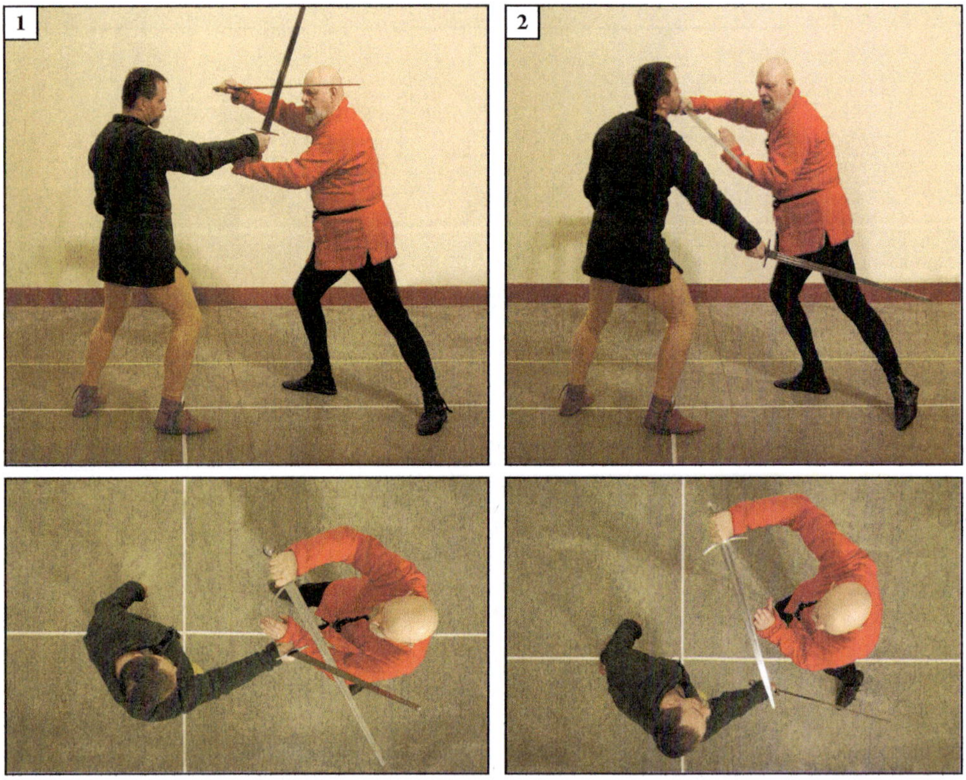

This play likely involves a less than fully extended cover, one which will allow the opponent's blade to slide free and to the scholar's left as the scholar steps toward his right (to the inside of the attacker's blow) and closer.

He steps in, beneath his own blade (as suggested by the crouched position of the scholar). As he moves his left hand to grip his sword blade.

As the opponent's blade slides free and towards the ground, the scholar makes his strike: a thrust.

"You should be in armor," Fiore warns. It's good advice, since the commitment to the half-sword grip thrust leaves the scholar uncovered to the opponent's sword. Speed is of the essence, as embodied in Fiore's use of the word immediately in the text for this play.

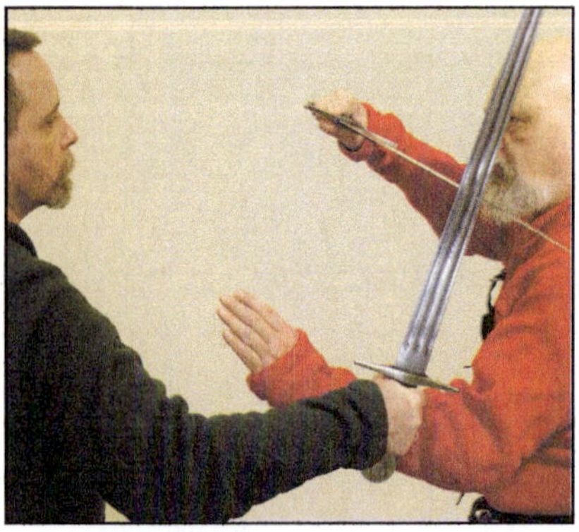

The scholar's shift to this technique may be triggered by the opponent's slipping sword taking his elbow out of reach of the scholar's incoming left hand.

The scholar shifts to the half-blade grip (*mezza mella*) to make his strike. He lowers his right hand as he places the point, ensuring his whole body strength is behind his thrust.

The danger is that the scholar is making a move without adequate cover. If the opponent reacts sufficiently fast, he can deflect the scholar's thrust and, since his sword is not controlled, strike.

At the right, the opponent, recognizing how the scholar is moving, has moved his left hand up to cover against the thrust. As he deflects the thrust, the opponent completes his counter strike.

Even an opponent who receives the scholar's thrust might strike reflexively, injuring an unarmored scholar whose action leaves him open on his left side.

I am the sword and I am lethal against any weapon; lances, axes and dagger are worthless against me. ... Come against me and feel the pain.

LESSONS OF THE SWORD

SWORD IN TWO HANDS

The sword in two hands section is commonly perceived as starting on folio 22 recto where two swordsmen, each standing in *Posta di Donna,* face each other. If it really does begin here, it would have the longest introductory section of any of the sections, starting with those two swordsmen facing each other and continuing with three sets of masters. Those of the first set all hold their swords differently. The second set are Instruction Masters who speak of the blows and thrusts one can do with the sword. The third grouping is twelve Fight Masters who show a variety of positions for the sword held in two hands. It is, however, only the last group who are truly the introduction for the sword in two hands section. The others belong to the sword in general, not sword in two hands specifically. Those first two fellows standing in sword in two hands positions confuse the matter. Fiore could have chosen another guard (*posta*) for them to stand in. They could be standing in almost any guard from the sword in one hand, the sword in two hands, or the sword in armor sections.

This text is the longest one in the illustrated portion of the manuscript. It is also the only occurrence of two figures spanned by a single block of text in the manuscript. The only other places a text block runs the full width of the page are on pages where the text applies to the page overall as with the dagger's Fight Masters (9 recto) and the segno page. This page structure is a clue that this pair is more general than specific, for the lessons in the two full-width paragraphs are not specific to sword in two hands.

Fiore begins this text by saying "we are two guards and we are alike but we are contrary to one another." He doesn't name the illustrated positions as *Posta di Donna* until nearly the end of this paragraph. Even then, he says nothing that is specific to *Posta di Donna.* The text concerns itself with guards in the abstract, although he does single out the point guards (*Posta Longa, Posta Breve,* and *Mezza Porta di Ferro*) as being a little different, contrasting them with the non-point guards.

In this paragraph Fiore introduces several concepts. Were he a modern instructor, some of these would have been presented long before this point. Indeed, he has in fact already used some of them in his instruction to specific plays. He describes the turns (*volta*) for which I provide interpretation on pages 25 and 26. In one of the most frustrating bits of the treatise, Fiore tells us that the sword can make all three turns (*volta*), but he does not indicate how the sword does these turns. Lastly, he names the "four more concepts" of his art, which are what we recognize as footwork. See the earlier section beginning on page 23 for an interpretation of these.

Continuing his general instruction, Fiore presents a set of masters offering six different ways to hold a sword. One of them, a fellow nearly identical to our old friend, the Master of the Sword in One Hand, quite plainly holds his sword with only one hand. His appearance alone should be enough to tell us we have not yet reached the section dedicated to sword in two hands.

The first four of these guards are not given names, although we are told something of their use and usefulness. The last two masters, standing in *Posta di Donna*, are nearly the same as the paired masters we saw before, the big difference being the very strange weapon held by the last fellow.

Sixth of the Sword-holding Masters

Some researchers want to take this drawing literally, imagining a Liberian student wielding such a monstrosity. Probably only for specialized combat, they would assure us. Fiore's text, however, makes it easy to see that the drawing is only an attempt to illustrate his words: "This sword is both a sword and an axe." This master is preparing to deliver a blow that German masters called the *mortschlag*, or murder stroke. In the *fechtbucher*, it is repeatedly illustrated as an ordinary sword used with hands on the blade. This grip allows the player to utilize the hilt of the sword like the heavy head of a poleaxe. I will cover some of how the sword is an axe in Lessons of the Axe.

The final group of this triple set of generalized masters contains four Instruction Masters. The first three of these speak of the *colpi*, or blows: *fendente*, *mezzani*, and *sottani*. Each concerns himself with one type, and each type consists of two blows: one from the right and the other from the left. The last master speaks of the *punte*, or thrust, of which he tells us there are five. He details the angles for all five: two high (one on each side), two low (one on each side), and one through the middle.

A difference in the drawing between the Getty and the Pisani-Dossi versions of the *Colpi Mezzani* Master has led some researchers astray. It has been posited that the fact that the figure in the Getty is turned with its side facing the viewer is something notable, an encoded message that *mezzani* strikes are something different than *fendente* or *sottani* strikes. That might be something to consider if this manuscript were intended to keep its information reserved only for the initiated. It is not. Fiore himself tells us that he has arranged things "to make the book easier to learn" and he says "The colored letters, the illustrations, and the plays will show you all the art clearly enough for you to understand it." In the prolog of the Pisani-Dossi manuscript, he is even more explicit, saying "I declare that it is intended to be very easily understood."

Getty's *Colpi Mezzani* Master

The *mezzani* strikes, as shown by the angle of the swords representing them, are essentially horizontal strikes. As such, a *mezzano* blow targets the side of the opponent. What better way of showing that than having the side of the target face the viewer to emphasize the point? It is, I think, very easily understood without resort to hidden meanings.

Pisani-Dossi's *Colpi Mezzani* Master

The four Instruction Masters with their seven strikes are directly related to the segno page, where seven swords overlay the master. They are the same strikes. The four come at the end of the sword in one hand section and the segno appears after the sword in two hands section. The connection between these masters and the segno joins the two sword subsections. The segno, situated as it is after some interstitial material with sticks and immediately before the sword in armor section, forms a bridge to the sword in armor section. It and the sword holding masters unite all three subsections pedagogically into a single, inter-related sword section.

Now let's look at the true opening of the sword in two hands section, the Fight Masters of sword in two hands.

Counting the Fight Masters

Fiore presents twelve masters. They are not all unique. Woman's Position (*Posta di Donna*) appears in both a left and right variant. Boar's Tooth (*Posta di Dente di Cinghiale*) appears in its normal iteration and in a Middle (*Mezza*) version with the weight on the back leg. This variation does not appear in either the Morgan or the Pisani-Dossi; those two manuscripts also have twelve Fight Masters, but substitute a third variant of Woman's Position for Middle Boar's Tooth. The Paris also shows twelve with a slightly different mix; it has two illustrations for Window Position[1] and two for Woman's Position.

What one guard can do, its opposite also can.

Why twelve? Twelve is a memory number, and a large one at that. In speaking with regard to practical working memory, Caruthers[2] observes that while total memory storage may be virtually limitless, there is a finite amount of material that can focused on and comprehended at one time. She notes that the typical limit for a grouping is somewhere between five and nine, which is less than Fiore's twelve. But twelve is not unfamiliar as a grouping number. We are used to dealing with groups of twelve in the number of months, Christ's apostles, and signs of the zodiac. Also, twelve remains a number one can count on one's hands (by adding the hand itself to the number of fingers).

Given the variations possible in the guards, the number could easily be more than twelve. Several guards are symmetrical; they can easily and safely be held in a right side and a left side version. In the Getty, Fiore gives us Woman's Position as one that fits this categorization, and the Paris shows us that Window Position (*Posta di Finestra*) also works this way. If Fiore had given us the alternate Window position in the Getty as well, he would have had thirteen, a very infelicitous number to the medieval mind.

Boar's Tooth Position held in the ordinary fashion and Middle Boar's Tooth with the heels-forward.

Also, as noted, Boar's Tooth comes in two variants, the standard and the heels-forward Middle Boar's Tooth. As Fiore tells us that all guards can make the Stable Turn (*volta stabile*), all ought to be able to take a toes-forward or heels-forward form. Presenting them individually would double the number of guards.

Further, some guards can be held with either foot forward, such as the so-called point guards Long

1 The depiction of Woman's Position on the right and Window Position on the right appear nearly identical as the sword in Window Position is depicted behind the head, as it is also depicted Window Position on the left. The sword behind the head in Window Position is, I believe, either an artist's mistake or an attempt to avoid obscuring the carefully drawn face.

2 To delve deeper into medieval memory processes, try Mary Caruthers, *The Book of Memory: A Study of Memory in Medieval Culture*, second edition, Cambridge 2008, but be prepared for heavy going.

Position (*Posta Longa*), Short Position (*Posta Breve*) and Middle Iron Gate (*Porta di Ferro Mezzana*). Frontal Position (*Posta Frontale*) and Two-horn Position (*Posta Bicorno*) fit this bill as well. What the five have in common is that they are held with the sword centered on the body. An alternate lead foot may affect where and how you play, but it doesn't prevent you from forming the guard. Adding the alternate foot forward forms would seriously increase the number of guards far beyond a useful grouping number.

So, why twelve? Because it is a good memory number and the smallest one that can include the unique guards. To make use of the powerful memory number, Fiore must fill out the number with variants, which he uses to advantage because they offer lessons that reinforce how the guards work.

LESSONS FROM THE FIGHT MASTERS

Each Fight Master offers details on a guard's nature, either as the guard is held or as play moves to or from it. None, however, is comprehensive in detailing all of the possible options a guard offers. Of course, given the nature of the art, that is not surprising. I will give some details for each of the guards (*poste*) in the interpretation section beginning on page 131, but here I'd like to make a few general comments about the guards.

In the text accompanying the set of two *Posta di Donna* guards, Fiore called out the point guards as different from the others, saying they are not direct contraries to themselves. From these guards, the primary attack threat is a thrust. The primary threat from the other guards is usually a blow. Indeed, Fiore is also sometimes very specific about a non-point guard's ability to make a powerful thrust. For some of the guards he says that they can make all seven blows of the sword; this is, all the cuts and thrusts.

The issue that the point guards have when opposing themselves is that "the most extended guard can reach the opponent first." For example, if both players adopt Short Position, one player may have an advantage over the other if he holds the position slightly more extended than the other player, or if he has a sword that is actually longer than the opponent's, or if he has a longer reach when his arms are extended. In each of these cases, the player with the advantage effectively has a sword that is longer than his opponent's, because his point will reach his opponent first. Getting your point to the opponent first is the way to win from a thrusting position. You merely have to ensure that his point does not find you a moment later.

When dealing with blows, there is more time and space to compensate for such minor differences such as weapon or arm length. This extra time allows the non-point guards to effectively oppose each other. They can come to the cross, providing defense for the player.

SORTING THE FIGHT MASTERS

At the end of each Fight Master's text, Fiore appends a single word, either *stabile*, *instabile*, or *pulsativa*. This division is another concept that Fiore doesn't define. The first two words are easily translated as stable and unstable. The third appears to be derived from the Latin *pulsatio* which means a knocking, striking, or beating. So guards tagged with *pulsativa* would be striking, or beating, guards.

By the tags on the drawings, Fiore divides the guards as follows:

- *Stabile*: Middle Iron Gate, Short Position, Boar's Tooth, Long Tail, Middle Boar's Tooth.
- *Instabile*: Window Position, Long Position, Two-Horned Position, Frontal Position.
- *Pulsativa*: Iron Gate, Woman's Position (Left & Right).

Short Position, however, is said in its text to have no stability. Could it be incorrectly categorized as *stabile* when it should be *instabile*? Omitting the "in" could be a simple scribal error.

What can we glean from these groupings? All of the *stabile* guards have the sword held with the hands low, but so does Iron Gate, which is defined as *pulsativa*. All of the *instabile* guards have the hands above belt level, but so does Woman's Position, which is *pulsativa*. All of the *stabile* guards have the point in line or close to it, except Long Tail, whose point is about as far from threatening as possible. All of the *pulsativa* guards cut along Fiore's favored *fendente-sottani* lines, but so does Boar's Tooth. All of the *stabile* guards are relaxed places to stand, but so is Iron Gate.

The only clear commonality is that all of the *instabile* guards are awkward to hold for any length of time as they are tiring for the arms. While the possible *instabile* guard Short Position is not particularly tiring to stand in, it does have the sword blade raised, which is more tiring to hold than when the blade is pointed down. When including Short Position, the set of instabile guards comprises those through which one tends to move, or stand in only for short periods of time.

At this time, I'm afraid, I have no good explanation of the how and why of these groupings.

LOOK AT ME AS A CROSS

Although he waits until the axe section to say it, Fiore tells us that all of *armizare* "features the defense of the cross." The crossing of the blades (*incrosada*) is where he starts instruction on the sword in two hands. If a strike from a guard is successful, the fight is often over. If that strike does not end the fight, most likely the swords will cross and a bind (blade-on-blade contact) will occur. The moment may be brief or extended. Even if brief, it will provide that instant of information to help guide the swordsman's next movement.

The whole art of fencing and of arms features the defense of the cross.

The Pisan swordmaster Filippo Vadi, Fiore's apparent lineal descendant, wrote in his *De Arte Gladiatoria Dimicandi* that "the art of the sword only consists in crossing, putting both strikes and thrusts in their rightful place, bringing war to those who oppose you".[3] You use the cross to close the opponent's line of attack, thereby defending yourself. Vadi has more to say on elements of making the cross, such as never letting your sword travel too far in making the cross and keeping your sword point toward the opponent's face, thereby maintaining a threat even in the cross. He notes that you should "when you cross blades, cross them resolutely." All of this is good advice and Fiore addresses much of it in his explicative manner by showing us these elements as part of plays.

Each of the Remedy Masters in this section starts with his blade crossed with his opponent's blade, as Fiore considers the cross crucial to understanding swordplay. In reconstructing his art, we must also consider this aspect in detail, whether the master gives us words to ponder over or not. In the real world of a fight, the distance between the opponents, the portion of the blade in the bind, and the body position of the players are determining factors as to how the play will proceed. These concepts are difficult to put into words. Explaining it is not a new problem, for Vadi says, "I can't show you this as well with my words, as I could with the sword"; something, alas, that he cannot do for us. We can take heed of the master's advice and study these elements carefully, sword in hand.

Fiore's scholar of the First *Largo* Master. Vadi says "If your foe crosses wide, thrust"

[3] Translation of this and all other passages from Vadi are by Luca Porzio & Gregory Mele, *Arte Gladiatoria Dimicandi: 15th Century Swordsmanship of Master Filippo Vadi*, Chivalry Bookshelf, 2002.

I am the sword ... I can become extended or with-drawn; when I get near the opponent I can enter into close play, perform disarms and abrazare. ...

PLAYING WITH *LARGO* AND *STRETTO*

The biggest lesson of the sword in two hands section is that swordplay is divided into wide play (*zogho largo*) and close play (*zogho stretto*). Unfortunately, Fiore never defines the terms, leaving us to divine the meaning from the examples he gives. *Largo* means *wide* and *stretto* can have several meanings, among them *close, narrow,* and *constrained.* The question is, how do these apply to the sword and to *armizare* in general? Fiore's bounty of scholars gives us quite a few examples to consider while trying to understand what he meant by *zogho largo* and *zogho stretto.* We also get two unillustrated paragraphs bridging between the *largo* and *stretto* plays, as well as the occasional use of the term *zogho stretto* elsewhere in the manuscript.

The term *zogho largo* appears for the first time in the sword in two hands section. He does not present a distinction between *largo* and *stretto* in the play of *abrazare,* dagger, or the sword in one hand. With the sword, we have for the first time a weapon than can reach the opponent at a range beyond that of the hand, and this is a key part of understanding what is going on. But if it is key, why does it not apply to the sword held in one hand? I think that, like the blows and the general *posta* instruction, it does. The sword in one hand section is structured for other purposes and Fiore covers the principles of *largo* and *stretto* in the sword in two hands section. He makes no *largo/stretto* distinctions in sword in armor, axe, or spear sections beyond mentioning that the player can go to close play; yet the axe and spear are both longer than a sword and have an even greater reach. For whatever reason, Fiore chose to present his core instruction on the difference between *largo* and *stretto* in the sword in two hands section.

Looking at what Fiore has to say, we see that *zogho largo* play includes "remedies and counters both from the *mandritto* and *riverso* side, counter-thrusts and counter-cuts to each action, with breaks, parries, strikes and binds" while *zogho stretto* has "every kind of parry, strike, entering and exiting binds, grapples, disarms and throws" as well as "the remedies and the counters to each action needed to attack and defend." We immediately see that *stretto* includes "grapples, disarms and throws" which are not listed among the *largo* actions and are all actions that involve body-to-body contact. As described, the *largo* plays are all weapon-to-weapon actions. So we start with a sense that *zogho largo* involves action where the weapon can interact with the opponent's weapon, and reach him while we cannot—or should not—reach him with our hand, while *zogho stretto* involves similar weapon action plus body contact actions.

Looking further afield for enlightenment, the natural first stop is within the Liberian tradition: Filippo Vadi. Although time separates them, tradition unites them. The Pisan master says, "The art of the sword only consists in crossing, putting strikes and thrust in their right place, bringing war to those opposing you." Porzio and Mele, in a footnote to their translation of this passage, comment that "Vadi underlines the fundamental principle of fighting from engagement (blade-to-blade contact) whenever the swords cross, a principle crucial to understanding Italian fencing through the nineteenth century." I think it may be telling that Vadi, who "acquired good knowledge from the practical experience and doctrine of many masters of arms in different countries," refers to bringing war (*guerra*). It calls to mind Liechtenauer's concept of *krieg* (war) in the context of close-range fighting. Remember that Fiore, too, says that he studied under German masters.

Vadi's most explicit passage on the subject goes as follows. "If your foe crosses wide (*crocia largo*), thrust: because you don't want to be divided from him. When he comes to the half sword (*mezza spada*) close towards him, as reason so requires, leave the long distance (*giocho*[4] *largo*) and assail him. … If you feel you haven't lost your cunning, leave the long distance (*largo*) for close combat (*stretto*), ... once you have done your cover, be quick to strike, at close (*stretto*) and wide (*largo*) you'll take down strength." The words in parentheses are the original Italian which I have inserted for words pertinent to the discussion at hand. You'll note that Vadi associates *largo* with both the crossing (*crocia*) and play (*giocho*).

Porzio and Mele translate *giocho* as *distance* rather than *play*. Is *distance* a suitable translation in Fiore's case? Speaking of the sword, Fiore says that "when I get near an opponent I can enter into close play." He clearly associates distance with *zogho stretto*: one can enter it when one gets near to the opponent. He also tells us that the dagger is "in love with close play" and dagger play occurs at close range. Comparing the sort of actions done in *zogho largo* to those done in *zogho stretto*, we see that most of the *largo* actions are done with the sword blade at an apparently wider distance than the *stretto* actions, which are done with the left hand (usually separated from the sword's grip) and executed with an apparent step to get even closer to the opponent. This all leads to a conclusion that distance should at least be a component of any definition of *zogho largo* and *zogho stretto*.

To refine our definition, we need to look at what plays Fiore presents and where he puts them. There are three masters with scholars in the sword in two hands section. Two belong to *zogho largo* and one to *zogho stretto*. The First *Largo* Master has a single scholar. The Second *Largo* Master is followed by sixteen scholars and a Counter Master, who replies to the last scholar and stands as the last play of *zogho largo*. The *Stretto* Master has twenty-one scholars[5] and two Counter Masters, who are specific to "the student who tried dagger plays against me" and are followed by the last seven scholars who concentrate on disarms. In each type of play, some of the scholars play directly from the cross and others are follow-on scholars, who complete the play of preceding scholars.

The scholar of the First *Largo* Master, who crosses at the point of the sword (*punta spada*), appears with his left foot forward as does his master. From the crossing, the master says that you can turn your blade and strike to the opponent's other side or make a thrust. The first master's only scholar is shown making such a thrust while, the cut goes unillustrated.

In this crossing, the blades are crossed above the middle. They are at the weak part where there is little or no leverage to remain in the bind. Thus, one of the players will win the bind and the other will lose. This sheds light on the reasons behind choosing one or the other of the masters actions. If the scholar wins the bind, his sword will be free to make the cut. If the scholar loses, his opponent's sword will remain in presence. An immediate thrust keeps the scholar's sword in the center and sends it sliding past the opponent's blade. Both plays occur comfortably in the weapon's zone, well clear of close contact.

First scholar of the Second *Largo* Master.

The Second *Largo* Master stands in a deeper crossing, where the swords meet at the middle of the sword (*mezza spada*). Like the first master, he stands with his left foot forward, and he also advises an immediate cut or thrust.

The Second *Largo* Master's first scholar makes a thrust similar to that of the first master's first scholar, the main difference being that his right foot is forward. I believe this is because the second master's

4 *Giocho*, like *gioco*, is a later form of *zogho* and still means *play*.

5 Curiously, in the Morgan, some of the *stretto* plays appear before the *Stretto* Master, right after the *largo's* "exchange of thrusts" scholars. The "breaking of the thrust" and subsequent *largo* scholars are absent, replaced by *stretto* scholars. Whether the error was made by the artist or the compiler of the pages, it seems to stem from confusion in the similarity between the eighth *largo* scholar and the first *stretto* scholar.

scholar has passed backwards with his left foot to keep the play at a wider distance, something the first master's scholar does not need to do because the players are already too distant for the opponent to step in and initiate close-range play. This scholar is working to keep the action at a wider distance. The instructions to make the master's cut to the opponent's hands rather than his head reenforces this idea.

The crossing of the blades at the middle puts the players at a measure where step can bring them body to body for close contact. Unfortunately, the Second *Largo* Master finds himself there with his left foot forward. He is not well positioned to step in himself, but his opponent is. Unless the master's students wish to accept close combat, they must do something about the situation. Looking through the scholars that follow, it becomes clear that maintaining the distance between the players is always on their minds.

Second and third scholars of the Second Largo Master

The second scholar takes advantage of the presence of his opponent's blade to grab it and neutralize its threat while he strikes the opponent. The next scholar adds a kick to the opponent's leg, very useful in forestalling a opponent who decides to forget about his sword and close in. It will disrupt his balance, possibly even knocking him down if he has already started to step.

The fourth scholar begins the curiously named "peasant's blow" play. Although the text describes it as being set up with a feint, the circumstances can arise any time the opponent comes hard enough to the cross that he pushes the scholar's sword wide. Such a push gives it the energy to come around quickly. The follow-on scholar puts that energy to good use. Note that the follow-on scholar makes his cut with extended arms.

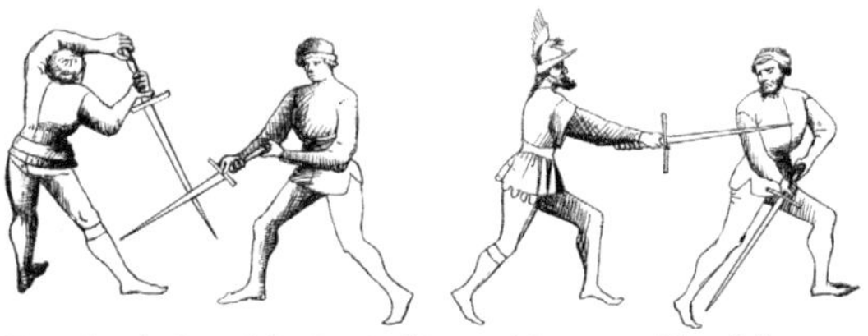
Fourth scholar of the Second *Largo* Master and his follow-on companion scholar

The sixth scholar provides a lesson in the geometry of the sword-player configuration. Attempts to cut to the leg are dangerous as the distance to the upper openings is shorter than that to the lower openings. In other words, the attacker's sword makes the hypotenuse of a triangle and the scholar's sword makes one of the legs. A triangle's legs, in anything but an equilateral triangle, are always shorter than the hypotenuse.

The seventh scholar responds to a full crossing (*tutta spada*) where the attacker's hands are high. This may be a situation that he creates himself by applying upwards pressure against a bound blade, or it might be because the opponent brings the blades up with the same pressure, seeking to clear his way to enter into close combat. However the players get to this point, the lower openings get uncovered. This allows a kick into those lower openings. Such a kick would likely halt an opponent trying to use the cross to move to close range.

Seventh scholar of the Second *Largo* Master

The attack that the next scholar, the eighth, deals with is a thrust rather than a cut. He executes the "exchange of thrusts" and acts on the inside line. Again note that he makes his action with extended arms. His follow-on scholar (the ninth) looks very like the first scholar of the *Stretto* Master. We'll look more closely at this in a bit. For now, it important to note that this play is a response to a thrust and a shift of focus.

Ninth scholar of the Second *Largo* Master

This is followed another technique against a thrust, the "breaking of the thrust," which acts on the outside line. The text notes that the previous scholar dealt with a thrust where the opponent's sword point was higher than his hands and that this one (the tenth scholar) is for a thrust where the opponent's point is lower than his arms. The play involves beating the opponent's sword to the ground and has three follow on scholars. The last of these (thirteenth scholar) involves the closest approach to the opponent made by any *largo* scholar as he shifts away to keep his opponent's body between the threatening sword and himself.

Tenth scholar of the Second *Largo* Master: breaking a thrust

Thirteenth scholar of the Second *Largo* Master: moving away from the blade

The second-to-last direct scholar plays "after beating the opponent's point or crossing his sword." We have here a scholar who can play whether the attack is a blow or a thrust. He makes a strike into the opponent's elbow "causing him to turn." The opponent in the illustration is shown being rocked back more than turned, although the follow-on scholar is definitely attacking an opponent who has been turned around. We will look at him more closer in a couple of pages.

The last *largo* scholar does what is essentially a thrusting variant of the peasant's blow, including the feinted *mezzano* blow to start the play. Also like the peasant's blow play, this action can come from pressure in the bind and need not be initiated with a feint. This scholar gets a Counter Master (the only one in the *largo* section) who ends the section.

Last scholar of the Second *Largo* Master

We will now start the close play of the two-handed sword. We will see every kind of parry, strike, entering and exiting binds, grapples, disarms and throws. We will also see the remedies and the counters to each action needed to attack and defend.

All of the direct *stretto* scholars (those who are not completing a play of a previous scholar but making their own action from the crossing at *mezza spada*) step in with their left foot to do their action. This is a standard move to close the distance when trying to execute a close-quarters technique such as grapple or a throw. One play is described as being derived from a dagger play, and few will argue that dagger fighting is anything other than close-quarters work. So I think one can conclude that actions of *zogho stretto* are close-quarters actions.

First scholar of the *Stretto* Master

The first scholar of the *Stretto* Master, as noted before, is definitely not the same play as that of the other masters' first scholars. It does, however, look remarkably like that of the eighth scholar of the Second *Largo* Master. The distance between the two players appears closer in the *stretto* play, as suggested by the placement of the players' lead feet and the angles of the arms and swords. The difference is not very much, which is not surprising as their blades cross at the same point, but the *largo* scholar's foot appears further from the viewer. This fits well with the circumstances from which these different plays arise. The *largo* scholar, we are told, is responding to crossing of the swords from an exchange of thrusts while the *stretto* scholar responds to one "from an over- or under-hand crossing," which is to say, from a cut. The *largo* scholar has already stepped forward (and off line) as part of the exchange of thrusts and driven his opponent's point wide and off line. The *stretto* scholar steps forward after the crossing and uses that pressure to drive the opponent's point away. Although that point may still be close to his body, its threat is eliminated. In both cases the scholars clear the way for their left hand to grasp the handle of the opponent's sword.

Second scholar of the *Stretto* Master

Third scholar of the *Stretto* Master

The next two scholars join the first in presenting a pattern of play we have seen before: playing to different pressures from their opponent. The first scholar's action can be initiated if the scholar is stronger in the bind or if the opponent tries to shift his blade to the scholar's left. The second plays while the opponent's sword stays near the center, using it as a pivot to move his pommel forward into a one-handed pommel strike. Note that he still needs his left hand to control the opponent's right arm to prevent the blade from hitting him as he closes. The third scholar does a similar strike. Either his blade is shifted to the right or he allows his opponent to do so by going soft in the bind. Because his opponent's blade is moving away, the scholar can safely make a two-handed pommel strike. If the opponent keeps moving after losing the resistance of the scholar's sword, the door is opened for the scholar to move wide from the blade, yet close to the opponent since the foe's body becomes a shield against his blade.

Fourth scholar of the *Stretto* Master, following on from the third

Fifth scholar of the *Stretto* Master

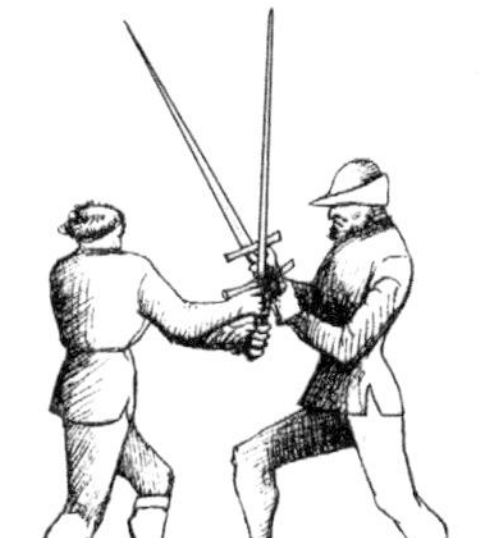

Seventh scholar of the *Stretto* Master

Following these are a pair of scholars (fifth and seventh) who react to upward and downward pressure against their blades in the bind. One scholar uses the downward pressure in the cross to whip his blade around and create a new cross on the other side of the opponent's blade as he moves in. The other makes a response to the opponent moving his blade up. Each of these direct scholars has a follow-on scholar who use his left arm in an enveloping technique; one traps his foe's sword and the other his arms.

Tenth scholar of the *Stretto* Master

Eleventh scholar of the *Stretto* Master

The next two scholars (tenth and eleventh) deal with an opponent who raises his pommel in the cross, such as he might if he were to seek to shift into Window Position. Fiore's scholar makes a grab at whatever part of the sword comes close to his left hand. The first of this pair takes the opponent's pommel, the target accessible when the opponent has his hands to the right of the cross. The second responds when the hands are to the left of the cross and grabs the opponent's blade. Once the opponent's sword is controlled, the scholar's sword is free to strike. Similar circumstances can come from an opponent striking a horizontal (*mezzano*) blow from the left (*riverso*) and the right (*mandritto*) respectively.

Thirteenth scholar of the *Stretto* Master

The next direct scholar (thirteenth) offers a play that "comes from a play of the dagger," the disarm of the First Remedy Master. The text goes on to say that one can also do the next play (the Middle Bind) of the same master, reiterating the close alliance between these two dagger plays. Interestingly, the two Counter Masters that follow this play seem to actually act against an attempt to execute the second play suggested rather than the first.

Counter Master to the thirteenth scholar of the *Stretto* Master

The next scholar, curiously, is shown as a Counter Master in the Morgan and the Pisani-Dossi. He does a grapple "to prevent him from trying any disarms or grapples of his own." He is essentially a response to the Remedy Master who is the *Stretto* Master and, thus, is a sort of general Counter Master. The scholars who follow may also fit the concept of variant scholars, given that they respond to variations in circumstances. So, did the artist mistakenly leave off a crown from this scholar and fail to mark him as Counter Master? Or is his presentation as a simple scholar an additional part of the approach that has the opponent in the Remedy Master's play a scholar rather than the master he is in the other two manuscripts? This is one of the cases where we cannot know Fiore's thinking, but I find the plays of this portion easier to understand when considering the scholar as a Counter Master punctuating the pedagogy.

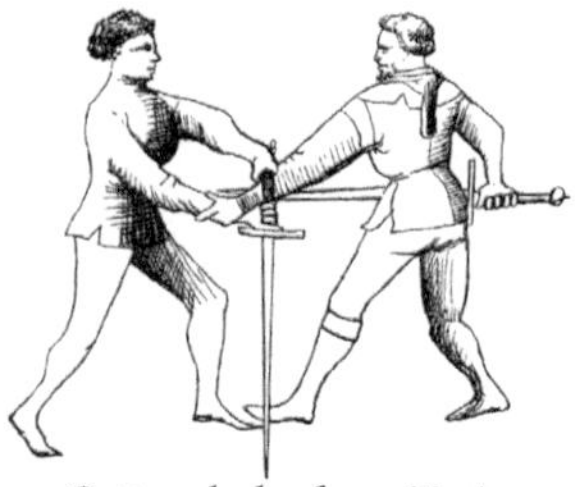

Getty scholar from 30r A

Corresponding play from the Morgan

The first of the scholars following the possible Counter Master responds to a *riverso mezzana* from the opponent with his own *riverso mezzano*. Swords coming to the cross in this situation would not be likely to have their points in presence as a threat to the opponent, so this does not seem likely to be the blow the *Stretto* Master makes. This is a variant situation.

The last four scholars are a set. Three deal with using the sword to make a high, middle or low disarm, respectively, while the last drops his own sword to make an empty-handed disarm.

Unlike the *zogho largo*, the *zogho stretto* does not end in half-blade grip. It doesn't have to, because Fiore covered the connection of unarmored and armored combat with the last play of sword in one hand section. Instead, the *stretto* section ends with an empty-handed scholar making a sword disarm. This is a visual reminder that you can do *abrazare* in the midst of a sword fight and refers the student back to *abrazare*: another internal link in the manuscript.

> ***... I can become extended or withdrawn; when I get near the opponent I can enter into close play ...***

From these plays we can see that *zogho largo* seems to be occurring when the distance between the players is wider rather than closer. This is the range at which a sword can be employed in full cuts with the arms extended, taking full advantage of its reach. If so, *zogho largo* would seem to be roughly analogous to the German *zufechten*[6] which Christian Tobler defines as "the first phase of combat where one closes with the opponent," which is to say when the combatant needs to take a step in order to strike the opponent.

Zogho stretto seems to occur when the distance between the players is shorter. With the sword, this play can only start after the crossing of the blades. Within this space, cuts are shorter, faster, and usually made without full extension of the arms. Within this constrained space, strikes need only be half strikes and can be made very quickly, so a player must maintain cover to avoid being hit. If so, *zogho stretto* would be analogous, at least in part, to the German *krieg* which Tobler defines[6] as "the second phase of a fighting encounter, when the combatants have moved to close range. The techniques used in this close combat are limited to those associated with winding (*Winden*) and wrestling at the sword (*Ringen am Schwert*)." It is worth noting that these are techniques Tobler mentions as being done from a crossing of the blades.

These Germanic correlations would seem to reinforce translating *largo* as *wide* in the sense of spread out and *stretto* as *close* in the sense of a nearby distance. Thus, one would expect that techniques would be more extended in *largo* while *stretto* would call for close-range techniques. A possible problem arises here, in that the *largo* scholars' actions include four in which the scholar uses something other than his sword to make the play. Specifically, they use what are normally considered close-quarters combat techniques. In two the scholar kicks the opponent, and in a third he grabs the opponent's sword grip. Perhaps more troubling is the elbow push done by the fourteenth scholar of the Second *Largo* Master. The elbow push, Fiore told us back in the dagger section, is "good in every close play of dagger, axe, sword in armor or sword unarmored." A quick look at this particular elbow push tells us that it is not quite like all the others because the recipient is being rocked back by it rather than simply being turned around. Thinking about how Fiore's actions derive from the basic *abrazare* guards, it looks as though the elbow is being turned with a Long Position strike rather than one from Boar's Tooth. In any case an *abrazare* technique is a close-quarters technique. So should this play be in *zogho stretto* rather than *largo*?

Fourteenth scholar of the Second *Largo* Master

[6] In Christian Henry Tobler, *Fighting with the German Longsword,* Chivalry Bookshelf, 2004.

First *Largo* Master

Second *Largo* Master

***Stretto* Master**

Before we decide, let's look a little further at the masters in this section. The two *largo* masters appear standing with their left foot forward, their blade crossed with that of their opponent. The difference between them is that the first master's sword is crossed at the point of the blade (*punta di spada*) and the second is crossed at the middle (*mezza spada*). The *Stretto* Master is shown with his right foot forward and his sword crossed at the middle with that of his opponent (*mezza spada*). There are two things to note: where the blades cross and which foot is forward. Both of the *largo* masters are left foot forward and cannot make a simple pass forward to bring their left hand into play for *abrazare* techniques. They are not in the correct place to make the sort of close-range plays we learned about in the *abrazare* and dagger sections. The *Stretto* Master is right foot forward and well positioned to do exactly that, putting him in the correct distance to make a close-range attack with a single step. The First *Largo* Master, with his crossing at the point, is clearly at a greater distance from his opponent than his companion *largo* master, with his crossing at the middle of the blade. So here at least we have a definite expression of distance, yet there are two masters for *zogho largo*, and each stands at a different distance from his opponent.

The First *Largo* Master has a single scholar. His scholar makes a sword attack directly from the crossing of the blades, yet Fiore says nothing about the strength of the bind between the swords. As anyone who has felt the pressure in the bind knows, it can differ and that difference affects where one can safely move one's sword after making the crossing. Surely Fiore was aware of this. He says that he studied with German masters and the closest thing we have to a contemporary German text, Hs. 3227a, elaborates on Liechtenauer's verse, saying[7] "he names five words; *vor, nach, weich, hart, indes.* On these five words hinge the whole art of Liechtenauer." Including soft (*weich*) or hard (*hart*) here is a pretty emphatic statement about how important understanding pressure is. Tobler's translation[8] of Sigmund Ringeck's glosses on the Liechtenauer verses makes clearer what the feeling (*fühlen*) of the swords and of being soft or hard in a bind is. "Therefore remember: if one binds against the others sword, you shall notice - right in the moment when the blades make contact—whether he is hard or soft. And as soon as you have noticed this, remember the word *indes*: this means that you should attack the next opening immediately and nimbly, hard or soft." In the *abrazare* and dagger sections (especially in the structure of the Fourth Remedy Master), Fiore demonstrates a sensitivity to pressure and the need to respond properly to it. It follows that he would be able to apply this crucial knowledge to using a sword. Yet he gives us no specific terminology or commentary concerning it as is found in Liechtenauer's verses, making it a bit harder to be sure one is correctly understanding some of his sword instruction.

7 In translation by David Lindholm and friends.

8 In Christian Henry Tobler, *Secrets of German Medieval Swordsmanship*, Chivalry Bookshelf, 2001.

Whatever the details of pressure in the bind, the Second *Largo* Master's first scholar does essentially the same thing, although he does it without stepping as the first master's scholar seems to do. With or without a step, the action is not surprising because all the same rules apply when the swords are crossed, whether at the point or in the middle. However, because of the shortened distance in which the Second *Largo* Master stands, he has more options, and thus more scholars.

The Second *Largo* Master and the *Stretto* Master are both crossed at the middle of the blade (*mezza spada*). This puts them at the same distance from their opponent, suggesting that the crossing at the middle of the blade is a transition point, a distance where a player can move from the *largo* to the *stretto*. Each of these masters has a different foot forward. Is this important? Very much so. Only the *Stretto* Master is positioned in such a way that he can initiate the step to get to a closer range.

Of course the *Stretto* Master's opponent is also positioned to make that step. The further consideration of weapon position comes into play. Fiore says "We have crossed our swords: this is the crossing from which we can make all the plays that follow. Both of us could perform each of them." The plays in question are, of course, the plays of *zogho stretto*, and only when the swords are crossed equally can this happen. If one player is not positioned as the other, one will have an advantage, and thus only one will be in a good position to execute a particular play. Later Italian masters such as Antonio Manciolino[9] seem to require that the sword points to, or remains close to, the opponent, and this is a valid concern with swords. The grip used in the axe or even the sword in armor requires a broader understanding of the situation than used by the more point-oriented fencers of later times. One can achieve an equal cross with an axe, shaft-on-shaft, with neither pointy end anywhere close to threatening the opponent, yet still be able to execute analogs of the sword in two hands *zogho stretto* plays. As a further note that Fiore does not link the word *stretto* with having the point on or near the centerline, one need only look to how he offers us two versions of Iron Gate (*Porta di Ferro*), one with the point held towards the opponent and one with it held off to the side. He calls them Middle Iron Gate (*Mezzana Porta di Ferro*) and Full Iron Gate (*Tutta Porta di Ferro*). Manciolino's guard names, where he distinguishes whether the point is on-line or not are *Porta di Ferro Stretto* and *Porta di Ferro Largo*. The later master is using the terms differently.

In Fiore's art, it is only in the sword and the axe, weapons whose length is longer than an arm but not longer than a man's height, that we get a distinction between *zogho largo* and *zogho stretto*. The many ways to grip these weapons and the multiple ways to apply them require us to distinguish not *where* so much as *how* we want to use it. What sort of play do we want to engage in? Do we wish to remain at a distance? Do we want protection as we close in to wrestling distance?

Thus, the play (*zogho*) you choose is a matter of distance, positioning, and intent.

Zogho largo describes play that is at wide distance (when you are too far to touch the opponent without a step) and stays at wide distance. It occurs when it is not your intent to close and you do not wish your opponent to close either.

Zogho stretto describes play that is at close range (where you can take no more than a step to touch your opponent's body with your hand) and stays at close range. It occurs when it is your intention to get close to your opponent or to let him get close to you.

---

[9] See Tom Leoni's *The Complete Renaissance Swordsman: A Guide to the Use of All Manner of Weapons*, Freelance Academy Press, 2010 and his on-line article at www.freelanceacademypress.com/articles.aspx.

HINTS OF FURTHER THINGS

As I noted in the previous chapter, the sword is a shield. Fiore shows us this in the plays of the sword in one hand and at the beginning of the sword in two hands plays he says, "I am expert in defense …." Vadi uses the words: "Your sword should be like a shield which covers you all" and in doing so, expresses a clear understanding that the sword must defend as well as attack. This is especially important if the swordsman is not wearing armor, for then he cannot afford to let a hit through. "With sharps and a gambeson,[10] a single failed parry can be fatal," says Fiore, "while in the lists a combatant wearing good armor can receive multiple hits and still go on to win the fight."

I am expert in defense and offense, and always strive to finish in those. …

The contemporary Liechtenauer tradition decries purely defensive fighting and espouses a simultaneous offensive-defensive strike. This is usually expressed in the so-called *meisterhau.* The always terse Fiore makes a statement that may indicate that he too values such action, at least for the sword in two hands. "I am expert in defense and offense, and always strive to finish in those." Let me repeat the last bit: "strive to finish in *those* (emphasis mine)." The goal, at the finish, is both: offense and defense. That one has to strive for them means that it is not always possible to achieve this ideal. The masters of the Liechtenauer tradition acknowledge this.

Certainly, one can achieve defense and offense in the form of a parry followed by a riposte as a two-time[11] (*dui tempi*) technique rather than the simultaneous actions (*stesso tempo*) of the German *meisterhau.* Some of Fiore's plays clearly work in *dui tempi.* Fiore's advice "to finish in these" may, however, be an opening to the simultaneous attack and defense concept of the German *meisterhau.* As you ponder this, consider also how little we would understand of Liechtenauer's teaching if we had only the master's verses and lacked the explanations of his student's' glosses.

Also in the manner of Liechtenauer's cryptic verses, Fiore tells us that the sword's art involves turning and binding. The Liechtenauer tradition calls the technique of turning the sword while in the bind *winden*, or winding. The swords' binding and this technique are inseparably connected, conjoined as Fiore's "to turn" is linked to his "to bind" in this verse. Fiore is not explicit about winding techniques, but among the *stretto* scholars are two who seem to be reacting to something very much like a winding technique. He also presents us with three undefined turns (*volta*) for the sword. Perhaps we should look to *winden* when we seek to understand *volta di spada.*

My art is to turn and to bind …

[10] Leoni translates the word *zuparello d'arme* as *gambeson. Gambeson* is as problematic in English as *zuparello d'arme* is in Italian. Multiple usages for the same words and changes over time have confused the application of these words. Fiore was fighting without armor and could be easily harmed by a sword; it seems likely the use here is a garment with little or no padding. It probably looked much like the garments worn by the unarmored players in the Getty.

[11] A fencing time is not an objective measure of time. It is the time (however many objective units of time it may require) that it takes to complete a single action. Thus, a *dui tempi* technique takes two actions (such as a parry and riposte).

IT'S ALL RELATED

Last scholar of the Second *Largo* Master

The last scholar of the Second *Largo* Master does a play called "false thrust or short point" which involves a feinted blow and the scholar grabbing his sword at mid-blade in order to place a thrust. The counter to the move shown in the illustration that follows has the Counter Master making the same grip. Observe that the last scholar grabs his blade very close to the middle and not as close to the point as many of the sword in armor scholars. This gives him lots of room between his hand and his opponent. Also note his extended left arm. This scholar is working to remain in wide distance. His sword point attacks, and if it does not strike, it remains an effective deterrent to any closing attempt on his opponent's part. This demonstrates a way to use of the middle-blade (*mezza mella*) grip in *zogho largo* rather than the *zogho stretto* favored by the armored players.

Specific Counter Master to the last *largo* scholar

Of course, his Counter Master has a response. He grips his blade closer to the point and steps in, forcing the threatening point offline and taking the play to *zogho stretto*. With that, he becomes a bridge both to the *stretto* portion that follows and to the sword in armor section.

In the text paragraph that follows the last play, Fiore notes than "these plays are all linked." The immediate reference is to the *largo* plays, and that is a useful and valid point. However, the visual and conceptual reference of those last two plays link the sword in two hands to the sword in armor.

In his closing paragraph to the *zogho largo* of sword in two hands, Fiore tells us that the plays "have remedies and counters both from the *mandritto* and *riverso* side, counter-thrusts and counter-cuts to each action, with breaks, parries, strikes and binds." This is one of his specific invitations to apply what he shows in one place to other circumstances and to look outside the illustrated offerings for more of the art. The act of applying the exemplars to circumstances not specifically illustrated is something that we should all see "can be understood very, very easily."

The last illustration of the sword in two hands section mirrors the first one of the sword in one hand section where the master stands in opposition to several figures who offer different types of attacks.[12] This takes us in a circle and unites the play of sword, whether held in one hand or two.

[12] In the Morgan there are two rather than three attackers. The swordsman with the blade above his head is missing.

FULL IRON GATE

(TUTTA PORTA DI FERRO)

PULSATIVA

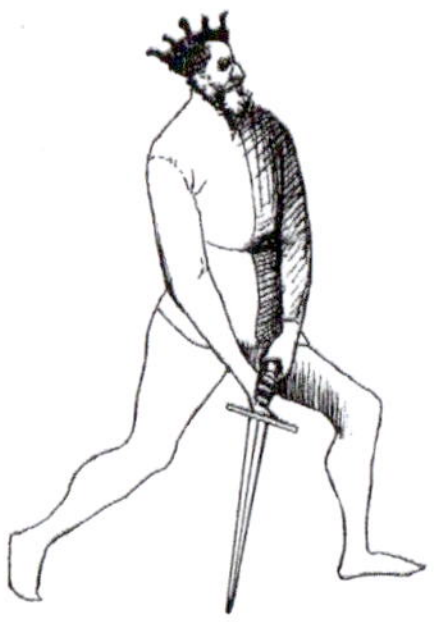

To find Full Iron Gate, hold your sword and stand as you would for the unarmed Iron Gate with the left leg forward. Your left hand should be in front of your groin area. With your arms relaxed, the sword's blade will naturally fall to your right. Your right hand should be as far forward as your left.

There is room for variation in the blade's position. It might be a little more forward or a little more back. It may be held so that the true edge or the false edge (or neither) is more forward. What is important is to be relaxed and comfortable. Holding your hands at an awkward angle will not achieve this.

Full Iron Gate is part of a set of low guards built around the unarmed position of Iron Gate. Each is adapted to what holding a sword in two hands does to your body structure. The others are Middle Iron Gate, Boar's Tooth, Middle Boar's Tooth, and Long Tail.

... The first is tutta Porta di Ferro (complete Iron Door), very strong, and good for waiting against any hand-held weapon (long or short), provided that your sword is of good quality and not too long. From this guard, you parry and pass, and come to the close. It can exchange thrusts and deliver its own. It can also beat thrusts to the ground, always proceeding with a pass and parrying any kind of attack. It can defend without much effort against anyone picking a fight with it.

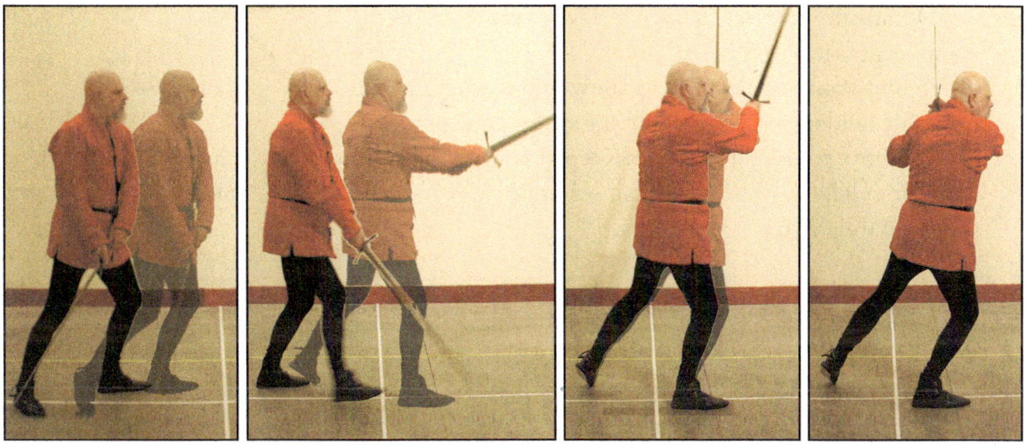

Full Iron Gate allows a strong *sottano* that can travel all the way up to Woman's Position on the left.

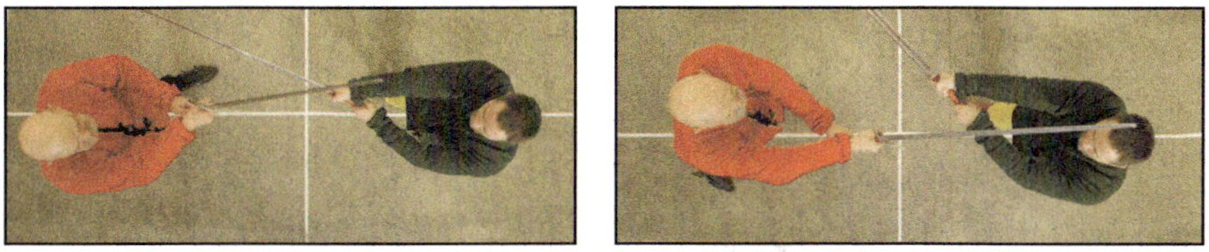

Displacing the opponent's sword requires a blade strong enough to withstand the contact and not so long that it cannot enter the space between you and the closing opponent. The rising *sottano* cut (left) displaces while leading with the false edge of the blade. You can immediately cut down with the true edge (right).

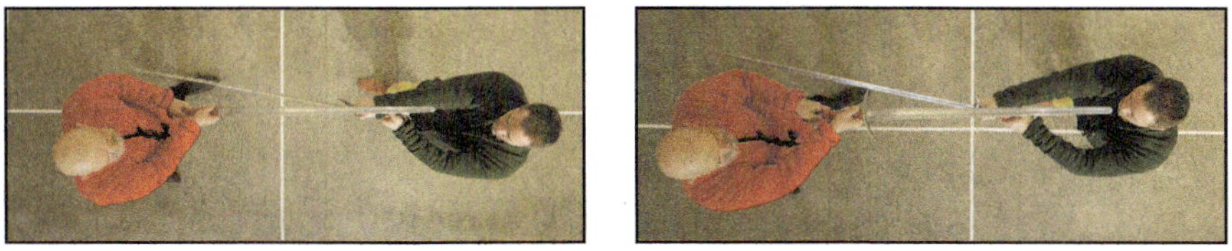

When deflecting with a thrust you cut into a position (usually Long Position) that lets you control the centerline while simultaneously taking his point off line(left). A step out of the way helps your defense but is not always necessary, or indeed possible in the time available. Once his point is dealt with, you can make you own thrust (right).

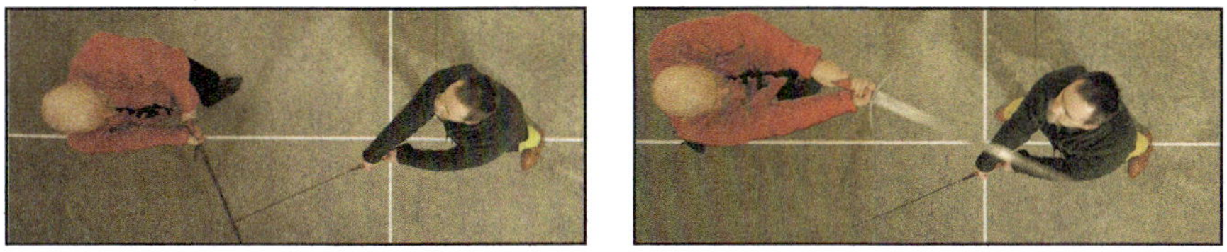

When breaking a thrust, a step out of the way (or even backwards) is necessary as your sword begins off the centerline and is therefore slower to meet the threat. The sword beats away the incoming blade (left), preferably into the ground, before making its own attack (right) with a true edge cut.

WOMAN'S POSITION
(POSTA DI DONNA)
PULSATIVA

This version of the guard is being held on the right. Woman's Position is a reciprocal guard and can be held on the left as well. Woman's Position is shown in several variations in the manuscript (see page 243).

To find Woman's Position as shown here, stand in Full Iron Gate holding your sword. Lift the sword until your right hand is above your right shoulder. Keep moving your left hand until it is higher than the right, lifting your left elbow until you can see under it. Now, make a Stable Turn (*volta stabile*) and shift your weight to your right foot.

Woman's Position is part of a set of high guards built around the unarmed guard of Frontal Position. Each is adapted to what holding a sword in two hands does to your body structure. The others are Woman's Position (left and right), Window Position (left and right), Frontal Position, and Two-horned Position.

This is Posta di Donna (Woman's Guard), which can execute all seven strikes of the sword and defend against all of them. It can break all other guards with its great strikes. It is also quick to exchange thrusts. Extend your front foot off the center-line and pass at an angle with the back foot. This leaves the opponent uncovered, enabling you to hit him.

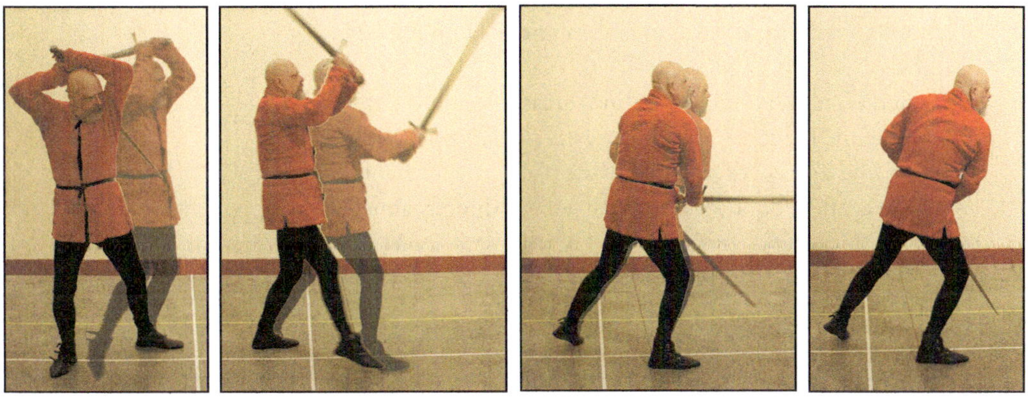

Woman's Position on the Right allows a powerful *fendente* down to Boar's Tooth. Left Woman's Position cuts down to Iron Gate or Long Tail. Both can cut down to Middle Iron Gate.

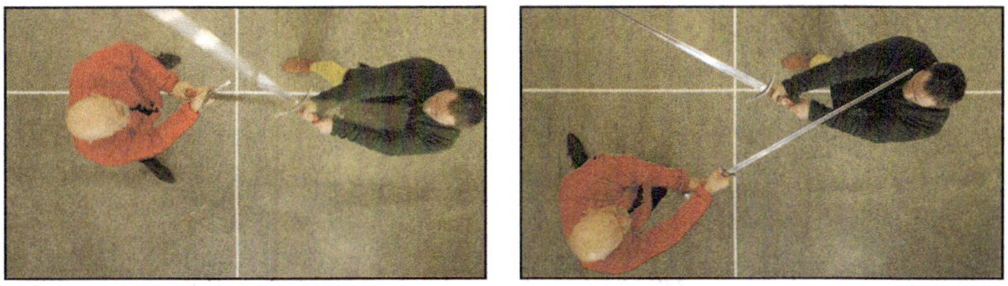

When breaking an attack, a step out of the way is an important part of your defense, needed because your sword starts well away from the centerline and from your attacker. How you step changes where you can hit. Distance and angle change the equation.

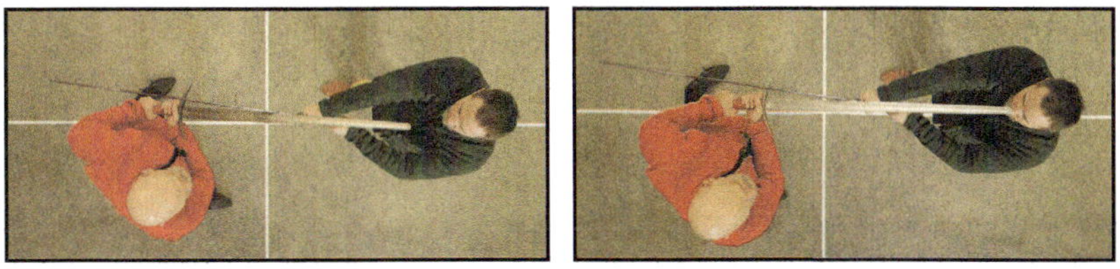

When exchanging a thrust, a step out of the way is necessary due to your sword's position, as noted before. Stepping to the outside of the thrust is best. Against a low-line thrust you need to come to a hands-low position such as Long Position.

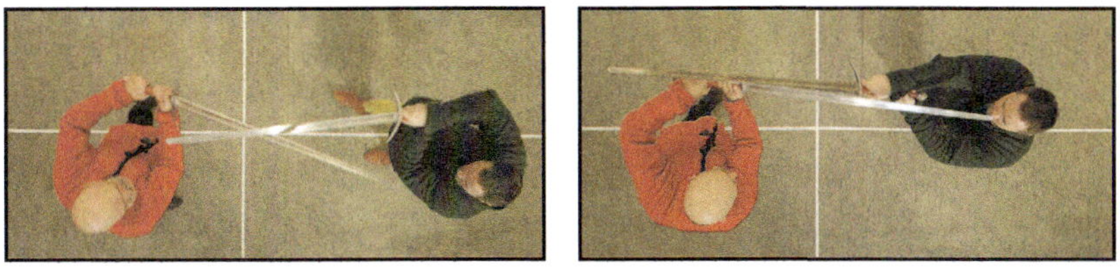

Against a high-line thrust you need to come to a hands-high position such as Window Position. If the attack comes in on your left, you need to lift your sword over your head as you step.

WINDOW POSITION

(POSTA DI FENESTRA)

INSTABILE

This version of the guard is being held on the right. Window Position is a reciprocal position and can be held on the left or right.

To find Window Position, stand in Woman's Position on the right as before. Make a Stable Turn (*volta stabile*) and as you do, raise your arms over your head. The blade of your sword comes forward, but not so far that the point is directly aimed at the opponent. Settle the blade parallel to the ground, above the level of your eyes. Don't block your vision!

Window Position is part of a set of high guards built around the unarmed guard of Frontal Position. Each is adapted to what holding a sword in two hands does to your body structure. The others are Woman's Position (left and right), Window Position (left and right), Frontal Position, and Two-horned Position.

According to the text for Two-Horned Position, Window Position can do everything Long Position can do.

This is the Posta di Fenestra (Window Guard), always quick to enact its tricks and deceptions. She has mastery of defenses and offenses. It can pick a good fight with all the guards, both the high and the low. It often goes from a guard to the other to deceive the opponent. It can deliver strong thrusts, and knows how to break and exchange them.

When held on the right, the wrists are crossed, something Fiore seems to avoid in the low guards. With the hands held back and the sword standing between them and any danger, the crossed wrists are not vulnerable as they would be with the sword held in a low position.

The categorization of Window Position as *instabile* suggests it is not a guard in which to stand for any long period of time, yet the master awaiting three attacks in Boar's Tooth says he could wait in other guards as well, including Left Window Position.

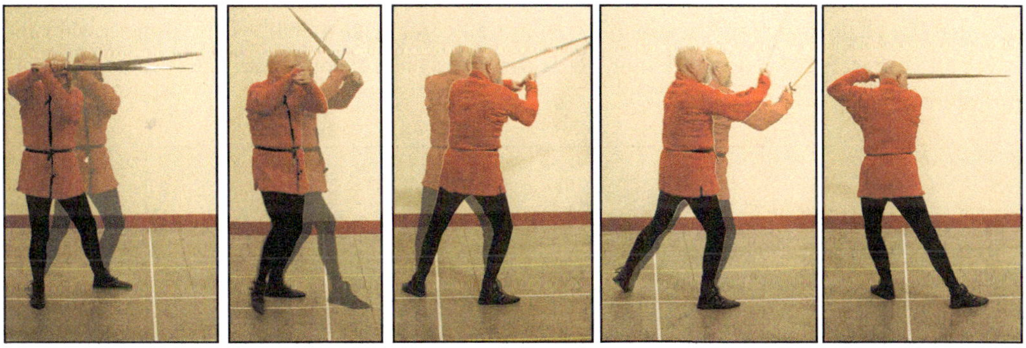

Window Position is set for action in the upper quadrants. Here, it goes from Right Window Position, around into Frontal Position, then withdraws into Left Window Position. Window Position is associated with *mezzana* cuts on the segno page of the Pisani-Dossi as both a starting and finishing position.

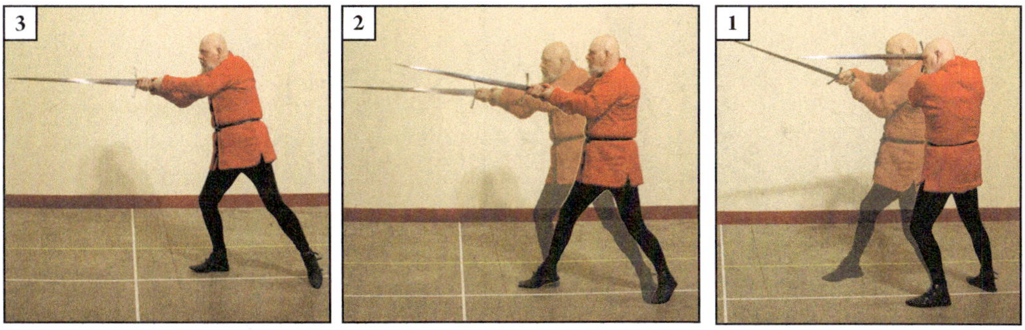

Window Position is also good for thrusts to the upper openings. Here, going from right to left, it extends out into Two-horn Position as a thrust along the centerline.

Here, the scholar strikes down from Window Position as he turns (*volta stabile*) and breaks the thrust aimed at him. While his opponent is dealing with the energy imparted to his sword, the scholar passes forward (*passare*) and makes his own thrust.

LEFT WOMAN'S POSITION

(POSTA DI DONNA LA SINESTRA)

PULSATIVA

This version of the guard is being held on the left. Woman's Position is a reciprocal guard and can be held on the right as well. Woman's Position is shown in several variations in the manuscript (see page 243).

To find Woman's Position as shown here, stand in Full Window Position as before. Lift the sword over your head so that the blade just clears the top. As you lift the sword, make a Stable Turn (*volta stabile*) and shift your weight to your back foot. Settle the sword behind your head, nearly to or onto your shoulder.

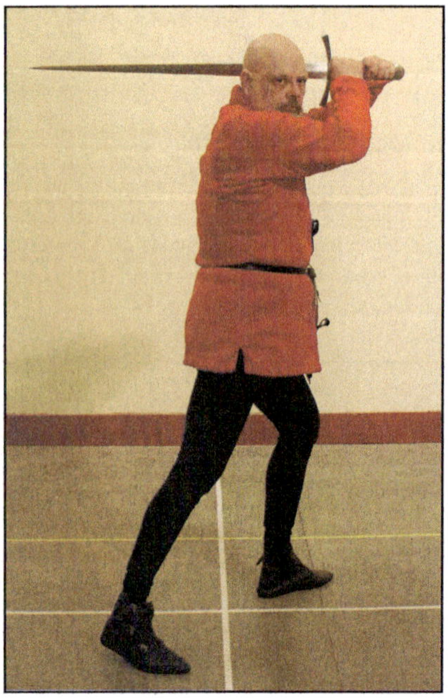

Left Woman's Position is part of a set of high guards built around the unarmed guard of Frontal Position. Each is adapted to what holding a sword in two hands does to your body structure. The others are Woman's Position (left and right), Window Position (left and right), Frontal Position, and Two-horned Position.

This is the left Posta di Donna, always quick to the defense and offense. She can deliver great strikes, break thrusts and beat them to the ground. Thanks to her knowledge of traversing, she enters the close play. This guard knows all these plays well.

Left Woman's Position is another guard to wait in, according to the master awaiting three attacks in Boar's Tooth. As such, it is clear that you should be able to deal with cuts, thrusts, and thrown weapons from this guard, presumably by using the "great strikes" that can come from this position.

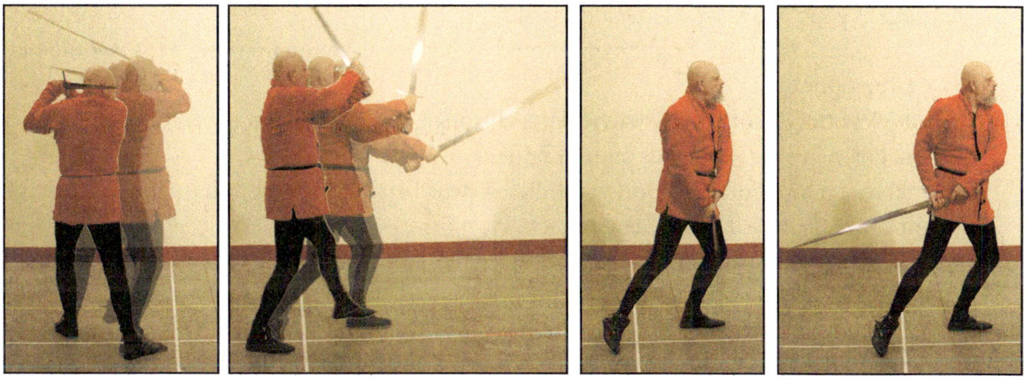

Woman's Position on the left allows a powerful *fendente* down to Iron Gate that can continue on to Long Tail. It can also cut down into Middle Iron Gate.

Left Woman's Position is noted as being able to enter *zogho stretto* "thanks to her knowledge of traversing."

Here, the scholar makes a turn (*volta stabile*) as he strikes into the incoming attack. Striking like this from Woman's Position puts the scholar's blade behind that of his opponent, driving it down and to his right. A step forward (*passare*) puts the scholar within reach of his opponent's elbow, which he quite rightly pushes. The scholar keeps his hand on his foe's elbow to control his sword arm while he makes his own strike. He could as easily keep blade contact and make an *abrazare* play with his left hand.

The close play that follows depends on the exact measure when the crossing of the blades occurs as well as on how the opponent responds to having his blade struck aside.

LONG POSITION
(POSTA LONGA)
INSTABILE

To find Long Position, stand as before in Left Woman's Position. Make a Stable Turn (*volta stabile*) while starting to bring both hands forward to the center of your body. Extend your arms and step forward (*passare*) as you do this. Your left hand should end at about sternum height. Your right hand should be higher, just enough to angle the sword point towards an opponent's face.

Long Position is something you will pass through in any extended-arms cut or thrust. It is also the position your strike hits your opponent.

Held as a guard, Long Position presents the sword's point in a way and a place that the opponent cannot ignore if he wishes to attack.

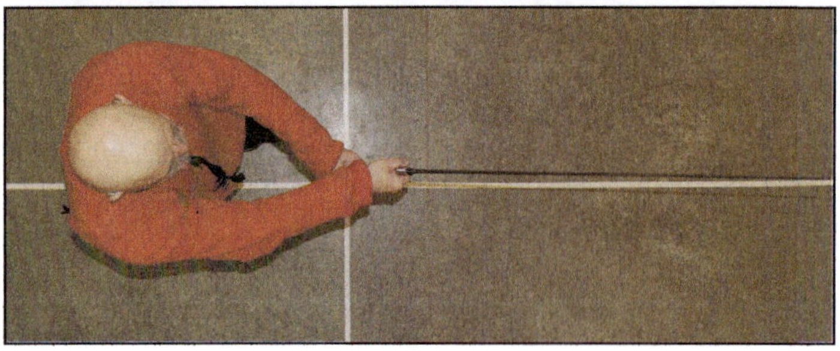

Long Position (like Short Position and Middle Boar's Tooth) is a point guard and Fiore tells us that "the most extended guard can reach the opponent first."

This is the Posta Longa (Long Position), full of deception. It can probe the opponent's guards to see if it can deceive them. It can strike with a thrust, knows how to avoid cuts, then deliver them when it is possible. More than other guards, it can employ deception.

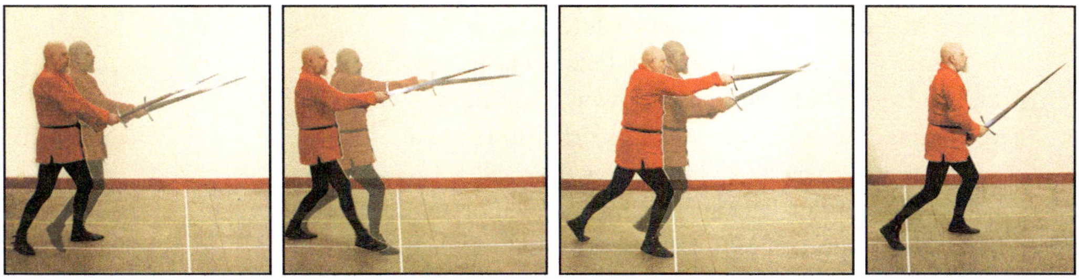

Long Position allows thrusts with a step. With another step you can return to an aggressive Short Position.

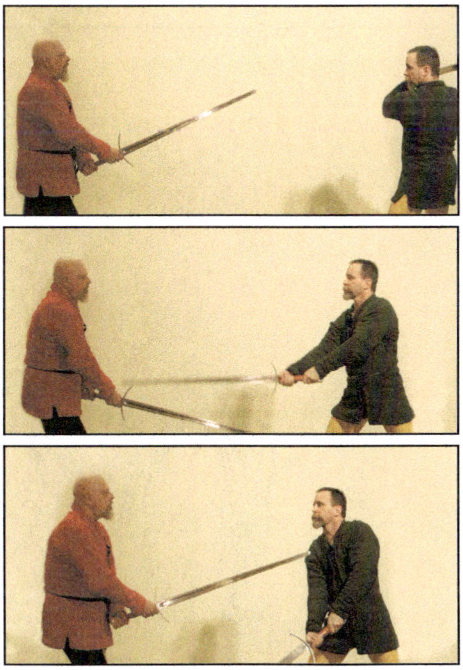

Even before the crossing occurs, Long Position can be deceptive. The extended blade seems to offer a chance to cross and bind. If an opponent seeks that bind, you can slip away before he gets there. As his sword strikes towards yours, drop the point lower, clearing the space where the blades would meet. When his sword moves past, unstopped by the resistance he was expecting, he will be open. Bring your point back up and attack.

When Long Position remains in the crossing, it can still deceive. If your opponent puts pressure against your point to force it out and down, yield to that pressure. As you yield, you can slip under his point then raise your blade on the other side of his and begin your thrust. If his blade remains close, remember to keep your own in place to ward against it and thrust in opposition.

Similarly, you can pull your point back. This offers more of the weak of your blade to him and can suggest to him that he is pushing your point aside. As before, your point returns on the other side of his blade.

MIDDLE IRON GATE
(PORTA DI FERRO MEZZANA)

STABILE

To find Middle Iron Gate, stand as before in Long Position. Lower your sword as you step forward (*passare*). Both hands remain in the center of your body and the sword points down to the ground. Your right hand should be at about groin height or a little below. This will mean you need to bend your left arm to maintain a comfortable position. It is important to be relaxed and comfortable.

Middle Iron Gate might at first appears to be a simple variation of Full Iron Gate, and like all the low guards, it is a variation. However, the difference is significant rather than simple.

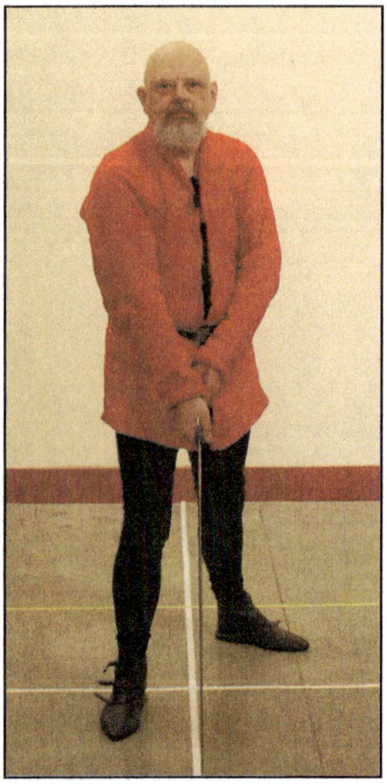

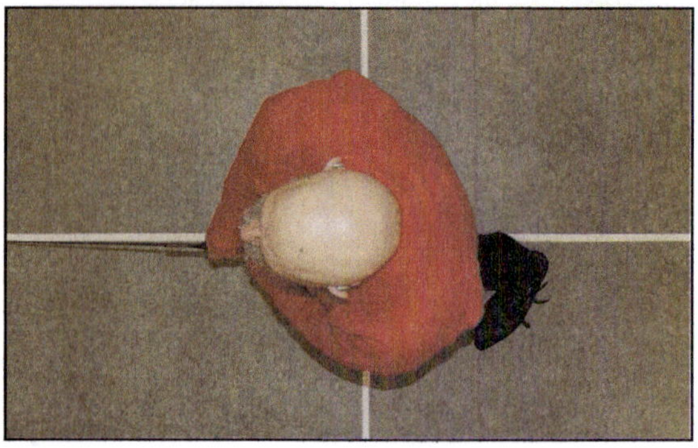

Middle Iron Gate is part of a set of low guards built around the unarmed position of Iron Gate. Each is adapted to what holding a Sword in two-hands does to your body structure. The others are Full Iron Gate, Boar's Tooth, Middle Boar's Tooth, and Long Tail.

Middle Boar's Tooth (like Short Position and Long Position) is a point guard and is covered by Fiore's caution that "the most extended guard can reach the opponent first."

This is Porta di Ferro Mezzana (Middle Iron Door), since it holds the sword in the middle. It is a good guard, but calls for a long blade. It delivers strong thrusts, beats away attacks low-to-high, then comes back down with a fendente to the head or arms, returning in this guard. It is called porta (door) because it's strong; it is a strong guard that is difficult to break without danger and without coming to the close.

Middle Iron Gate is held in the center of the body and can be held with either leg forward. Changing the lead foot is something Fiore's other low guards cannot do without significantly changing the swordsman's structural positioning.

Fiore notes that this guard is hard to break without coming close. Much like Long and Two-horned Positions, one must get safely past the point to make an attack and by then you are in close range.

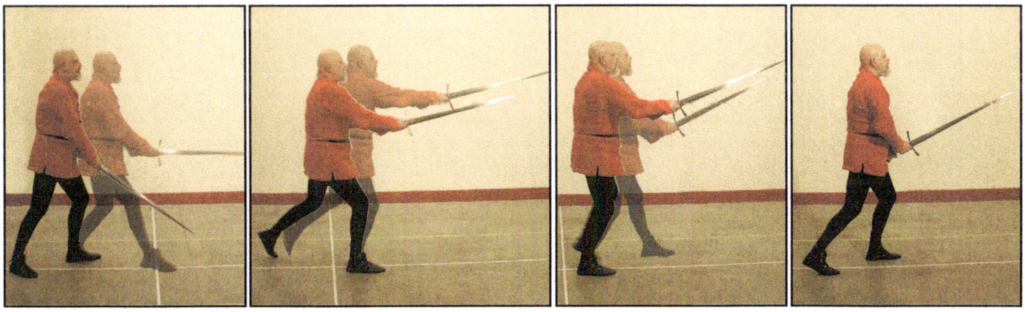

Middle Iron Gate offers a strong centerline thrust. Here, the scholar is shown recovering to Short Position, but you can recover into almost any guard.

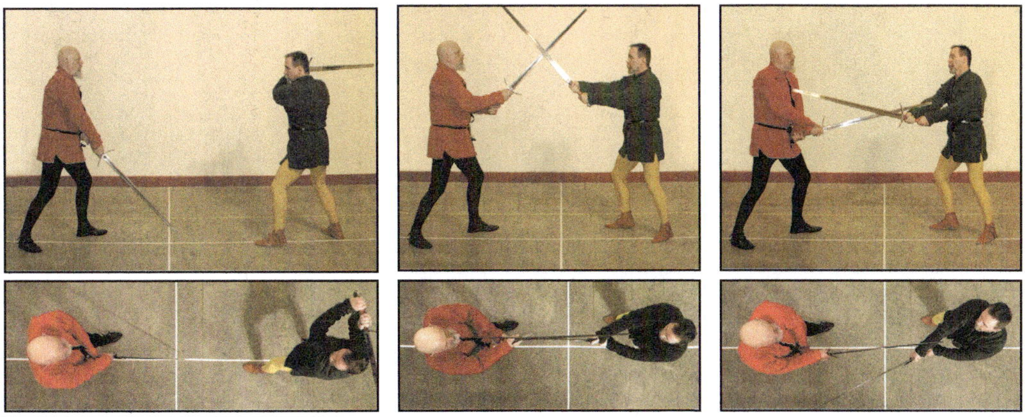

Moving from low to high, a *sottano* cut with the false edge beats away the incoming strike. You can then return with a downwards (*fendente*) strike, to the head if he is close enough or to the arms if he is not. This response will deal with thrusts as well as strikes.

SHORT POSITION
(POSTA BREVE)
STABILE

To find Short Position, stand as before in Middle Iron Gate. Raise your sword point as you step forward (*passare*). Your left hand should not rise, but your right hand will. The sword tip should stop at about chest height. Keep your elbows in close to your flanks.

Short Position is a place you will pass through during any shortened-arms strike, which is a strike in which you do not extend your arms fully. It is also where you will be when such a blow hits your opponent.

If you end in this position, you are likely close to your opponent. He may have closed more than you expected, resulting in you shortening your defense to create cover, or you may have

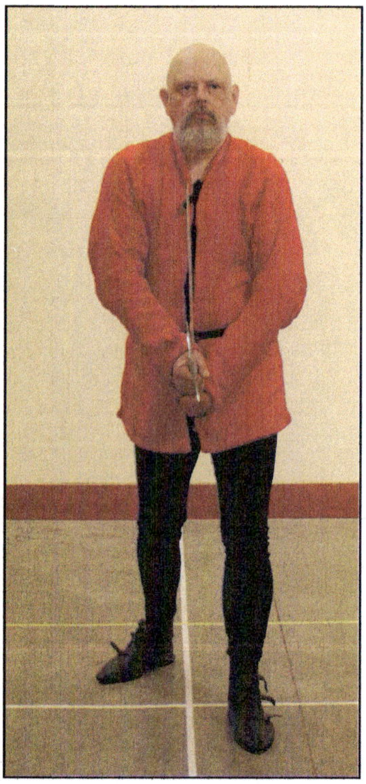

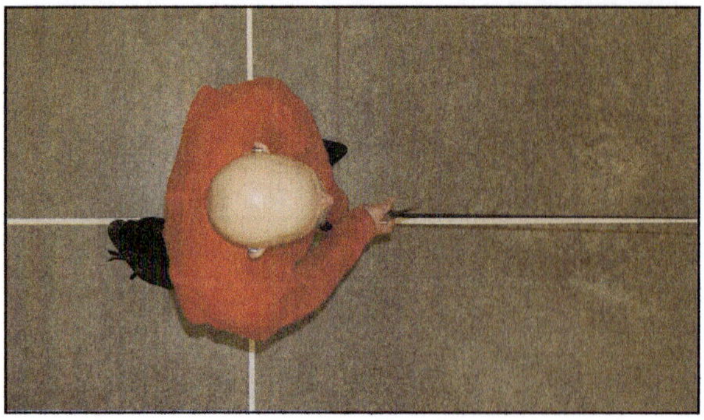

Short Position is a point guard and Fiore tells us that "the most extended guard can reach the opponent first."

This is the Posta Breve (Short Guard), which calls for a long blade. It is a deceitful guard, which has no stability. It too remains in motion and probes the opponent for an opportunity to thrust and pass forward. This guard is better in armor.

deliberately struck to this short range. These blows are commonly seen when the fighters are close together and are commonly thrown from a crossing at the half sword (*mezza spada*).

Fiore calls this guard "deceitful" much as he does Long Position. Their relationship is close. The difference lies in how extended your arms are.

When speaking of the dagger guards, Fiore said that those which could not cover long were "better in armor," and here as he gives the same advice for Short Position. As with the dagger, you play with your arms at less than full extension; thus your opponent likely is—or will get—close. Your reaction time will be limited and you are better off having armor that can protect you in case you don't sufficiently cover against an attack.

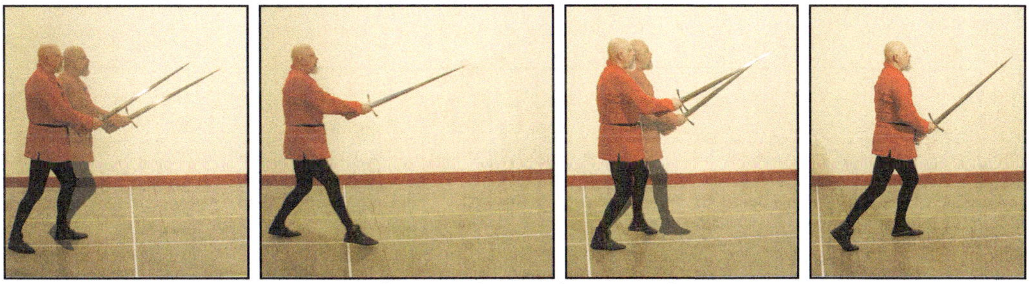

Short Position allows easy thrusts and returns to Short Position. Cuts from Short Position must be shortened cuts.

Short Position is a likely place to be when crossed at the mid-blade. You can take advantage of the situation by using elements of the art beyond what is in the plays.

Shift to Frontal Position and collect his blade with your cross. As you shove it clear, move your left hand on top of his elbow. Press it down and thereby control his sword. Your sword is now free to strike him.

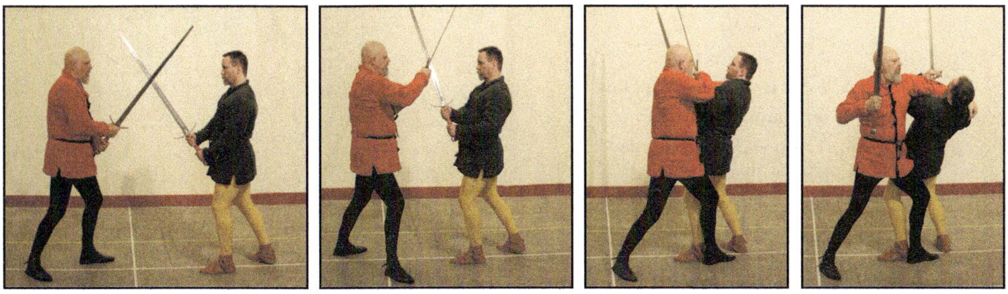

Shift to Frontal Position with a step to your right. Press down on his blade and clear the way for your arm. Step forward and extend into *abrazare's* Long Position on the left to throw him.

BOAR'S TOOTH
(DENTE DI CINGHIARO)
STABILE

To find Boar's Tooth, stand as before in Short Position. Step backward (*retornare*). Bring your left hand back and snug it up against your hip. As you move, lower your right hand until the sword's tip points at the ground. The blade should be parallel to your left leg or point a little further from the center; your right shoulder will drop to allow this.

The sword's presence on your left side means that its action in any defense will make it a threat to an opponent trying to close in.

Boar's Tooth is part of a set of low guards built around the unarmed position of Iron Gate. Each is adapted to what holding a sword in two hands does to your body structure. The others are Full Iron Gate, Middle Iron Gate, Middle Boar's Tooth, and Long Tail.

This is Dente di Cinghiaro (Boar's Tooth), since it learned its offenses from the boar. It can deliver strong underhand thrusts all the way to the opponent's face without stepping; it then comes back down with a fendente to the arms. Sometimes, it can deliver a thrust to the opponent's face, point up, while quickly extending the front foot, and recover with a fendente to the head and arms; then it immediately delivers another thrust with the extension of the front foot. It defends well against the close play.

Boar's Tooth allows a strong *sottano* up to Woman's Position on the right.

To the left, the scholar thrusts, without stepping, toward the opponent's face, then cuts down to his hands.

Above, the scholar thrusts while advancing his lead foot. Then he cuts down, returning his foot to the starting position to generate power. He immediately advances and thrusts again.

While the leg and arm positions of the Boar's Tooth master in the Morgan are close to those of the Getty drawing, his torso (judged by the central seam/closure of the garment) is notably more turned to the left. This shoulder shift will bring the sword point out wider.
The Pisani-Dossi version displays a more upright stance and less widely spaced feet. In addition, the master's left arm appears more tucked in, with the hand rotated for a more comfortable grip.

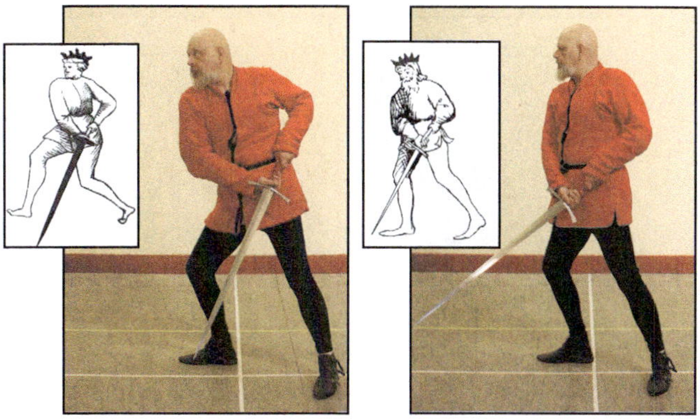

LONG TAIL POSITION
(POSTA DI CODA LONGA)
STABILE

To find Long Tail Position, stand in Boar's Tooth as before. Move both hands forward and across in front of your body. When they reach the other side, bring your left hand in toward your hip. As you do, shift your right hand further back, letting the sword swing out and around until it extends behind you like a long tail.

Long Tail, like Full Iron Gate, is held on the right when using the sword in two hands. While Full Iron Gate has a counterpart on the left in Boar's Tooth, Long Tail does not. There is no way to hold the sword in both hands on that side with its point to the rear without badly stressing the left wrist. Conceivably one might stand with

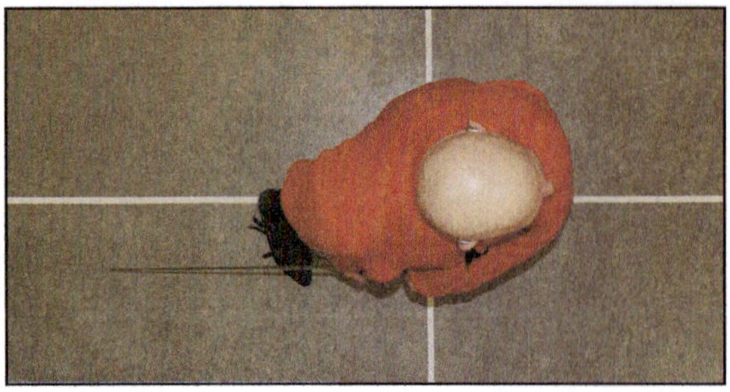

Long Tail is part of a set of low guards built around the unarmed position of Iron Gate. Each is adapted to what holding a sword in two hands does to your body structure. The others are Full Iron Gate, Middle Iron Gate, Boar's Tooth, and Middle Boar's Tooth.

This is the Posta di Coda Lunga (Long Tail Guard), extended backward to the ground. It can thrust forward, parry and strike. If it passes forward with a fendente, it enters into close play without fail. This guard is good for waiting, since it's easy to shift from this one to others.

the blade pointing out to the left (as the point stands out to the right when in Full Iron Gate), but Fiore neither shows nor implies such a guard.

This guard is easy to wait in, offering an easy transitions to most other guards that can confound an attacker expecting your sword to be too far from your defense. Sometimes a step will be necessary to respond with the proper guard.

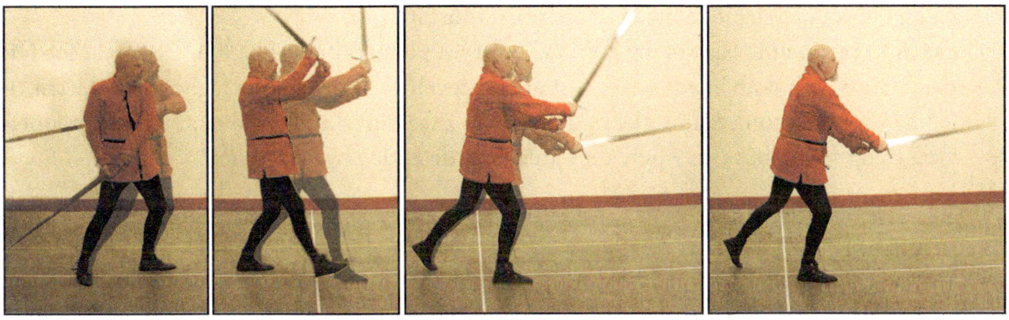

Long Tail Position can make a *fendente* by moving up to Woman's Position and then cutting towards Long Position.

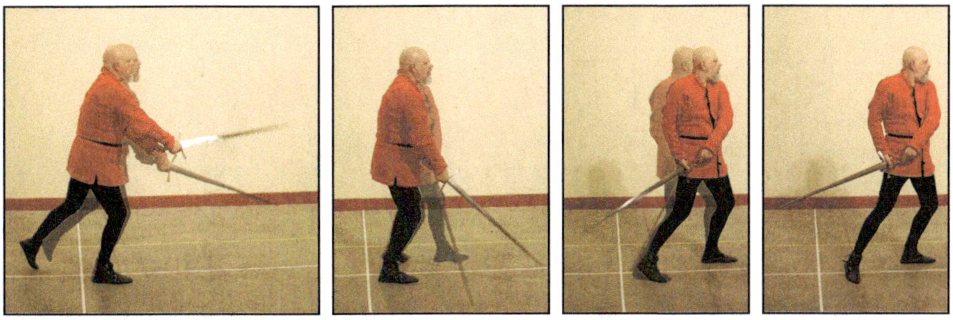

The motion can continue from Long Position and moving down to Iron Gate before continuing back into Long Tail.

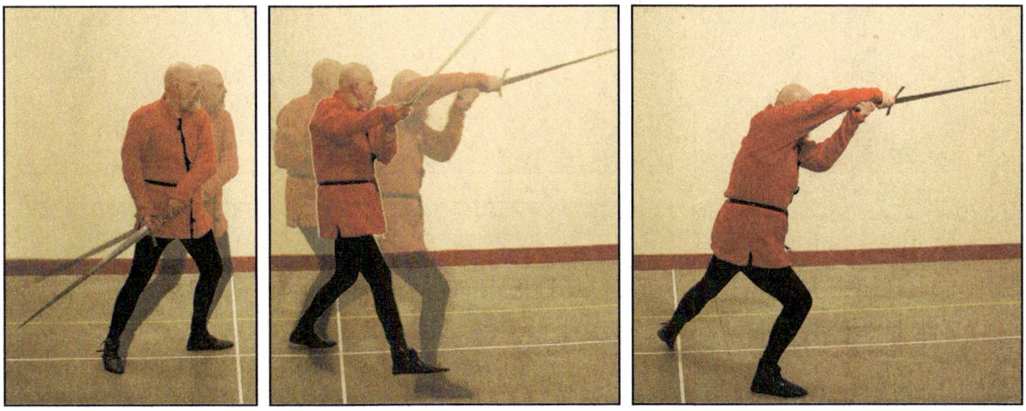

Thrusts can come out of Long Tail Position. Here, a high line thrust moves up and over on its way. To gain time to move the sword around, you often need to pass back as you initiate your thrust to keep safe from an opponent who is moving in.

TWO-HORNED POSITION
(POSTA DI BICORNO)

INSTABILE

To find Two-Horned Position, stand in Long Tail Position as before. Bring both hands forward and up, allowing the sword to swing outward and around. As the sword nears the center line, the plane of the blade should be perpendicular to the ground. A loose grip is what allows the left hand to comply; the pommel will rotate in your palm. Let your left hand rotate in sympathy, turning it to the right around the back of the pommel until your fingers have shifted to the top of the pommel. Finish with both hands near chest or chin level, the right slightly higher than the left. The left hand should snug against the right forearm. The point should be directed at an opponent's face. Keep your elbows in where they are better defended by your sword.

Two-horned Position is part of a set of high guards built around the unarmed guard of Frontal Position. Each is adapted to what holding a sword in two hands does to your body structure. The others are Woman's Position (left and right), Window Position (left and right), and Frontal Position.

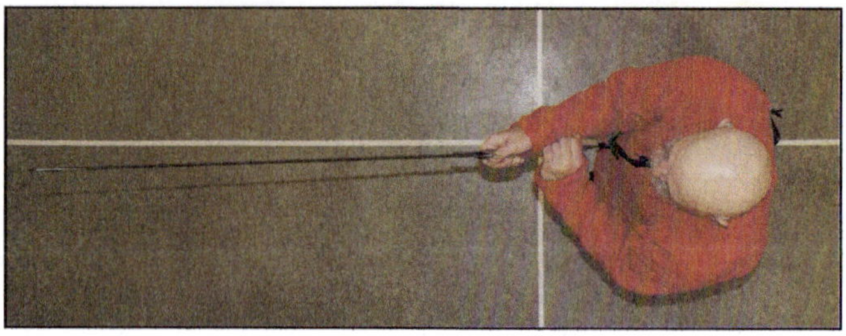

This is the Posta di Bicorno (Two-horned Guard), which stays closed so that the point stays on the centerline. It can do all that the Posta Longa can, which is also true of the Fenestra and the Posta Frontale.

The text says that Two-horned Position can do all that Long Position can do. When you follow that guidance, remember that this guard is neither as extended as Long Position nor as withdrawn as Short Position. This can affect your play.

Another feature of this guard is that your closed hand position makes the extended sword quite strong against pressure trying to push it aside. Among other things, this makes it very good in an exchange of thrusts.

The other manuscripts show this guard held with the right foot forward. Like the other centerline guards, Two-horned Position may be held with either foot forward.

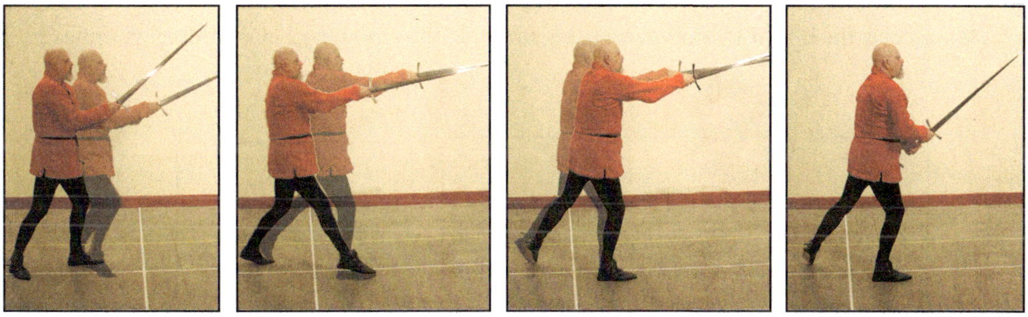

Two-horned Position is a centerline, point-forward position whose primary threat is a thrust.
Here, the thrust is made with a pass forward and the scholar recovers to Short Position.
Below, are detail shots of the left hand rolling into position.

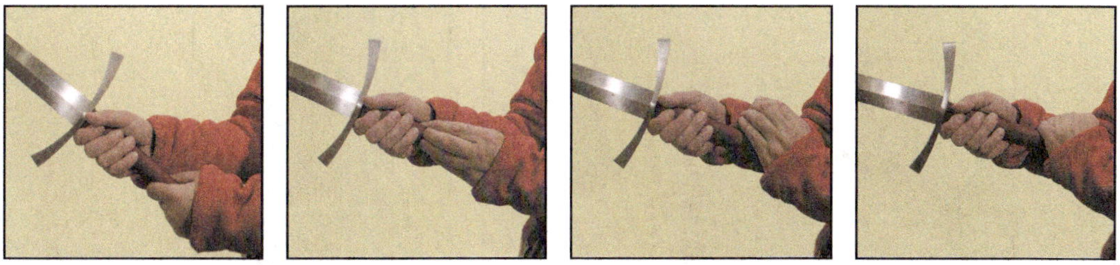

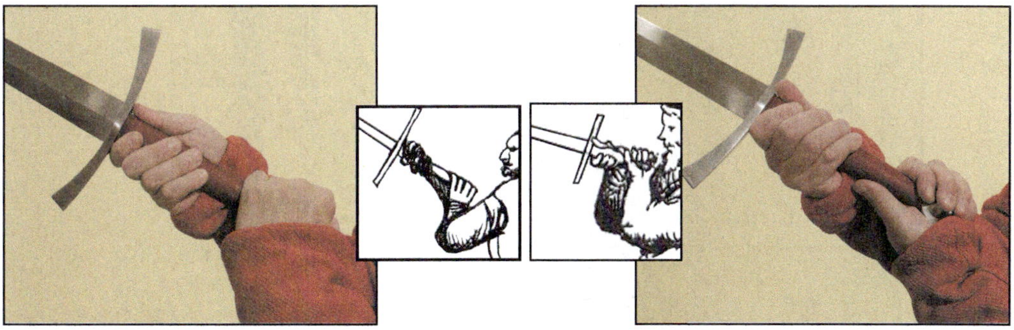

The Getty and Morgan manuscripts agree on the master's hand position (left) but the Pisani-Dossi shows a very different hand position (right).
Practice indicates that this is an alternative grip that may be easier for some students to achieve.
Incidentally, the Paris manuscript clearly shows the master's left hand cupping his sword's pommel.

FRONTAL POSITION
(POSTA FRONTALE)

INSTABILE

To find Frontal Position, stand as before in Two-horned Position. Raise your right hand, rotating it so that the palm faces up. Your left hand needs to be loose on the pommel; it will essentially reverse the motion you made to go into Two-horned Position. Turn it towards left and around the pommel while shifting it forward as you return to a more normal grip. As your hands turn raise the tip of your sword, pulling your right hand a little closer to you.

The drawing shows the sword's crossguard just above eye level. In practice, the height will vary according to need. The crossguard must protect your head.

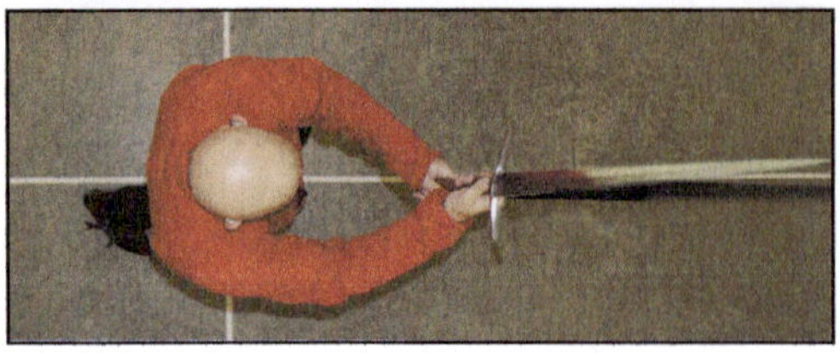

Frontal Position is part of a set of high guards built around the unarmed guard of Frontal Position. Each is adapted to what holding a sword in two hands does to your body structure. The others are Woman's Position (left and right), Window Position (left and right), and Two-horned Position.

This is the Posta Frontale (Frontal Guard), which some masters call the Guard of the Crown. This is good for crossing the opponent's sword, as well as against thrusts. Against a high thrust, cross the opponent's blade while passing out of line. Against a low thrust, also pass out of line, beating the thrust to the ground. You can also operate this way: against a thrust, pass back while delivering a fendente to the head and arms down to Dente di Cinghiaro, then immediately follow with one or two thrusts with the extension of the front foot, and finish with a fendente that gets you back in that guard.

According to the text for Two-Horned Position, Frontal Position can do everything Long Position can do. While you can come into this position with your point as a threat, arriving in it reduces or eliminates that threat. Because of that, this guard does not offer the same provocation that Long Position does.

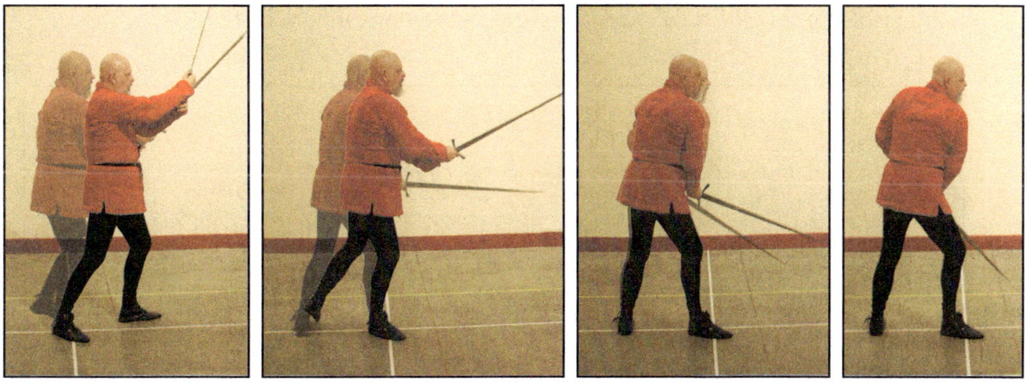

Frontal Position makes close range cuts (here a *fendente mandritto*) down to Boar's Tooth. Often you may have to pass back to create space.

Frontal Position holds the center against a high-line thrust by deflecting it. Once you clear the point, make a cut.

Frontal Position holds the center against a low-line thrust by breaking it. Once you clear the point, make a cut.

MIDDLE BOAR'S TOOTH

(DENTE DI CINGHIARO LO MEZZANO)

STABILE

To find Middle Boar's Tooth, stand as before in Frontal Position. Bring the sword tip down, turning the blade so the true edge is down. Step backward (*retornare*). As you do, bring your left hand back towards your hip. Keeping the sword point in the middle, make a Stable Turn (*volta stabile*) to your left. Keeping your sword's point in the middle will prevent you from snugging your left hand to your hip as you do in Boar's Tooth, which would pull your sword's point away from the center.

As held here, Middle Boar's Tooth uses a heels-forward orientation. Like all guards, it can do the Stable Turn (*volta stabile*) and present in a toes-forward orientation.

Middle Boar's Tooth is part of a set of low guards built around the unarmed position of Iron Gate. Each is adapted to what holding a sword in two hands does to your body structure. The others are Full Iron Gate, Middle Iron Gate, Boar's Tooth, and Long Tail.

This is middle Dente di Cinghiaro. ... It is called middle because it is in the center of the body; what the other Dente di Cinghiaro can do, this can do as well. And just like the boar strikes at an angle, from this guard the sword always strikes at an angle to the opponent's. From this guard, always attack with thrusts, uncover your opponent, mess up his hands and sometimes his head and arms.

Middle Boar's Tooth is similar to Middle Iron Gate of the dagger; both are a version of their respective guard that places the point in the centerline while keeping the body turned away.

Fiore's advice to "always attack with thrusts" from this guard makes it clear that thrusts are the strongest, and most likely, attacks from guards with the point on the centerline.

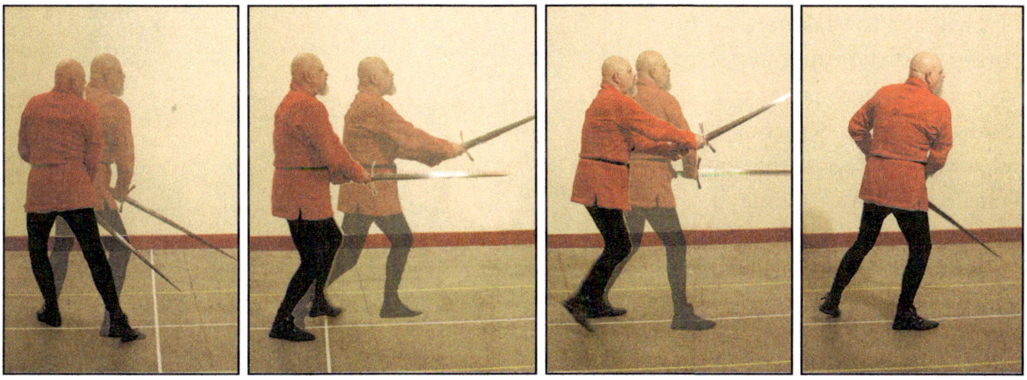

Middle Boar's Tooth makes a powerful thrust from below. Here, it begins with a Stable Turn, then a pass while thrusting to Long Position. The scholar recovers in Boar's Tooth. He could return to Middle Boar's Tooth by making a Stable Turn.

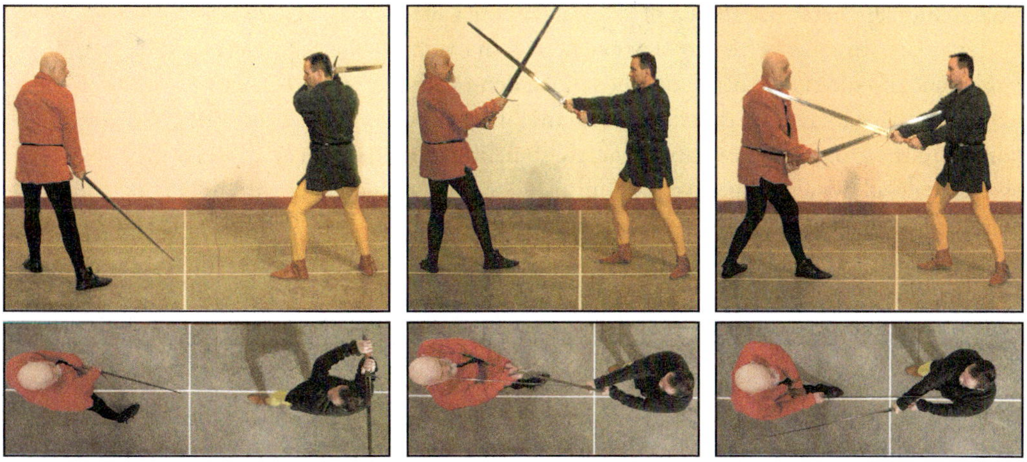

Because Middle Boar's Tooth can do what Boar's Tooth can do, it can do what the Boar's Tooth master does against three sorts of attacks. Here, the scholar starts by shifting his lead foot off line. He then cuts up, using a rising cut (*sottano*) with the false edge to beat away the incoming attack. This strike is powered by a Stable Turn (*volta stabile*). With the opponent uncovered, he returns with a downwards cut (*fendente*), again powered by a Stable Turn.

The First *Largo* Master's sword crosses at the point

Here begins the play of two-handed sword, in wide play. This Master has crossed his sword at the point with this opponent, and says: when I am crossed at the points, I quickly turn my sword and strike the opponent on the other side with a fendente to the head and arms; or I thrust to his face, …

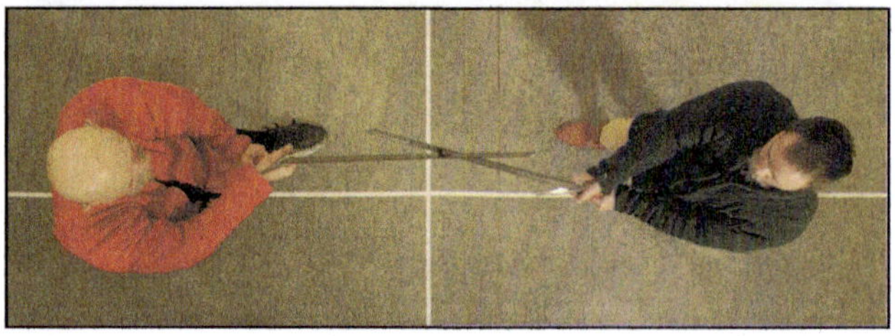

The swords cross above the midpoint of the blade. If you are in proper measure to hit each other, your points will end high.

Leverage is weak here for both parties, and you cannot establish a proper bind because of that. This makes it very likely that one or the other will move across the centerline with his blade. And this may happen quite quickly.

If he moves your blade, quickly shift it to the other side of his sword and cut down without stepping, using a twist of your torso to power the cut. His head or arms are your target, which the sword can conveniently reach. Be certain to keep your hands low so that your blade will be in position to intercept his sword should he generate his own attack from the crossing.

If you are stronger in the crossing and start to move his blade off the center line, drop your point and slide along his blade. The scholar demonstrating this thrust (in 25rD) has his hands relatively high as he thrusts. Indeed, the Morgan version shows the scholar's sword parallel to the ground and his elbows nearly straight and wrists slightly canted down. This sword angle allows a stronger part of your blade to remain in contact with his, giving you a leverage advantage that allows you to keep his sword displaced as you thrust to his face.

Whichever move you make, do not step in. This is *zogho largo*, where you want to play wide and stay wide.

THE CUT

THE THRUST

The Second *Largo* Master's sword crosses at the middle

Here we are crossed at the middle of the sword, in wide play. As soon as the cross is made, I glide with my blade over his hands, and if I pass with the right foot out of line, I can push a thrust to the opponent's chest, as you will see directly.

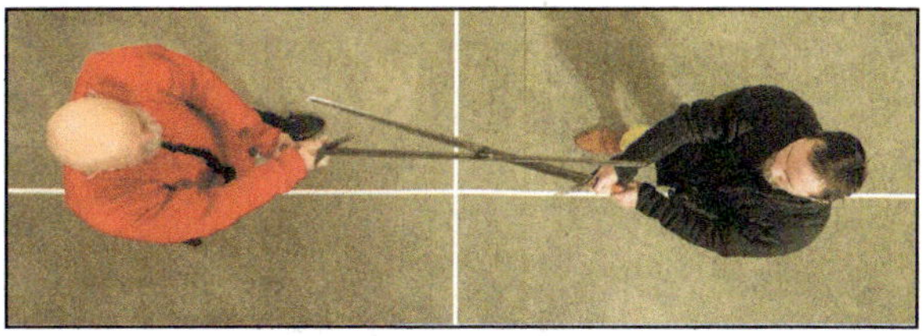

The swords cross at the mid-point of the blade. Crossing at this point puts you in danger of having your opponent initiate close play. The plays of this master, as Fiore presents them, are for when you want to play wide and stay wide.

If the crossing is close to equal, which is to say if your opponent is neither especially strong nor weak in the bind, you can slip your blade down along his and cut his hands or arm. Unlike what I showed on the previous page, this time your sword remains on the same side of his.

If your opponent is not neutral in the cross, what you do will depend on his strength in the bind and your understanding of what he might do next. Remember, your goal is to remain at distance and to keep him from closing that range.

The alternative play from the cross involves stepping out of the way and making a thrust. Your sword must remain where it can offer you cover against his weapon.

Cut to hands

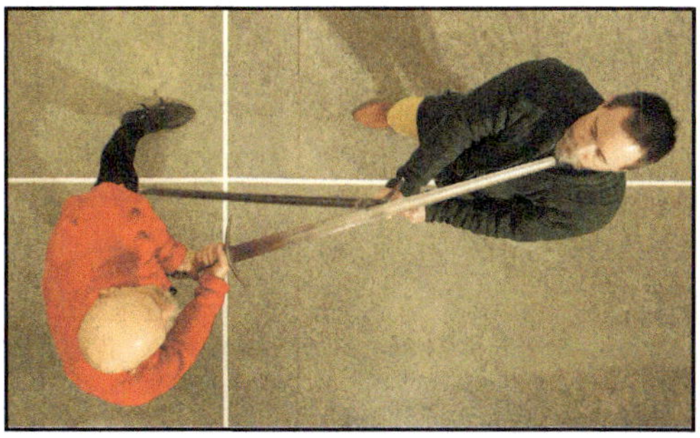

Step and thrust

He is in the center and giving neutral to weak pressure

... first I wounded the opponent's arms, then I placed a thrust into his chest.

If his sword is moving away, the thrust is made easily with a step on your part. If his blade is still on yours, you must make your thrust in opposition, turning your blade so that the cross will protect you from the threat of his blade.

His pressure puts his point to your left

... I should step forward immediately and grasp his blade as shown, so that I can strike him with a cut or thrust. ...

Your attack is made at the same time as the grab. As the two actions are nearly simultaneous for you, you will hit him before he can react. Even so, you must be prepared to let go if you feel him pulling or pushing on the blade. Moving your hand in the direction of his pull/push makes your release safer.

He leaves the bind and tries to cut low to your leading leg

... withdraw the foot you have forward or pass back, and deliver a fendente to his head ...

Withdraw your lead foot as soon as you recognize that he is going low. If you take your foot no further than your other foot, you should be able to strike him in the head. It is simple geometry; he is making the hypotenuse of a triangle with his sword while you are making a shorter leg with yours. If you make a full pass backwards, you may take yourself too far back to hit him. That's okay, because you still have a leg and can fight on.

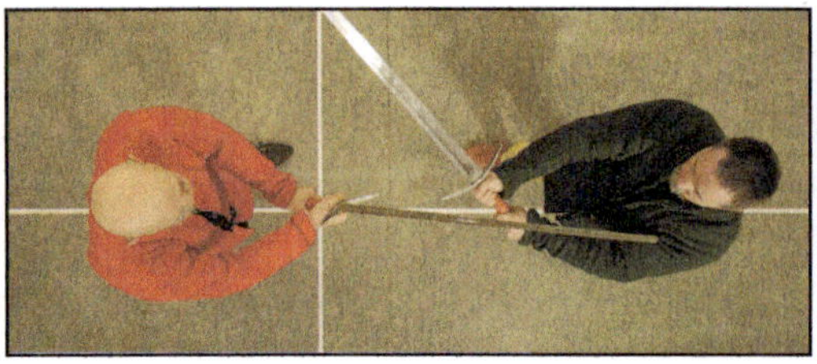

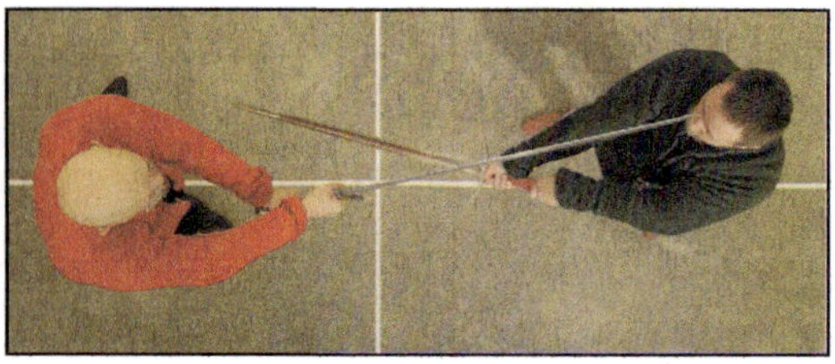

He forces his sword in or up

I'm kicking you in the balls to give you pain and make you miss your parry. …

Strong pressure in the bind may be a sign of an untutored swordsman or he may be preparing to shift to *zogho stretto*. A kick will forestall his coming in.

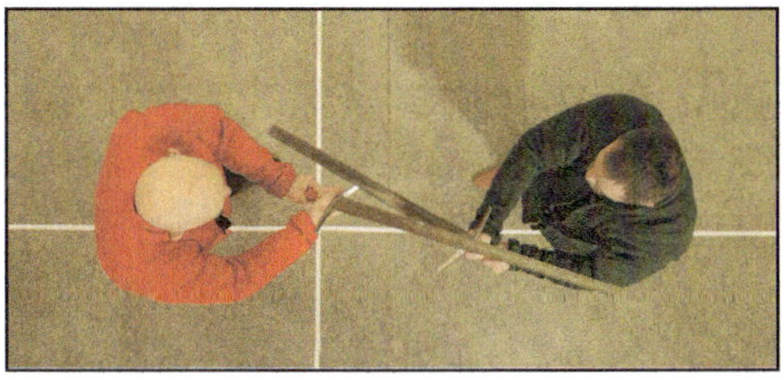

He gives strong pressure or tries to force your sword to your right

Let his sword glide to the ground, and immediately respond with a fendente to the head or arms, or with a thrust to the chest …

Following the mechanics of the "peasant's blow" play, you allow your blade to be pushed aside and you use the energy provided to turn your blade around to the other side of his. In this case, his sword is unlikely to go far, so instead of stepping across in the space between you, simply twist in place, using your torso to power your attack. Be sure to make your cut or thrust in such a way as to keep your sword positioned so that if his blade comes back at you, you will have cover against it.

A small step back with your rear foot can offer additional safety and keep the play wide.

Both options start with him displacing your sword.

The upper sequence ends in the cut and the lower in the thrust.

The Second *Largo* Master's sword crosses at the middle

... Wait for the peasant to launch his cut with his sword. As you wait, stand in a narrow stance with your left foot forward. When he attacks, step with your left foot offline to the opponent's right, then perform an oblique pass with your right foot, catching his cut with the middle of your sword. Let his sword glide to the ground, and immediately respond with a fendente to the head or arms, ...

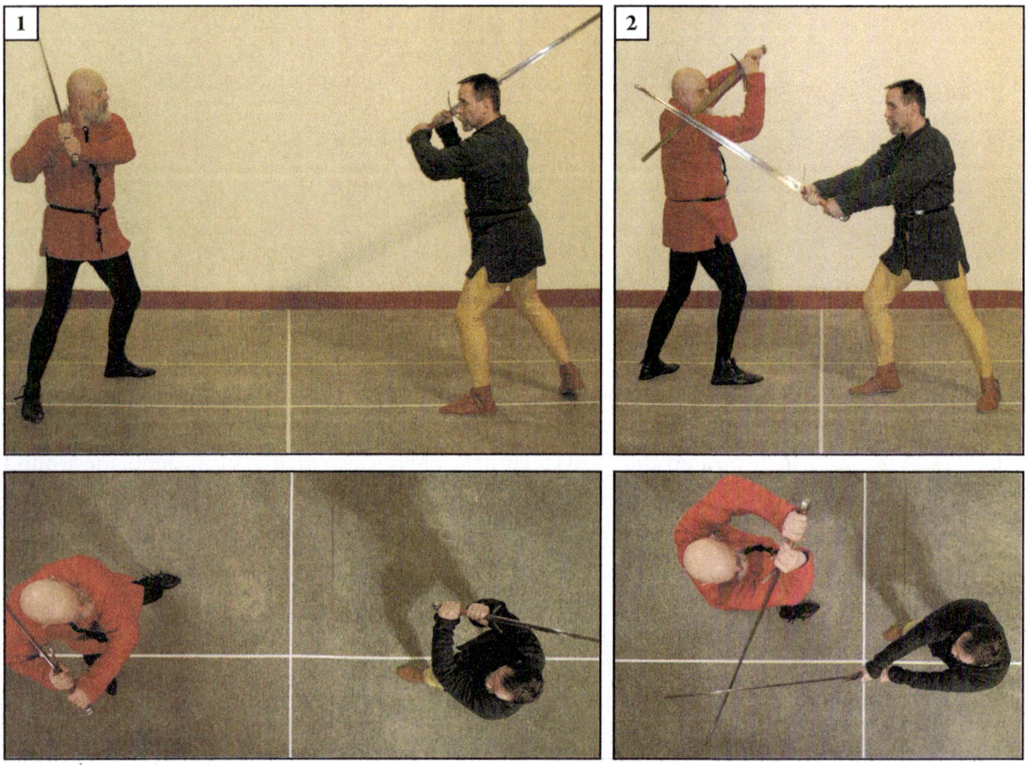

The text accompanying this play indicates that it doesn't exactly start from the crossing of the blades, but it uses the crossing for its effect.

You start in a "narrow stance," by which I think Fiore means your feet are closer together than usual. As he starts to move, step with your lead foot off line and to your left as has already been done in the first picture above.

Immediately pass obliquely across to the same side as you bring your sword in to meet the oncoming blade. You do not, however, intend to stay at the cross. As you come to the crossing, push your pommel forward and let the energy of your opponent's strike push your blade out and down.

As this happens, step back with the foot you just brought across and direct that energy around and into a cut. The tighter the circle through which you guide your blade, the more powerful a cut you will make. The step back keeps you at distance from your opponent.

Fiore's stepping instructions have led to differing interpretations about where and how to step. As this is a *zogho largo* play, you should step so that you maintain your distance from your opponent. The step with your right foot will go across the line, but only briefly takes you closer to your opponent, as shown in the interpretations below. Your first step offline with your left foot will determine whether your cut hits head or arms; you will need to vary how far forward and how far offline you step according to your opponent and the circumstances of the encounter.

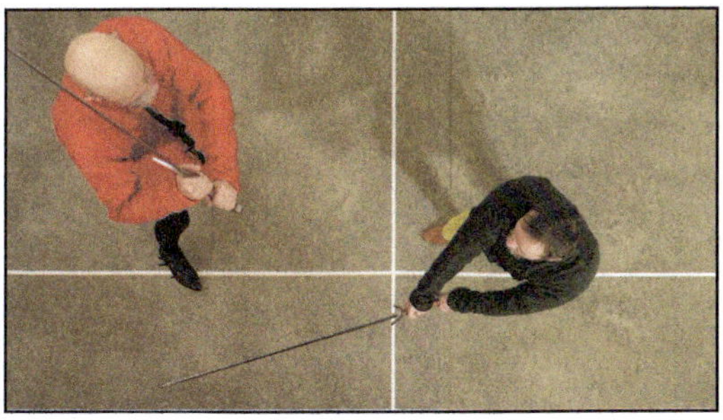

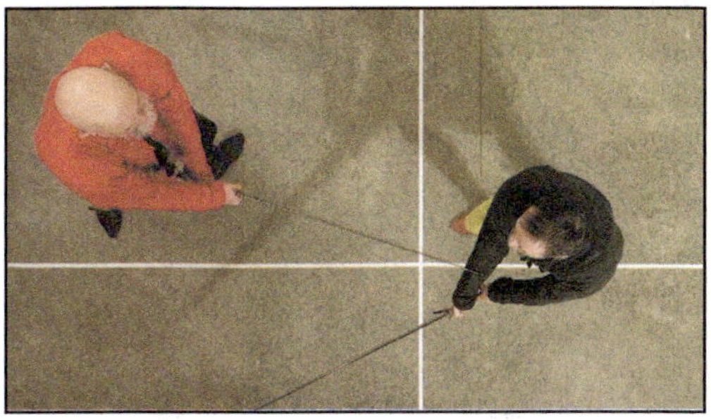

... now, I have put my point into the opponent's chest.

Instead of a cut, you can bring your sword around and thrust. Be sure to keep your hands low and point high so that you are well placed to respond to him if he tries "to counter with a *riverso.*"

... If the opponent tried to counter with a riverso under my arms, I would immediately step forward with my left foot, place my sword over his and he wouldn't be able to do anything.

If he is quick to cut back up (*riverso*), you can bring your sword down on his blade rather than directly attacking him. This will establish your dominance over his blade and allow you to go for a follow-on play such as those that come after the breaking of a thrust. See page 172.

The Second *Largo* Master's sword crosses at the middle

This play, called exchange of thrusts, is done this way. As the opponent attacks you with a thrust, step out of line with your front foot, then pass obliquely also offline, crossing his sword with your arms while thrusting in his face or chest with your point high, as shown.

This response is an exchange of thrusts; he makes one and your action drives his point wide and positions your point to come in on the centerline.

As this is a play of the Second *Largo* Master, your left foot is leading. Move it offline—but not forwards—as he starts to thrust. Keep your hands low and point high, meet his sword blade. As the blades slide across each other, you should be on a stronger part of the blade than he is. Your step across the line with your right foot will emphasize this. Keep your hands to your left side so that you will be "crossing his sword with your arms." This action, with the power of your body behind it, will shove his point away while you take on the proper structure to hold your point steady on target. Your opponent should impale himself on it.

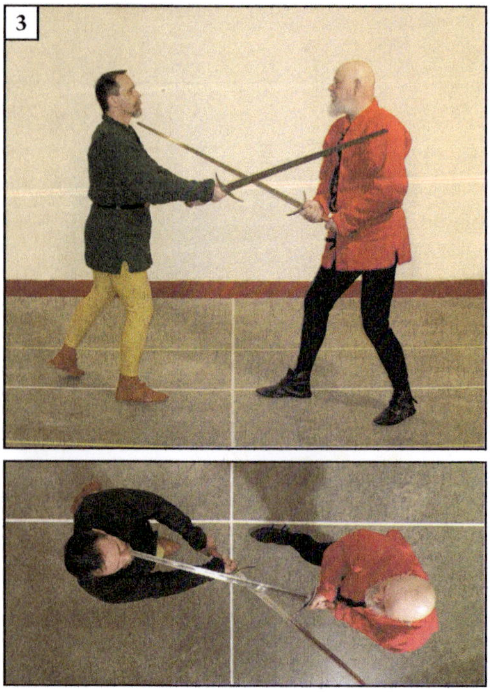

This play derives from the exchange of thrusts we just saw. Let's say the student in the play before me didn't immediately thrust to the opponent's face; let's say he instead hesitated with his point without directing it to the opponent's face or chest, because the latter was in armor. In this case, the student should pass forward with his left foot and grasp the opponent in this manner. Next, he should use his sword to strike, since the opponent's sword has been grabbed and he cannot escape.

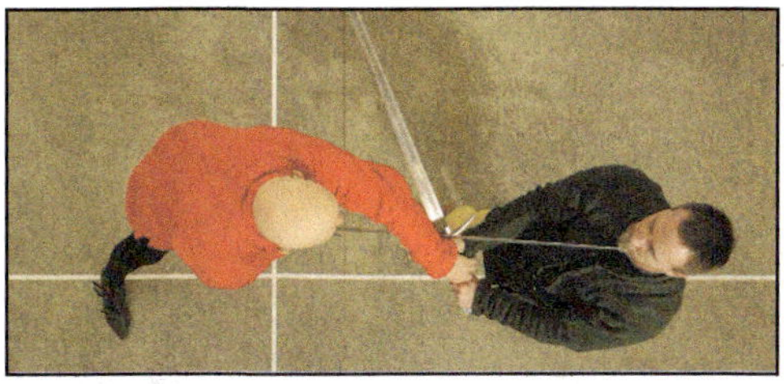

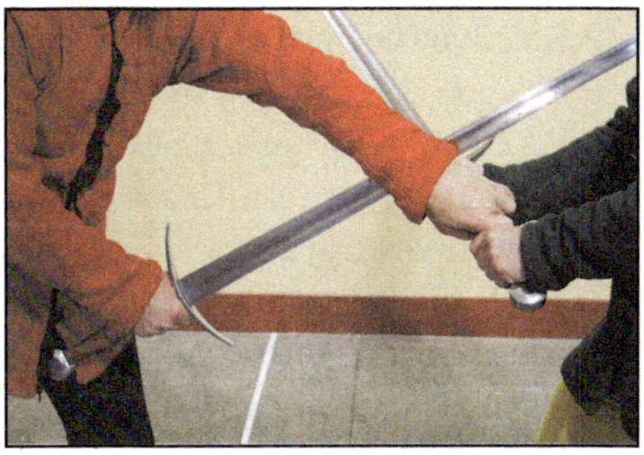

This play is related to the previous one, covering a change in response if you do not get your point on-line, or hesitate long enough that your opponent begins to recover from having his point shifted off-line. The drawing suggests that you might not have made the step with your trailing foot to structure your body for the counter-thrust.

In any case, you have succeeded in getting your opponent's thrust offline, but have not actually exchanged his thrust for yours. Having lost the momentum, you must do something to recover the initiative.

Your must keep pressure on your opponent's blade. Step forward with your left foot, using your body weight to control his blade. You need your body, because you are about to release one of your hands from your sword handle. Reach with your left hand over your sword and grab the handle of your opponent's sword. You now have control of his sword and can slide your blade back and free from his. Strike him without hesitation.

The Second *Largo* Master's sword crosses at the middle

This is another way to defend against a thrust. ... you need to step and pass offline .... In this play, which is called breaking the thrust, the student has his arms high, makes a fendente while stepping and passing offline and throws the opponent's thrust sideways, almost at mid-blade, to beat it to the ground. Then, he immediately goes to the close play.

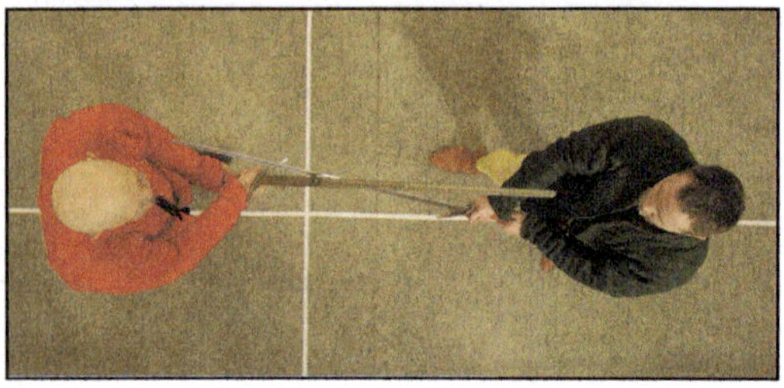

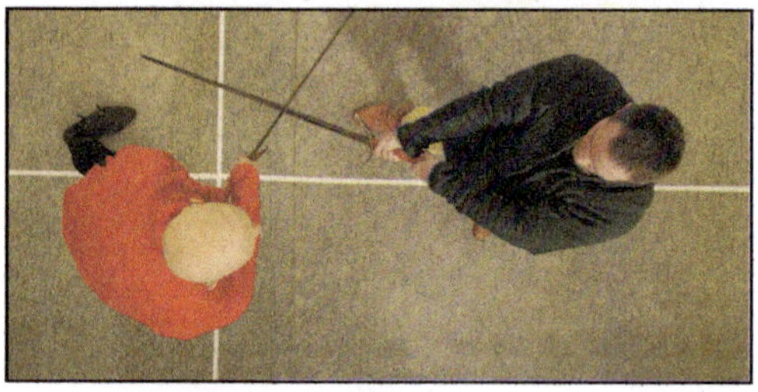

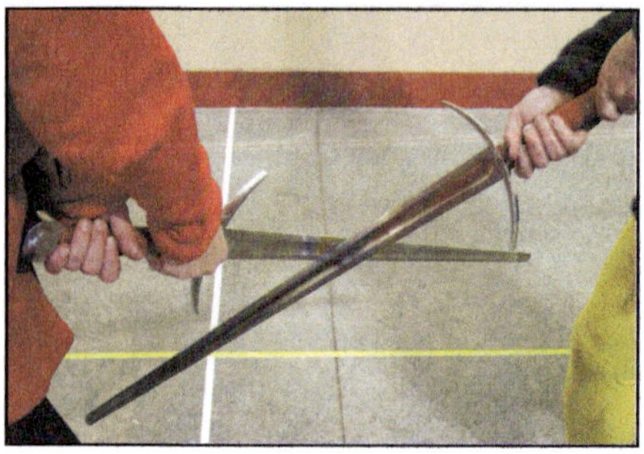

This play introduces the "breaking" of a thrust, which you do by striking into it and beating it away. The text says that you should be starting from a position where your arms are high, which suggests one of the upper guards, a seemingly different starting position than the crossing of the *Largo* Master.

Here we follow the directions of the text. Assume you start with a left-foot lead as your opponent begins a thrust. Step forward (*passare*) offline to the right as you cut downwards (*fendente*) into his blade.

The text calls for immediately going to close play. If you have driven his blade to the ground, you can safely pass in with your left foot and initiate close play because you have removed the threat of the opponent's sword.

The breaking of a thrust can be done with a right-foot lead as well, but with all directions reversed.

However, if your intent from here is to play wide and stay wide, you should pay attention to the follow-on scholars on the next page.

... After beating his sword to the ground, I forcefully place my right foot on his sword, ... as soon as I have done that, I strike him under his beard or in the neck with my false edge, and immediately come back with a fendente to his arms or hands, ...

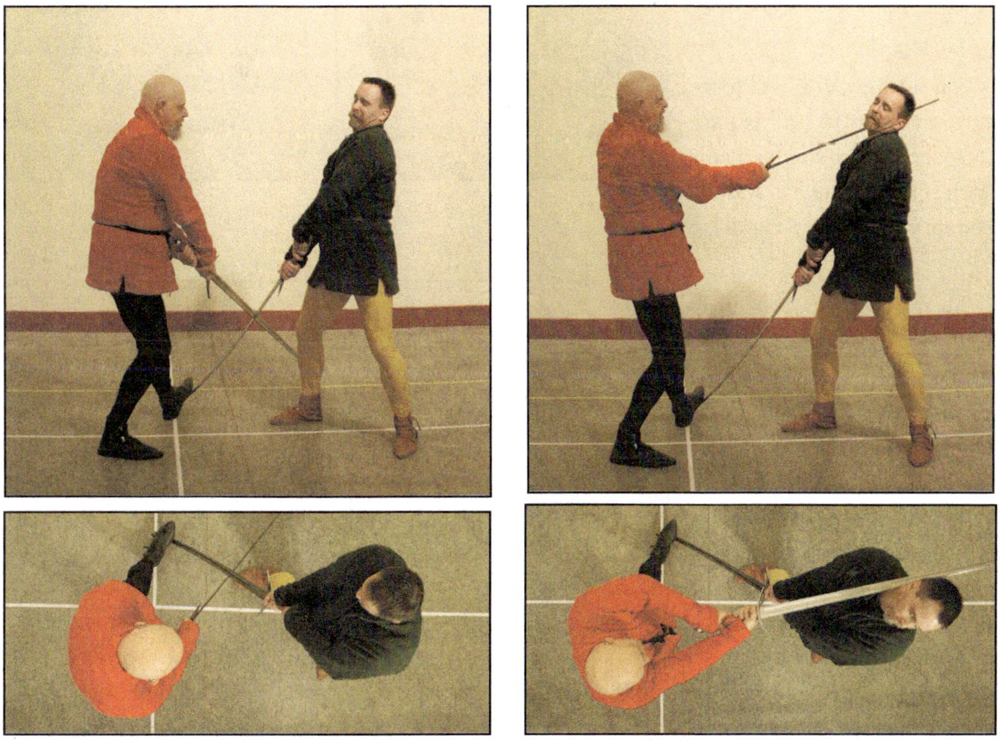

Once you have broken the thrust, you can stomp the blade with your foot. This ensures that it remains down and unthreatening. The text says "right foot" but the foot you use will depend on where his point ends up. In a real fight, you would want to stomp hard on the blade, but for training you don't want to break your partner's blade, so go easy.

Lift your blade from his, cutting up under his jaw. Return with a downwards cut against his arms.

This play can be done whether you break his thrust so that his sword point goes on the ground to your left or to your right.

Alternatively, you can use the energy from the cut you used to break the thrust to power around, circling and cutting down to his head.
As in other circumstances, you can thrust instead of cutting.

The Second *Largo* Master's sword crosses at the middle

Playing wide and staying wide is the name of the game in *zogho largo*. Whatever your opponent does from the cross, you want to keep him from closing.

If when you grab his sword, you kick to his lead leg as you hit him, you will forestall any attempt on his part to close to *zogho stretto*. If you catch him after he has started to step, you may even knock him down.

If he raises his sword in the cross, he offers his lower openings to a kick attack. His groin is a soft target, even in armor.

That lifting of the sword, however, may not be a peasant's mistake. He could be trying to set your sword aside so he can safely close. Your kick will forestall any attempt to close, even if you miss his groin. Note the scholar in the drawing is not leaning backwards; your kick must maintain an upright or forward-oriented body structure. This allows you to resist his advance even though you are only standing on one foot, and you also stay balanced if you are in armor.

The text with this scholar says his play can come "after beating the opponent's point or crossing his sword." So however you get your chance to make the elbow strike, you use it to keep your opponent at bay.

By making this strike using the *abrazare* guard of Long Position, you rock your opponent back and keep him literally at arm's length. If your opponent has already started to step, he will likely be turned by this strike since he would momentarily be on one foot. His step is using the natural pivot point of the ball of his grounded foot, and the force of your strike redirects the action of that pivot.

... I feint a strong mezzano to the opponent's head. As he forms his parry, I lightly strike his blade, then immediately turn my sword to the other side, grasping it almost at mid-blade with my left hand. I can then place a quick thrust to his throat or neck. ...

The text says this play starts with a feinted strong *mezzano* blow, but it can be done from the crossing of the swords if the pressure conditions are right. Strong pressure from him to move to your right will produce a displacement if you do not resist him. This corresponds to the circumstances of his defensive response the threatened strong *mezzano*.

To do the play, do not resist the pressure, however it is generated. Shift the blade around, moving the point to the other side of his blade. As you do, bring your right hand down and back as you step to your left and let go with your left hand. As your blade clears his, grab your blade near the mid-point with your left hand. Extend your left arm as soon as your point is on target with his face or neck. This must be done very quickly.

The counter

... I turn mine around his in the same manner, while with an oblique pass I find the opponent's uncovered side. I then can put a thrust in his face. ...

To counter, he makes the same move you did. With his sword on top, he has superior leverage and can control you sword as he thrusts at your face.

Into *zogho stretto*

If you do not wish to stay in *zogho largo*, you can step forward to help drive your thrust home. If play continues from here, it will be *zogho stretto*.

THE *STRETTO* MASTER'S SWORD CROSSES AT THE MIDDLE

We have crossed our swords: this is the crossing from which we can make all the plays that follow. Both of us could perform each of them. ...

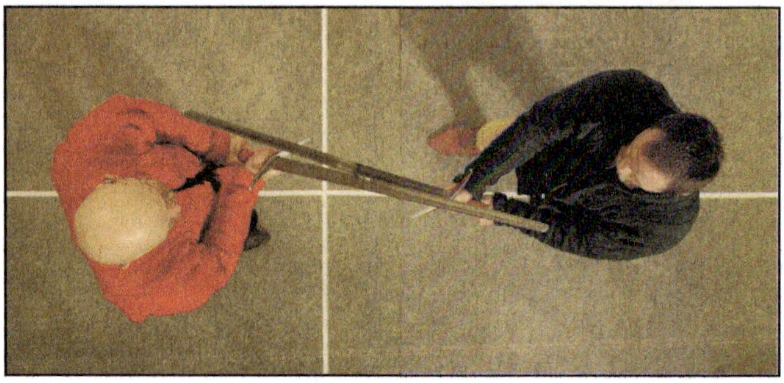

Unlike in the *largo* crossing at mid-blade (*mezza spada*), both players in Fiore's drawing have a right foot lead. This means each is capable of making the step that will allow them to touch their opponent's body, which is to say, each can enter *zogho stretto*.

The first scholar of this master tells us that his play "... can be executed with the one- and two-handed sword, and can come from an over- and under-handed crossing." Since he is a scholar of his master, it follows that his master may make over- and under-handed crossings.

If you come to the cross from a lower guard by making a rising cut (*sottano*) that leads with the false edge, you will find yourself in an underhand crossing; your false edge will be against his blade. If you come from a high guard by making a downward blow (*fendente*), you'll be in an overhand crossing with your true edge against his blade.

UNDER-HAND CROSSING

OVER-HAND CROSSING

A general counter to the *Stretto* Master appears in the sixteenth play

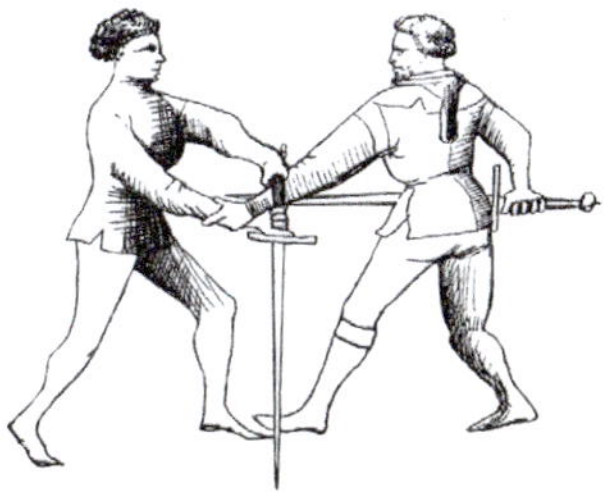

If I cross into close play with someone, I can immediately do this grapple to prevent him from trying any disarms or grapples of his own. I can strike him with thrusts or cuts without any danger.

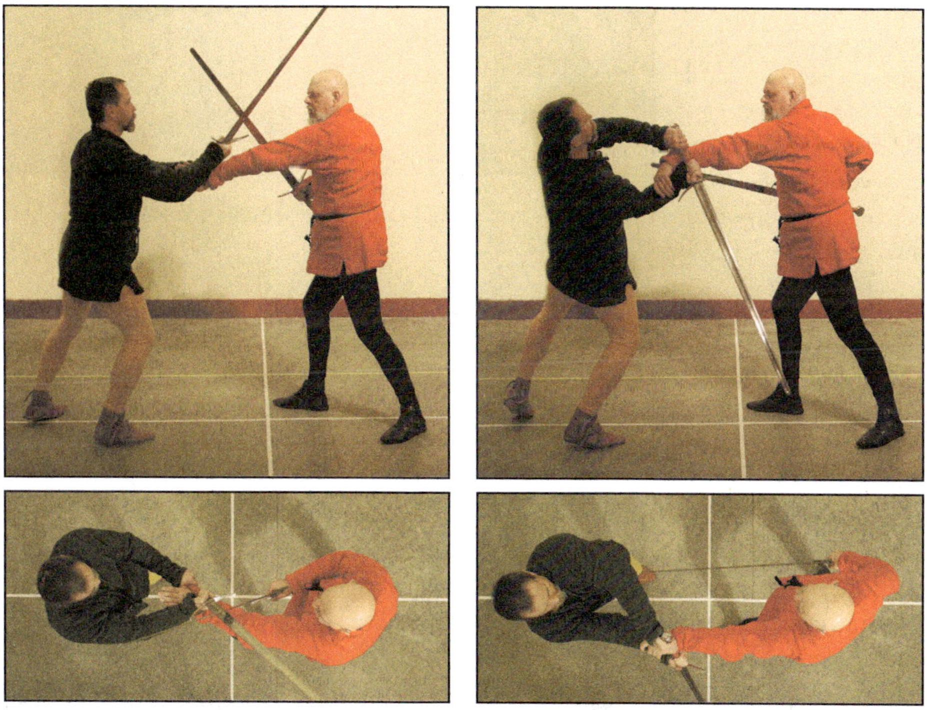

Although this play is shown with a scholar rather than a Counter Master, his action is that of a Counter Master because he answers the Remedy Master and prevents his and his scholars' plays.

From the crossing, reach under his sword's handle with your left hand to grab his right wrist. Once you have the grip, step in and rotate your hand as though your were starting a dagger disarm. The pressure of your arm against his handle, supported by your body as you step, pushes his sword wide.

If he keeps his left hand on his sword, he will have enough strength to prevent a disarm, but he will be tied up. While he struggles, cut or thrust at him with your sword.

The scholar's hand reaches under the opponent's sword handle, heading for his arm.

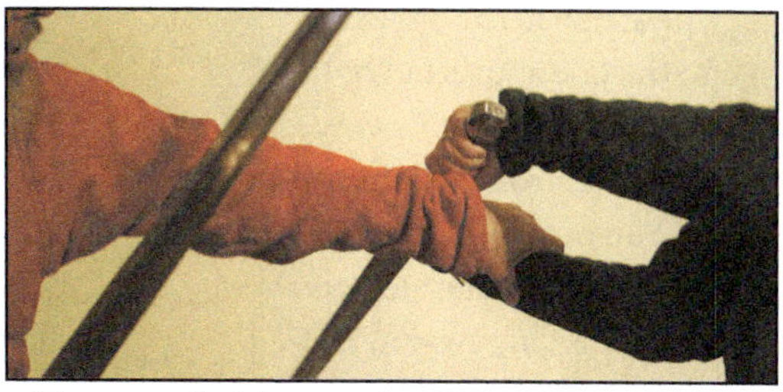

Having reached the arm, the scholar takes his grip and twists.

He is weak in the bind or shifting to your left

. . . . I pass with my left foot, while going with my left hand over my right arm and grasping the handle of the opponent's sword between his hands; that is, at the center of the handle. I can now strike him with a cut or thrust. . . .

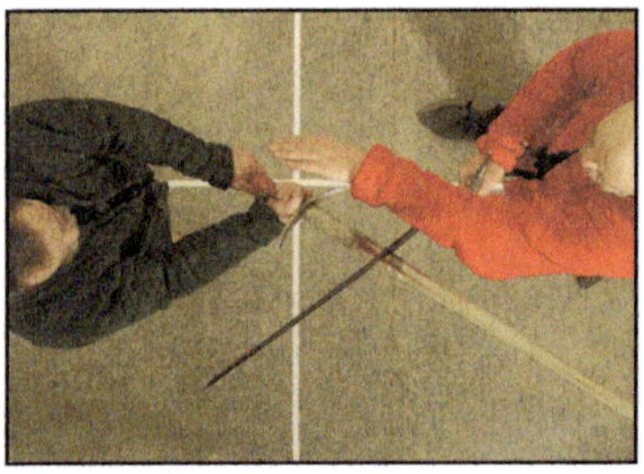

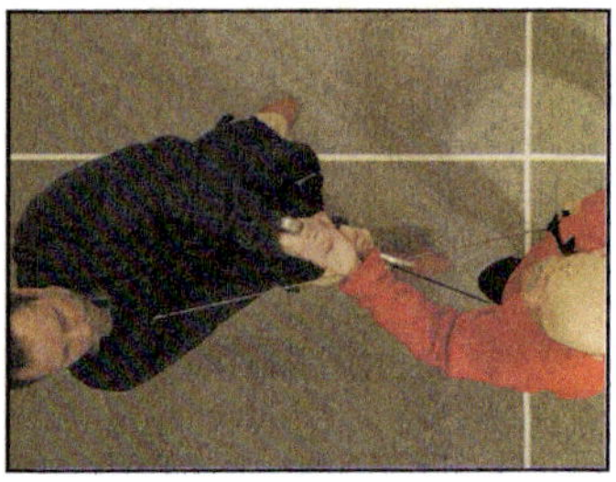

If he is not going far enough left, encourage him with the pressure of your blade, supported by your body as you step forward. As you step, reach over your sword with your left hand and grab his sword handle. With his sword controlled, you can strike him as you wish, or do as the scholar does and thrust beneath your own arm.

He stays in the center with pressure

. . . Grasp the opponent as shown and strike him in the face with your pommel. You can also cut a fendente to his head before he can parry.

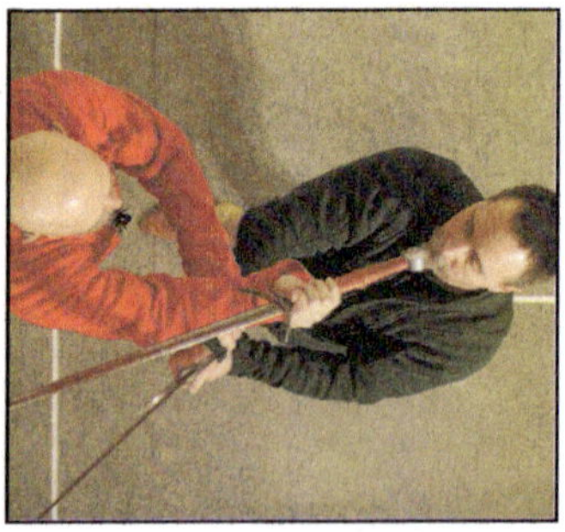

Using the blade contact point as a pivot, raise your sword hilt beside his blade. Your left hand goes to his arm, to control his sword when your blade leaves his. Shove your pommel into his face as you step forward.

He is strong in the bind or shifting to your right

Here's another pommel-strike. You can do it at once, and if his face is uncovered, do it without fear. . . . If you want, you can also whip your sword around his neck, . . .

The action here is very similar to the one above, but both hands remain on your sword. This yields a stronger pommel strike. You can do this because his sword is far enough to your right or is moving away in that direction.

He lifts his hilt in the bind; it is on your left

If someone parries on the riverso side, grasp his left hand and his whole pommel with your left hand and push him backward; then you may strike him with thrusts or cuts.

The necessary pre-condition here is that the opponent's hilt in the crossing is on your left side. If he raises it, shoot forward with your left hand, stepping into Long Position, and drive his sword high with your grip on his pommel. Your sword is now free to cut or thrust.

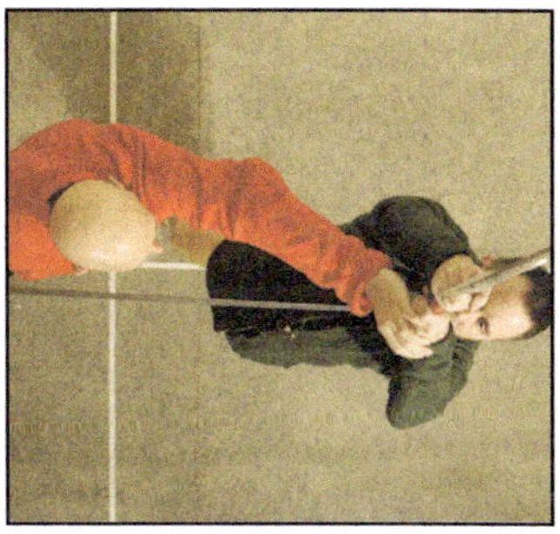

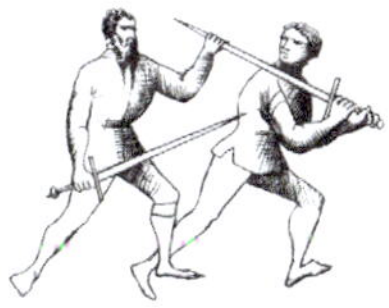

He lifts his hilt in the bind; it is on your right

If someone parries from the mandritto side, grasp his sword with your left hand as shown and strike him with a thrust or cut. If you want, you can cut his face or neck with his own sword as you see in the picture. …

A parry from the *mandritto* side will leave the opponent's hilt on your right side, away from your grasping hand. If he lifts his hilt now, the target for your grab is his blade. Get it before it can threaten you, again stepping into Long Position to force it away, and strike immediately.

He lifts his sword

… I put my hilt between your hands, and lift your arms with your point high. I will now throw my left arm over your arms, to my left, and strike with your sword under my left arm …

If he lifts his whole sword in the bind, go along with him, rotating your pommel forward and slipping it between his hands. Use this control to keep his point high as you put your left arm to go over both of his arms, enveloping them.

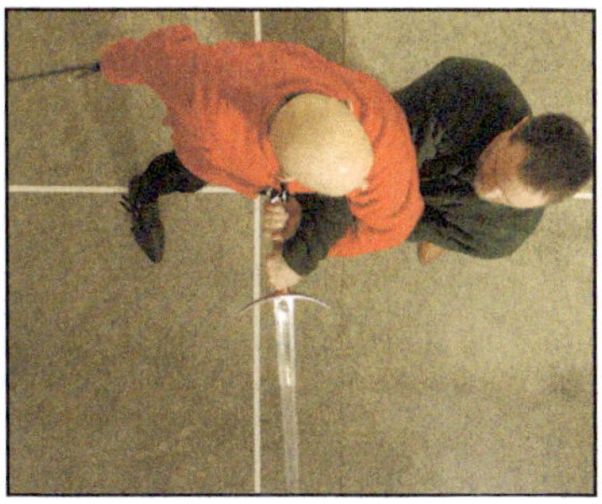

The *Stretto* Master's sword crosses at the middle

This play comes from a play of dagger—the first Remedy Master. In that, the left hand was used to disarm the opponent by placing it under the dagger; similarly, the student here places the left hand under the opponent's right hand to disarm him. Or, he can then place the opponent either in a middle bind, as the play that follows the first Remedy Master of dagger mentioned above. And that bind belongs to this student.

From the crossing, shoot your left hand in under his sword handle and grab his wrist. Your sword must remain on his while you do this or he will hit you. Grip his wrist and seek *abrazare's* Long Position. As you are twisting his wrist, you draw right hand back as you would while preparing to strike as in the dagger disarm play, letting the sword blade trail behind. You might hit him as his sword leaves yours; this is a benefit. If you do not, your sword should be well positioned to thrust into his face. Do so.

If your hand goes too deep to make the disarm, you can go for the Middle Bind (*ligadura mezzana*). Slip your hand behind and under his elbow. Make a Stable Turn (*volta stabile*) as you seek Boar's Tooth *abrazare* position on the left. This creates the Middle Bind (*ligadura mezzana*).

Note how his sword's handle lies over your arm as a dagger does when positioned for the corresponding disarm.

This alternative Middle Bind treats the sword like the forearm of a dagger-armed attack, placing pressure at the wrists.

I am the Counter, and … I won't believe my eyes if I see the opponent still standing after I'm done with him.

As he goes for the Middle Bind, shift your left hand to the blade of your sword while using your right to lay your blade against his shoulder. This new grip links your two hands, giving you the structure used when reversing this lock while using a dagger. Levering the blade against his shoulder, reverse the bind against him by moving your left hand down and your right up. You can do this with a Stable Turn (*volta stabile*) or you can step across in a Half Turn (*mezza volta*) to add even more power to your binding.

I am the Counter … Slitting his throat would be going easy on him. And I can also throw him to the ground as quickly as I want to.

As he starts the Middle Bind, release your left hand grip and roll your right hand over towards your center. Tilt your sword down over his shoulder and grip the blade with your left hand. To make the play in the drawing, as soon as you have your grip, advance (*accressere*) into *abrazare's* Frontal Position. This will force your blade's edge into his throat. If he is unarmored, a simple shift will slit his throat. If he is protected from that, you can make your advance a deep one and use your blade to force his head back. This will over-balance him and send him into a backwards fall.

This sequence shows a variation where the countering player passes in (*passare*). The blade edge is still forced into the throat. He essentially advances into *abrazare's* Long Position while using the locked-up arm as a pivot point for rotating his victim out of balance.

The *Stretto* Master's sword crosses at the middle

The High Disarm

Your left arm goes over both of his. Press down and to your left while using the handle of your sword to apply pressure against his blade, forcing it to the right.

This is a high disarm. I hold my sword and push forward with the left hand, squeezing his arms until he abandons his weapon. Then, I can give him a good dose of strikes. The student after me shows the opponent's sword on the ground.

The Middle Disarm

Your left hand goes between his. Press into his wrist and up while using the handle of your sword to push right and down.

This is a middle disarm—if you can do it. The turn of the sword is the same as in the first, although the grapple is different.

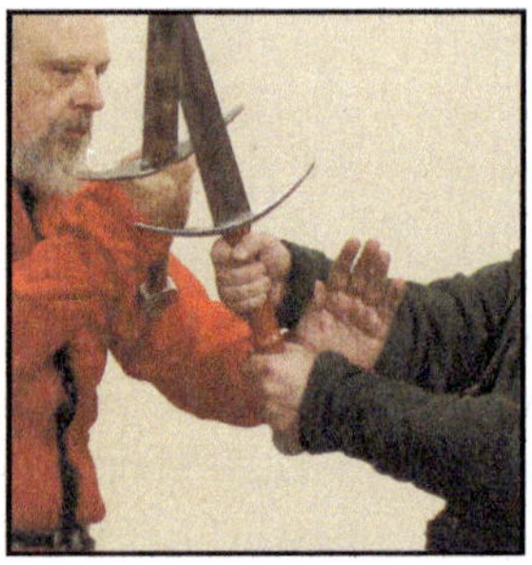

The Low Disarm

Your left hand grabs the pommel of his sword. You will pull up and to the right as you lever right and down with the handle of your sword against his blade.

This is another disarm, called low. This is similar to the way the low and high are performed, that is, the path of the sword is like the others. I use my right hand, pressing forward and giving a turn to the handle; the left hand must follow this turn.

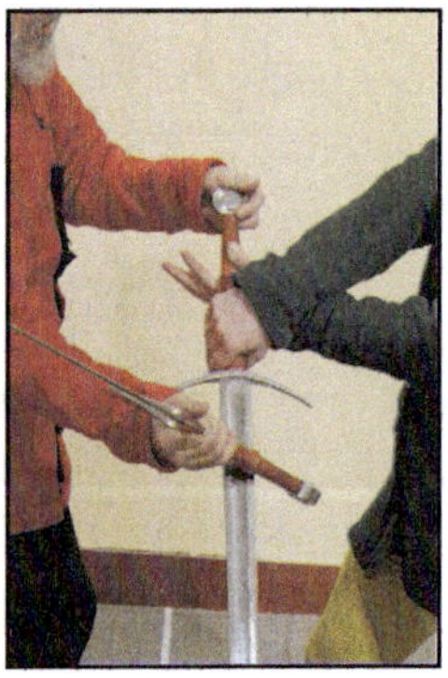

The Empty-hand Disarm

Here's another disarm. When you are crossed in close play, put your right hand under your sword and grab that of the opponent almost in the middle, nice and straight, and immediately drop your sword. Grab the underside of the opponent's pommel with your left hand and give it a good turn to the left, which will cause him to let go of his weapon.

While at the cross, let go of your right hand grip first (an unusual move for Fiore). Shoot it under your own sword and grab his about mid-blade. Then drop your own sword and grab his pommel with your left hand and begin the turn. Do this all very quickly!

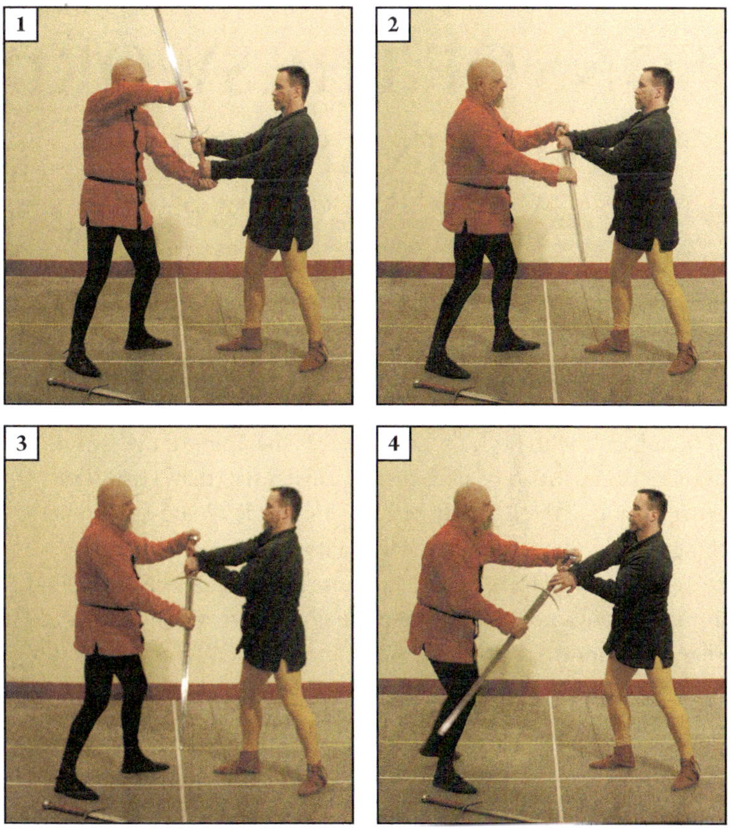

... the path of the sword is like the others ...

The path of the sword is the same in all of these disarms. Rotation starts in a plane parallel to the plane of the opponent's shoulders. This twists his arms and locks up his grip. When your left hand nears the top of its circle, he should be thoroughly jammed. At this point a 90° shift of direction will rip the weapon from his grasp. Passing back with your lead foot as you do this adds energy to your move and does not expose your elbow (or worse, all of you) to his counter-attack as would using a turn (*volta*) in the direction you have been turning the sword to power the disarm.

Handheld weapons give us no worry, and we defend handily against cuts and thrusts that may come our way.

LESSONS OF THE SWORD

SWORD IN ARMOR

The sword in armor section is the first in the Getty where the players are illustrated wearing armor.[1] It begins with six Fight Masters. All but one of these hold their sword with one hand on the blade and the other on the grip. This grip is called half-blade[2] (*mezza mella*), although the Germans refer to it as half-sword (*halbschwert*). Most of the players using this grip hold their hands with the thumbs towards each other. Some hold their hands with both thumbs towards the point of the sword. The differences in the grip seem to be more preferential, or perhaps circumstantial, than significant with respect to technique. In fact, the first scholar of the Remedy Master shifts his left hand around between the cover and the action, something rather unlikely to happen in reality.

The odd Fight Master out is *Porta di Ferro Mezzana*, whose master holds his sword in the usual sword in two hands way. This master looks no different than the one shown among the sword in two hands masters save that he wears full armor.

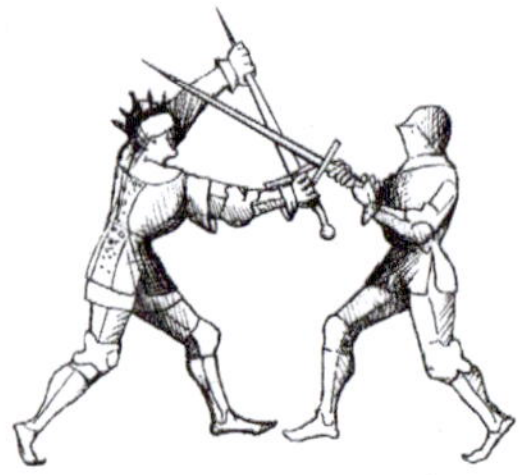

Remedy Master of the sword in armor (33rD)

This section's only Remedy Master is shown making the cross against a player who has made a thrust, presumably from *Porta di Ferro Mezzana*. Of the fifteen plays that follow, only eight are direct scholars (and one of those may be something else). One is a general Counter Master and another is that master's scholar.

The first scholar does a familiar action. His master's cover has intercepted the incoming thrust and set it aside, and the scholar immediately thrusts. We have seen this in the other sections of the sword. Here Fiore reinforces

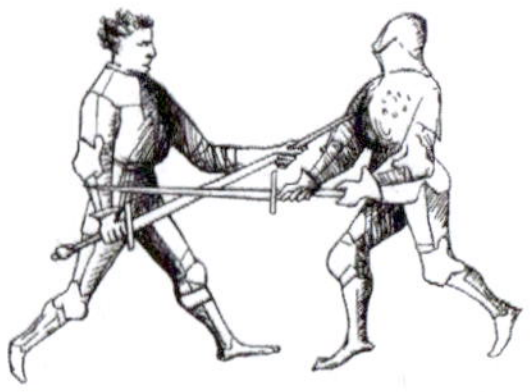

First scholar of the sword in armor (33rD)

[1] The players in this section of the Morgan, however, are not shown wearing armor.

[2] Unfortunately Fiore gives us no clear terminology for this grip. The phrase *mezza mella* appears in Vadi to describe gripping the blade. It is worth noting that he uses blade (*mella*) rather than sword (*spada*) in this context.

The sixth scholar plays against the opponent's shift to the right (34rA)

The seventh scholar plays against a left shift with his crossguard (34rB)

The eighth scholar plays against a left shift with his pommel (34rC)

the lesson while covering the slightly different mechanics of doing it with the half-blade grip.

Armor being armor, it can resist attacks. The next three scholars offer different ways to deal with resistant armor. One opens the opponent's visor and tries again. One turns the opponent with an elbow push and tries the strength of his back armor. The third goes for a the Lower Bind (*ligadura sottana*), which his follow-on scholar completes.

The next scholar (above left) introduces the leverage mechanic for using a sword in the half-blade grip to make a throw. The following pair (above center & right) use the other end of their sword against the opponent, offering a use of the sword's crossguard or pommel to strike. Taken together, these scholars deliver the important lesson that the half-blade gripped sword works at both ends, often pivoting around the middle to bring one of the other into play.

These first direct scholars also combine to give Fiore's usual lesson in pressure response. The first scholar can thrust more or less in the center because of the opposition of his blade. The scholar using his blade tip to throw (again, above left) plays more easily when the opponent tries shifting to the scholar's right while the two scholars that play with their hilt end (again, above center & right) deal with a shift to the left.

The ninth scholar[3] plays against an opponent using the half-blade grip (34rD)

The ninth scholar, according to the text, ought to be a follow-on companion to the pommel-striking scholar, offering the knowledge that a throw can be done from that side as well. The text, however, does not acknowledge that the position shown is notably different. Here the opponent is also holding his sword in the half-blade grip, as he will be doing against the rest of the scholars. The scholar achieves his throwing position by moving his pommel under the opponent's left arm as he pivots on the blade. He forces his foe's arm up and hooks his neck with the pommel.

The next two scholars make the point that they cannot use their swords effectively. They "resort to wrestling with the sword" and demonstrate the two basic ways a sword in the half-blade grip can be used to generate throws and create locks. The first uses the bar of the sword's blade as a link between his hands to make a grip around the opponent's head for a throw. The second uses the blade end to create a leverage point against his opponent's arm. He could almost as easily use the pommel end as the ninth scholar does for a throw.

The thirteenth scholar may be a Counter Master (34vD)

The last scholar (right) at first appears to be another scholar resorting to wrestling. However, in the Morgan, the corresponding play is the last one and the acting party is marked out as a Counter Master. Although still marked as a student's play, this is also the last play of sword in armor in the Pisani-Dossi. As the last two plays of the Getty's sword in armor section do not appear in

[3] The drawing is modified from the Getty's to show the scholar's blade beneath his opponent's and to thereby bring it into line with the corresponding drawings in the other three manuscripts.

either the Morgan or the Pisani-Dossi, this suggests that the Morgan's Counter Master is intended to be a general Counter Master. Experimentation with the play suggests that it can work both from the opponent's position in the Remedy Master's play and from a crossing where both players hold their swords in a half-blade grip. The path from each starting position is somewhat different. The mechanics of this play are strongly related to one in the *stretto* portion of the sword in two hands section, the sixteenth play after the *Stretto* Master. In this play, the active player levers against the sword's grip rather than the opponent's arm. Interestingly, while this also is a scholar's play in the Getty, both the Morgan and Pisani-Dossi show it as a Counter Master's play. If considered as a counter, this play fills the niche of a general Counter Master and seems to separate the *stretto* scholars into principal and variants groups as noted previously. The strong relation in mechanics argues that the sword in armor play ought to be a Counter Master as well. Fiore has used multiple general Counter Masters before (see First Remedy Master of the dagger), so doubling up on the masters in this section is a possibility. The play is placed where a Counter Master should be in the Morgan and the Pisani-Dossi and where one might be in the Getty. Along with the strong affinity to the similar *stretto* play, this argues for promoting this scholar to a master, despite the fact that only in the Morgan is he a crowned master.

Tenth play after the Stretto Master in the Pisani-Dossi (carta 23a C)

The last two plays are a Counter Master, who "is the counter to the Remedy Master and all his students," and "the student of the Counter Master." The Counter Master's technique is the familiar elbow push. The student strikes the turned opponent, although here the text calls out targets specifically vulnerable while in armor: in the right armpit (as illustrated), the back of the head under the aventail, under the skirt, and in the back of the knees.

The last two positions on the last page of the sword in armor section each have a drawing of a peculiar sword along with text to describe it. The first is "equally a sword and an axe" and its blade is unsharpened except for the last six inches or so. Despite its sword-axe nature, this is not quite the same as the notional weapon depicted in the hands of the last Sword-holding Master. This second sword has a dedicated gripping place on the blade. Its crossguard and pommel are "sharp, strong and well tempered" unlike typical fighting swords. These weapons would seem to be specifically optimized for fighting in armor and, although Fiore does not say so, may be intended for use in formal combats such as deeds of arms or judicial duels.

Fighting in Armor

Much ink, real and digital, has been spilled debating which medieval weapons can and cannot penetrate medieval armor. While the fine details can, and will, be argued about for a long time, some general statements can be made.

Mail armor (not the butted junk you may have seen destroyed by weapons on television) resists cutting very well, especially when worn with padding beneath. Padding helps its resistance to penetration by points as well, but thrusts and other point impacts can punch through mail. Mail's flexibility means it will deform under impact pretty easily.

Plate armor is rigid and doesn't deform except under significant force. It is better than mail at standing up to a point and significantly better at resisting cuts. A large part of plate's resistance is due to its curvature, which helps prevent edges and points from catching and thereby transferring the full force behind the blow. Like mail, plate is more vulnerable to point impacts than cuts.

Fiore's described attacks against armored men are preferentially targeted at weaker points in the armor (such as armpits and the backs of knees where the defense, if any, is mail) or intended to slip past or around the armor (as in the previously described attempt to slip under an aventail or skirt of mail). To end a fight, these are the targets one must seek. Even then, the armor may be too strong to penetrate, and so Fiore advises things like moving it (lifting a visor) or ending the fight with *abrazare* techniques.

Surprisingly, few researchers consider whether damage can be caused if the armor is not penetrated. Much is said about softening up an opponent in *abrazare* with strikes to open the way for more decisive techniques, but few acknowledge that similar techniques can be used in armored combat. Surviving linings from helmets are quite thin and, while offering some shock resistance, they cannot compete with modern impact-resistant foams in lessening shock. A strong, double-handed blow to the head will get someone's attention. It is also true that powerful blows against flexible mail can damage the tissue beneath, even break bones, without actually damaging the armor. Since Fiore is advocating pommel strikes to an armored man's head, he must think that there is some advantage to be gotten from making an attack that is unlikely to defeat the armor.

IT'S UP CLOSE

Using the half-blade grip to make a cross, as the section's Remedy Master does, puts the player fairly close to his opponent, whom he can touch by taking no more than one step. Most of the scholars' plays involve advancing even closer.

The half-blade grip cannot actually strike long. While it is true that cuts can be made with the portion of the blade extending beyond the user's hand, that blade is of necessity shorter than the sword's full length and the linked grip prevents it from outreaching a man's arm. Looked at in a certain way, this grip means you have a downwards-grip dagger in one hand and an upwards-grip one in the other. Certainly that's how those ends can be used, modified by the fact that each hand is rigidly linked to the other by a sharp bar, of course. And a dagger is a notorious short-ranged weapon that is "in love with close play." The fourth Sword-holding Master, who uses the half-blade grip, says he is a good guard that can "fend off a dagger": another sign that this grip finds its utility in *zogho stretto*.

Although the last scholar of the Second *Largo* Master tries to use this grip in its extended form, this grip is essentially of *zogho stretto*. That scholar conveys the one way to try to use the grip at *largo* and it is immediately dismissed by the Counter Master, who ends the *largo* section of the sword in two hands by shifting his own grip to half-blade and taking the action to *zogho stretto*.

IT'S ALL RELATED

By now, you should know that I am going to point out that the *Porta di Ferro Mezzana* master represents a link to the techniques of sword in two hands. Further, the last Fight Master, standing in *Posta de Croce Bastarda*, can also be found among Sword-holding Masters, who are their own statement of the sword instruction unity.

Porta di Ferro Mezzana (32vD)

Sword in armor general Counter Master (35rA)

The Counter Master's text in this section provides us with a rule: "every counter performed against a Remedy Master is equally effective against the Remedy Master's students." To make sure we understand the universal applicability, Fiore specifically says this means "with the lance, the axe, the sword, wrestling and the rest of the art." This Counter Master uses the elbow push, which in the dagger section was said to be "good in every close play of dagger, axe, sword in armor and sword unarmored." This combined instruction makes the elbow push as close as it gets to a universal counter technique.

SHORT SERPENT POSITION

(POSTA BREVE LA SERPENTINA)

To find Short Serpent, start with you hips squared up against your opponent and your left leg forward. Turn your torso to the right, opening your hip structure in a classic Iron Gate stance. Keeping your shoulders aligned with your hips, grip your sword with your right hand on the handle just below the crossguard and your left on the blade just above the mid-point. If you follow the drawing, both of your thumbs will be toward the point. Hold the sword low and to your right side. The part of the blade between your hands should be near your hip. This will mean your left arm is across your body.

It is not clear whether Fiore thought this position could be held in a left-side version, which would entail the pommel being forward rather than the point. Mechanically it should work. The function of such a position could be filled by True Cross Position.

... I am the Posta Breve la Serpentina (Short Serpent Position) and I consider myself better than the others. If I give you a thrust you'll surely bear the mark.

Rather than having your right side refused in a typical Iron Gate body position, you can stand in an analogue of Half Iron Gate with your hips squared up. This will reduce the potential power held ready but increase response time to your left side.

Held as it is on the left, this position has tactical affinities with Iron Gate as held with the sword in two hands. Its attacks and defenses tend to come from below and move from the scholar's right towards the center.

Many strikes are possible from this position. It can mimic High Serpent Position in reverse, going from low to high. It also allows a strong strike with the pommel done with a Half Turn (*mezza volta*).

The Pisani-Dossi (shown here) and the other manuscripts show the sword held differently. The sword's blade is gripped close to the crossguard, creating a longer "point." The sword seems to be held further forward and closer to the center as well, making it more reminiscent of Short Position (although the point is presented more like Long Position) than Iron Gate. Possibly the pommel is rested against the armor in an effort to prevent the sword from rocking back as it meets resistance and thus dissipating some of a thrust's power.

The mid-blade grip does not allow powerful cuts with the blade, but it excels at strong thrusts. The forward gripping hand stiffens the blade and allows you to put your entire body weight behind the point. It is still unlikely to penetrate plate armor, but it will seriously challenge mail armor. Thrusts from this position will find good targets in the armpit (as shown to the left) or the neck.

TRUE CROSS POSITION
(POSTA DI VERA CROCE)

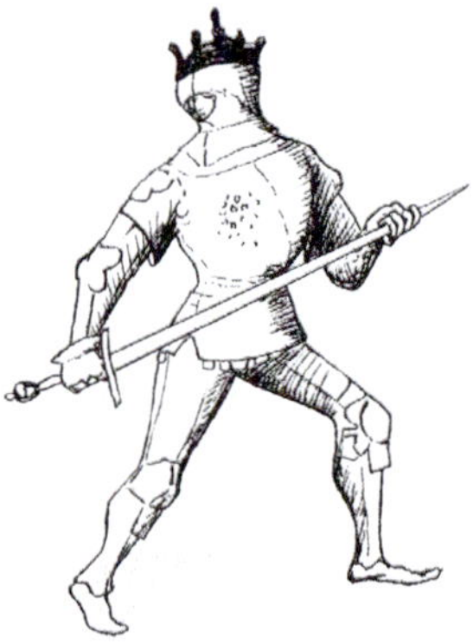

To find the True Cross, step forward (*passare*) from Short Serpent so that your right leg is forward. Make a Stable Turn (*volta stabile*). Bend your left elbow as you do, raising your hand to about the height of your rib cage. Keep your head turned toward your opponent.

In this position you are holding the sword in such a way that it presents no immediate threat. However, much like the Long Tail position adopted by the Master of the Sword in One Hand, this guard is coiled for action. Motion from it will make cover and set up a strike.

It is not clear whether Fiore thought this position could be held in a right-side version, which would entail the point being forward rather than the pommel. Mechanically it should work. The function of such a position could be filled by Short Serpent Position.

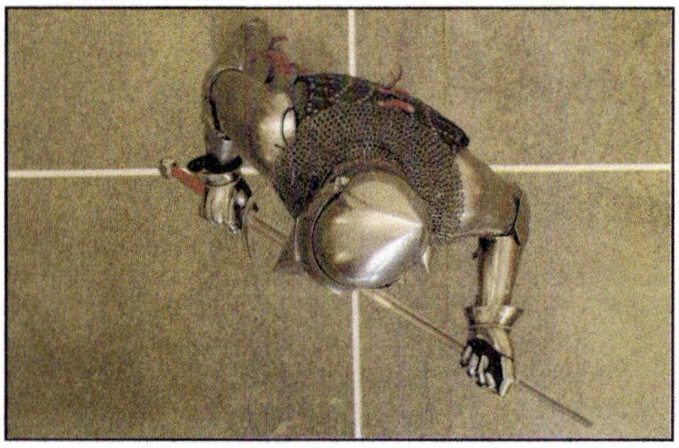

I want to use the Posta di Vera Croce (True Cross Position) against you. Your thrusts cannot reach me: I will parry while passing and strike you without fail with a thrust. Neither you nor the other guards worry me much: I know my fighting pretty well, and I can't fail my crossing. For this is what the art requires you to do without screwing up: passing, crossing and striking.

This position is probably called True Cross because making cover from it creates a strong and safe cross and Fiore says the position "can't fail my crossing." The name's allusion to the religious virtue of the True Cross of Christ and its link to salvation is probably not coincidental in this context. I doubt Fiore's medieval readers would fail to see a connection.

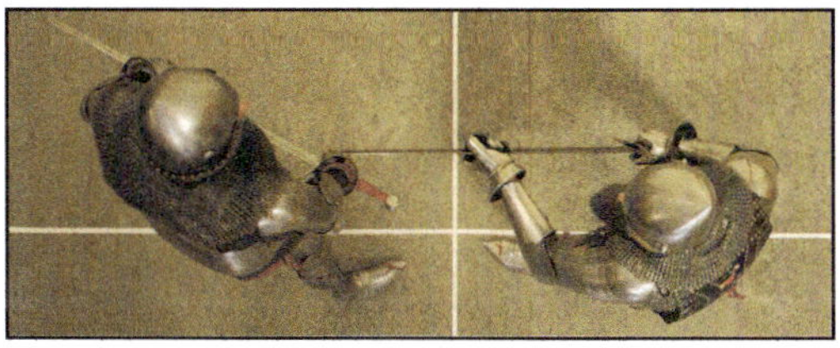

True Cross sets aside thrusts easily. The scholar moves with a pass (*passare*) and makes his cover. From there he can makes his own thrust while keeping his blade in opposition to his opponent's.

Here the scholar has missed his intended target of the armpit as his opponent turned. His point, however, has slid on the armor and entered under one of the lames.

HIGH SERPENT POSITION
(POSTA DI SERPENTINO LO SOPRANO)

To find High Serpent Position, begin in True Cross Position as before. Make a Stable Turn (*volta stabile*) and step (*passare*) with your left foot. As you move, change your left-hand grip so that the thumb is toward the sword's pommel. Once in the new grip, raise both hands above your head while continuing to bring the sword around until the point is toward your opponent. The sword blade should end parallel to the ground.

This guard is linked to Short Serpent Position by the shared word *serpent*. Each of the guards threatens with the point and you can place a solid thrust from both of them. Were you to let go

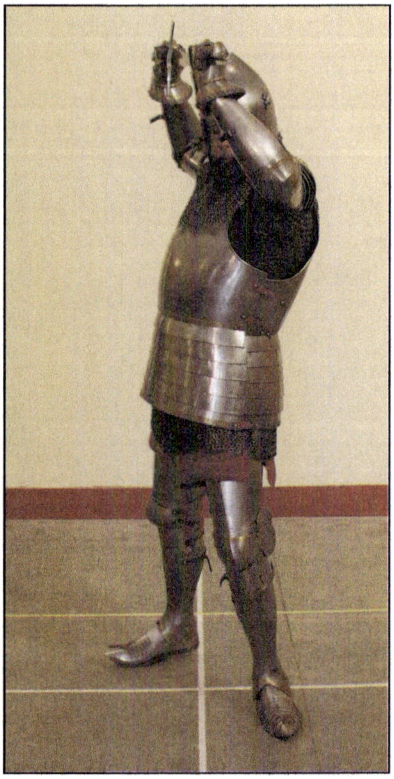

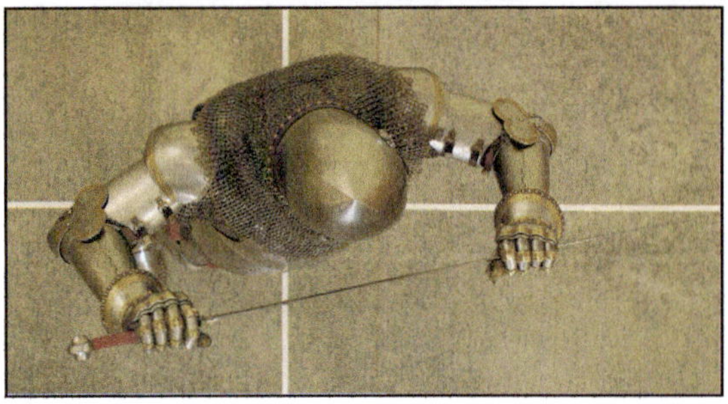

It is not clear whether Fiore thought this position could be held in a left-side version, which would entail the point being backwards rather than the pommel. Mechanically it should work.

I am the Serpentino lo Soprano (High Serpent), high and well armed. I throw strong underhanded thrusts, since I am high and get back low. I'll throw a good thrust while passing. I know my art well. I couldn't care less about your cuts, since I know my stuff and I can give you a good dose of thrusts.

of your blade grip and thrust forward with a single-hand thrust, the blade would seemingly flicker out from your guard like a serpent's tongue.

High Serpent need not attack high. With a pass (*passare*) off line, the scholar shifts his arms to make a thrust that comes in deceptively.

A simple turn of the torso brings the blade in to block a downward cut in a move similar to that of the Remedy Master of the sword in armor.

The same turn with a lowered right hand catches and deflects a thrust, relying on the armor for protection.

Passing obliquely to the right, the scholar voids the incoming thrust.

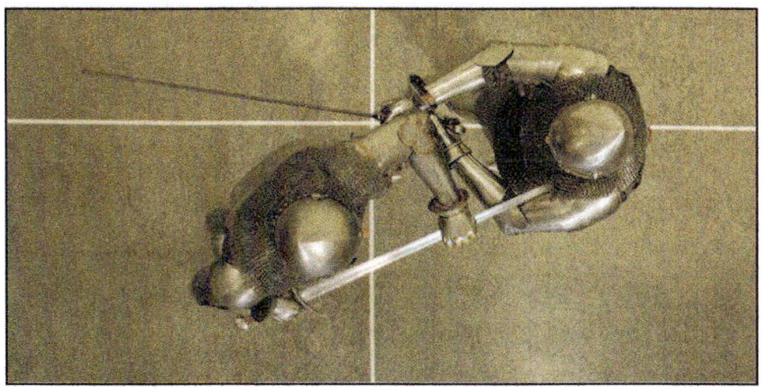

With a pass inward, the scholar finishes with a strong thrust to his opponent's upper left opening.

MIDDLE IRON GATE
(PORTA DI FERRO MEZZANA)

To find Middle Iron Gate, stand in High Serpent Position as before. Let go with your left hand grip. Move your right hand down to a position in front of your groin area; you will need to turn it as you do. Bring your left hand to join your right on the sword's handle. Step forward (*passare*) with your right foot. Your sword should stop on the centerline, point towards the ground.

This guard is identical to Middle Iron Gate for the sword in two hands. Like that guard, it can be held with either leg forward.

Middle Iron Gate is a point guard and Fiore tells us that "the most extended guard can reach the opponent first."

They call me the middle Porta di Ferro (Iron Door), since both in and out of armor I deliver strong thrusts and pass off line with my left foot while giving your face a good taste of the point of my sword. I can also place the point and edge of my sword between your arms, putting you in a middle bind—like the one pictured and named earlier.

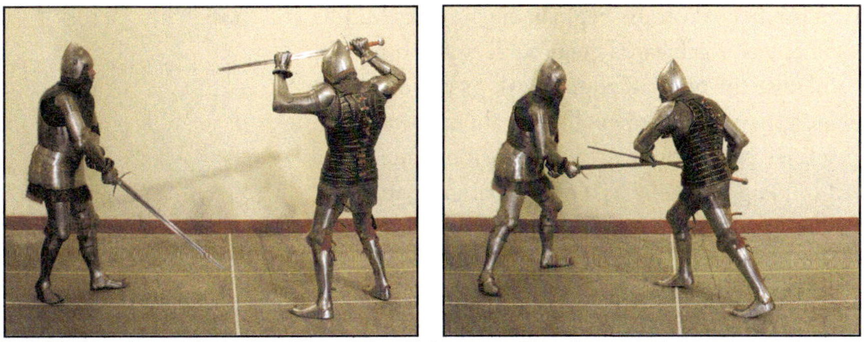

Middle Iron Gate makes strong thrusts. The scholar steps off line (*accressere*) to set up an advantageous angle. Raising his sword point he can let a closing opponent run on it. If the opponent does not oblige, the scholar can step forward to make the thrust in any case.

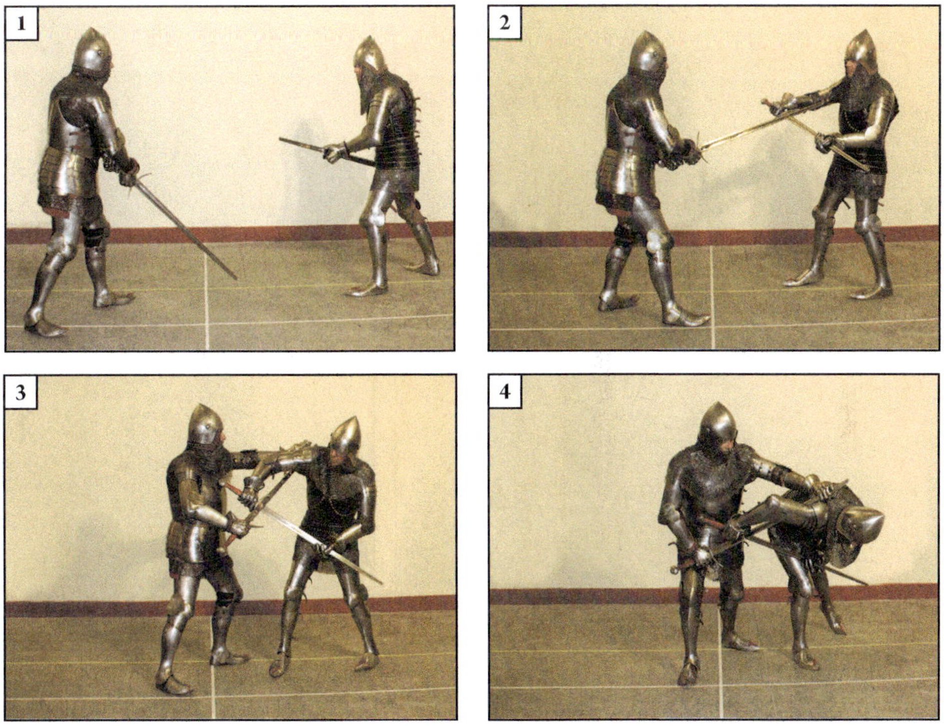

Middle Iron Gate can take advantage of its extended blade. By slipping the point past an opponent's arm, the scholar can place the blade where his arm might have difficulty going. A shift of grip and a Stable Turn (*volta stabile*) can create the Middle Bind (*ligadura mezzana*).

Note the similarity of the action to this Counter Master from the sword in two hands section (shown here reversed).

ARCHER'S POSITION
(POSTA SAGITARIA)

To find Archer's Position, begin in the previous Middle Iron Gate. Pass backwards (*retornare*) with your right foot and raise the point of your sword. As you do, take a left-hand grip on the blade with your thumb away from the pommel. Note: the very similar position among the Sword-holding Masters has a different right-hand grip, one with the thumb towards the pommel, but the posture is the same.

Like the other point-forward, mid-blade positions, Archer's Position makes its thrust with a pass (*passare*). The pass powers the attack, using the strong body structure to put body weight and momentum behind the point.

You can throw your sword using this grip, which is likely the source of the name.

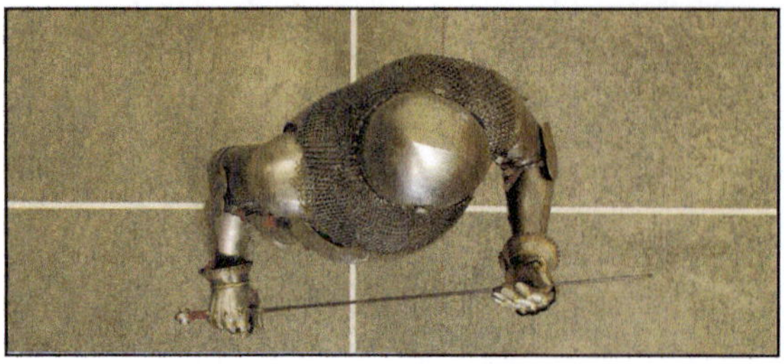

While it is theoretically possible to hold this position in a left side version, a throw from that side would launch an unwieldy missile with low damage potential.

They call me Posta Sagittaria (Archer's Position): I give strong thrusts while passing off line. Any attack or cut coming my way I can foil with a good parry and immediately deliver the counter. This is my art, and I never depart from it.

Archer's Position uses thrusts. The scholar passes off line to set up an advantageous angle (2). His point slips behind that of his opponent. His point comes in over the arm of his opponent (3). As he strikes home, his body structure and momentum collapse the defender's arm (4).

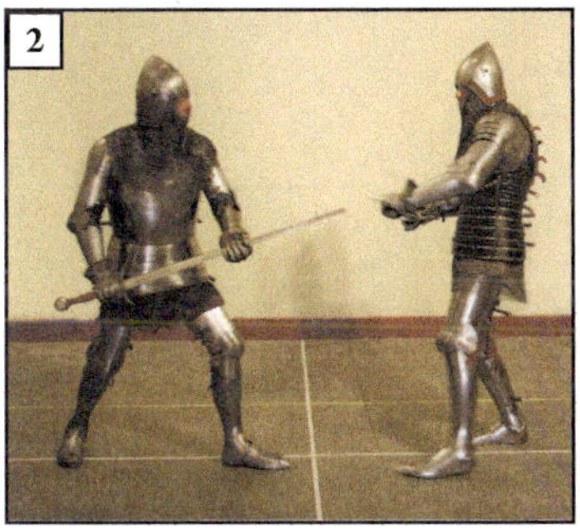

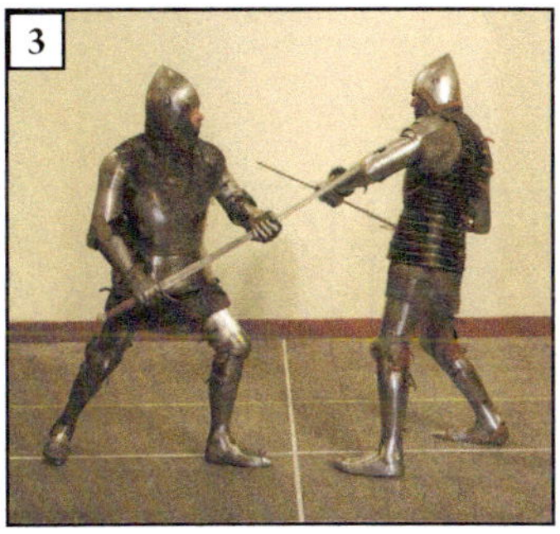

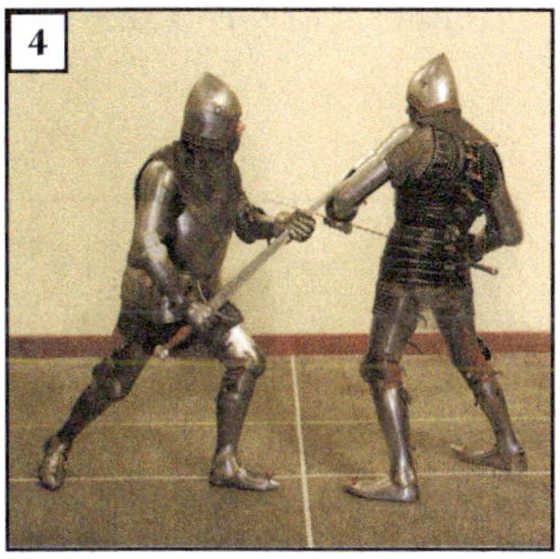

Archer's Position offers the opportunity to launch the long thrust. While it might be effective put into the uncovered face of an armored man, it is difficult, to say the least, to generate enough force to penetrate armor. Against an unarmored man, however, it is a different story.

The scholar covers against a pommel-strike attack, catching it between his hands. The attacker can throw this attack because his own hand is protected by armor.

With a Half Turn (*mezza volta*) the scholar raise his own pommel ...

and strikes his opponent's face.

BASTARD CROSS POSITION
(POSTA DE CROCE BASTARDA)

To find Bastard Cross Position, start in Archer's Position. Shift your right-hand grip around so that the thumb is towards the point of your sword. Pass forward (*passare*) with your right foot and bring the pommel forward. Your right hand should end roughly over your right knee. The sword should be approximately parallel to the ground and nearly or completely perpendicular to the centerline.

This is a centered position and as such can be held with either foot forward.

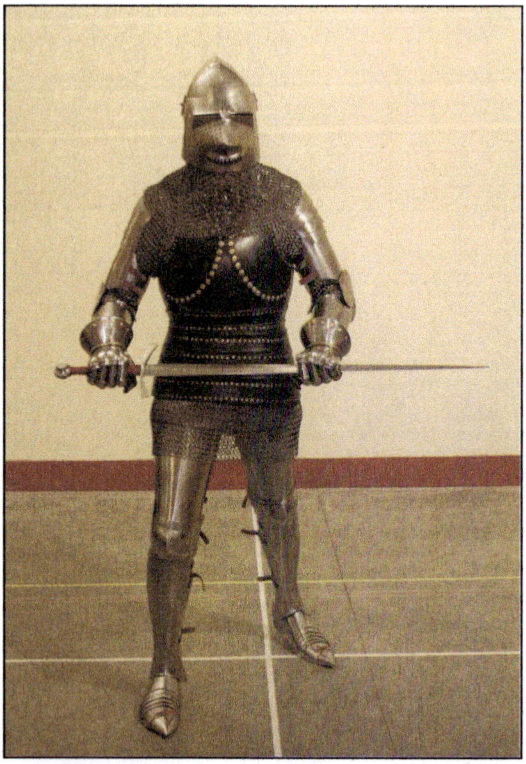

Learning the Guards

The instructions to "find" the sword, ax, and spear guards are written sequentially. This allows you to build a beginner's drill of moving through the guards in the order of their appearance in the Getty manuscript.

Posta de Croce Bastarda (Bastard Cross Position) is the bastard child of the Posta di Vera Croce: anything it can do, I like to also do. I parry, thrust and cut well, usually while voiding attacks off line. I always have a good stock of attacks that I can deliver.

The text for this position tells us that is a variant ("the bastard child") of the True Cross Position. Naming it this way suggests that it is not a good as the True Cross Position, but Fiore says that it can do anything that True Cross can do. Indeed, Bastard Cross is versatile and actions from it are quite close to those from True Cross. What they lack is the power generated by the refused hip position of True Cross. Bastard Cross trades that power for the quicker response time from the central position, something that can be vital in an armored fight where your vision may be restricted resulting in an equally restricted window of response time.

The scholar here starts in True Cross (1), but he moves into Bastard Cross to meet his opponent's thrust. He is not in a position to set it aside even as he meets it, so he shifts his left hand further forward to deflect the incoming point (2). His opponent tries to dominate him with body structure and press down on his blade and the scholar responds by beginning to roll up toward High Serpent (3). Displacing his opponent's efforts to the side, he makes a pass (*passare*) and drives his own point in as he shifts to High Serpent (4).

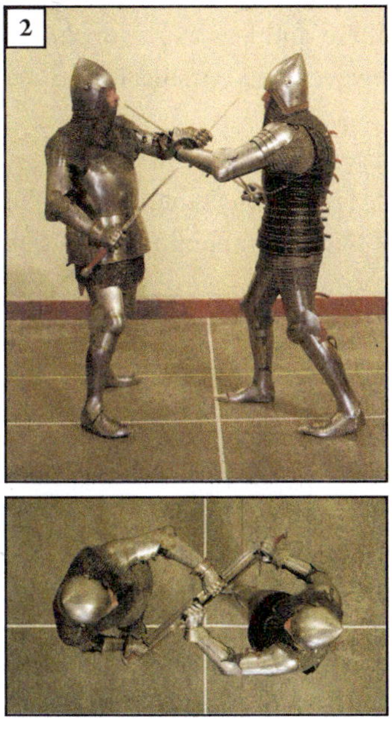

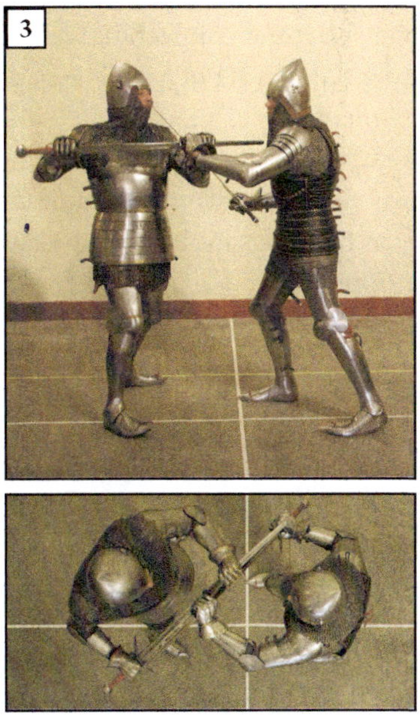

The cover of the Sword in armor Master is built from modified *abrazare* Positions

I came out of the Posta di Vera Croce with this parry, while passing obliquely off line. What I can do from this parry I can easily show through my students, as they complete my plays. Those who fight to the bitter end will surely show their art.

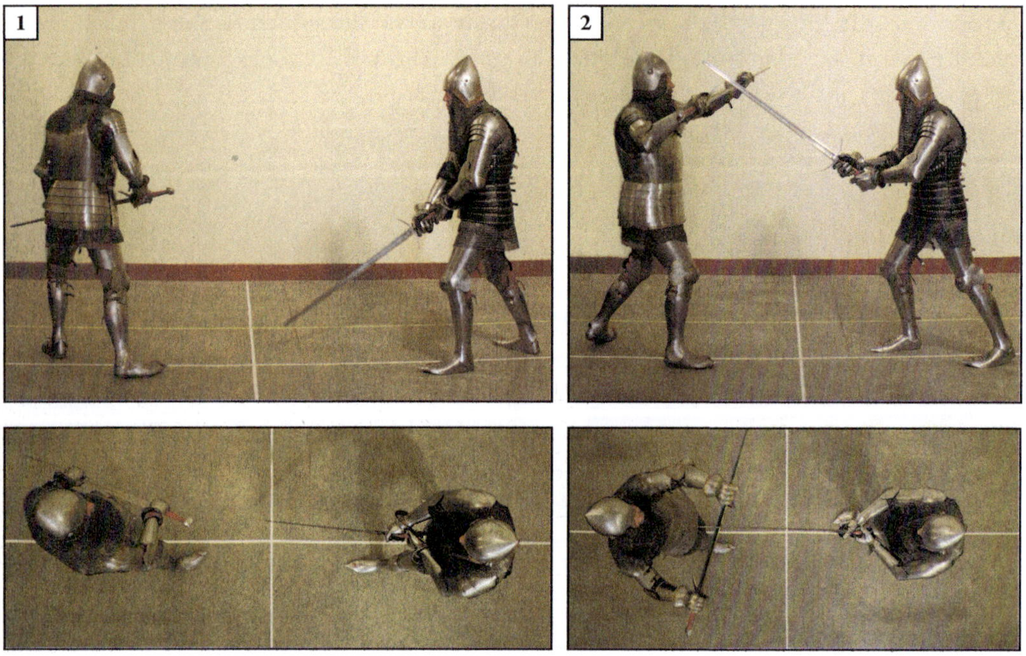

The cover made by the Remedy Master has the structure of *abrazare's* Frontal Position. The linkage provided by the blade allows the master's hands to be farther apart than in the *abrazare* position yet retain the strong structural connection with his torso and legs as he forces the incoming point up. The master's action is not a static block, however, and remains in Frontal Position for the merest of moments.

The master starts in True Cross Position. He may begin action with a step off line but armored fighting is often already close and there may not be time. He makes a Stable Turn (*volta stabile*) and passes (*passare*) as he brings his blade into contact with the incoming point. His rising hands help take the opponent's point off target and his step also provides a measure of safety.

Note the contact point of the blades. This will be changing immediately.

Observe how the scholar's turning pressure has shifted the contact point of the blades.

His left hand continues to rise and his torso turns slightly toward the opponent, using the mechanics of *abrazare's* Boar's Tooth Position. This action further drives the incoming point away. It also is the start of his own counter-attack.

As the master continues this turn, he brings his sword point down. Part of

I am the first student of the Master just before me, and I deliver this thrust straight from the parry. This same thrust can come immediately from the Posta di Vera Croce and Posta di Croce Bastarda: as the opponent attacks with a thrust, the Master or student who is placed in one of these guards (or poste) should lower his body and pass off line, crossing the opponent's sword and with the point high against the enemy's face or chest. And, as shown here, the sword needs to be kept low while doing this.

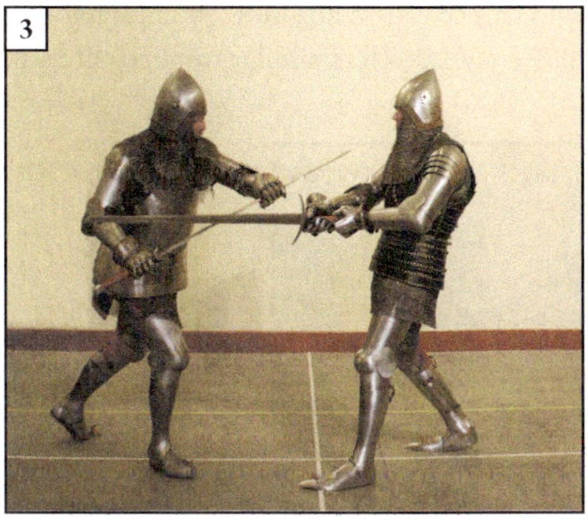

this comes from his hand motion and part from dropping his center of gravity a little. As his blade remains in contact with that of the opponent, these actions help to keep the opponent from interfering with what is to come.

As soon as the master's point comes into line with a suitable target (such as the opponent's armpit or neck; the face is good, too, if he is not wearing a visor), he thrusts. Full body alignment is important for the power necessary to penetrate armor. If the opponent is close enough, an increase step (*accressere*) can do the job. If he is further away, a pass (*passare*) will be necessary. In either case, the master's sword slides along the opponent's as his point seeks its target.

If your opponent's sword slips free, he is likely to try to bring it up to push your point away. You can counter this by raising your right hand, shifting toward High Serpent Position, and continuing your thrust.

The cover of the Sword in armor Master is related to dagger positions

Despite the Remedy Master's statement that his play "came out of Posta di Vera Croce," you can cover in a similar fashion from any of the guards in which you hold your sword in a mid-blade (*mezza mella*) grip. Note how similar the grip and position in the Short Serpent is to the dagger guard of Middle Iron Gate, Doubled (*Mezzana Porta di Ferro Doppia*). This is the dagger guard which goes most easily into the Sixth Remedy Master, who can cover on all sides. By applying that principle, we can see that the mid-blade grip with the sword offers similar opportunities in combat with swords.

Short Serpent

The scholar steps off-line to the outside and covers. Because he is armored, he can catch the incoming blade with the portion of his own blade that is in front of his hand and bend it against his wrist.

High Serpent

The scholar passes across with his back foot and makes his cover. The high position needs to travel a significant distance and he needs time to make the cover.

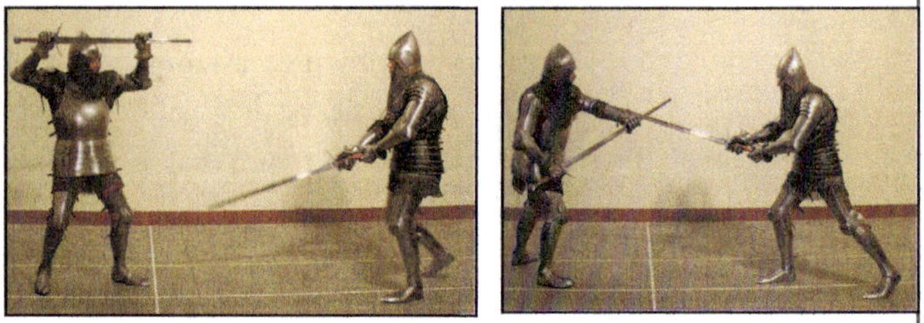

Archer's Position

The scholar uses a turn (*volta*) to deflect the incoming point. If he needs to, he can pass back (*retornare*), buying time, to make his cover.

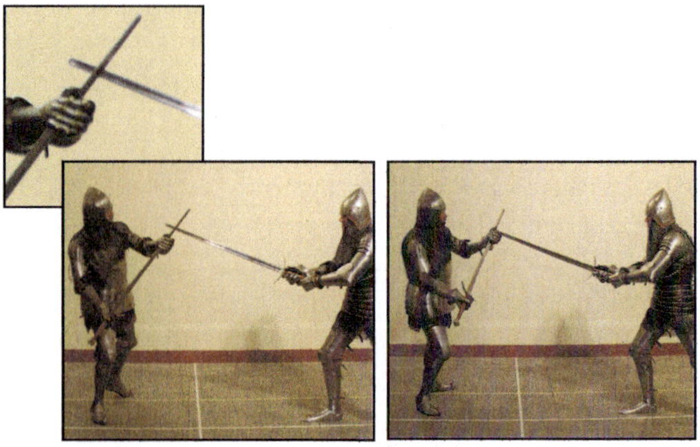

With a sword in mid-blade grip, you can attack as you cover

Whether you are playing against another mid-blade (*mezza mella*) grip or a conventional sword in two hands grip, you must make cover against an attack. Despite the statement of the scholar in play 34r A that the plays come "from the first Master from the Posta di Vera Croce or Bastarda," his and the next several plays can come from the other guards as well. Also, judging by what we know of Fiore's basic principles and the way the opposing players are shown with different grips on their swords, you can also play against an opponent using either a mid-blade or a sword in two hands grip.

If you do not wish to be hit, you find yourself in a crossing. Just as it was with the sword in two hands, this is a situation where the pressure will determine the proper action.

When I come out of the guard into a tight parry and I can't strike you with a cut, I deliver a thrust. If I can't do either, I strike you with the guard or the pommel of my sword—depending on my preference.

You make the cross as you cover with your point leading. If you come a little deep, you cut him as part of the motion.

You make the cross as you cover with your pommel leading. If you come a little deep, you hit him with your crossguard as part of the motion.

You make the cross as you cover with your point leading. If you come in a little shallow, you are set up for a thrust as part of this motion.

You make the cross as you cover with your pommel leading. If you come a little shallow, you hit him with your pommel either as part of the motion or as a follow-on strike.

If you have not hit him as part of the cover, but have been stopped at the cross, you must feel his intent through the blade. By shifting as appropriate to avoid his strength, these actions can come into play.

A crossing can be made with the mid-blade grip

And when I am also in close play and the opponent thinks I will use my sword, I can instead resort to abrazare as long as I can see an advantage. If I don't I can strike him in the face with my hilt as I've said before.

The crossing made when both players have mid-blade grips and cross their blades between their hands places you in *zogho stretto*.

When the situation allows you to move to your left (left pictures), you can step in and put your point past his neck.

When the situation allows you to move to your right (right pictures), you can step in and put your pommel past his neck.

In both cases, a deliberate or incidental strike to his face only helps. In both cases, you place your lead leg to the outside of his. In both cases, you throw him to the ground.

The mid-blade grip offers an option not available when playing against the sword in two hands grip. The opponent's raised left arm can allow you to enter beneath it to set your pommel against his neck. Your armor protects you from incidental contact with his sword point. Note that the drawing shows the scholar's blade over his opponent's, which may be an error as achieving that position is awkward and slow at best.

When I realize that my point can't reach the opponent's chest or face (because of his visor), I can remove the visor and thrust into his face. ...

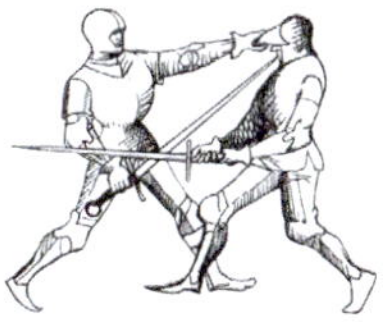

Visor latches for helmets do not appear in the archeological record until after Fiore's time. This play takes advantage of the lack of a secure catch.

This situation arises when your initial thrust fails to pierce his visor. Without withdrawing, the scholar moves his left hand to the opponent's visor and lifts it, making him vulnerable to a single-handed thrust to the face.

... When the student is in that guard and the opponent comes against him and attacks, the student passes off line and give a thrust to the other's face, as you see here.

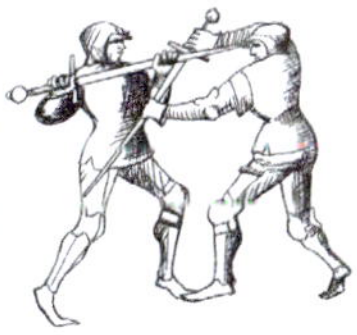

The scholar here has passed offline and turned his sword to get the angle for his thrust. His arm takes over the job of maintaining pressure on the opponent's blade and the scholar relies on his armor to protect his arm against being cut as he sets up his thrust.

If the cross is on the blades between the hands, a similar move can be made which keeps blade-on-blade contact so that the scholar's arm does not contact the blade, and thus does not need armor.

... This Counter Master places his left hand behind the opponent's right elbow as the latter performs the parry of the Remedy Master. The student then gives him a forceful turn ...
... As soon as the opponent has turned, I immediately strike him from the back, under his right arm. I can take my pick: I can hit him in the back of the head (from under the mail coif), or in his buttocks (with all due respect!), or under the knees, or anywhere else I see an opening.

The text and drawings here are the Counter Master and his scholar, but earlier in the section, one of the Remedy Master's scholars also makes the elbow turning play after his attacks fail to penetrate the armor so that he "can then see if the back of his armor is equally strong."

The armor on the back might actually be thinner or less complete, and thus less strong. Certain weak spots are also available from behind, as Fiore notes.

I am the axe, heavy, cruel and lethal, and I deliver bigger blows than any other handheld weapon.

LESSONS OF THE AXE

Despite moving to a new weapon, Fiore does not begin this section with a paragraph extolling the virtues of the axe (*azza*). The usual bluster does not appear until the second to last paragraph in the section, but when it does, the axe lays claim to making "bigger blows (*colpo*) than any other hand-held weapon." Hefting a quality reproduction of such a weapon makes it easy to believe that the axe is "heavy cruel and lethal." Most of its mass is concentrated at the head end, and that makes it capable of truly terrifying downward blows.

The Getty's axe section opens with six Fight Masters. The other manuscripts only have four guards, omitting Long tail (*Coda Longa*) and Window Position (*Posta di Finestra*). Of the guards they have in common, there is an issue. The Getty's drawing of what the text calls True Cross (*Posta di Vera Croce*) looks much more like the position called Bastard Cross (*Posta di Croce Bastarda*) in the sword in armor section. Oddly enough, the *Croce* position illustrated in the Pisani-Dossi and the Paris[1] looks much more like the sword in armor's *Posta di Vera Croce*. Are we looking at an artist's mistake in the Getty or a textural one? The Pisani-Dossi agrees with the Getty about which sword position is *Vera Croce*, making it look as though the artist is to blame. So we should assume that the axe position illustrated in the Getty is *Posta di Croce Bastarda*.

Of course *Vera Croce* and *Croce Bastarda* are closely related. Their difference lies mostly in the body positioning (the key difference is hip positioning, not the more obvious foot orientation). One of the plays in the sword in armor section notes that it "comes from the

The Getty's *Posta di Vera Croce* (35vB)

The Getty sword in armor *Posta di Croce Bastarda* (33rB)

The Pisani-Dossi's *Croce* position (carta 27a position B)

The Getty sword in armor *Posta di Vera Croce* (32vB)

[1] The axe section is absent from the Morgan.

first Master from the Posta di Vera Croce or Bastarda," which makes it clear that a proper cover can be made from either.

Another of the guards raises an identification issue as well. The text accompanying the fourth Fight Master calls it Iron Gate (*Porta di Ferro*). Its companion master, which opposes it, says that is opposing Boar's Tooth (*Dente di Cinghiaro*), a different guard entirely. The Pisani-Dossi drawing identifies itself, although in a dialect spelling, as Boar's Tooth. We will ignore this obvious scribal error and refer to the guard as Boar's Tooth.

THE SWORD IS AN AXE, THEREFORE ...

Sword-holding Master 6 (22vD)

The axe is a sword.

The Fight Masters of the axe tell much of the story. Four of the axe guards bear the same names as sword in two hands guards: Woman's Position (*Posta di Donna*), Boar's Tooth (*Dente di Cinghiaro*), Long Tail (*Coda Longa*), and Window Position (*Posta di Finestra*) and the other two share names with sword in armor guards: Short Serpent (*Posta Breve la Serpentina*) and True Cross (*Posta di Vera Croce*). There are no unique axe guards.

The axe's True Cross guard specifically claims to be able to do the same play as "the first student of the Remedy Master of the sword in armor." Window Position for the axe has "no stability," which is to say it is *instabile* (whatever that truly means), as is its corresponding sword position. These two instances tell us that the same dynamics are at work in the axe and the sword when working from the same positions, but it is the text for Boar's Tooth that makes the reciprocal relationship between the sword and the axe explicit. In referring to this position and its partner, Fiore says, "For we have faced one-another many times before, sword or axe in hand." Whether with sword or axe, the play is the same from these positions.

Axe play can have *zogho largo* and *zogho stretto* as can the sword. Certain grips encourage its use in one mode over the other. Actions from the guards related to those of the sword in two hands are more likely to be *zogho largo* and those from guards corresponding to those of sword in armor more likely be *zogho stretto*.

As we saw in the sword in one hand section, we can make expansions to the illustrated material by looking at related material, for example, the two axe guards shared with the sword in armor. In the sword section, there are two *Croce* and two *Serpentina* guards. Fiore even says in the Bastard Cross's text that "anything it (True Cross) can do, I can do" while the High Serpent's text reports "I am high and get back low" to "throw strong underhanded thrusts" which presumably end in a position much like Short Serpent. Because the sword is an axe, and vice versa, the similarly named sword in armor guards Bastard Cross (*Croce Bastarda*) and High Serpent (*Serpentino lo Soprano*), although not explicitly shown as axe guards, should also be viable for the axe.

Similarly, closely related guards of the sword in two hands should translate into axe play. For example, symmetrical positions should be transferable to the axe. Thus a version of both Woman's Position and Window Position held on the left side should work. This is, I think, embedded in Fiore's drawings of the axe positions, with Woman's Position shown on the right and Window Position shown on the left. In addition, the usual rule that positions (*poste*) can do the Stable Turn (*volta stabile*) and the Half Turn (*mezza volta*) also applies.

But for all their similarity, there are differences between the weapons due to their construction. The axe has a heavy head. This makes an axe balance very differently from a sword, especially when held near the butt end. The heavy head can be powerful in a strike, which Fiore acknowledges in the text with the Sword-holding Master who holds his weapon like an axe, saying "weighty things can be of great impediment to those that are light." The weighty head of an axe can demolish light defenses and can crash through lightly held parries.

The weight of the axe can affect play against other weapons. Fiore spells it out in a play from the axe's Boar's Tooth master where the text describes action done with a sword rather than an axe. The attack comes from Woman's Position, suggesting a powerful, downwards blow enhanced by the weighty head of the axe. The response is to step out of the way and enter forcefully, grabbing your sword at half-blade to give him a thrust to the face. The sword is used in a deflecting mode here as it is ill-suited to directly opposing the heavy axe.

The heaviness of the axe's head is shown in the first play of the axe. While Fiore tells that the axe can do a play from the True Cross like the first scholar of the sword in armor, what he shows us as a starting play is both players' axe heads low or on the ground. Because of the axe's heavy head, a downward trend of the heads in a wide cross is a situation far more common with the axe than the sword and can easily take both heads to the ground. This very low crossing is, in many ways, a desirable outcome for the player who sends his opponent's axe there. An axe head on the ground is a far weaker threat than one anywhere else.

The axe's haft offers more opportunity for one to slide along the other and when head meets head, they can catch on each other; something sword points never do.

The axe also has no crossguard. This means that sword positions like Frontal and Two-horned, which rely on the crossguard to protect the user, are not available to the axe. For centerline defenses the axe relies on its shaft to block and deflect. In such actions, the hands are only protected by the axe-man's gauntlets and his skill; he must avoid putting his hands in harm's way.

The plays of the axe section are very reminiscent of the plays of the sword section, as they should be. The axe is a sword in the sense that it shares techniques within the art, but one must never forget that an axe is not exactly the same weapon as a sword.

A CONVERSATION BETWEEN GUARDS

"Everything she says she can do to me ..." "... I can do better to her."

It is in the axe section that the paired Fight Masters have the most to say about each other. Two explicitly refer to their partners as being opposed. One goes further, getting a bit snarky about the other, and says "everything she says she can do to me, I can do better to her." This interplay that lets us see there is something more than random pairing in the Fight Masters who face each other.

The paired guards offer some insight into how Fiore thought the various positions (*poste*) interact. The rest of the text that accompanies the snarky quote above makes it very clear that the player is facing, if not actually waiting, for an attack from an opponent in Woman's Position while in the Boar's Tooth Position. The text from True Cross states that the player in this position is awaiting an attack and will respond as does "the first student of the Remedy Master of the sword in armor," who faces a thrust from his opponent. It is no coincidence that True Cross faces Short Serpent, whose text boasts of its powerful thrusts. The texts for the last pair of axe positions, Long Tail and Window Position, do not explicitly speak to how they relate. However, the action described for Window Position would void "one of my (Long Tail's) fendente" and strike at the then uncovered opponent.

When you look at any of the paired positions (*poste*) in the manuscript, keep in mind how they might interact. I don't know that Fiore is suggesting that one is an ideal counter to the other, but he is certainly suggesting that one can be used against the other.

SHORT HAND INSTRUCTION

The axe portion of the manuscript is a short section of only ten drawings. Unlike all of the other sections, the plays do not begin with a Remedy Master, or even a Fight-Remedy Master. The first play after the Fight Masters depicts a scholar[4] as the acting player. The only crowns appear in the last two drawings. These end the section with two crowned masters advocating actions that can be only categorized as tricks, or maybe ninja techniques. These Trick Masters, with their binding rope and blinding powder, function as the section end points, but they do not offer realistic combat options. Perhaps they are meant to show Fiore was a font of exotic and esoteric knowledge as well as practical and useful techniques.

Of the eight plays with scholars, three of them are clearly stated as following-on from the scholar before them. This leaves five to make Fiore's points about axe play. By this point in the manuscript, Fiore has introduced almost all of the art, either implicitly or explicitly. The sections can now focus on specific elements that apply to a specific weapon. Direct and indirect connections link to previous teaching. By now, Fiore expects a student to have understood earlier principles. Applying those principles to new weapons and circumstances is expected. The axe section is an ideal example of this compacted instruction.

The first play acknowledges that the heads of axes will often go to the ground. At the same time it acknowledges that play is somewhat different from sword play because of the axe's haft. It is not as easy to play to either side, especially without shifting grips.

First play of the axe section (36vA)

The second play is unique to the Getty. The Pisani-Dossi and Paris manuscripts go immediately to what is the Getty's third play. That play and its start from a low cross is a direct parallel to the very similar sword in two hands play that involves the breaking of a thrust. Together the second and third demonstrate proper action: if your axe is under his, close and throw him, but if your axe is on top, strike him quickly.

The other two direct scholars (plays five and six) offer a bind and a disarm, respectively. Like the previous axe scholars, they function more as reminders of principles learned in other techniques in previous sections. There are some subtleties related to the nature of the axe present, to be sure. By and large, however, the plays of the axe section are more like chapter headings to remind us to refer elsewhere for details. We get five things to remember: crossing, throws, strikes, binds, and disarms. This is not a new pattern.

IT'S ALL RELATED

The "sword is an axe" reflexive statement is the most obvious of the axe section's windows into other parts of the art. The conversations of the axe's Fight Masters and their implications for other Fight Masters throughout the manuscript is another of the interactive elements. And the axe section ends, as the unarmored sword section ended, in a play in which the scholar has abandoned his a weapon and is attempting an unarmed technique, returning us again to the foundation of the art, *abrazare*.

Not a play of *abrazare* but the last scholar of the axe section (37rD)

2 In the Paris, this scholar is crowned as a master, but not in the Pisani-Dossi. The Morgan has no axe plays.

SHORT SERPENT POSITION
(POSTA BREVE LA SERPENTINA)

To find the Short Serpent, start with you hips squared up against your opponent and your left leg forward. Turn your torso to the right, opening your hip structure in a classic Iron Gate stance. Keeping your shoulders aligned with your hips, grip your axe with your right hand near the butt-spike and your left below the head. Both of your thumbs will be toward the head. Hold the axe low and to your right side. Your left hand should be behind your hip and the shaft near it. The right arm is not extended as it was in the sword in armor version; it is bent at the elbow with the hand at about waist level. This brings the head a little higher and closer to the centerline.

Stepping the Guards

Stage 1

Stand in a guard.
Cut (or thrust when in a point guard) to Long Position.
Return to guard.

Stage 2

Step as your cut (or thrust).
Start with straight steps forward, then do steps backward, oblique steps forward then backward.

I am the Posta Breve la Serpentina, and I consider myself better than the others. Take one of my thrusts, and you'll definitely bear the mark. This point is very strong, and can penetrate breastplates and cuirasses; come on, defend yourself and let's try it.

Short Serpent, like True Cross, shares a name with a guard from sword in armor. Although named the same as the guard for sword in armor, this position is drawn more open, a little refused on the right side to allow more potential power to be held ready. Unlike the case with its sword in armor counterpart, the other manuscripts do not show it differently, presumably because of the physical reality of the axe prevents it from being held extended from the center of the torso.

Be wary of the extra bits of the axe. It can't slide as easily as a sword.

The tactical options of this guard are essentially the same as those for the corresponding guard of the sword in armor. Indeed, the boasting is nearly identical with the addition of a claim to be really good at penetrating armor. Being stiffer than a sword, the axe may be able to live up to that claim.

It is not clear whether Fiore thought this position could be held in a left-side version. If you simply switch lead legs and shift the axe over to the left side, the head will be backwards rather than the butt-spike. We see similar reverses of the weapon in the sword in armor.

Alternatively, since the manner of gripping the double-ended axe is such that you could achieve a left-side version by shifting your grip so that your right hand is near the head and your left near the butt-spike, ending up with the head forward. Having the right hand near the head is the more common grip illustrated by Fiore.

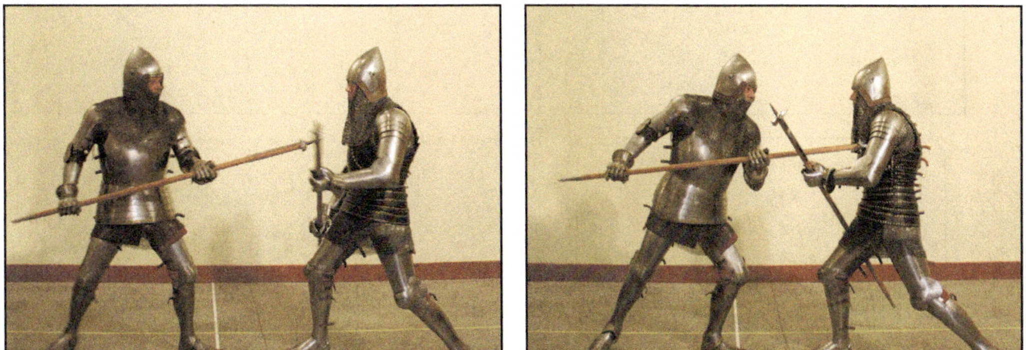

Short Serpent makes powerful thrusts and offers good strength to press them home against opposition.

TRUE CROSS POSITION
(POSTA DI VERA CROCE)

The Pisani-Dossi's *Croce* (carta 27a position B)

The Getty's *Vera Croce* (*35v b*)

Fiore gives us a significant interpretation issue with this guard. As drawn in the Getty (inset) it looks far more like Bastard Cross than True Cross. The Pisani-Dossi and the Paris manuscripts draw it more like the sword in armor's True Cross. I think that the Getty's artist picked the wrong model, so …

To find the True Cross, pass forward from Short Serpent so that your right leg is forward. Make a Stable Turn (*volta stabile*). Raise your right arm a little as you do. Thus, bringing the head of the axe to about shoulder height. Keep your head turned toward your opponent.

Guard Transitions

Stage 1

Stand in a guard.
Move your weapon smoothly to another guard, stepping or turning as necessary.

Stage 2

Stand in a guard.
Make an attack (cut or thrust as appropriate), stepping if necessary.
Continue smoothly to the destination guard.

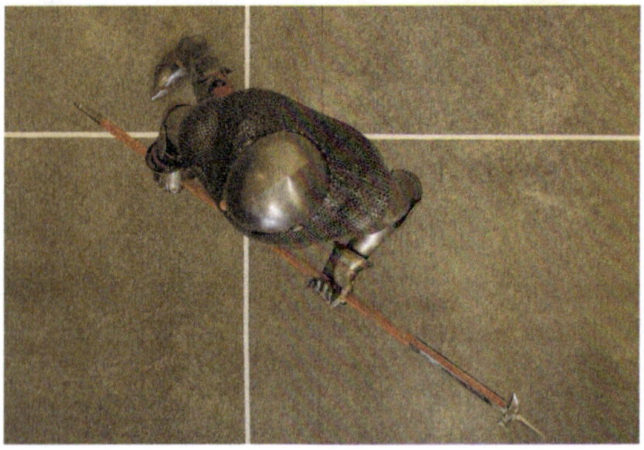

I am the Posta di Vera Croce, since I defend myself with the cross. The whole art of fencing and of arms features the defense of the cross. Go ahead and attack, I'm waiting for you. With my axe, I can perform the same thrust with a pass as the first student of the Remedy Master of the sword in armor.

In this position the butt-spike is forward, but is not much of a threat as it is pointed down. Like its sword in armor counterpart, this guard is coiled for action. Motion from it will make cover and, in doing so, make or set up a strike.

True Cross, like Short Serpent, shares a name with a guard from sword in armor. The tactical options of this guard are essentially the same as those for the corresponding guard of the sword in armor.

It is not clear whether Fiore thought this position could be held in a left-side version. A change of lead leg and a Stable Turn to the right will set up a right-side counterpart. The head will be forward rather than the butt-spike, but that is hardly a problem.

Given that Fiore tells us the Bastard Cross can do with the sword in armor what the True Cross does, we can expect that the axe can be used in its own version of the Bastard Cross. Given the nature of the guard, it could be held with either leg forward. Given the nature of the axe, it could also be held with the head on either side.

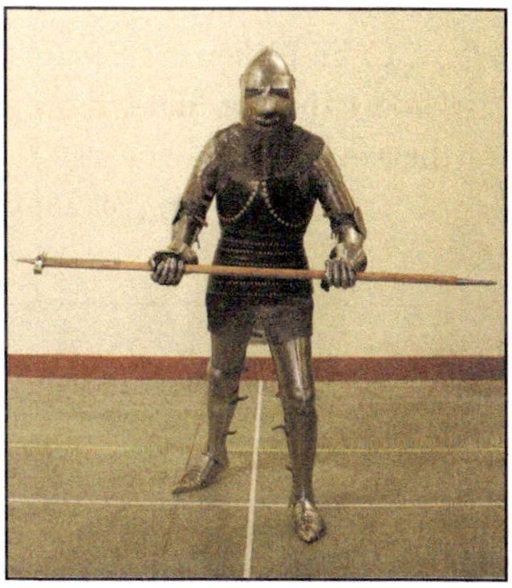

Right Bastard Cross with the axe with the head on the right.

As the text says, the axe guard of True Cross "can perform the same thrust with a pass as the first student of the Remedy Master of the sword in armor."

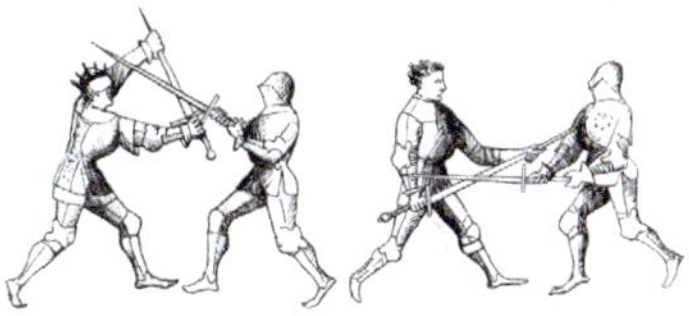

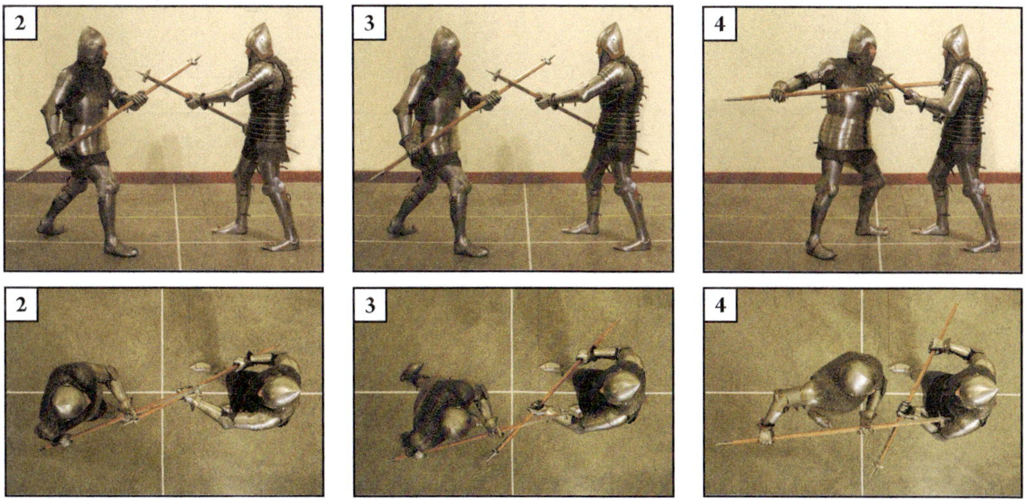

WOMAN'S POSITION
(POSTA DI DONNA)

Woman's Position is one of four axe guards that share names with guards from sword in two hands. The others are Boar's Tooth, Long Tail, and Window Position. This version on the guard is being held on the right. Woman's Position, as it was for the sword, is a reciprocal guard and can be held on the left as well.

To find Woman's Position as shown here, stand in True Cross as before. Slide your right hand to about the middle of the axe haft. Shift your left-hand grip to a point between your right hand and the butt-spike. Make a Stable Turn (*volta stabile*) then a pass (*passare*) with your left foot so that it is forward.

GUARD TRANSITIONS
STAGE 3

Stand in a guard.
Make an attack (cut or thrust as appropriate), stepping if necessary.
Continue smoothly to the destination guard.
Cut (or thrust) from the destination guard, stepping if necessary.
Continue smoothly to the origin guard.

I am the Posta di Donna, and I oppose the Dente di Cinghiaro. If the Dente di Cinghiaro waits for me, I can make a powerful strike by passing with the left foot, stepping off line and entering with a fendente to his head. And if the opponent comes forcefully with his axe under mine, if I can't strike his head I can do so to his arms or hands.

Make another Stable Turn and, as you do, lift the axe over your head. Settle the axe just above your shoulder with the shaft slanting up slightly; the head should be approximately even with the top of your helmet. Your weight should be on your back foot.

The tactical options of this guard are essentially the same as those for the corresponding guard of the sword in two hands.

With the axe, this guard can be as easily adopted on the left as it can with the sword.

The axe's Left Woman's Position.

Woman's Position allows a powerful *fendente* down to Boar's Tooth. Be sure to extend your arms enough that the butt-spike clears your body as you strike. Once the strike is complete, you will have to adjust your hand position if you wish to mimic the illustrated version of Boar's Tooth.

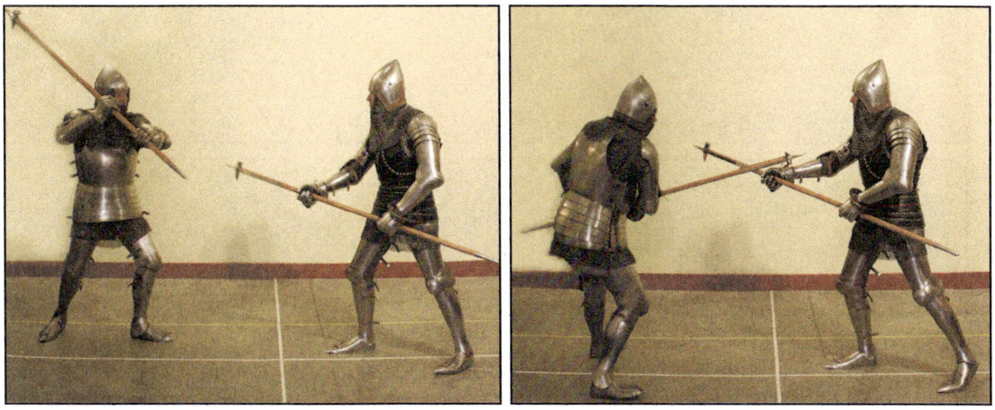

If your opponent tries to deflect your strike by coming up under the stroke, shorten your strike, making the rotation a little faster, and strike the opponent's arms instead of his head.

BOAR'S TOOTH POSITION
(DENTE DI CINGHIARO)

Boar's Tooth is one of four axe guards that share names with guards from the sword in two hands. The others are Woman's Position, Long Tail, and Window Position. To find Boar's Tooth, stand as before in Woman's Position. Step backward (*retornare*). Bring your left hand back and snug it up against your hip. As you move, lower your right hand until the axe's head points at the ground. The plane of the hammer and beak should be parallel to your left leg or point a little further away from the center. Your weight should be on your front leg.

To match the drawing, you need to choke up on the axe. Loosen your left-hand grip and slide the axe back until your right hand meets your left, then slide your left hand back and take

GUARD TRANSITIONS

STAGE 4
Drill as per Stage 3 Guard Transition but make all steps backward.

STAGE 5
Drill as per Stage 3 Guard Transition but make all steps oblique.

STAGE 6
Drill as per Stage 3 Guard Transition but make all steps backwards and oblique.

If a Posta di Donna opposes me, the middle Porta di Ferro, I know her play and she mine. For we have faced one-another many times before, sword or axe in hand. And here's what I think: everything she says she can do to me, I can do better to her. … Anyway, between the two of us there's little to choose from, except in trickery.

hold of the shaft. You may need to repeat this action to get close to the drawing if your haft is a long one.

The tactical options of this guard are essentially the same as those for the corresponding guard of the sword in two hands.

For example, the axe head's presence on your left side presents a threat to an opponent trying to close, much as the sword's point does.

Unlike the sword, the axe would seem to offer a Right Boar's Tooth option, with a shift in grip and lead leg, that would not change the principles of play.

A possible Right Boar's Tooth for the axe, which might be possible because of the way you grip an axe. With the sword, the position on this side would be Iron Gate, which doesn't have to deal with a haft's butt end.

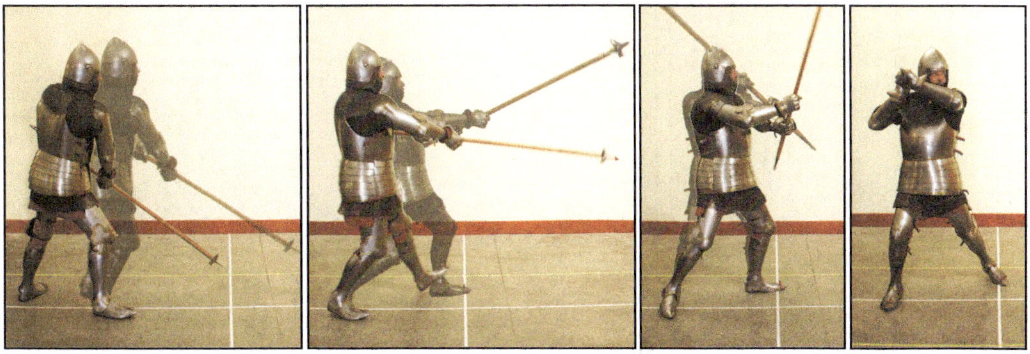

Boar's Tooth allows a strong *sottano* up to Woman's Position on the right.

There is an interpretation problem regarding this guard as well. The text with the drawing calls it Middle Iron Gate (*Porta di ferro mezzana*) but the text of its opposing guard refers to it as Boar's Tooth. As you can tell from the title of this page, I am inclined to believe it is a textual error in the Getty, because the Pisani-Dossi has the same opposing pair and uses Boar's Tooth. In addition this position holds the weapon well to the left, an arrangement associated elsewhere in the Getty with Boar's Tooth.

The possibility exists that the intent was that this position be Middle Boar's Tooth, to be held with the axe head on the centerline.

LONG TAIL POSITION
(POSTA DI CODA LONGA)

Long Tail is one of four axe guards that share names with guards from sword in two hands. The others are Woman's Position, Boar's Tooth, and Window Position.

To find Long Tail Position, stand in Boar's Tooth as before. Step back (*retornare*) so that your left foot is leading. As you step, let the axe move around you. Its head will want to swing behind like a long tail. While it is swinging, slide your right hand down to your left. Re-establish your grip and slide your left hand closer to the butt-spike. Make a Stable Turn (*volta stabile*). Keep looking straight ahead through the process. Your weight should be on your back leg, and your left arm should be stretched across

SIDE TRANSITIONS STAGE 1

Stand in a guard on one side.
Step and make an attack to Long Position.
Recover to the same (or corresponding guard on the other side.

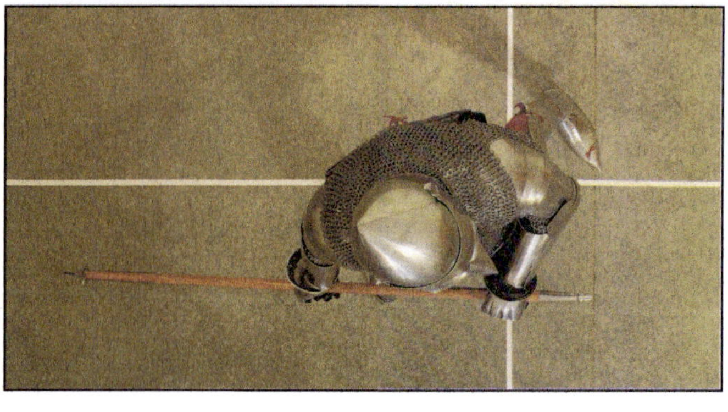

I am the Coda Longa, against a Posta di Fenestra, and I can strike at any time. One of my fendente can beat any axe or sword to the ground, placing me in a strong position for close play. You will now see my plays: please be so kind as to examine them one by one.

your body and back, along the line of the axe haft. To keep this alignment, the axe head may have to be pointing more at a diagonal rather than straight back.

The tactical options of this guard are essentially the same as those for the corresponding guard of the sword in two hands.

It should be possible to hold a Left Long Tail Position. As when trying to assume this guard on the left with the sword in two hands, the position would cross your arms. This is less dangerous with the axe than with the sword for much the same reason that Left Window Position can stand with the wrists crossed: you have a point projecting a threat towards the opponent. Further, the manner of gripping the double ended axe is such that you could shift your grip so that your left hand is near the head and your right near the butt-spike. Fiore shows such a grip in Short Serpent Position, indicating that we may be expected to change our grip on the axe as needed. Still, such a grip will be slightly weaker (assuming you are right-handed) as you will not have your stronger hand near the heavier end of the axe.

Long Tail Position can make a strong *sottano* strike up to Left Window Position, then relaxed into Left Woman's Position

WINDOW POSITION
(POSTA DI FENESTRA)

Window Position is one of four axe guards that share names with guards from sword in two hands. The others are Woman's Position, Boar's Tooth, and Long Tail. This version of the guard is being held on the right. Window Position with the axe is a reciprocal position as it is with the sword and can be held on the left or right.

To find Window Position, stand in Long Tail Position as before.

Make a Stable Turn (*volta stabile*) and as you do, raise your arms over your head. The head of your axe comes forward, but not so far that the point is directly aimed at the opponent. Settle the shaft parallel to the ground, above the level of your eyes. Don't block your vision!

SIDE TRANSITIONS

STAGE 2

Drill as Stage 1 Side Transition, but make steps backwards.

STAGE 3

Drill as Stage 1 Side Transition, but make steps oblique.

STAGE 4

Drill as Stage 1 Side Transition, but make steps backwards and oblique.

They call me the left Posta di Fenestra, and I keep the right arm withdrawn. We have no stability. Each seeks deception: you think I'll attack with a fendente, but I pass back instead and change guards. So, while I started to the left, I will enter to the right, and I can quickly perform the plays we will now see.

The tactical options of this guard are essentially the same as those for the corresponding guard of the sword in two hands. However, when we remember that Fiore categorizes Window Position as *instabile,* we can only think that the axe's Window Position is even more unstable, given the heavy head that you are trying to keep up there.

It seems likely that this guard can be held in a right-side version. If you simply switch lead legs and shift the axe over to that left side, you will have two choices. You can take the head backwards and leave the butt-spike forwards. This puts the lighter, faster end forward but reduces the resistance to strikes by an opponent's axe head. Alternatively, you can keep the axe head forward, but this crosses your arms. With the hands held back and the axe head standing between them and any danger, the crossed wrists are not as vulnerable as they would be in a low position. This is comparable to the situation with Left Window Position for the sword in two hands. An additional option presents itself with the axe because of the weapon's double-handed grip: you hold the head forward and shift your grip to have the left hand forward and the right back.

Left Window Position allows a *mezzano* around to Right Window Position (wrists crossed). This Right Window Position can easily flip back into Long Tail Position by bringing the axe head back over the head and then down.

Axe blows deliver bigger blows than any other handheld weapon

These are the plays through which these guards fight. Each guard wants to try them, certain to win. If you can beat the opponent's axe to the ground as shown, by all means do it. Also do the others as long as the opponent does not stop you with a counter.

A fully powered blow from the axe can be devastating. You cannot trust that your armor will protect you, so you must try to stop or deflect an incoming axe head. If you can bring your opponent's axe head to the ground, you will neutralize its greatest threat. While it is true that you can make this attempt from any of the axe guards, some combinations work better than others and the details will vary.

Each player stands in Woman's Position on the Right and each makes a downward blow (*fendente*) as they might in a similar situation with swords. The axes will come to a cross. If they stay high, continued play will be similar to that of swords. Axes being axes, mass and momentum are likely to take over take over and send both heads the ground. Done this way the final positions are not advantageous for the player whose axe is below to shoot his axe through his opponent's legs. The player on top can strike up.

If one player starts an attack and the other must react, he can make a more defensive-minded pass backwards (*retornare*) while making his downward blow. In this final position, the relative leg positions are different as each player has the same leg forward.

The player in Boar's Tooth attacks, making a typical thrust with an advance (*accressere*). The scholar in Woman's Position responds, passing back and striking down to drive his opponent's weapon to the ground. The players have opposite legs forward, but in a mirror image to the drawing in the manuscript.

THESE ARE THE PLAYS THROUGH WHICH THESE GUARDS FIGHT

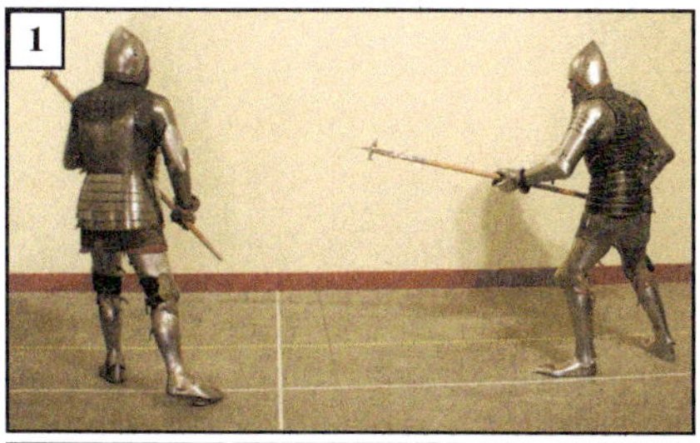

The player in Short Serpent attacks, shooting a thrust forward. The scholar in True Cross responds, passing back as he deflects the incoming axe head and carries it to the ground.

The player in Woman's Position attacks, making a standard downward blow (*fendente*). The scholar in Boar's Tooth responds, striking up to deflect the incoming axe head from behind and using his turning motion to guide his opponent's weapon to the ground.

The player in Long Tail attacks, making a truly powerful downward blow (*fendente*). The scholar in Window Position responds, passing back and catching the incoming axe head from behind. Both axe heads crash to the ground.

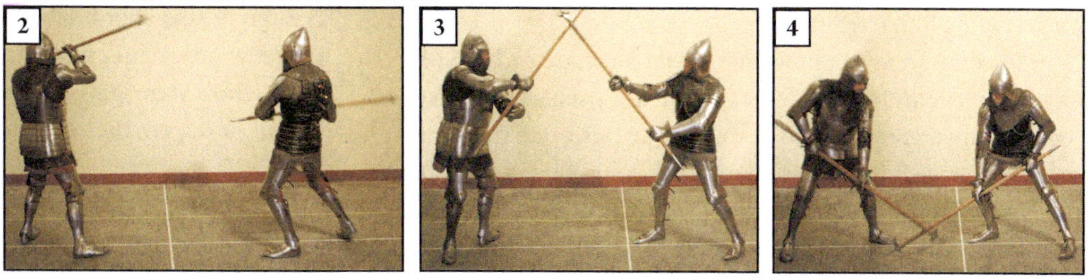

Here's a student who thrusts his axe between the opponent's legs, while covering his eyes with his left hand. When the opponent can no longer see and tries to turn, he will fall down for sure.

The scholar shoots his axe haft forward as he steps.

The scholar's axe haft levers over his opponent's left thigh and behind his right knee.

When the axe heads in a crossing go down and your axe is beneath his, this play is easy. It is easiest when the players have opposite lead legs.

Shoot your axe haft forward, sliding it through your lead hand as you guide it between his legs. As your rear hand nears your lead hand, you should release the rear grip and pass forward (*passare*). You want to step to the outside of his lead leg. Your free hand shoots forward and up. A strike here helps disorient him. Finishing with your hand across his vision slits blinds him, encouraging him to panic.

In the play above, the scholar uses his cuirass (left) to lock his axe into his body structure, rather than his thigh as shown in the drawing and the picture above.

Your motion in stepping will drive your axe head deeper between his legs and start to lever the haft against his legs. You must lock it against your body to keep a strong position. This arrangement's leverage is immense. It will break your opponent's balance. Applied to completion, this move will topple him. Pushing his head back only exaggerates the effect.

Safety note: The lever created in this action is extremely powerful. It may cause limb damage either before or during the resulting fall.

Do not execute this play to completion!

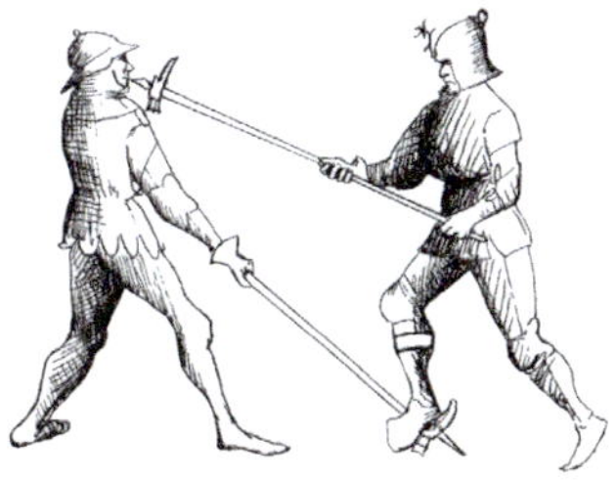

This play can be performed by the student before me too, when he is in close play (as you can see). Place your left foot on the opponent's axe while pulling yours back and thrusting into his face.

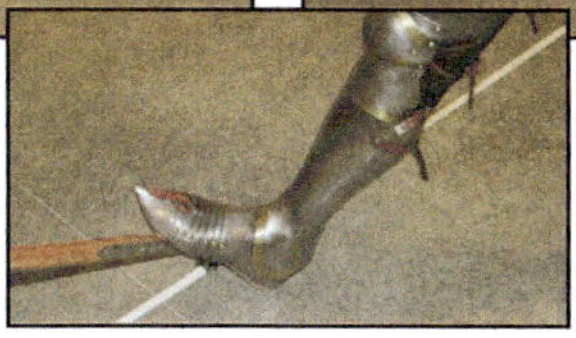

The scholar's foot pins his opponent's axe head.

When crossing axe heads go down and your axe is on top of his, it is free to rise up and strike. Having your lead leg the opposite of his is the best.

Using whichever foot is nearest, stomp on his ax head to ensure it stays down. As you do, raise the head of your own axe and turn your torso to strike or to set up a thrust.

Make your attack as quickly as you can. Aim at a lightly armored target since you will not have full power. Fiore specifies the visor, which is indeed thinner, but possibly also because a rising thrust might slip beneath the visor's edge.

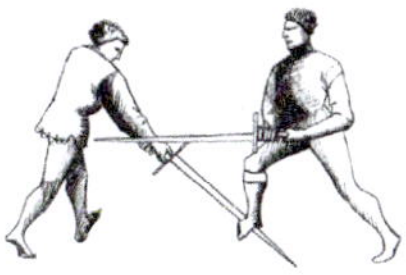

Eleventh and twelfth plays of the Second *Largo* master (27rA & B)

This play is a direct analog of a *largo* play in the sword section that comes from a low crossing and has a follow-on scholar who stomps his opponent's weapon and strikes. The *largo* play, however, is shown against a thrust while the axe crossing does not specify what attack it answers. Further the sword is an all together handier weapon than an axe. For one thing, it does not have a shaft that can get in the way of shifting across the your body as an axe does. The sword blade can whip up from the cross in a cut; it is harder to do that with the axe, especially if one wants to penetrate armor.

Fiore acknowledges that this thrust may not have sufficient force to penetrate armor with the follow-on scholar. Having failed to penetrate the visor, this follow-on scholar steps in, lifts it, and thrusts again at the exposed face. His opponent seems to be in the process of pulling back on his axe to extricate the head from beneath the scholar's foot, an action that gives the scholar time to act.

The third play of the sword in armor (33vA) represents the same solution to an impenetrable visor. Note how the scholar also uses his blade to ward against his opponent's sword as he acts.

This grapple allows me to strike you in the head with my axe. I'll use my left arm to place you into the strong low bind, which is the one from which the opponent can be placed in the most danger of death.

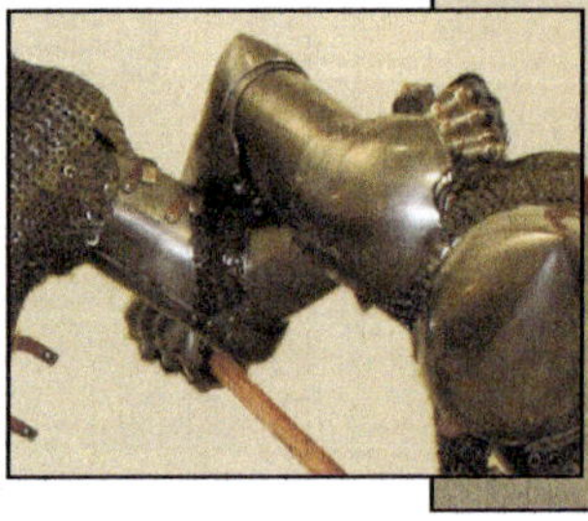

As with other weapons, when the opportunity presents, you can release your grip and go for a bind. Here, the scholar has found a chance to slip his left arm past his opponent's elbow and create the Middle Bind (*ligadura mezzana*). With the bind achieved, wide motions are necessary to bring the ponderous ax into play.

The axe can make the binding and control plays that use leverage more powerfully than the sword, for it has a longer lever arm.

An axe can also mimic a dagger's play, or how you might use your open hand against a dagger. Here, it uses the mechanics of the First Remedy Master's disarm.

Unlike the sword, the axe has extended portions on both ends, adding the possibility of significant strokes with the butt of the weapon as well as the head. While butt strokes will not cut, they can apply significant concussive force.

I'll use a mezza volta to disarm you of your axe. That done, and while I am still turning, I'll strike you in the head just like the student we'll see next. I believe you'll fall dead.

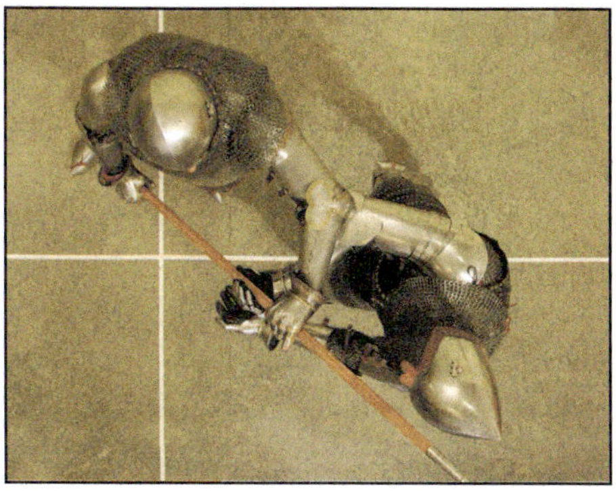

It may happen that you find yourself in a position where your axe is more a hindrance than a help. Perhaps, as here, you have lost your grip with one hand and your opponent is threatening to put you into the Middle Bind (*ligadura mezzana*) as preparation for smiting you right and proper.

To avoid the bind, you must drop your axe so that you can slip your arm free. That leaves you without an axe, however. Luckily, there is one coming your way—all you have to do is catch it. Fortunately you are close enough to him that his axe strike cannot be at its full strength.

Having grabbed his axe shaft, you can twist it as you did in the sword in two hands disarms.

Of course, once you have his axe, you know what to do with it. In case you don't, the follow-on scholar shows you.

… I want to pull you to the ground by your visor. And if I wanted to, I could do the same with wrestling—which is the better way to do it, and which is something I'm good at.

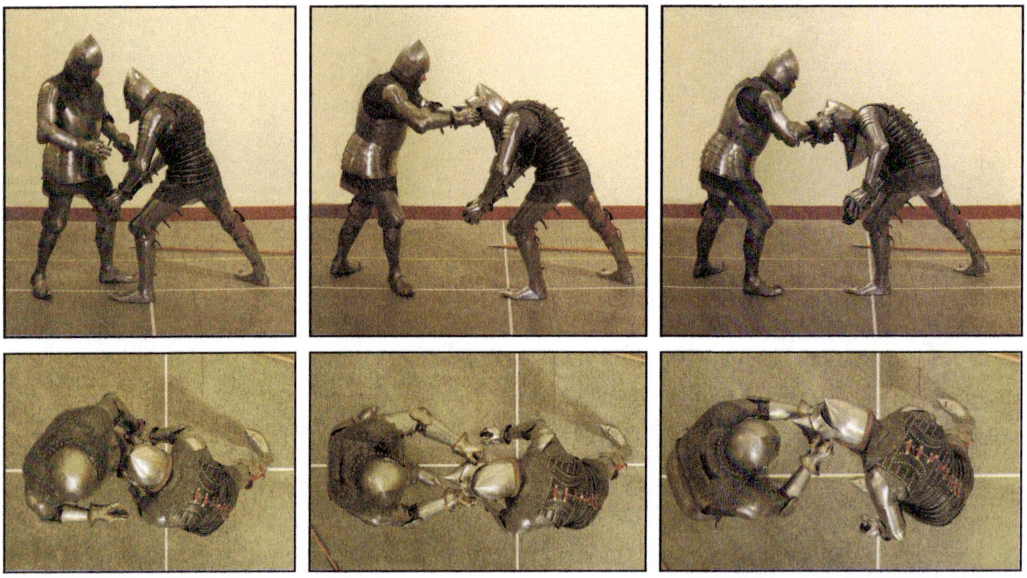

In this play the scholar of the axe has found himself and his opponent without their weapons. His opponent, possibly because the previous action has left him bent over (otherwise he is foolish), attempts to grab the scholar's leg to take him down. The scholar beats him by grabbing his helmet and, with a quick Full Turn (*tutta volta*) sends his foe to the ground.

A new lesson here is that you can use your opponent's armor against him. You could just grab his helmeted head and throw him, but lifting his visor improves your leverage against his neck and makes the throw easier.

As always, it's a fight. Your opponent is your foe, not his weapon. This play reiterates several lessons. One is the geometry lesson of the sword in two hands: the distance is shorter to the head than it is to the leg. Another is that *abrazare* is for armored combat as much as for unarmored.

Grabbing the helmet directly will also work, but provides significantly less leverage.

Safety note: The grip on the visor that Fiore advises gives you tremendous leverage against your victim's neck. A strong twist could snap a neck. This is not a move to be tried without great care given to your partner's safety!

The axe, like a sword, is longer than a man's arm. This puts it in the category of weapons that can play both wide and close. In its play, it will mimic the sword. In the wide play, its strikes will follow the sword's.

Woman's Position allows downward blows (*fendenti*).

... I can defend with the pulsativa guards of the sword. ...

All is done with prudence

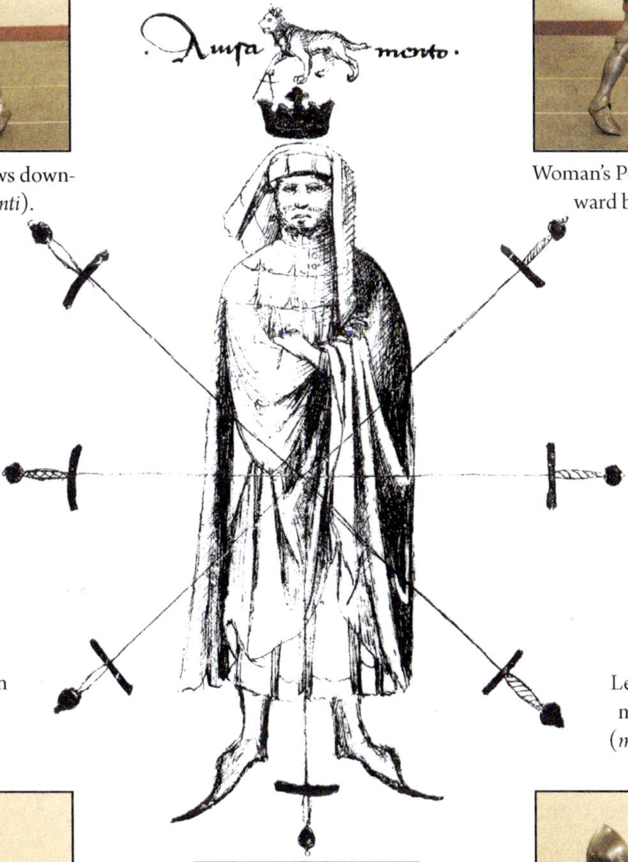

Woman's Position allows downward blows (*fendenti*).

Right Window Position makes middle blows (*mezzani*) to the left.

Left Window Position makes middle blows (*mezzani*) to the right.

Long Tail allows upwards blows (*sottani*) from right to left.

Short Serpent makes the thrusts (*punte*).

Boar's Tooth allows upwards blows (*sottani*) from left to right.

THE AXE IS A SWORD

If you are on the receiving end of it once, you won't want to try it again.

LESSONS OF THE SPEAR

The spear (*lanza*) section is only three pages, even shorter than the axe section. It departs from Fiore's pattern of instruction and illustration by presenting three Remedy Masters, all of whom do the same play. Each master appears facing an opponent, each figure in a separate layout position on the page with the accompanying text only over the master. Then he shows an alternate guard, again with an opponent in a separate drawing. A third guard follows, as does a third opponent. All of these *poste* are held to the right side of the master's body. They all do the same play, which is drawn with both players in the same illustration space. A counter follows.

Three more Fight Masters are next, each sharing a drawing with his opponent. This does not indicate plays occurring at a different distance; it is a space-conserving measure in the manuscript and allows the spear instruction to appear on three rather than four pages. Each of this second set of masters holds a guard on left side. Again, they all do the same play, essentially a high-line version of the previous play done on the other side. No counter is shown, but one is described in the last text block. Surprise! It's the same butt stroke used by the Counter Master to the first play, done on the other side.

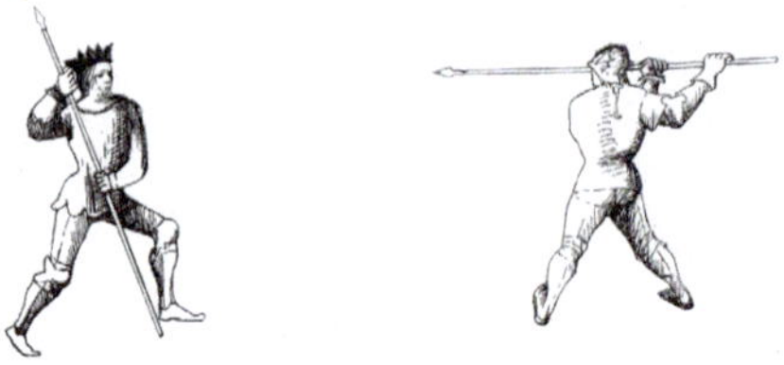

Tutta Porta di Ferro (39rAB)

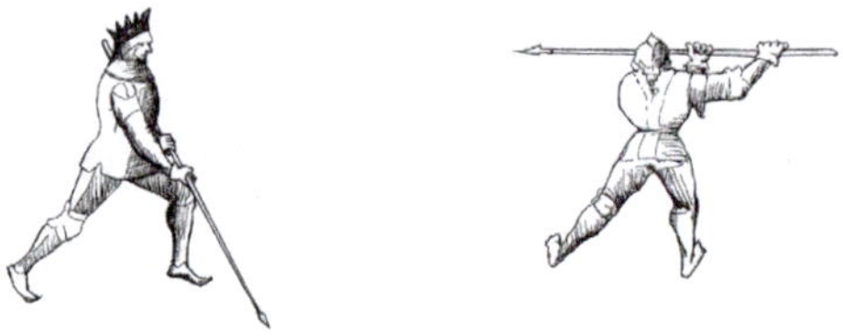

Mezza Porta di Ferro (39rCD)

Posta di Fenestra on right (39vAB)

The scholar of spear on the right (39vC)

Dente di Cinghiaro (40r a)

Posta di Vera Croce (40rB)

Posta di Fenestra on left (40rC)

The scholar of the spear on the left (40rD)

GET THE POINT

Each of the plays in this section is against a thrust and makes its own thrust because "the lance can only strike this way." Even in the counter, the move is not usually a percussive strike, but a strike with the tip (i.e., a thrust). "This is why the butt of my lance should be capped with a point of iron."

Why can the spear "only strike this way"? Is it because the spear's point is the only effective strike against players armored as the Getty's are? The players in the Pisani-Dossi and the Morgan are not. Could the prohibition mean *decisive* strike? A butt stroke would be a nuisance strike against an armored man, as would a slash with a spear point's edge. Or does this mean, as I think likely given the treatise's structure, that this is the only strike a spear may strike at the distance at which a spear plays, but where other weapons do not?

A LONG DISTANCE GAME

The representation of distance between players on foot is greater here than in any other section. The spear is the longest of Fiore's weapons, the first to be notably longer than a man is tall. Even a short spear is a long weapon, and the spear plays work "whether their lance is long or short."

A spear's reach is its special feature and what Fiore is most interested in this deep into the treatise. That reach sets play at a wide distance, so there is no *zogho stretto* for the spear—as a spear. If the play starts too close, the True Cross Master tells you what to do. Pass back (*retornare*) and keep it wide as you exchange his thrust.

IT'S ALL RELATED

At several points in this section Fiore refers to the sword. First, he mentions that the spear takes the guards of the sword, although they are clearly adapted to the long length of the spear. Here he tells us that you can use a sword to make these plays and offers tactical advice on how to set aside attacks when you have a shorter weapon.

> ***... Any off-line guard with the short lance or a short sword is enough to wait for any long hand-held weapon. Right-sided guards will parry and, while parrying, pass and strike with a thrust. Left-sided guards will parry and beat aside, and strike with a cut—but are not as good for answering with a thrust.***

The Counter Master of the spear (39vD)

The counters to these plays involve reversing the spear. Where did we learn to strike with the non-pointy end? Back in the sword section. And that is where we can look for details in how to do more than just strike with the butt. The difference here is that because of the longer length of the spear, the butt strike occurs while the player is further from the opponent.

And that, as Fiore says "can very well suffice as to the lance." We have completed the combat on foot and will move to dealing with mounted combat.

FULL IRON GATE
(PORTA DI FERRO)

... I am the first, who is set in tutta Porta di Ferro, to beat away the lance of the opponent; I will pass obliquely out of line with the right foot, and crossing his lance I will beat it away to the left. As long as you pass and parry in uninterrupted sequence with your strike, this action can't fail.

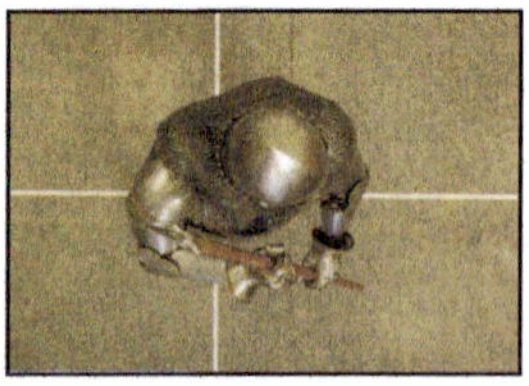

To find Full Iron Gate, hold your spear in both hands, the right nearer the head and just below your eye line. Your left hand should be about elbow height. Both thumbs should be towards the head and the butt near the ground. Take the usual stance, left leg forward and weighted. Your hips should be open and ready to power an action. Pull your right hand back toward your shoulder and let the butt drift out and to your right.

From here, you will make the play by stepping off line with your right foot while bringing your right hand out and across. You must be careful to clear your left knee with the butt of the spear.

HALF IRON GATE
(PORTA DI FERRO MEZZA)

I am situated in mezza Porta di Ferro ... I will parry while making a step, and strike you without fail.

To find Half Iron Gate, start in Full Iron Gate as before. Close your hips, rotating your right hip forward until your torso is squared up towards the opponent. As you do, lower your right hand and let your left go backward along with the spear's butt. Your right arm should be fully extended, but not locked up. Your right hand should end a little forward of your lead knee.

From here, you will make the play by stepping off line with your right foot while bringing your right hand up and across.

RIGHT WINDOW POSITION
(POSTA DI FENESTRA)

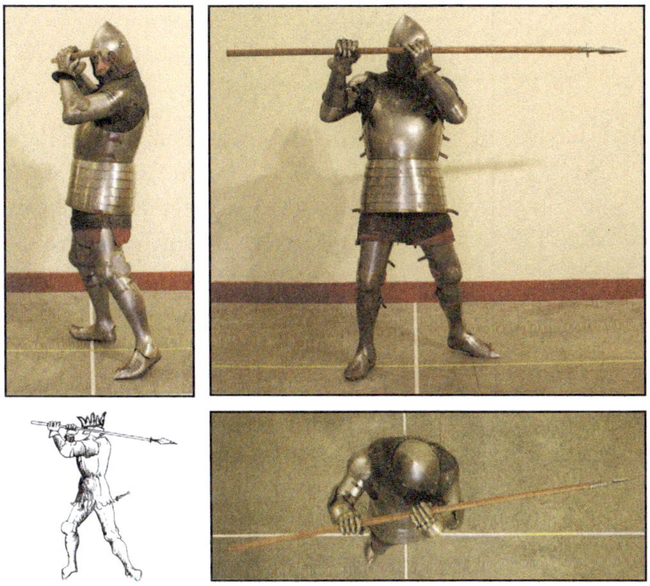

The postion held in the photos is a variation of the *posta* imposed by the constraints of this particular armor.

I am the noble right Posta di Fenestra, ... I can easily perform the exchange of thrust, and beating your weapon to the ground will work without fail. ...

To find Right Window Position, start in Half Iron Gate as before. Make a Stable Turn (*volta stabile*) while simultaneously bringing your right hand up and your left across until your right is about head height, where you can look under the spear shaft. Your left continues moving, coming around and up until it is behind your right hand.

From here, you will make the play by stepping back with your left foot and making a Stable Turn as your bring the spear's butt around and the point in line.

The three guards we have just seen ... should finish their actions with this play. This play ends their actions and their art—as I strike this opponent on their behalf.

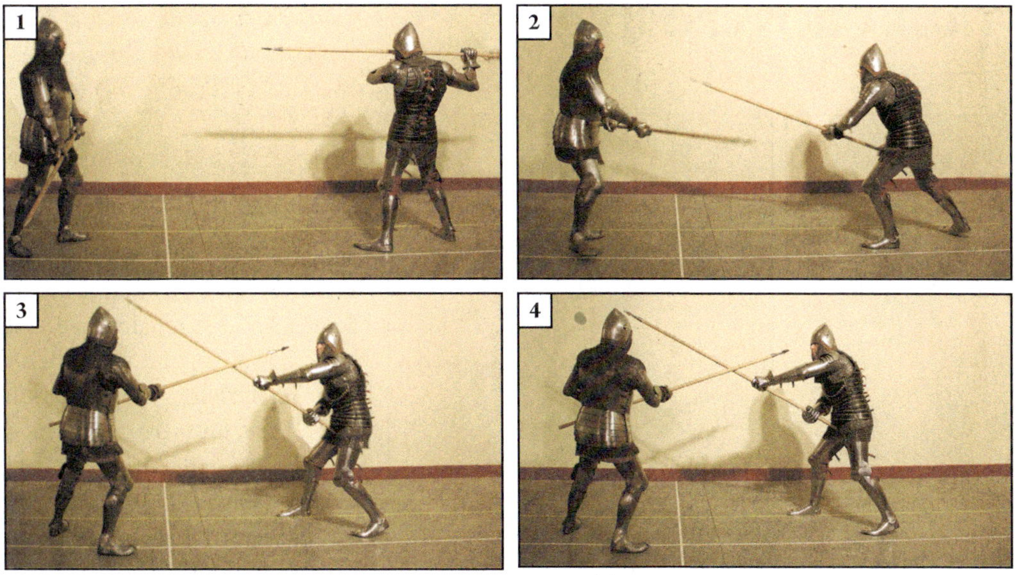

The scholar steps offline, bringing his spear up and around to parry (2). Shaft-on-shaft contact drives his opponent's point off target (3) and allows the scholar to place his point into the oncoming opponent (4). The opponent's height and distance determine where your point needs to be. Adjust accordingly, even if it means using your left hand to pull your spear shaft back through your lead hand. If so, keep pressure against his shaft to keep his point away.

BOAR'S TOOTH POSITION
(POSTA DI DENTE DI CINGHIARO)

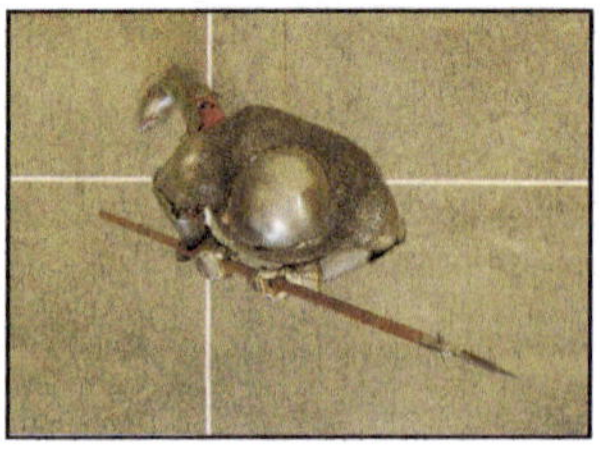

... I am the first, the Dente di Cinghiaro. ... We pass out of line by first stepping offline with the foot that is forward. And all of us ... come together with a thrust after the parry, since the lance can only strike this way.

To find Boar's Tooth Position, stand in Right Window Position as before. Make a Stable Turn (*volta stabile*) and step forward (*passare*). Bring your hands down and around until they are in front of you, your right hand just about chest height. Make another Stable Turn and shift your weight onto your back foot. Your spear shaft will come to a new angle as your turn.

From here, you will make the play by stepping off line to the right with your lead foot with a Full Turn (*tutta volta*) with your moving foot ending behind your pivot foot. Your left hand will whip around and up to about shoulder height as your body turns to present your point at the opponent's face.

This move creates a beat against the opponent's shaft rather than a thrust in opposition as we saw from the other side.

TRUE CROSS POSITION
(POSTA DI VERA CROCE)

I am waiting in Posta di Vera Croce, and you are too close to me. I pass backward with my front foot (the right) while beating your lance out of line to my right. My point won't miss, while yours will.

To find True Cross Position, stand in Boar's Tooth Position as before. Bring your left hand down and out until the spear point is just below horizontal. Your right hand should rise a little, until that elbow is at about a 90° bend.

From here, you will make the play as you did from Boar's Tooth, but this time both of your hands must rise as your turn.

LEFT WINDOW POSITION
(POSTA DI FENESTRA)

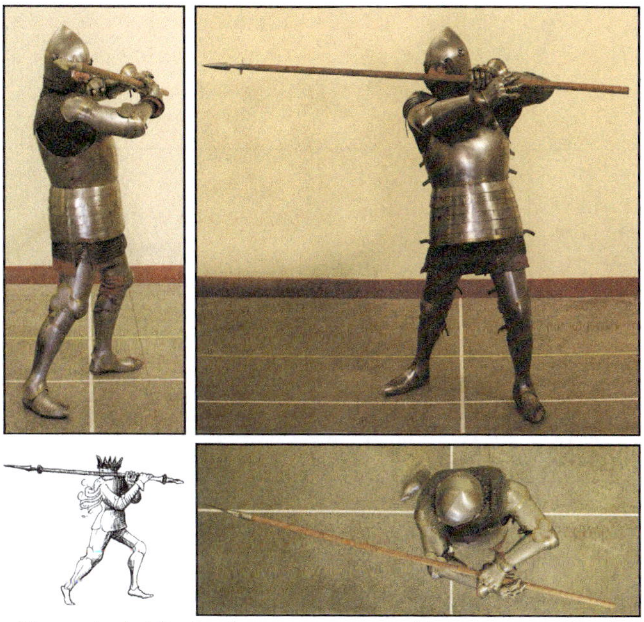

The postion held in the photos is a variation of the *posta* imposed by the constraints of this particular armor.

I am ready in left Posta di Fenestra, … I will keep my point high and my arms low, pass offline to the riverso side with my back foot …

To find Left Window Position, stand in True Cross Position as before. Bring your left hand up while keeping a loose grip on the shaft. Push up with your right hand until it reaches your left. Let momentum keep the spear turning. Shift your left hand grip to a place on the shaft behind your right as the spear's point comes down. Stop the spear just above your eye line.

From here, you will make the play by stepping as you did from Boar's Tooth. Your left hand will swing down and rise as it comes around into Right Window Position.

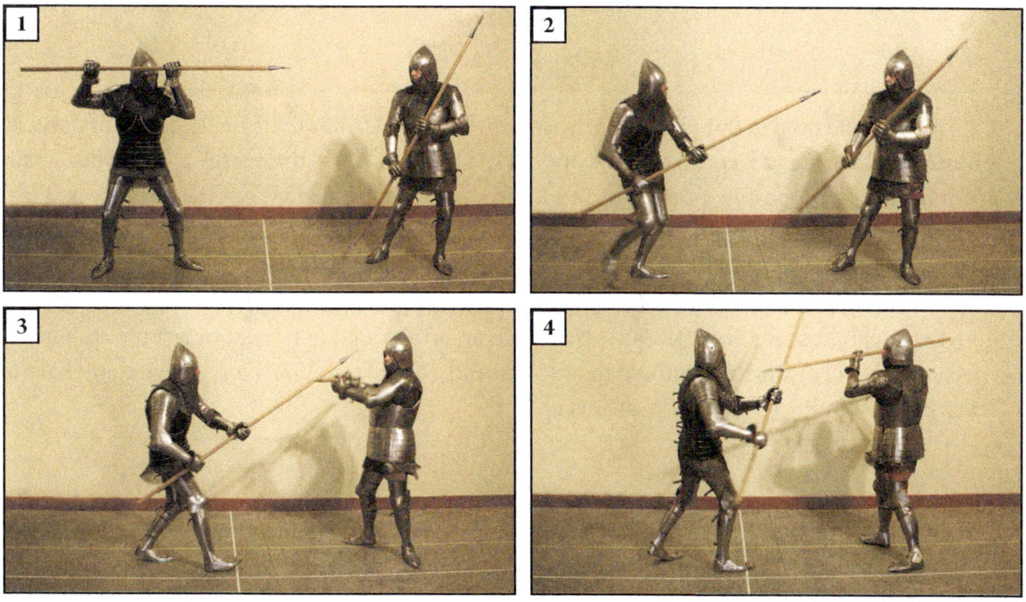

The scholar (on right) steps offline (2), making a Half Turn; the lead foot changes with the turn. He brings his spear around with him, raising his hands so that his shaft is high (3). The snapping action beats away the opponent's point. The scholar then places his point (4), thrusting if the opponent does not just run onto said point.

Note: When done from Left Window Position, you will not look like the drawing without shifting your grip shift as part of the move.

The counter moves to Window Position on the right

This is the counter of the three Masters of lance, who finish the play just before. Here is how this is performed. When the Masters think they have pushed my lance out of line, I turn my weapon and strike with the butt. This is why the butt of my lance should be capped by a point of iron. I care little for the plays of these Masters.

The principle used in this counter is the same whatever side it is done on. When your point is beaten or set aside (2), you accept the opponent's action and use the energy to turn your spear around, bringing the butt end forward (3). You can make strike directly if the distance is short enough (4); this is the most instinctive action. Of course, the butt can strike along all seven lines of attack as a sword does. Fiore's drawing implies that the Counter Master has brought the tip of his spear butt on line and thrust it into his opponent's face.

Even a blunt spear butt can cause trauma in an unarmored opponent or against an unprotected face, but against an armored man you would do well to follow Fiore's advice and have a sharp iron capping the butt of your spear.

If he strikes into your advancing point, use the energy to help turn your spear around. If you present little or no resistance, his point will not come online for an immediate thrust.
If you find yourself at too great a measure to strike him with the butt of your spear, thrust at him with the foot instead.

A spear is a long weapon and can be an awkward one to manipulate. Shifting your lead foot or your grip can be tricky and you should practice until you can make changes swiftly and smoothly.

Maintain a good grip

You should always grip your spear with your hands sufficiently far apart to make it balance well enough that you can easily make minute and quick adjustments of the forward point. This will allow you to fence with the tip against an opponent where all the principles of pressure and response apply as they do in the crossing of swords.

An exchange of thrusts.

Exchange hands

To exchange hands, slide the one furthest from the balance point of the spear closer to the other. Re-grip the spear shaft and move the previously stationary hand to the other side of the hand you just moved. Cup the shaft as soon as you can and slide the hand to its new position before taking hold again.

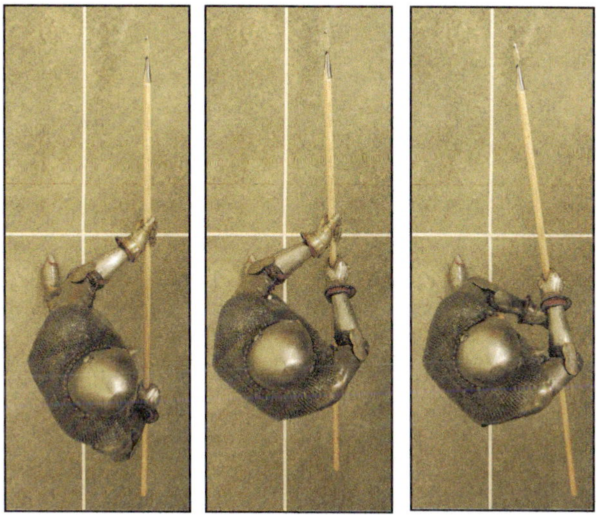

Shifting sides

To shift sides, loosen the grip on your lead hand. Slide the spear in the grip of your rear hand forward so that your rear hand is just behind your lead hand. Your spear point creates a threat. Shift your lead hand behind the other and grab the shaft. As you do this, shift the butt across in front of you. Pull the spear back through the loose grip of your new lead hand. You can make this shift while stepping forward or back.

I am the noble weapon called the lance ... if I do my task from the beginning I will defeat axe, sword and dagger.[1]

LESSONS OF MOUNTED COMBAT

The mounted combat section has three parts: lance (*lanza*), sword (*spada*), and *abrazare* on horseback. There are no Fight Masters and the section jumps right into a Remedy Master of the lance (using *Dente di Cinghiaro*) and his Counter Master. Both of these masters hold their lance points forward and the Counter Master, like a good general Counter Master, is a punctuation point. The three crowned masters in the following three plays each holds his lance differently. The first two use Woman's Position (*Posta di Donna*) on the left; one plays against an opponent with couched lance and the other against one who will throw his. The third master is riding away from his opponent and points his lance back over his shoulder. He is said to be unarmored, but the Pisani-Dossi shows him as fully armored as his pursuer.

All of the lance plays take up two illustration spaces, one for each rider. The text accompanies the master's block.

Next come a series of sword-against-lance plays. The first sword-armed master holds an unnamed position that "is also good against all other handheld weapons—that is, axe, staff, sword, and so on." Two Counter Masters have responses to him before another sword-armed master faces a lance while in Boar's Tooth (*Dente di Cinghiaro*). His Counter Master does the same thing that the first Counter Master does to the first sword-armed master; he puts his lance point into the horse before the sword-armed master can deflect it.

Like the lance plays, the sword-on-lance masters and the sword-on-sword masters that follow them use two illustration spaces. Clearly the positions are adopted before the horses close to contact. The sword-on-sword plays begin with the swords crossed. As the riders are no longer closing towards each other, each play takes a single illustration space.

The sword-on-sword portion begins with two Remedy Masters in the same guard: Long Tail (*Coda Longa*). The first is for when you ride to the opponent's right side and the second for when you are on

[1] This quote is from the Pisani-Dossi.

his left. The guard, we are told, "counters all the blows on both the mandritto and riverso side, and is usable against right- or left-handed opponents."

The nine following plays occupy a single illustration space each, the nearer horse obscuring much of the farther one. Six scholars use sword against sword, grab the opponent's sword and use the sword arm to grapple with him. The seventh is a specific Counter Master. The eighth play is a general Counter Master who counters "all the plays before this." The ninth play, shown as a scholar, counters "the play we just saw" and ends the sword-on-sword portion.

The first play of mounted *abrazare* identifies itself as *abrazare,* but the player is only a scholar in all of the manuscripts except the Paris. It is the first of four plays and all except the last have a Counter Master.

This is followed by a single page with a master on foot, using a weapon called a *ghiavarina* (a bladed variant of a spear), who stands against a mounted opponent. His two students each use a different end of their weapon to put paid to the mounted opponent.

The mounted combat section ends by returning to two mounted opponents. One is a master using a rope trick and the other a "play" that doesn't seem to be a technique at all. They share their page with what is clearly the closing paragraph of the treatise.

PACE OF THE HORSE

In mounted combat, horsemen must ride toward each other if they wish to engage. Once engaged, their horse will act as their legs, and govern not only the distance at which they will stand from their opponent but how quickly they can change that distance. To say that what the horse does is important is only to state the obvious.

The horses depicted in this section are shown in one of two stylized gaits, with little subtlety in the depiction of weight distribution or leg positioning comparable to the drawings of men on foot. In one of the gaits, the horse's front legs are together and raised and its rear legs are together and either outstretched behind it or gathered beneath it. In the second, one front foot is raised and the others all remain in contact with the ground. The first is likely a canter and the second a walk. The horses of all swordsmen and wrestlers appear in the second gait. Most of the lancers' horses are in the first; three of the five facing swordsmen are in the second gait.

Lance-on-lance combat appears to be expected to take place at higher speeds, and sword-on-sword and wrestling at slower speeds. The latter would almost certainly include the riders maneuvering their horses to optimize the angle of approach. Fiore, however, gives no instruction on how to handle one's horse or how to direct it, other than indicating the direction of travel relative to the opponent or whether you pass to the left or right.

It has been suggested by some that Fiore omits truly basic material either because "everyone knows that" or because presenting it to an experienced patron would be insulting. If so, riding and maneuvering a horse must be very basic to a mounted combatant. Yet it is vital. Dom Duarte (king of Portugal, avid horseman, and advocate of arms training) in his fifteenth-century treatise *Bem Cavalgar* tells us that when equivalent swordsmen fight on horseback, the better horseman will win.

GETTING THE POINT

Fiore tells us that when guards stand in point, the longer one wins, and the lance is by far the longest weapon he deals with. Yet Fiore also shows us in several places how to deflect an incoming point, and tells us that we can do it with a shorter weapon. Here he shows us what happens when that point can score before it can be deflected. Pity the poor horse.

This is a lesson that goes beyond the problems of defending your horse. If you extend any part of your anatomy (and when mounted the horse is your legs, and so is essentially part of your anatomy) outside the defensive zone of your weapon you risk having it hit. This issue is an especially important concern in dagger fighting.

BEAT IT

A big concern of mounted combat, especially as opponents close, is that there is something between you and your opponent: the front half of the horse. Even in closer ranges, the horse's head and neck fill part of the area where you might swing your sword. Naturally, you don't want to hit your own horse, nor do you want your opponent to. A deliberate attempt to cut to the horse while within range of the an enemy's sword is only going to leave you open to that enemy's sword. Your life for his horse's life is not a good trade. You must defend as well as attack, and the presence of the horse just complicates matters. In this, Fiore does pay attention to the horse.

> ***Bear in mind that thrusts and riversi must be beaten out to the side, and not upward; fendente should similarly be beaten out to the side, lifting slightly the opponent's weapon.***

As the sword is used to defend, the mounted swordsman must be careful not to direct his opponent's sword into his horse. Incoming attacks from your left side "must be beaten out to the side" or they will redirect into the horse. Similarly downward blows must also "be beaten out to the side" but the swordsman must work to raise the enemy's weapon as he does so, to ensure that the blade's path will be wide of the horse.

TWO SINGULAR INSTANCES

There are two things that appear in this section that do not show up elsewhere in the Getty.

One is a play where the advice is to not do it if the opponent is armored. In it, the Counter Master attempts to foil his opponent's attempt to throw him from the saddle with a technique similar to the that of the Third Remedy Master of the dagger's second scholar. As in that play, the mounted opponent has managed to get outside his foe's weapon and has placed his arm around his foe's neck. Here, the Counter Master strikes with his false edge, down and over the opponent's horse and into his leg. Against armor, this is too weak a blow to cause a wound, or even much of a distraction; against an unarmored man, it's a different story. In addition, the opponent's likely natural flinch response to the wound may well signal his horse to turn in the Counter Master's direction, thereby eliminating the pressure needed to make the throw.

Seventh play of mounted sword (44vC)

The other unique appearance is that of a Contra-counter Master, although he is not crowned as such. This player, who wear the garter of a scholar, is described as doing a "counter to the play we just saw." That play is a Counter Master, and a general Counter Master at that, since he "counters all the plays before this—especially those of mounted sword and their masters in Coda Longa." The text and sequencing make it clear that this apparent scholar is, in fact, an uncrowned Contra-counter Master. He doesn't appear as Fiore describes such masters in the prolog, but he definitely fills the role, especially in regard to being rare. All hail the singular, uncrowned Contra-counter Master!

Ninth play of mounted sword (45rA)

A WEIRD ENDING

The last two illustrations featuring mounted plays appear on the second-to-last page of the manuscript. The first of these features a master with a lance and returns to the two-illustration-space format used in the beginning of the section. The second has two mounted swordsmen who share a single illustration space with each other and a portion of a castle. The page also contains a text paragraph over the last, unfilled illustration space.

The master uses a trick: he has "tied one end of a strong rope to his horse's saddle. The other end is tied to the foot of his lance" and he intends to use this arrangement to pull his opponent off his horse. This fellow is clearly similar to the Trick Masters of the axe, and like them, he ends the instruction of his section with something one cannot normally do in battle.

The second illustration is of a sword-wielding scholar (so he doesn't belong to the Trick Master who precedes him) who is dealing with a "rascal" who is "running away from me towards a fortress." The fortress reference explains the appearance of scenery, something unique in the manuscript. Further, this scholar is chasing, striking, and needing to "get away, since his friends may give me grief"; he is not executing any particular technique such as we have seen in the other plays throughout the manuscript. Something else is going on here. What it is isn't exactly clear, although several lessons in prudence seem embodied in the text.

The last text says "here ends the book by the student Fiore." It was probably intended to accompany the drawing on the next leaf, that of two horses tied to a tree, whose design is too wide for a single space.

The last illustration (47rA & B)

IT'S ALL RELATED

As noted before, the sword on horseback portion provides several named positions using the sword in one hand. To further connect things, the text of the unnamed position (which should be left *Posta di Donna*) says it is "good against all other handheld weapons—that is, axe, staff, sword, and so on" and thereby suggesting several mixed-weapon encounters that are not shown in the manuscript.

The second sword master to play against lance does an action that involves "parrying and striking in a single turn of the sword." Here, Fiore makes explicit the sort of action he implied when he told us that the sword is "expert in defense and offense" and will "always strive to finish in those."

Distribution of Imagery in *Il Fior di Battaglia*

Section	Folios	FM	RM	SCH	CM	CCM	Other
Abrazare	6r-8r	4	1	12	3	0	0
Baton	8v	0	0	4[1]	0	0	0
Dagger	9r-18v; 38	5	9	52	19	0	5[2]
Dagger vs. Sword	19r-20r	0	4	4	1	0	0
Sword: in one hand	20r-21v	0[3]	1[3]	11	0	0	1[4]
Sword: in two hands	22r-31r[5]	19	4	37	1	0	5[6]
Sticks	31	0[3]	2[3]	2	0	0	0
Segno	32r	0	0	0	0	0	1
Sword: in armor	32v-35r	6	1	14[7]	1	0	2[8]
Axe	35v-37v	6	0	8	0	0	0
Spear	39r-40r	6	0	2	1	0	0
Mounted[8]: Lance	41r-42r	0	4	0	1	0	0
Mounted: lance vs. sword	42r-43r	0	2	0	3	0	0
Mounted: Sword	43v-45r	0	2	7[9]	2	0	0
Mounted: Abrazare	45r-45v	0	0	4	3	0	0
Mounted: Mounted vs. Foot	46r	0	1	2	0	0	0

[1] Two of the scholars are referred to as students of dagger masters
[2] These are Instruction Masters
[3] The Remedy Master also serves as a Fight Master
[4] This shows the opponents of the Remedy Master
[5] This count includes the masters at the "traditional" beginning of the sword in two hands section
[6] Four of these are Instruction Masters; the other shows the opponents of a Remedy Master
[7] One of these is a scholar of the Counter Master
[8] These are illustrations of specialized swords
[9] The last two drawings in *mounted combat* are omitted from this chart; see page 241

FM = Fight Master
RM = Remedy Master
SCH = Scholars
CM = Counter Master
CCM = Contra-counter Master
Other = Other illustrations

GLOSSARY

Abrazare – The art of unarmed combat techniques.
Accressere – A step that increases distance between the feet without changing lead foot.
Armizare – The art of arms.
Azza – A shafted weapon with an ax or hammer head, beak and spike.
Contra-counter Master – The player who defeats the action of the Counter Master, shown wearing a crown and garter.
Counter Master – The player who defeats the action of the Remedy Master or one of his Scholars, shown wearing a crown and garter.
Daga – A dagger.
Discressere – A step that decreases distance between the feet without changing the lead foot.
Fendente (pl. Fendente) – A downward blow, nearly vertical.
Fight Master – A figure who gives instruction on the art especially with regards to attacks and *poste*, shown wearing a crown.
Guardia – A position to stand in and/or move through; said to be the same as a *posta*.
Lanza – A spear.
Mandritto – A blow struck from the player's strong side, usually the right.
Mezza Spada – The middle of a sword blade; the crossing of the blades near the mid-point.
Mezza Mella – Half-blade, a sword grip with one hand (left) on the blade at or forward of the mid-point.
Mezza Volta – A half-turn; a passing step made while performing an action.
Mezzano (pl. Mezzani) – A blow, either upwards, downwards, or horizontal that is not a *fendente* or *sottano*.
Passare – A passing step where the trailing foot becomes the lead foot.
Player – A person acting within the art.
Posta (pl. Poste) – A position to stand in and/or move through which you use to injure an opponent or to defend against an attack; said to be the same as a *guardia*.
Punte di Spada – The point of the sword; the crossing at the weak part of the blade near the tip.
Remedy Master – The player whose action thwarts an attack, shown wearing a crown.
Retornare – A passing step where the lead foot becomes the trailing foot.
Riverso – A blow struck from the player's weak side, usually the left.
Scholar – A player who makes the plays of a master, shown wearing a garter.
Sottano (pl. Sottani) – An upwards blow, near vertical.
Spada – A sword, either with a single or hand-and-a-half grip.
Tutta Spada – The whole of the sword; used here in reference to a crossing of the blades below the mezza spada on what is modernly called the forte.
Tutta Volta – A full turn where one foot moves around the other, (which does not change position) while performing an action.
Volta Stabile – A stable turn, made without changing the position of the feet.
Zugadore – A player, usually the opponent.

Woman's Position is the most pictured guard in the Getty manuscript, showing both left and right versions as well as a high version. Especially when compared across the manuscripts, the drawings show quite a bit of variation, particularly in those of Right Woman's Position, which is arguably the most common one to be adopted by a right-handed fighter. Even fencers untutored in the art will adopt a version of this guard, as it offers probably the strongest blow a right-handed fighter can make.

Right Woman's Position appears with different weapon angles, different arm positions, different spread of feet in stance, different depth of stance, and as Fiore says it should, the heels-forward and heels-back variants that result from a Stable Turn.

What are we to make of these variations? I think we are seeing an expectation that there will be variation in a stance. Some will be due to individual preference, and some to individual capability. In a fight, some might even be due to an opponent not truly understanding the art. In short, Fiore lumps together these variations into a single position.

Why? A true master can play deceptively, attacking from an unexpected direction, but not all of your opponents will be true masters. Even so, there are many variables that can occur in a fight. Where you hold your weapon and how you stand can be influenced by your opponent's positioning, aggressiveness, and speed, as well as by your own capabilities and intent. What remains important is the quadrant in which a fighter is likely to play from a particular position. Fiore's *posta* instruct about and respond to the most likely probabilities. He doesn't seem to care about achieving a "perfect" version of a guard.

HIGH WOMAN'S POSITION
(POSTA DI DONNA LA SOPRANA)

Getty   Getty   Getty

Pisani-Dossi   Morgan   Paris

LEFT WOMAN'S POSITION
(POSTA DI DONNA SINISTRA)

Getty   Pisani-Dossi

RIGHT WOMAN'S POSITION
(POSTA DI DONNA DESTRA)

Getty   Getty   Getty

Pisani-Dossi   Pisani-Dossi   Pisani-Dossi   Morgan   Paris

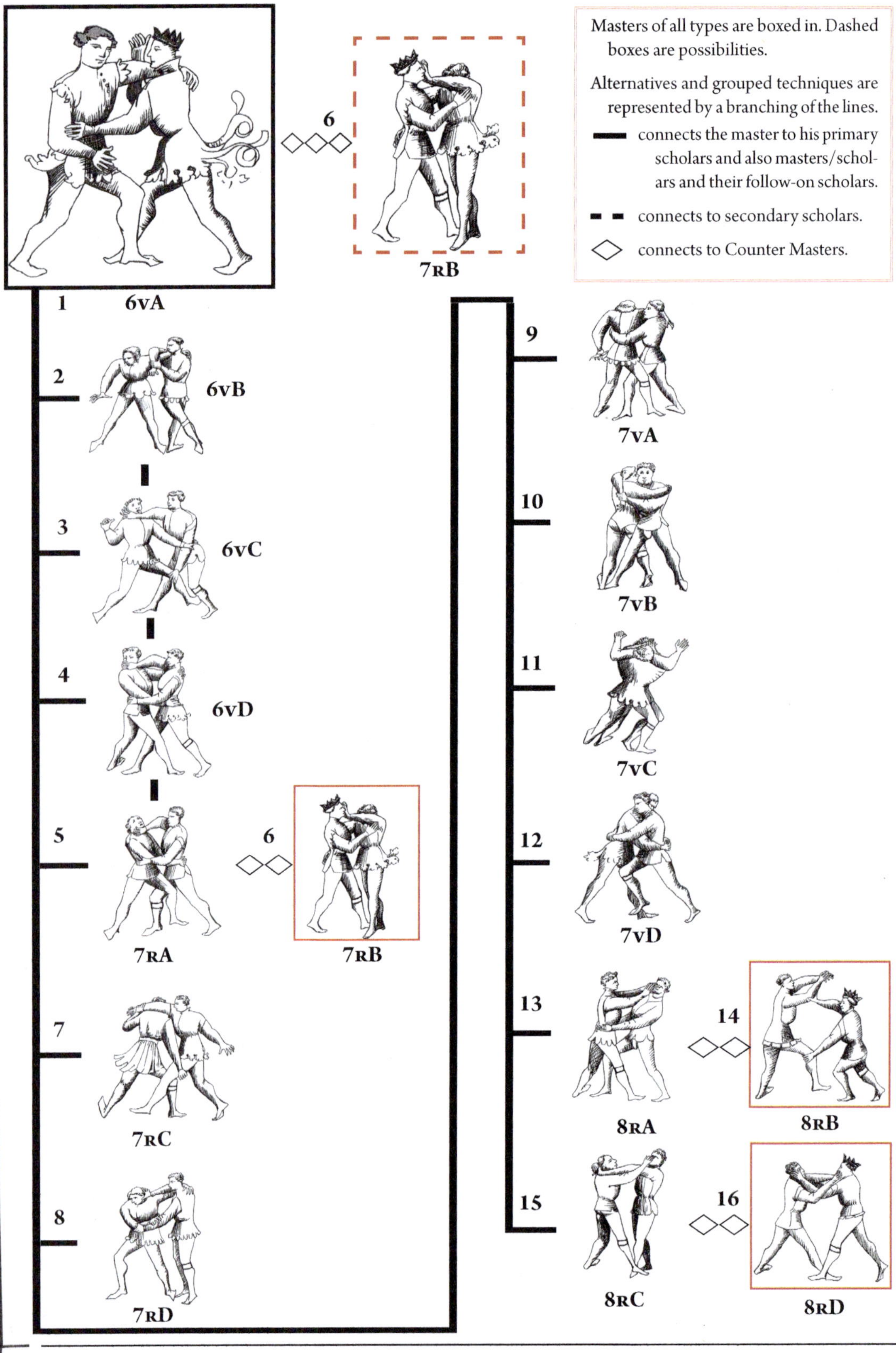
Masters of all types are boxed in. Dashed boxes are possibilities.
Alternatives and grouped techniques are represented by a branching of the lines.
connects the master to his primary scholars and also masters/scholars and their follow-on scholars.
connects to secondary scholars.
connects to Counter Masters.
1
6vA
6
7rB
2
6vB
3
6vC
4
6vD
5
7rA
6
7rB
7
7rC
8
7rD
9
7vA
10
7vB
11
7vC
12
7vD
13
8rA
14
8rB
15
8rC
16
8rD

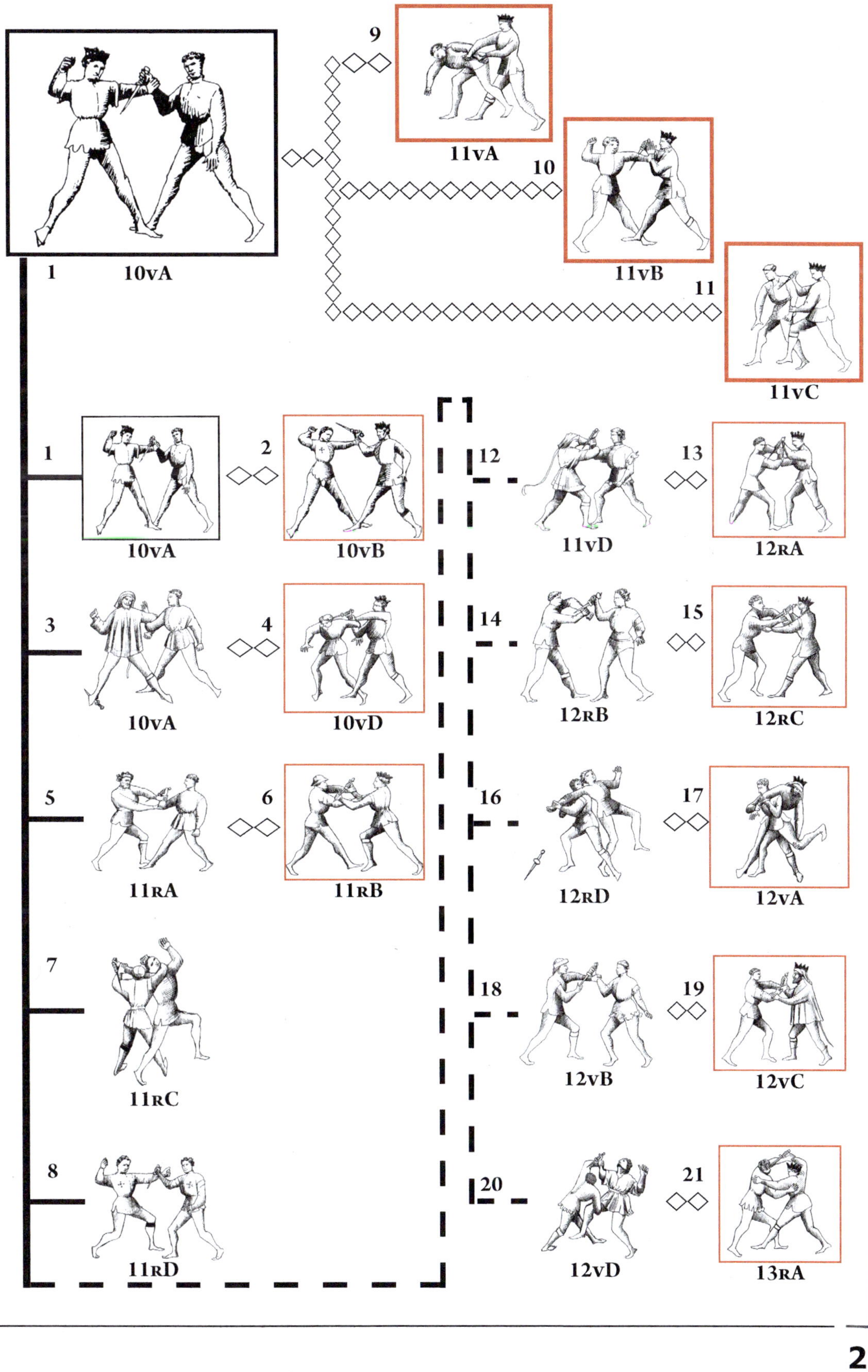
10vA
1
9
11vA
10
11vB
11
11vC
1
10vA
2
10vB
3
10vA
4
10vD
5
11rA
6
11rB
7
11rC
8
11rD
12
11vD
13
12rA
14
12rB
15
12rC
16
12rD
17
12vA
18
12vB
19
12vC
20
12vD
21
13rA

1 13rB

2

13rC

3

13rD

4

13vA

"I can play to the right and the left."

Scholars of the First Remedy Master

Scholars of the Third Remedy Master

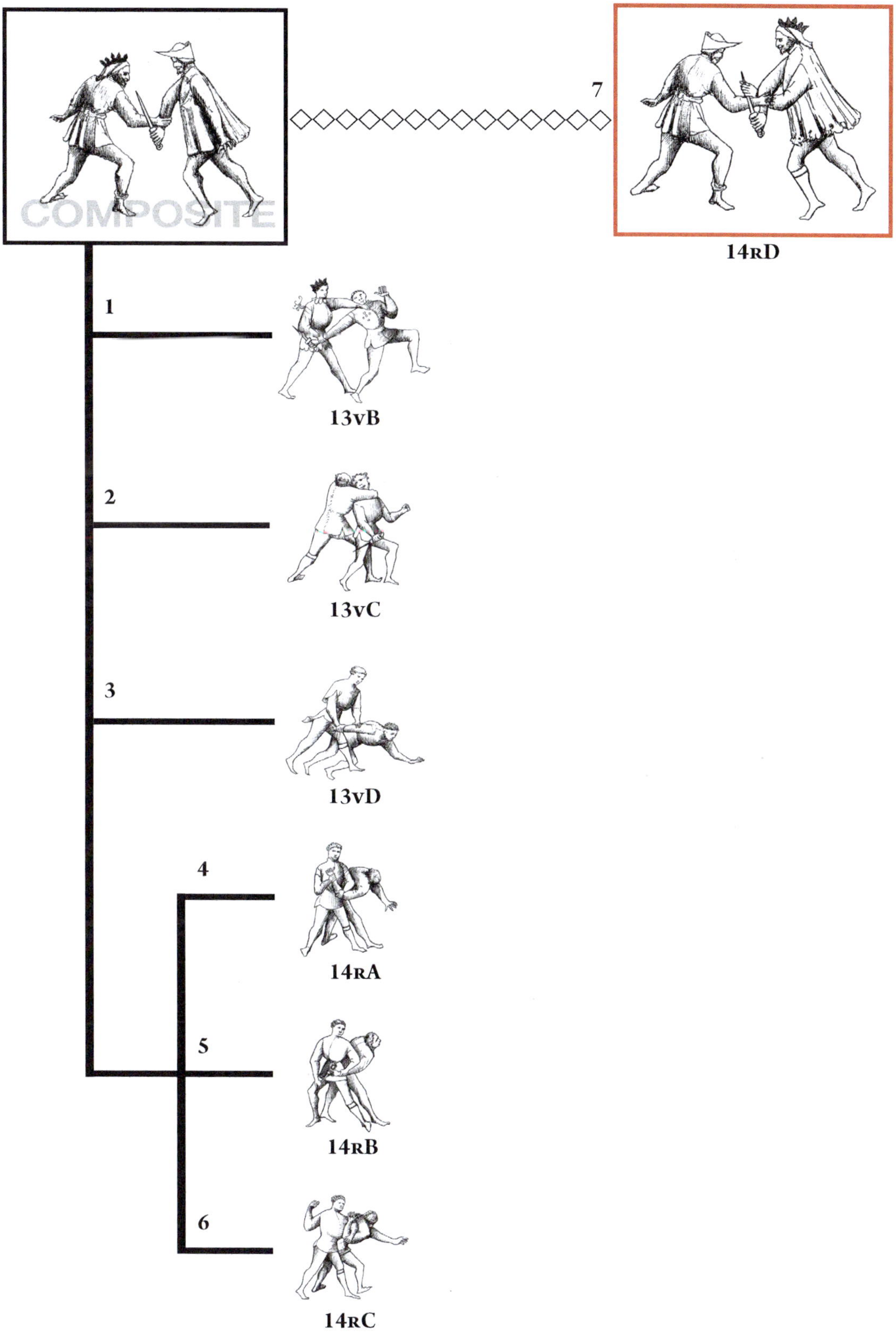
COMPOSITE
7
14rD
1
13vB
2
13vC
3
13vD
4
14rA
5
14rB
6
14rC

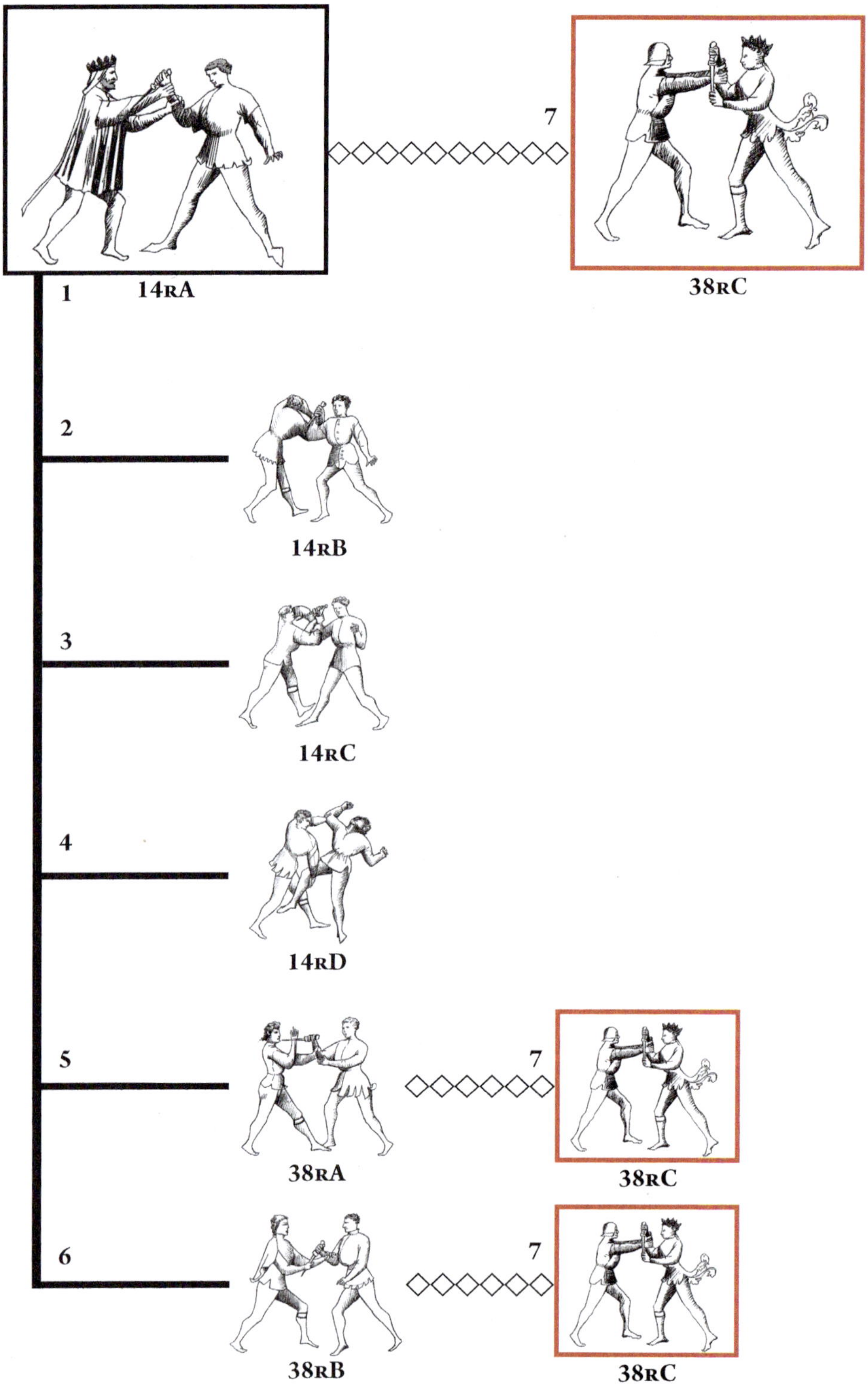
1
14RA
7
38RC
2
14RB
3
14RC
4
14RD
5
38RA
7
38RC
6
38RB
7
38RC

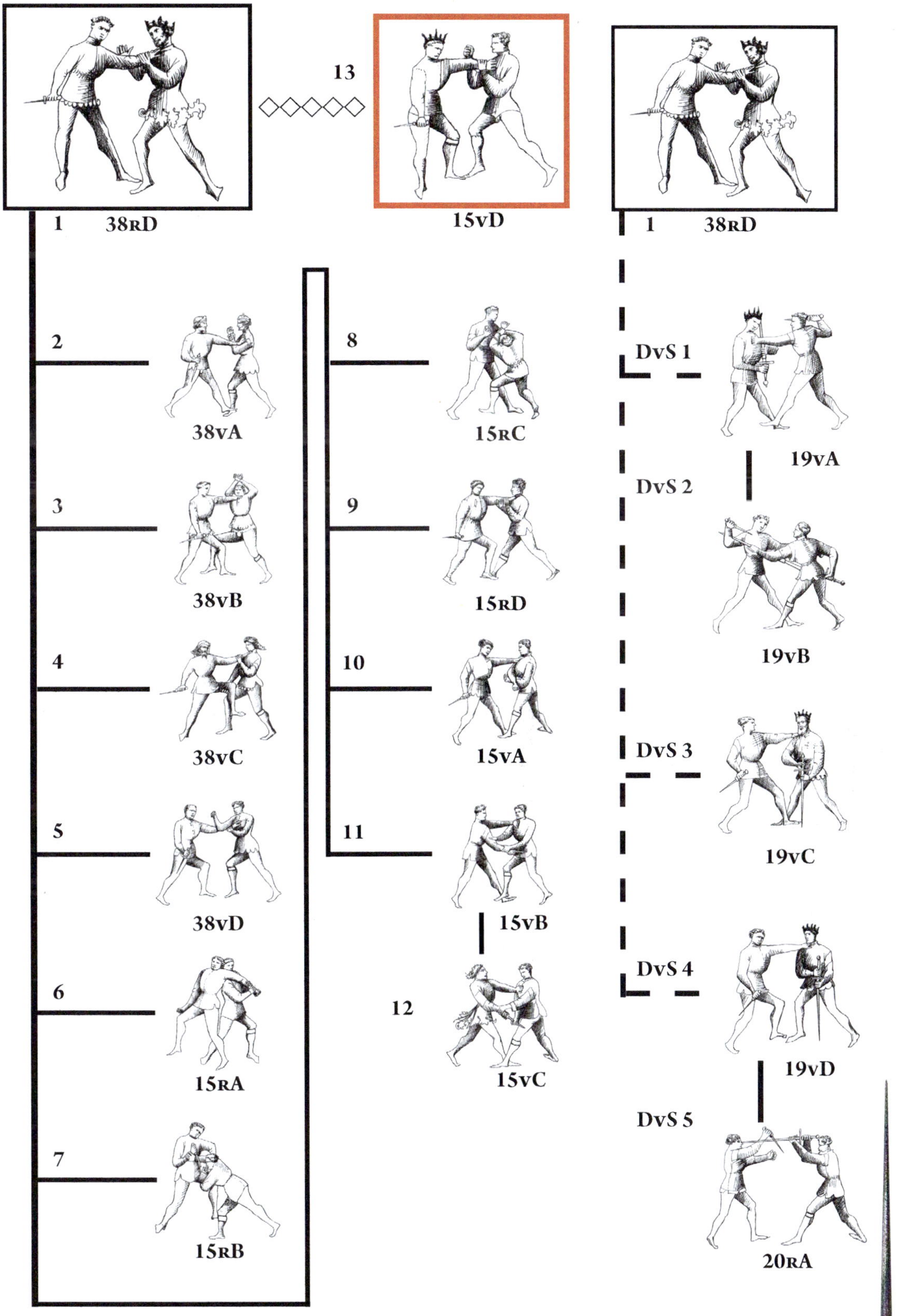
1
38rD
13
15vD
1
38rD
2
38vA
3
38vB
4
38vC
5
38vD
6
15rA
7
15rB
8
15rC
9
15rD
10
15vA
11
15vB
12
15vC
DvS 1
19vA
DvS 2
19vB
DvS 3
19vC
DvS 4
19vD
DvS 5
20rA

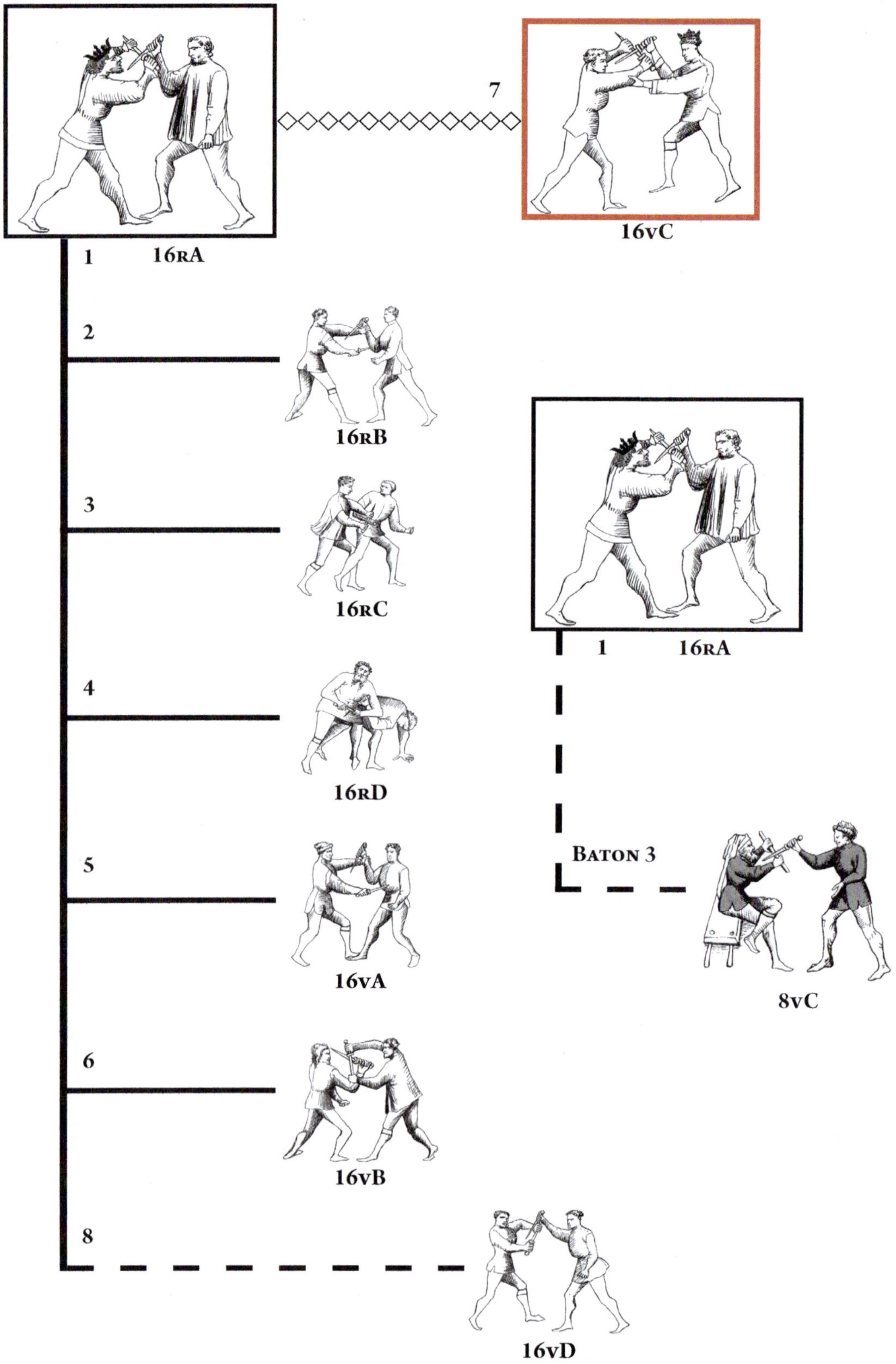
7
16vC
1
16rA
2
16rB
3
16rC
4
16rD
5
16vA
6
16vB
8
16vD
1
16rA
Baton 3
8vC

17rA

1 ◇◇◇◇◇◇ 2

17rB

EIGHTH REMEDY MASTER OF THE DAGGER ORGANIZATION

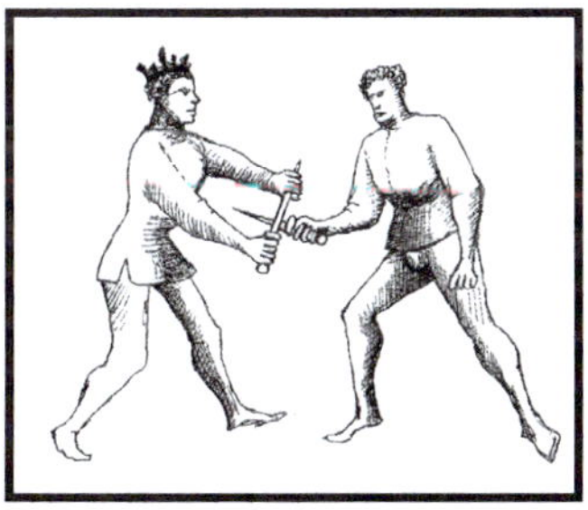

1 17rC

2

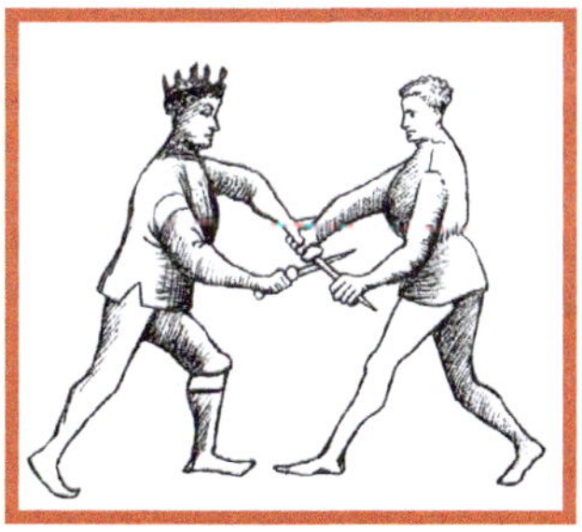

17rD

3

17vA

4

17vB

1 17rC

Baton 4

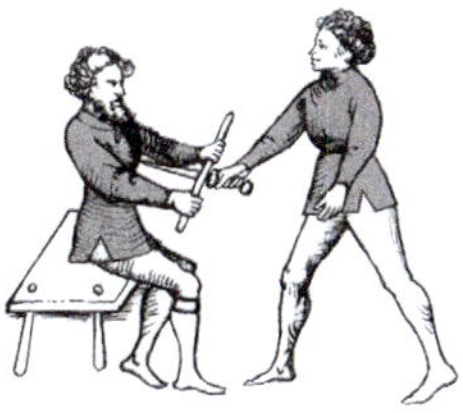

8vD

Written in Play 10: When the player has grabbed the right hand with the dagger with his left hand then immediately (you) grabs his dagger near the point and pulls it or draws it towards himself with strength ... or else puts the dagger point to the elbow ...

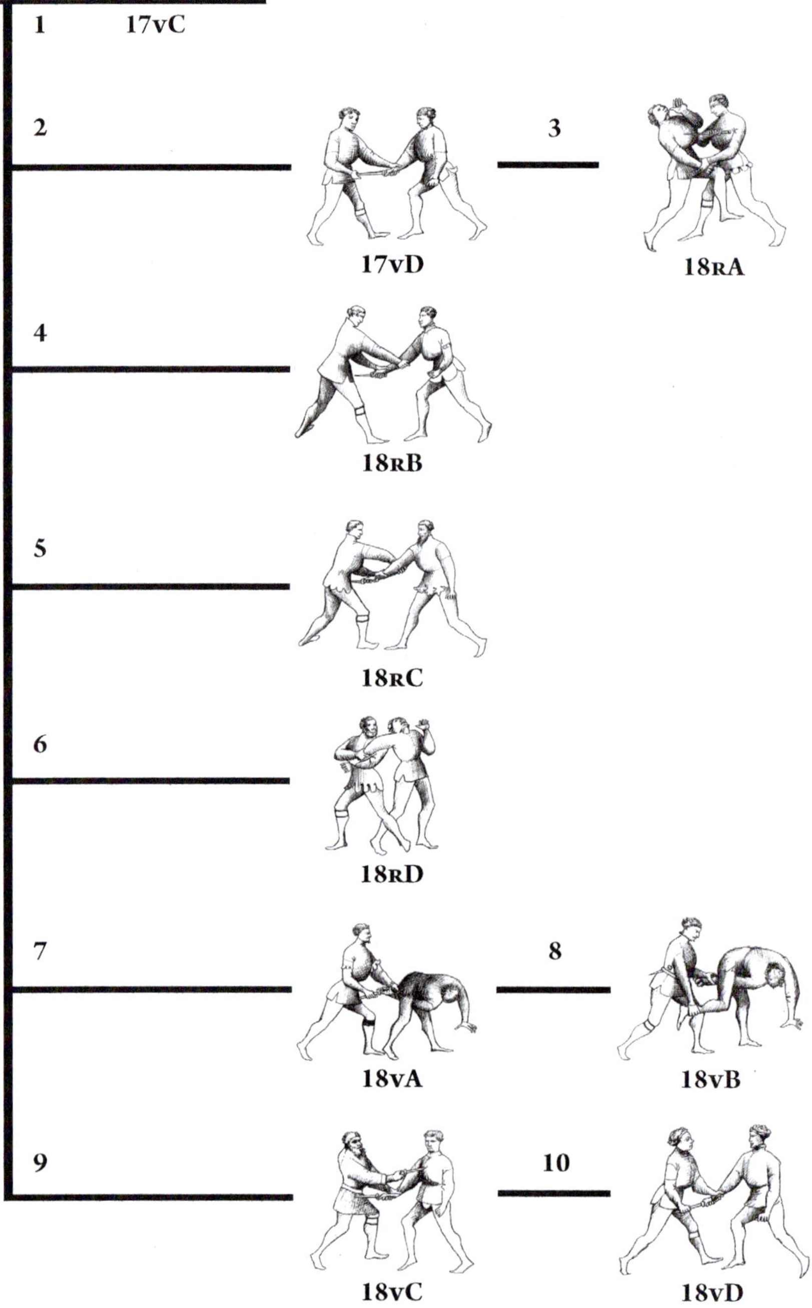

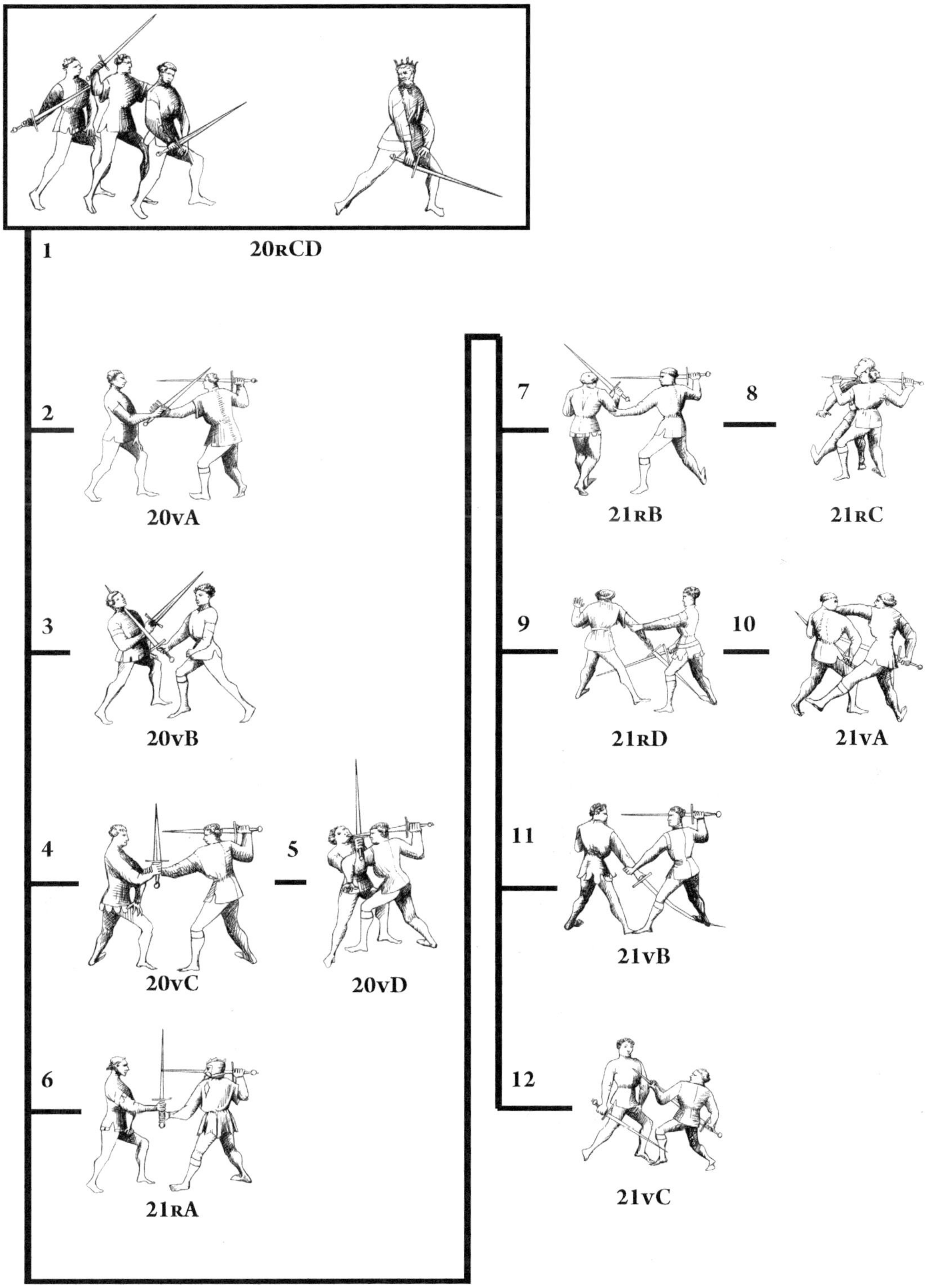
1
20rCD
2
20vA
3
20vB
4
20vC
5
20vD
6
21rA
7
21rB
8
21rC
9
21rD
10
21vA
11
21vB
12
21vC

Crossed at *punte di spada*

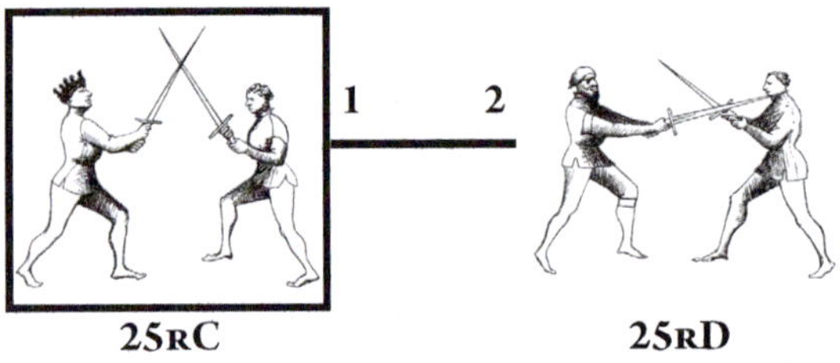

Crossed at *mezza spada*

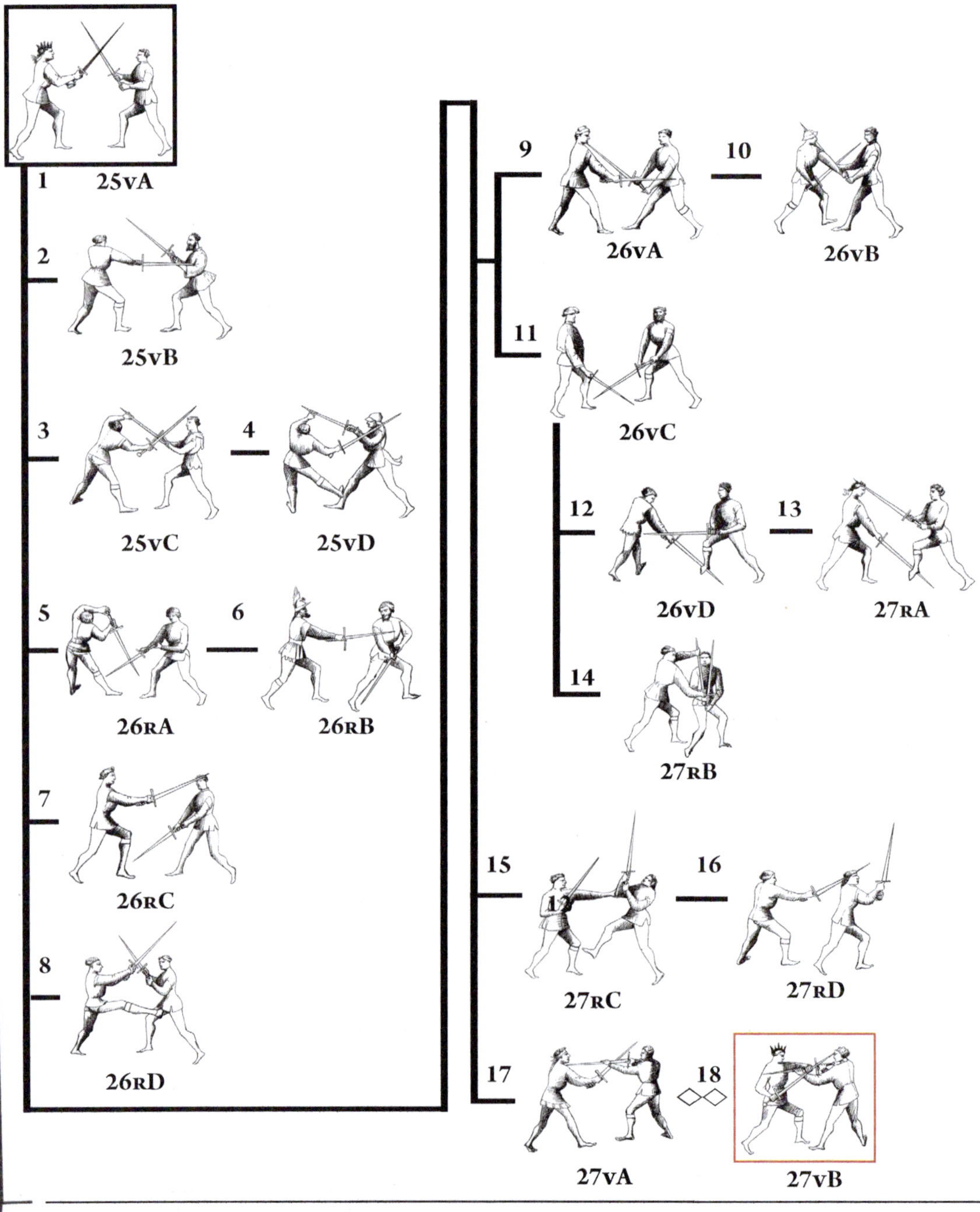

CROSSED AT *MEZZA SPADA*

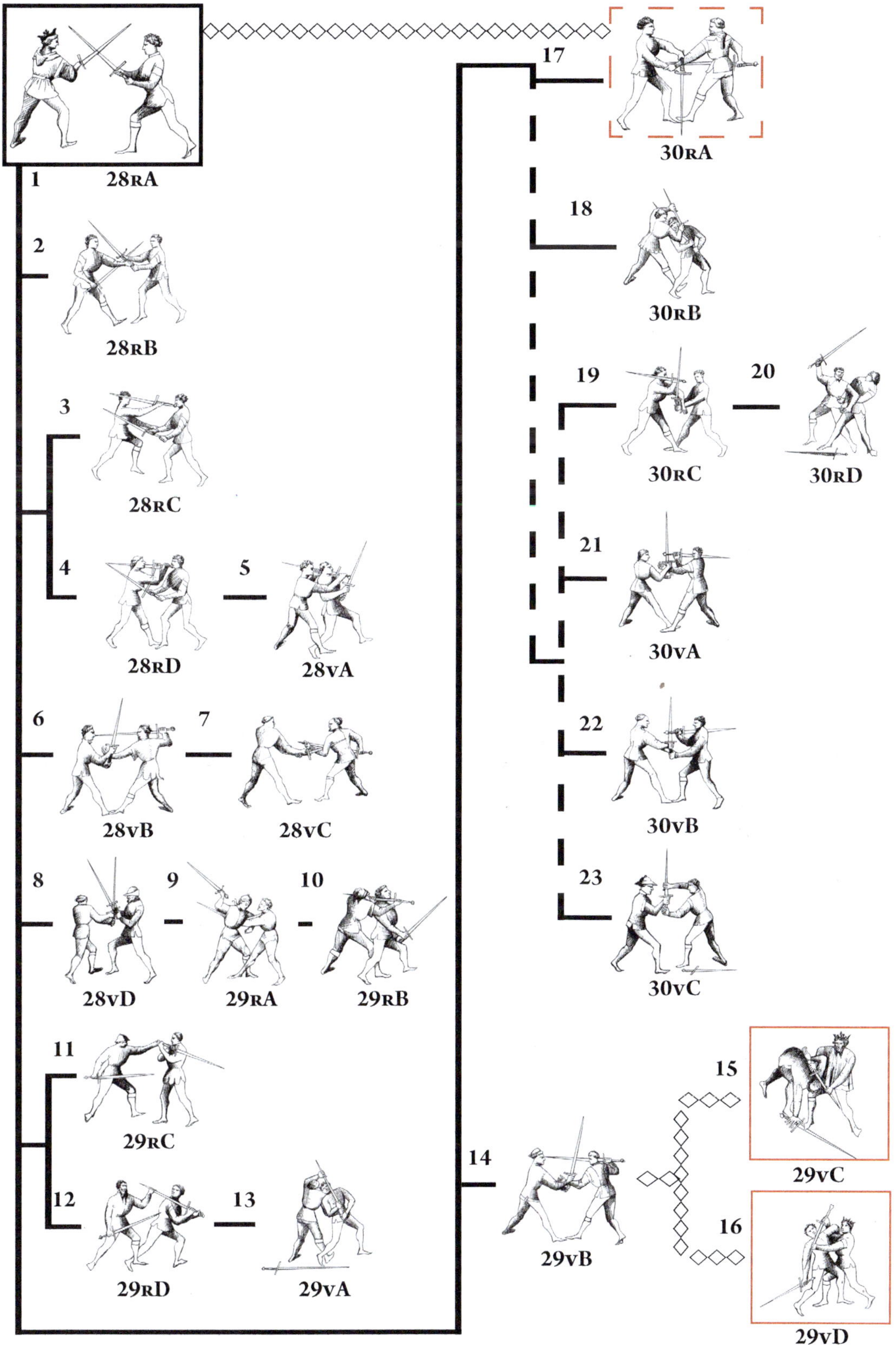

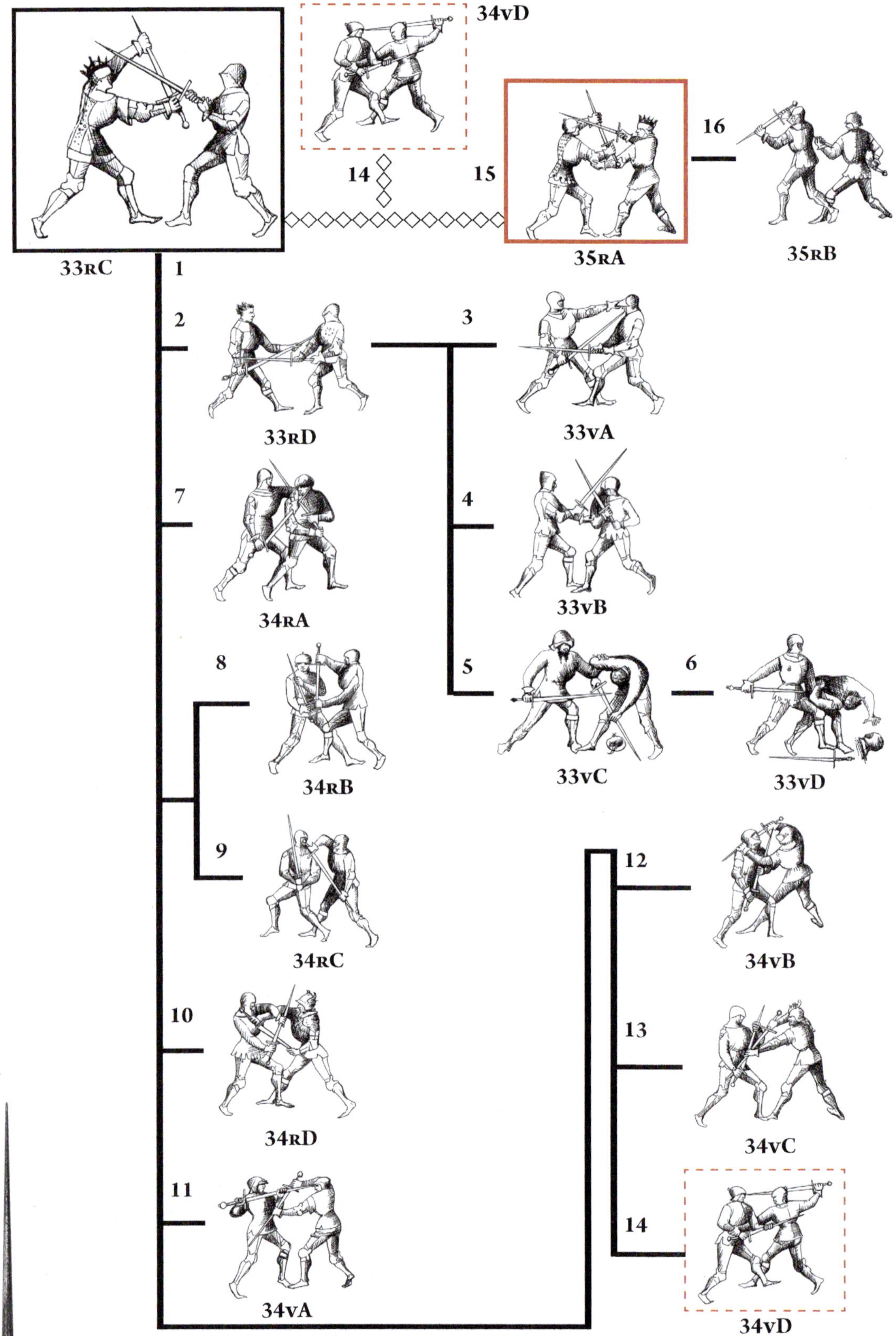
34vD
14
15
16
33rC
35rA
35rB
1
2
3
33rD
33vA
7
4
34rA
33vB
8
5
6
34rB
33vC
33vD
9
12
34rC
34vB
10
13
34rD
34vC
11
14
34vA
34vD

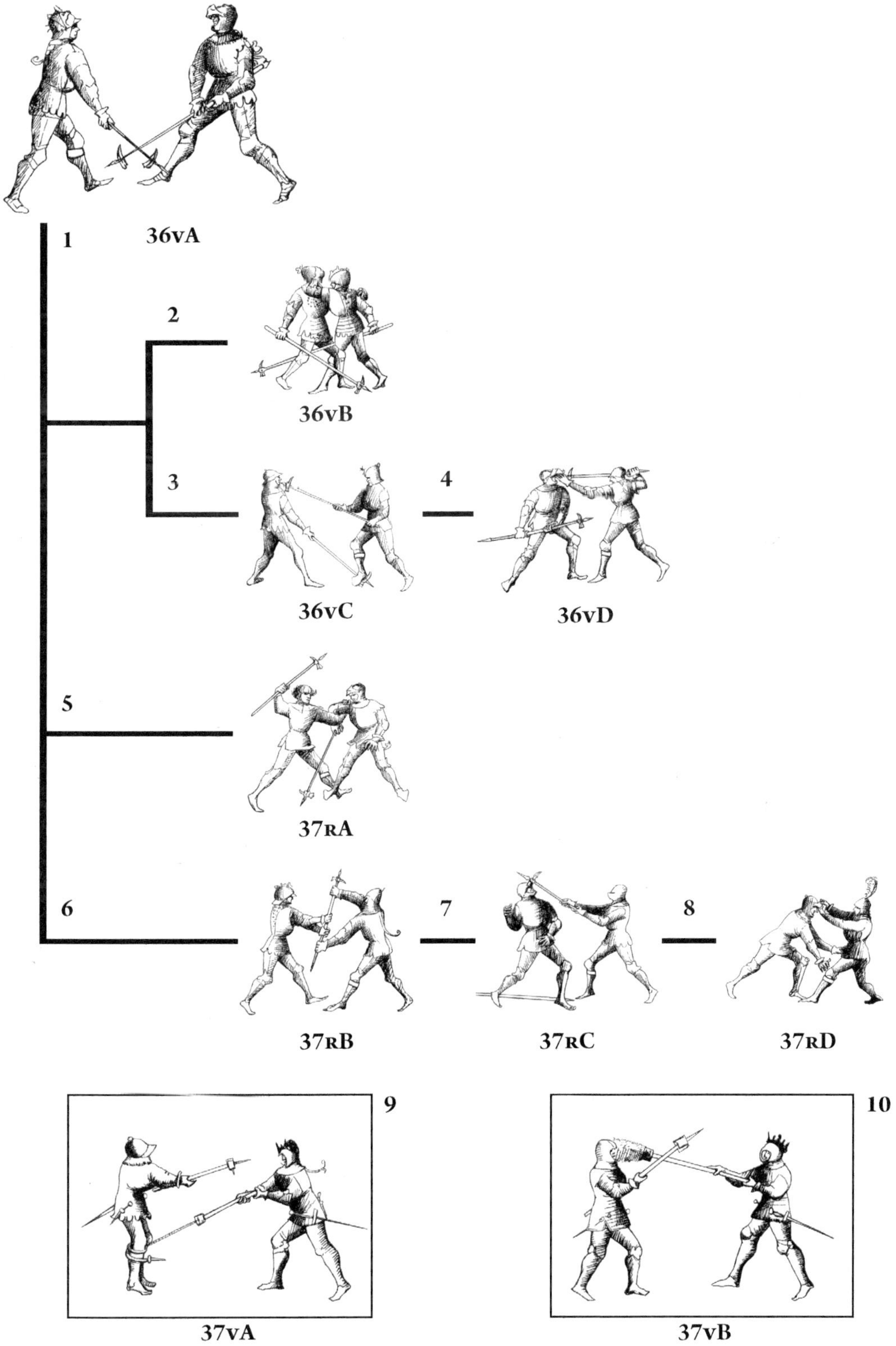
36vA
1
2
36vB
3
36vC
4
36vD
5
37rA
6
37rB
7
37rC
8
37rD
9
37vA
10
37vB

39rAB

1

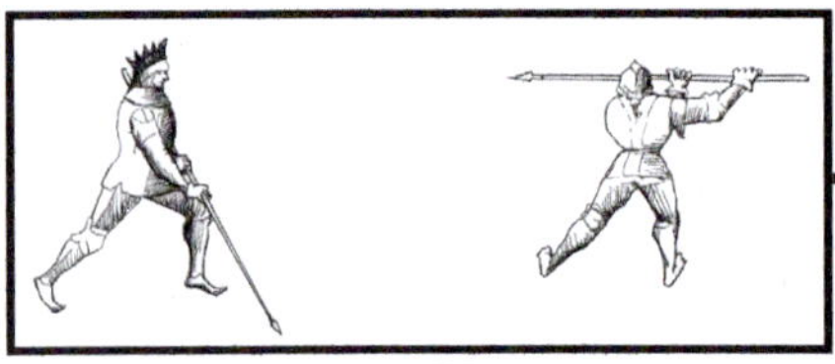

39rCD

2

39vAB

3

4

39vC

5

39vD

40rA

6

40rB

7

40rC

8

9

40rD

Written in Play 9:
The counter of this thrust is easily performed; when the point of the lance breaks, always turn the lance and strike with the butt.

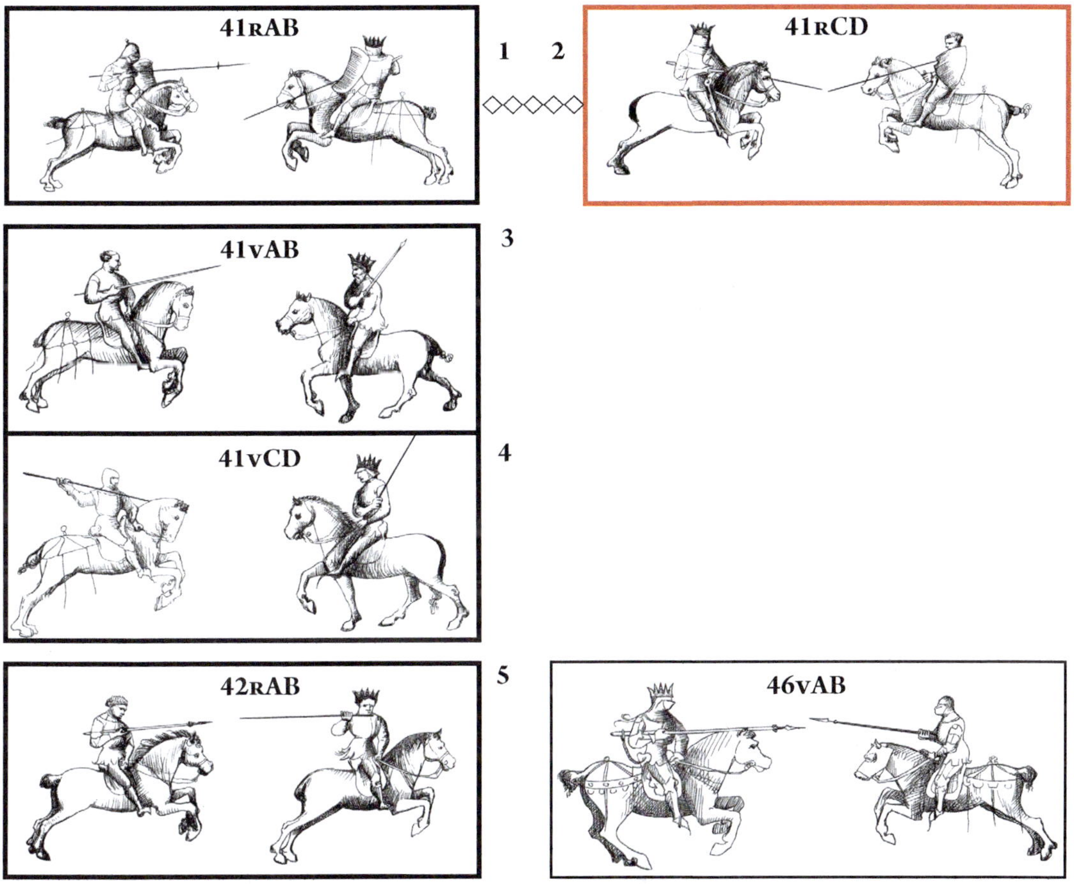

MOUNTED LANCE VS. SWORD ORGANIZATION

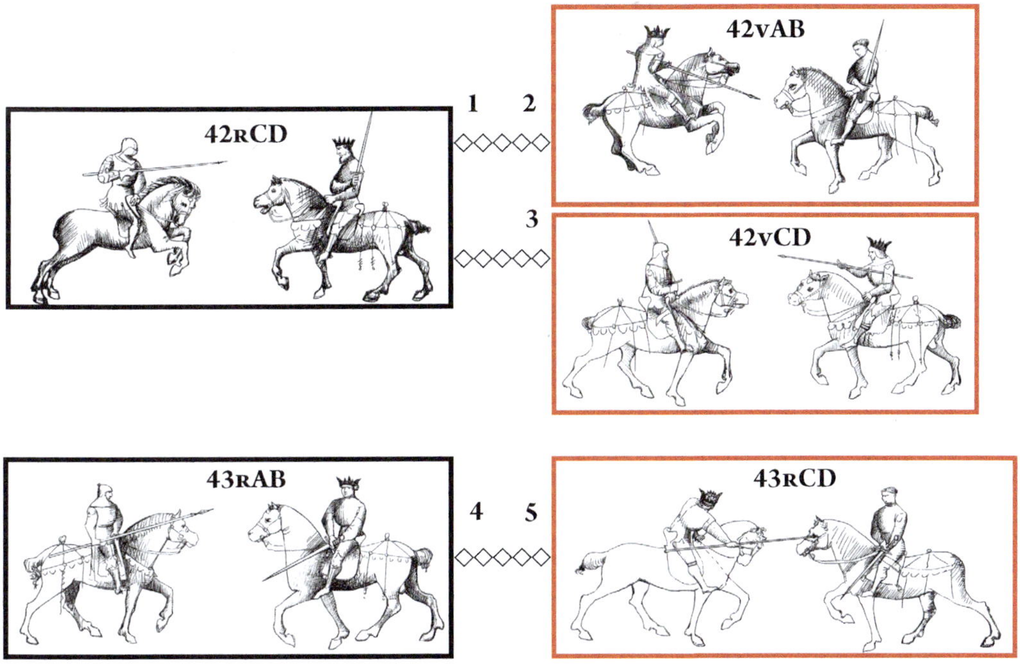

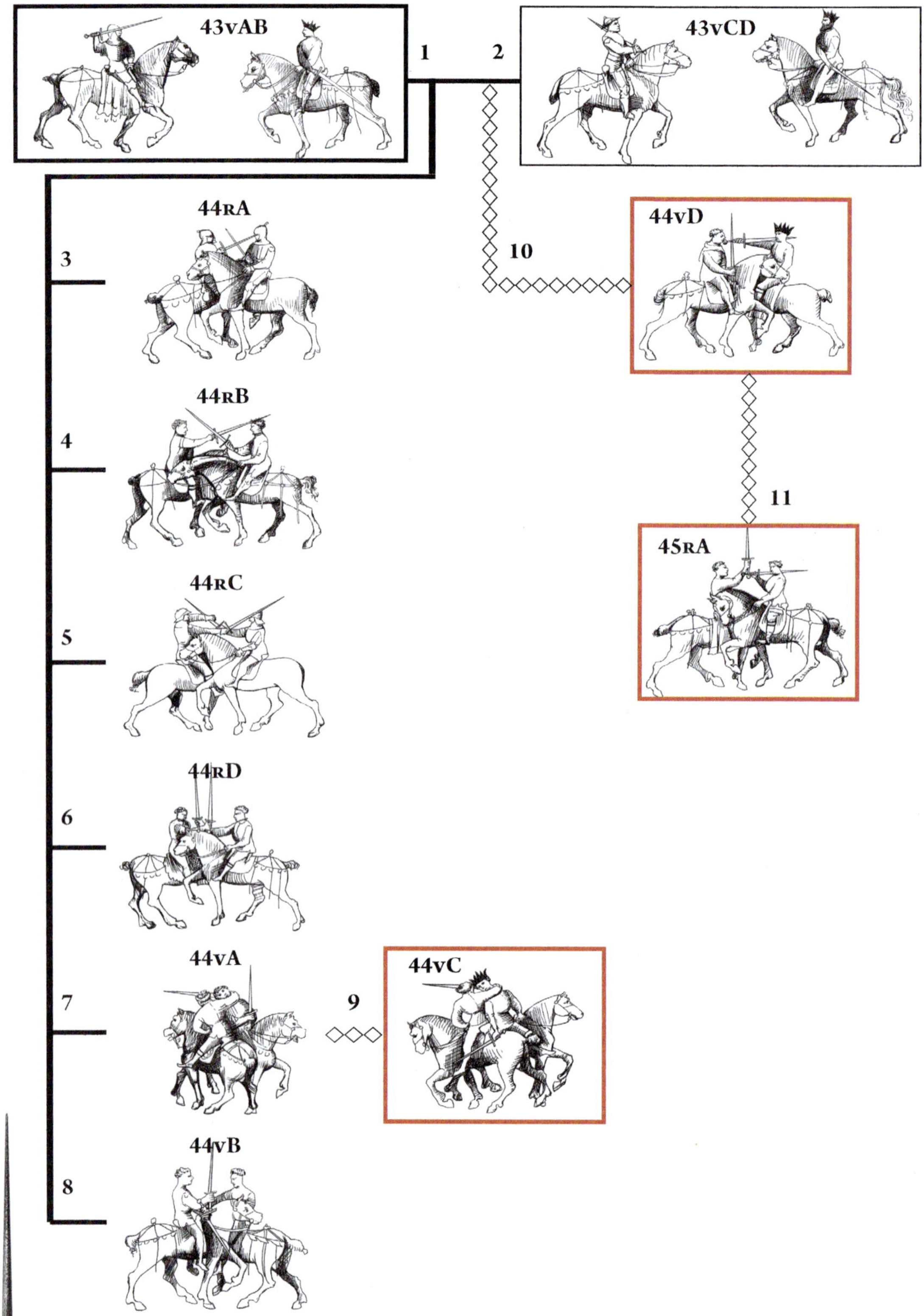
43vAB
1
2
43vCD
44rA
3
10
44vD
44rB
4
11
44rC
5
45rA
44rD
6
44vA
7
9
44vC
44vB
8

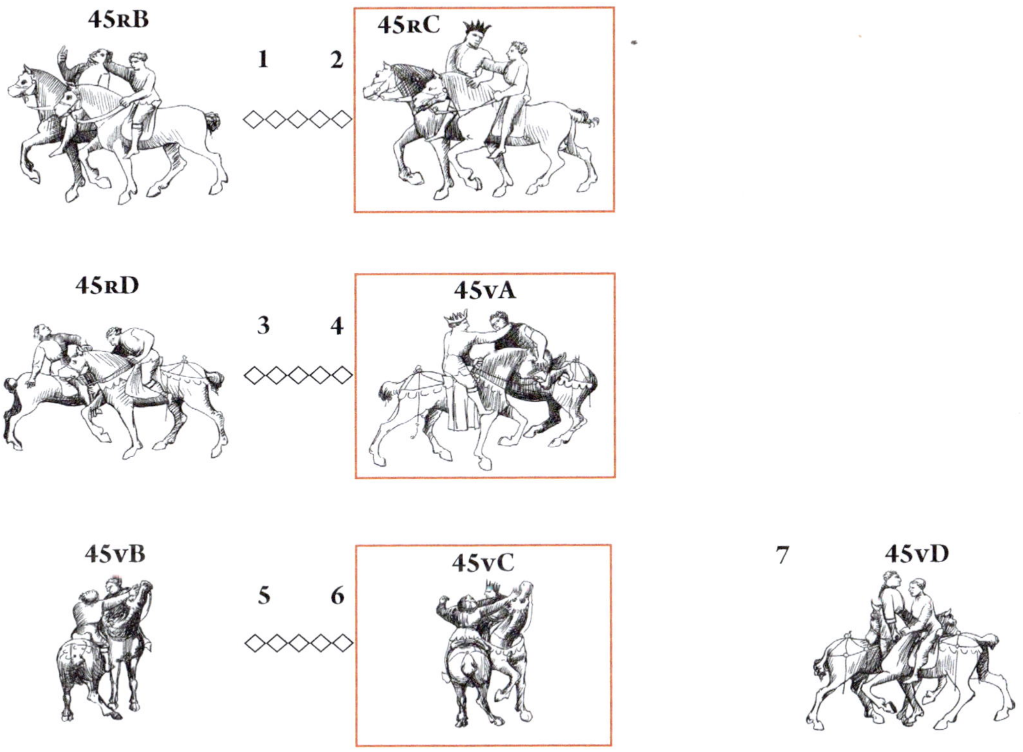

MOUNTED VS. FOOT ORGANIZATION

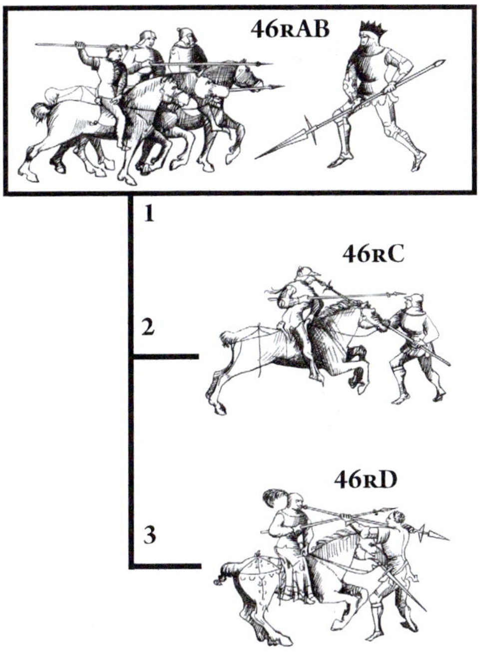

9780982591178